the
babycenter®
essential guide to
your baby's first year

We believe in the journey of Mommyhood.

We believe in packing up the **almighty diaper bag** and multi-tasking with a hands-free breast pump. We believe in that **one little sock** that always, always, always gets kicked off. We believe in **soothing night lights** that allow everyone to sleep peacefully.

We believe that the right products make the journey of Mommyhood a little bit easier. (And Daddyhood, too.)

Free shipping every day.* www.babycenterstore.com

the babycenter®
essential guide to your
baby's first year

expert advice and mom-to-mom wisdom from
the world's most popular parenting website

Linda Murray, Anna McGrail, Daphne Metland,
and the BabyCenter Editorial Team

RODALE

To Mary McDermott Scott
Whose love of family inspired us all

© 2007 by BabyCenter

All rights reserved. No part of this publication may be reproduced or transmitted in any form or by any means, electronic or mechanical, including photocopying, recording, or any other information storage and retrieval system, without the written permission of the publisher.

Rodale books may be purchased for business or promotional use or for special sales. For information, please write to:
Special Markets Department, Rodale, Inc., 733 Third Avenue, New York, NY 10017

Printed in the United States of America
Rodale Inc. makes every effort to use acid-free ♾, recycled paper ♻.

Illustrations © 2007 by Mark Watkinson
Photographs on pages 20, 56, 105, 119, 151, 208, 230, 283, 297, 330: © Anke Weiss
Photograph on page 235: © Comstock
Photographs on pages 129, 259, 305, 311: © Getty Images
Photograph appearing in The Bottom Line sidebars: © Getty Images
Photograph on page 359: © Anna Palma
Book design by Joanna Williams

Library of Congress Cataloging-in-Publication Data

The BabyCenter essential guide to your baby's first year : expert advice and mom-to-mom wisdom from the world's most popular parenting website / Linda Murray . . . [et al.].
    p.   cm.
Includes bibliographical references and index.
ISBN-13 978–1–59486–411–7   paperback
ISBN-10 1–59486–411–X   paperback
   1. Infants—Care—Popular works. 2. Child care—Popular works. I. Murray, Linda, date
RJ61.B123   2007
649'.122—dc22   2007015915

Distributed to the trade by Holtzbrinck Publishers

2   4   6   8   10   9   7   5   3   1   paperback

We inspire and enable people to improve their lives and the world around them
For more of our products visit rodalestore.com or call 800-848-4735

contents

part three: settling in
4–6 months

part four: on the move
7–9 months

part five: first steps, first words
10–12 months

part six: first-year health guide

acknowledgments

The authors wish to thank everyone whose efforts and talents contributed to giving birth to this book.

Jim Scott, BabyCenter's vice president of editorial, whose keen, consistent editorial and parenting insights helped keep our vision clear.

Bruce Raskin, executive editor at BabyCenter, whose enthusiasm and indefatigable editing helped keep us and the project on course.

Writer and parenting expert Paula Spencer, who played a strong role in the book's development and made sure that it reflected the cares and concerns of its audience.

Our medical reviewers, pediatricians Nancy Showen, MD, and Paul Young, MD, who reviewed and helped us clarify the medical and baby development information in these pages.

The many writers, editors, and BabyCenter community staff who contributed so many important sections and details to the book: Chess Thomas, who combed through academic journals and papers to track down the real facts and figures on child health; Scott Adler, BabyCenter's managing editor, who vetted and added words of wisdom to all the new dad material; Jennifer Scully, who helped with research; Heidi Kotansky, who added key links to babycenter.com; Katie Motta, who worked tirelessly in developing the polls throughout the book; and, in alphabetical order, our team of dedicated community managers and administrators who hand-picked the many insightful quotes from our bulletin boards to create the Buzz throughout the book: Lisa Bartels, Melissa Byers, Heather Davis, Laura Larsen, and Katie Schiavo.

Our agent, Jeff Kleinman of Folio Literary Management, who consistently provided excellent guidance and advice.

The staff at Rodale, including our editor, Mariska van Aalst, who brought to bear not only her considerable talents as an editor in helping to shape this book, but her firsthand knowledge as the parent of a 4- and 1-year-old; our project editor, Lois Hazel, warm and wonderful doula to books and babies alike; our copy editor (and mother of a 2-year-old and a brand-new baby), Jennifer Reich, who asked all the right questions; and our designer, Joanna Williams, who translated the BabyCenter look and feel to the book page with the same care she shows to her own 3- and 1-year-old.

introduction

If you're a new parent looking for expert advice, there's no short-age of sources. *The BabyCenter Essential Guide to Your Baby's First Year* is a special kind of resource, because it offers not only the collective insights of trusted experts, but also the wisdom and support of moms and dads who've been there, too. Millions of parents around the world visit BabyCenter's family of Web sites and books for its comprehensive advice and guidance, and to share their firsthand experiences. This guide reflects the distinctive reassuring authority that we're uniquely able to provide.

what's in this book

We'll take you step-by-step through the amazing journey of your baby's first year, telling you not only what you *need* to know but *why* you need to know it. The book is easy to use because it's divided into 3-month stages. That way, you can always find information that's appropriate for your baby's age. The sleep needs of a newborn, for example, are very different from those of an almost 1-year-old.

Within those 3-month stages, we've divided what-you-need-to-know information into repeating sections on:

- Your baby's development
- Feeding

- Sleep
- Baby care
- You (because being a good parent means taking care of your needs as well as your baby's)

There's a wealth of useful information just for dads, too, who have unique questions about their new role.

You may wonder why we've chosen not to organize the book month-by-month, but instead describe the broader 3-month stages. The reason is because babies go through the same developmental steps in roughly the same order, but they develop at slightly different rates. We'd like to encourage you to think about your baby's development in terms of milestones rather than months. That way, you can relax and enjoy what comes next without worrying and obsessing about why your baby hasn't walked yet or isn't sitting up exactly when your best friend's baby is.

Of course, if you do find yourself worrying, check out our **by the numbers** pages. We've included the results of a whole range of polls, quizzes, and surveys from the BabyCenter Web site. It's incredibly reassuring to realize that other people's 4-month-old babies don't necessarily sleep through the night, or that you aren't the only one who stands by your baby's crib checking whether she's still breathing! It's also useful to know that although 50 percent of parents have sex again within the first 2 months of having their babies, fully 20 percent haven't gotten around to it when their baby is older than 2 to 3 months. Phew!

Also worth noting: All of the poll results, many of them international, were provided to BabyCenter by parents *who had a baby at that age*. These parents aren't simply recalling, nor are they predicting; they're reporting from actual, current observations. And that means you're getting a unique snapshot of baby development and family life as it's truly experienced and lived by parents right now.

Our **decision guides** cover the hot topics that parents feel strongly about. Some topics are so hotly debated that we've summed up the reasons for and against each issue to help you make parenting choices that are right for you and your family. For example, what are your options when it comes to:

- Breastfeeding or formula feeding?
- Co-sleeping with your baby?
- Crying and sleep training?
- Returning to work?
- Following a schedule or going with the flow?

We've also included an in-depth **first-year health guide,** loaded with information to inform your day-to-day decisions and organized to help you easily find answers to the most common problems you're likely to encounter.

One thing we've carefully avoided is trying to frighten you with a list of every rare health problem or ailment, because in those instances you'll want specialized advice and information. The BabyCenter Web site is a good place to begin such a search. It's a lucky parent, though, who gets through the first year without her baby catching a cold, so you'll find vital tips and tricks for dealing with very common health problems such as sniffles and sneezes. Of course, whenever you have concerns about your baby's health, don't hesitate to call your baby's doctor.

Scattered throughout the book are our **worry meters.** These are questions and common worries that may seem too simple to ask anyone about, but that often concern new parents. Your health-care professionals may appear to dismiss such worries—they see new babies every day—but when you notice that your baby's hands are blue or that she makes little noises at night, it will bother you. So our worry meters tell you whether something is no big deal or a probable concern and, if the latter, what to do about it.

babycenter insights

This book taps all the resources of babycenter.com, with its millions of members who inform us about the most front-and-center issues that parents care about today. It's the feedback we get from all these real moms and dads that guides us in understanding just what parents want to know—and when they need to know it. For example: When did their babies roll, sit up, crawl, walk, or smile? How often do their babies cry? When did they first sleep through the night? When did they first have a taste of solid food? What are parents worried about? What do they enjoy most about being parents? What sorts of support do they need?

You'll see how your experiences and feelings, and your baby's development and behavior, compare to others. And if you've ever wondered if you're the only one feeling a particular way (whatever the topic), chances are you'll find out in these pages that you're not alone.

As a new parent, when *you* are ready to share what you've learned, we invite you to visit the babycenter.com bulletin boards and add your two cents. You'll be participating in the network of support for parents who are traveling the same path as you—and at the same time.

a note on style

Throughout the book, we use *he* and *she* interchangeably when referring to your baby, and we've tried to balance that usage. Likewise, your healthcare provider may be a pediatrician or a family doctor; you'll know best who to turn to for help, even though we may use a different term.

When it comes to the main caregiver, we recognize that increasingly these days it's not always Mom, and families don't always have a mom *and* a dad. Whatever your family set-up or parenting arrangements, you'll still experience that universal and unique

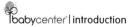

bond between parent and child, and this book addresses all of our common needs and concerns.

parenting your way

Parenting is an art, not a science. Every parent and all families are entitled to make the choices that are right according to their own beliefs and standards. This isn't a book about rules and regulations or the approaches of well-known experts. It's about information, support, and the many possible ways of doing things. We'll help provide you with the background to make your choices with confidence.

Learning how to be a parent takes time and effort. Learning what sort of parent you *want* to be takes knowledge, experience, and a helping hand from other parents. If this book gives you the confidence to best enjoy your baby's first year, we'll have done what we set out to do.

part one
the firsts

getting to know you

first meeting

"Unforgettable." That's how most new moms describe the moment when they first hold their babies in their arms. Some moms laugh, some cry, some do both, and a good number are too stunned to do either. How you react will depend on your personality and the circumstances of your baby's delivery.

How soon after delivery will you be able to cuddle your newborn? That varies from mom to mom. Some women—typically those with uneventful vaginal deliveries—get to hold their newborns immediately after delivery (with the cord still attached). But many women, including those who have Caesarean sections, have to wait a few minutes while they or their babies get needed medical attention.

If you're handed your newborn right away, she'll be slippery and wet, and she can get cold quickly, so you both may be covered with a towel or blanket. While you're holding your baby, the nurses will wipe her and put on a covering to help keep her warm. If you have to wait a few moments to hold your baby, she'll probably be brought to you swaddled snuggly in a blanket. Either way, it's surprising how huge your baby will feel to you—was this new person really inside you just a few minutes ago?

If your baby is adopted, you share one key thing in common with giving birth: In that first meeting with your child, you'll develop

babycenter **buzz**
welcome to the world

"I know that when I finally look into his eyes, it will be like no other moment in my life. I'm really looking forward to that first meeting. I hope that means that we won't have any trouble bonding, because I think we're already almost there."—**Leah**

"My little guy was born 2 days ago, and I can honestly say I fell in love with him from the moment I saw him. I couldn't even speak without tearing up. I try to hold him close every chance I get because just looking into his little eyes makes me feel more wonderful than anything else I've ever felt."
—**Jeffrey**

"For me, the bond hit after they brought my baby to my room. I kissed his forehead, and he opened his eyes and stared directly into mine. For an instant, it was like we could see into each other's souls. My little boy has me completely hooked on him. I love him more and more with each day that passes!"—**Amanda**

"My baby arrived 9 weeks prematurely, so I never saw her for 2 weeks as she was really sick and so was I. The first time I saw her, I burst out crying with happiness. I've never felt so much love for anyone in my life. After waiting for the 2 weeks, I thought 'what if she doesn't bond with me?' But as soon as she grabbed my finger tightly with her tiny hand, I knew she knew she was mine!"—**Sinead**

"As soon as I held my baby boy in my arms, I felt an indescribable love."
—**Erin**

an entirely new perspective on life. The world will never look the same.

skin to skin

One of the most important things you can do after your baby is born is spend some time in skin-to-skin contact. Holding your baby close helps you get to know each other. It keeps your baby warm and her temperature, heart rate, and breathing regular. It also calms your baby and makes her feel safe. Your healthcare provider will leave you, your baby, and your partner, as well as any other birth witnesses or supporters, alone for as long as you like. Many men are surprised by how emotional they feel when they finally get to hold their babies in their arms. Even dads who keep it together during labor and delivery and who stay very calm and in control while other people are around start to cry when the three of you are alone together.

wakeful babies, tired moms

Babies often go through a wakeful phase just after birth, opening those big eyes as if taking in every last detail of the strange new world around. Your baby's sight isn't yet well developed, but he may turn and gaze at your face. He can best focus on things about 8 to 15 inches away, the distance from his face to yours when held in your arms.

On the other hand, your baby may be sleepy and unresponsive after the birth, especially if you've had a long labor. The experience was just as tiring for him as it was for you. After he's had some rest, it's time to try skin-to-skin contact again.

If you're exhausted, then no matter how much you've been looking forward to your baby, that initial meeting can seem anticlimactic at first. You may feel too worn out or overwhelmed to get very excited. Don't worry. "Bonding" with a new baby isn't an instant

help with breathing

It's not uncommon for a newborn to need a little help breathing just after birth. If your baby has trouble making the switch from amniotic fluid to air, medical staff will give her oxygen, and perhaps suction her breathing passages clear of mucus. Chances are she'll need only a few minutes of treatment before being brought back to you.

process for everyone. As you get to know your baby and touch, hold, feed, and care for him, your bond will deepen.

how newborns look

Newborns aren't the plump, smiling cuties you see in baby magazines. If you're not prepared, some aspects of your baby's appearance may even be alarming. So here's what to expect.

Pointy head. Squeezing through the birth canal gives your baby's head a pointy, almost cone shape. This isn't dangerous or permanent, and it usually disappears within a few days. Babies born by Cesarean section usually have more rounded heads right from the start.

Soft spots on your baby's head. The soft spots (fontanelles) on your baby's head are there to allow the skull to compress enough to fit through the birth canal. The rear fontanelle can take up to 4 months to close, while the front one takes between 9 and 18 months. If your baby doesn't have much hair, a pulse may be visible at the fontanelles. This is normal, and it's often more visible when your baby cries or fusses. By about 18 months, your baby's skull bones will have fused together.

The cord. Before birth, your baby received all the nourishment he needed through the umbilical cord. Once it's cut, the stump of the cord remains attached to your baby. Your baby's doctor will likely remove the plastic clamp used to seal the cut cord after about a day (or it may detach on its own). Within about 1 to 2 weeks, the stump will blacken, dry up, and fall off, leaving behind your baby's belly button, a wonderful reminder of how you were once attached. You needn't do anything special to the stump while it's healing; just keep it dry. Applying alcohol to the stump is no longer considered necessary.

Your baby's skin. If your baby was born early, she may have thin, rather red-looking skin (red because of the blood vessels that show

(continued on page 8)

just for dads

welcome to the family

It's not every day your life undergoes such an intense event as the birth of a child (an experience that's no less extraordinary if you're a repeat visitor to the delivery room). But many expectant fathers haven't thought about what happens *after* their babies are born, so becoming a dad can be a bit of a surprise, not to mention down-right overwhelming.

First, the actual birth can be a real eye-opener—literally and figuratively. But if you take a step back and let go of any urge to try to take complete control of the situation (or, for that matter, even to keep your cool), it can be one of the most wonderful events of your life. Fortunately, the delivery room staff will take care of the practical matters, and if you do feel like bursting out in tears of joy, no one is going to mark that down in your permanent record. While many dads feel overwhelmed with love when their babies are born and are ready to defend mom and baby from the rest of the world, a sudden sense of terror is also common. Some dads are hit by exhaustion, worry, and uncertainty about how to "do the dad thing." But don't worry: You'll become an expert soon enough.

what you can do on the road to experthood

- At your baby's first cry, don't race for the hallway to make tell-the-world phone calls or to hand out cigars. After who-knows-how-many hours of labor, your partner—not to mention your baby—will appreciate your presence. This is your chance to get family bonding off to a great start.
- If you don't want to cut the cord, no sweat. If you don't want to take a picture of your mother-in-law with your wife 5 seconds after the birth, not to worry. Don't feel pressured to do any-thing that interrupts this incredible moment in time. It's your baby, too, and your memories. Soak it in first and then chroni-cle your mother-in-law's congratulatory smooch.

- Babies are tiny. Stating the obvious? Maybe, but for some first-time dads, the fantasy of life post-birth focuses on playing catch in the park or attending ballet class recitals, not gingerly holding a naked, fragile blossom of new life. Rest assured, that tiny baby will grow into your star runner or graceful gymnast—with many amazing stops along the way.
- Should your baby need to go into the nursery or neonatal intensive care unit (NICU) for any reason, take a deep breath and redouble your support and advocacy for your partner. She'll be anxious—and want constant updates—in a way you've never experienced before. And if she had a c-section, you'll be her foot soldier. If it's possible to take digital photos of your baby in either the nursery or NICU, do it and bring them to your partner ASAP. You'll be a hero.

underneath it). Her skin may also be covered with lanugo, a fine, downy hair, and vernix, a cheesy, white substance that protected her skin in the amniotic fluid. Full-term babies usually have only a few traces of vernix in the folds of their skin.

If your baby arrived late, she may have a slightly wrinkly appearance and very little, if any, lanugo. Sometimes what remains of the vernix looks like a white powder on the skin.

About half of all babies are born with milia, tiny white pimple-like dots on their faces. These disappear in time. Your baby may also have a birthmark. These range from temporary discolored patches to permanent splotches in a variety of colors from pink and red to brown and even blue. The most common are red "stork bites"— sometimes more sweetly referred to as "angel kisses" when found on the forehead or nape of the neck—that are dilated capillaries near the surface of the skin that fade by toddlerhood, though some last longer. If you're concerned about any marks on your baby, talk to your baby's doctor.

Gray-blue hands. A new baby's blood circulation takes up to 48 hours to settle down, so her hands and feet may feel cold.

Enlarged genitals. Whether you have a boy or girl, your baby's genitals could be swollen from the extra dose of hormones you passed on just before birth. This is temporary! Baby girls may have vaginal discharge, too, which can be bloody.

Swollen breasts. Many babies—boys and girls—have swollen breasts, along with a milky discharge from the breasts. It is caused by exposure to maternal hormones in utero and will disappear within a few weeks.

first checks
and tests

In the first hours after birth, your doctor or midwife will give your baby a complete physical examination, checking his heart, lungs, eyes, spine, skin, hips, central nervous system, head circumference, and everything else. Use this opportunity to voice any concerns about your baby and to ask questions.

apgar

The first test carried out on your baby is the Apgar assessment. It's done 1 minute after birth and then again after 5 minutes (and, in a few cases, after 10 minutes as well). The name comes from its developer, Dr. Virginia Apgar, and is also an acronym for the five main areas being checked: **A**ctivity level, **P**ulse, **G**rimace (response to stimulation), **A**ppearance, and **R**espiration (breathing). When the numbers are added up, the highest possible score is 10. Most healthy, full-term infants score between 7 and 10. The purpose of this test is to decide whether your baby needs immediate medical attention; it doesn't predict future mental or physical health. In the excitement of delivery's aftermath, you may not even be aware that your baby is being scored.

vital statistics

After you've had a chance to say a quick hello to your baby, she'll be weighed and measured, footprinted, and probably photographed.

vitamin k and eye drops

Vitamin K plays a role in making blood clot. A small number of newborns don't have enough vitamin K, the lack of which can cause minor problems such as nose or mouth bleeds, or even major problems such as stroke or death. That's why your newborn receives an injection of vitamin K shortly after birth. Your baby will also have antibiotic ointment or drops put into his eyes within the first hour of birth to prevent eye infections (some of which can lead to blindness); this is a legal requirement in most states.

cord blood

After your caregiver clamps your baby's cord, she may take a sample of blood from it to determine your baby's blood type. The blood may be used for other tests as well. If you chose while pregnant to bank cord blood, after the cord is cut, your doctor, midwife, or nurse will insert a needle into the umbilical vein still attached to the placenta to draw out blood for this purpose. Your baby won't feel a thing after the cord has been cut. The blood in your baby's umbilical cord contains stem cells, which can be used to treat certain conditions later in life, or be a match for a sibling who needs treatment. Cord blood can be frozen and stored.

Cord blood retrieval and storage is not standard practice. Cord blood may be donated to a public bank or stored privately for your personal use. Private cord blood banking is expensive and not recommended by the American Academy of Pediatrics because in most diseases for which stem-cell transplants are currently used, your baby's own cord blood is unsuitable. In the rare case that such a transplant is necessary, a stem cell match may be located through the public cord-blood banking system.

pediatric check

In the first day or two after the birth, your baby will have a full once-over by a pediatrician or your family doctor. The check includes looking at the shape of your baby's head; examining his ears, eyes, mouth, hands, and feet; and listening to his heart and breathing. The doctor will turn your baby over to check his spine and manipulate his hips to ensure that the joints are stable. Any birthmarks will be examined and some of his reflexes tested. The most common test is the Moro reflex, which is done by gently allowing your baby's head to flop a short distance. Your baby will respond by flinging out both arms with his fingers spread and stretching out his legs. He may also cry a little. Your baby will probably also receive his first hepatitis B vaccine before discharge.

newborn screening tests

Every state requires by law its own list of newborn screening tests. These tests are important because they help uncover serious, even life-threatening disorders that have no apparent symptoms. Only about $\frac{1}{10}$ of 1 percent of all children will actually have a disorder. But identifying these children early and getting them the proper treatment can save their lives.

The tests are primarily blood screenings, and one sample of your baby's blood is enough to do the entire battery of tests. The blood sample is drawn (usually from the heel) before your baby is discharged from the hospital. If you're discharged within hours of birth, or if you give birth at home, you need to make arrangements to have these screenings done within the week, ideally on day 2 or 3 and no later than day 7. Some disorders don't show up within the first 24 hours.

The American College of Medical Genetics recommends 29 key screening tests, and an additional 25 are possible. What your baby will be screened for depends on the state he's born in. The list includes an alphabet soup of metabolic, blood, and other disorders, including:

- **Phenylketonuria (PKU):** The inability to process the amino acid phenylalanine, which accumulates and damages the brain.
- **Sickle cell anemia:** A blood disease more common in people with African, Mediterranean, Asian, and Caribbean heritage.
- **Congenital hypothyroidism:** A thyroid disorder that affects brain growth and development.
- **Cystic fibrosis:** One of the most common inherited disorders in the United States, it causes lung and digestive problems that shorten life span.

Depending on where you live, you may be asked to give your consent before your baby receives these tests. You may have the right to refuse tests (but not be asked permission), or your baby will be given them whether you want them or not.

newborn hearing tests

A hearing test is almost always among the initial screens. It's recommended by the March of Dimes and the American Academy of Pediatrics, but it is state law only in some states. The most commonly used test is the otoacoustic emission (OAE) screen. This involves placing a small, soft-tipped earpiece into the outer part of your baby's ear and playing quiet clicking sounds. In a hearing ear, the organ of hearing (the cochlea) should produce sounds in response to the clicks. These are recorded and analyzed by the computerized screening system. A hearing test usually takes only a few minutes and can be done at the bedside, often while your baby is sleeping. It doesn't hurt. Because hearing problems can affect your baby's development and ability to speak, finding and treating problems early is very important.

chapter 3

first time in your arms

Brand-new babies tend to curl up, folding in their arms and legs, much as they did in utero. This isn't surprising, since they were curled up like that for months. At first, picking up and holding your baby might make you nervous, but you'll soon be doing it without a second thought. Handling your baby is one of the key ways that you'll get to know him. Use slow, firm movements, which babies find most reassuring.

supporting your baby's head

Your new baby's head is relatively big and one-quarter the length of his body (when he's grown, it will be one-eighth). At birth, his head is too heavy for his back and neck muscles to lift, so you'll need to support it for him until he can do it by himself at around 3 months.

picking up your baby

Let your baby know you're about to pick him up by talking to him or touching him first. Then . . .

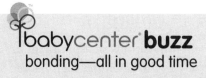

babycenter buzz
bonding—all in good time

"The night my little guy was born, as soon as I heard him cry, I cried with him. I haven't been able to keep myself from holding, kissing, and cuddling him."—**Michelle**

"Mothers shouldn't feel pressure to have that automatic bond the moment they first see their children; everyone is different! It took me a couple of weeks to bond with my son. Birth was a huge adjustment, but once we both got a little settled, that's when we bonded. Every day we grow closer and closer."—**Allison**

"I had a horrible pregnancy and labor that ended with a c-section, so I didn't feel that immense love at first. I loved him but not in the way it was described to me. It's important for new mothers to understand that sometimes, for one reason or another, you don't bond with your baby right away. We need to stop this stereotyping of how things *should* be in the beginning, because it's false."—**Silvia**

"I ultimately felt the bond with my daughter when I woke up in recovery after being put to sleep for my c-section. I think that being put to sleep and not being able to see my daughter's birth made that first moment a very powerful one in our bonding as mother and daughter."—**Molly**

- Slide one hand under his head, supporting his neck with the palm of your hand and his head with your fingers. The top of his back will rest on your wrist.
- Slide your other hand under his bottom, either between his legs or from the side. His bottom will now be resting on your palm and his lower back will be supported by your fingers.
- Give your baby a moment to get used to the support that your hands are giving him.
- Lean over him and gently lift him toward you.
- Hold him close to your body as you stand upright.

ways to hold your baby

Babies like to be held in positions that put them in full body contact with the person who's holding them. Some holds to try:

On your shoulder. Using one hand to support your baby's head and the other to support his bottom, lift your baby so his head is resting on your shoulder and his body is upright.

This is a good position for comforting your baby, burping him, or carrying him when he's asleep. Later, you'll be able to use one arm to support him, freeing your other arm to do something else, such as answer the phone or eat your dinner. As your baby gets older, this position also gives him a grand view of the world around him.

Cradling. Hold your baby in your arms so his head rests just above the crook of one arm and his bottom is supported by the other.

As you get more confident, you'll be able to cradle your baby with just one arm supporting both his head and neck. This is a good position for making close eye contact and singing to your baby.

Babies have an instinctive fear of being dropped, and they'll react with the startle or Moro reflex whenever that feeling overcomes them. You're most likely to see it when you move your baby from one position (say, in your arms) to another (on a mattress). Keep your movements gentle and controlled, and your baby is likely to be much happier.

putting your baby down

Putting your baby down is basically the gentle reverse of picking him up.

- Lower your baby gently until the arm that's supporting his head and back is resting on the mattress.

- Lower his bottom, if it's being supported by your other hand, then give him a moment to get used to his new position.
- Gently slide your hands out from underneath him.

others holding your baby

It's fine to let friends and family hold your baby, provided they aren't visibly sick (coughing or sneezing, for instance). Newborns' immune systems aren't yet mature enough to fight off germs and infections. It's smart to take the added precaution of asking everyone to wash their hands first. But practically speaking, hand-washing isn't always possible and chances are your baby will be just fine. If your baby was delivered prematurely, however, hand-washing is a must to help avoid germs.

first feeding

Just after your baby's birth, when you're in skin-to-skin contact, is a good time to try a first feeding. Holding your newborn close against your skin will usually cause her to root around in search of your breast and make sucking noises. Your baby may even crawl to your breast and take her first drink, or she may just smell your breast and lick the nipple. Early skin-to-skin contact can increase the rate of successful breastfeeding, so take some time to get to know your baby this way if breastfeeding is important to you.

There's no need to force your baby to breastfeed. While some babies feed within minutes of birth, others just drop off to sleep. That's fine. Either way, spending time together soon after delivery helps establish and promote breastfeeding.

When you do start feeding, you can help your baby by making sure she's in a good position first, and then help her to attach to your breast well. (See page 73 for more about ways to get your baby positioned and latched onto your breast correctly.)

Some newborns are slow to get the hang of breastfeeding, particularly those who are very sleepy in the first days. (This may be the case if you had a difficult labor or certain labor medications.) If your baby is drowsy, try keeping her in bed with you during the

babycenter buzz
beginning to breastfeed

"She came out sucking away at her hand and hasn't really stopped since. I immediately put her to my breast, and she nursed for a good 30 minutes."
—Christina

"I got to breastfeed him right away, and we started off nicely. The nurse helped me latch him on that first time. After that, I didn't need any help. The next day, my nipples started getting a little sore, but I tried to look past that. Finally, that's the reason I quit breastfeeding; it hurt too much."
—Anonymous

"I felt very relaxed whenever I was nursing, and that one-to-one time with my baby was very special and rewarding."**—Kathy**

day for lots of skin-to-skin contact. She may also wake up and feed more often if she can smell you and your milk than if she's tucked into a crib.

after a c-section

In theory, if you've had a c-section, you should be able to breast-feed just like a woman who's had a vaginal birth, but circumstances often conspire against you. You'll be in the hospital longer, you'll find it more difficult to pick up your baby, and staff might be busy and have less time to help you. But don't give up hope. Many women do successfully breastfeed after a c-section; they just need extra help at first. It may be easier to lie on your side with your baby on the bed facing you. Your partner or a nurse can help by holding your baby in the right position for the first few feedings. If you prefer to sit up, put a couple of bed pillows or a nursing pillow on your lap and place your baby on them. This will take the weight off your incision and help bring your baby up to your breast.

formula-feeding

If you've chosen to formula-feed your baby, a nurse will give you a bottle of formula to offer to your baby soon after birth. Don't be surprised if she also asks you to breastfeed your baby at least once. This isn't to second-guess your decision but to allow your baby to get some of the benefits of colostrum. This is the very concentrated and rich first breast milk that contains vital antibodies that help protect your baby from infections. (See page 72.)

feeding a premature baby

Breast milk is the safest and best food for a preterm baby. Your baby won't be able to drink it straight from your breast, but hospital staff will show you how to pump your milk. Sometimes a preemie needs extra nutrients added to the breast milk. If breastfeeding isn't possible, your baby will be given formula specially designed to meet the nutritional needs of premature babies.

first diaper change

Okay, you've got the baby in one hand, the diaper in the other—now, which hand are you going to use to wield the wipe and the diaper rash ointment? Welcome to the world of baby care.

Changing that first diaper can be a bit daunting, especially since the first bowel movement your baby produces is an unusually black and sticky one. It's called **meconium**, and it's your baby getting rid of all the waste that's built up in the colon during the months of swallowing amniotic fluid.

Gradually, as your milk comes in, the poop will turn to the yellow, soft consistency that's normal for a breastfed baby. Formula-fed babies have poop that's thicker, darker, firmer, and stronger smelling.

Your baby will need diaper changes from the first day. Many moms and dads have never changed a diaper until they face their own baby. But as the job needs doing 7 to 10 times a day on average, you'll soon be able to do it blindfolded.

what you need
- A plastic changing mat, covered with a towel or flannel blanket to take away the chill

- Baby wipes (or toilet paper and lukewarm water; some parents use a clean, damp washcloth)
- A new diaper

how to do it

Always put your changing mat on a wide and secure surface. The floor is a good place, as your baby can't roll off it, but you'll need to kneel down to avoid straining your back. If you use a changing table, never leave your baby unattended on it, and use the safety strap to keep your baby from wriggling off.

The basic routine will always be the same:

- First, get rid of the mess, which is easily done. Unfasten the diaper, fold it over, and gently set your baby's bottom back down on the clean outside of the diaper.
- Grasp your baby's legs in your nondominant hand, and lift slightly, so just your baby's hips are off of the floor or mat.
- Using your other hand, hold the wipe on your flattened palm and fingers and wipe his bottom clean. Always wipe a girl's diaper area from front to back to help prevent urinary infections. Experts now say you should wipe a boy the same way, for

the same reason. You'll have to work carefully and gently to clean stool from skin folds. You may need several wipes.

- Put the dirty wipes inside the diaper, fold the diaper over, and throw away!
- Once the area is dry, put on a new diaper. Pick up your baby's legs in the same fashion as with cleaning, then lay the clean diaper underneath your baby's bottom, with the tabs under her back, positioned just beneath the waistline.
- When changing a boy, point his penis down when you put the new diaper on. If it's pointing upward, urine could leak out of the top of the diaper. (You'll probably be treated to at least one glorious arc of urine from your son over the diaper changing years, and if that happens, just wash it away.) An uncircumcised penis requires no special cleaning or care.
- If you aren't using newborn diapers that have a cut-out area for the umbilical stump, roll the top of the diaper under the stump to allow it to air-dry until it falls off. Some doctors still recommend the once-standard practice of using a cotton ball dipped in rubbing alcohol to further keep the stump clean and dry, but there's no evidence that this causes faster healing or fewer infections than plain old air-drying.
- Wash your hands.

There's an optional middle step of providing your baby with a barrier cream such as zinc oxide to prevent redness and rashes. Redness is caused when your baby's skin stays in prolonged contact with moisture. In the early days, however, you'll probably be changing diapers so frequently that barrier cream isn't necessary. One of the best preventatives for redness is to let your baby have some diaper-free time, which also gives him a chance to kick freely.

chapter 6

first night at home

You won't be the first parents in the world who, when left alone for the first time with your new baby, nervously feel like there's been some kind of mistake. *Surely they're not going to leave us in charge? We don't know anything about babies! What if she stops breathing? What if we drop her? What if . . .*

During that first night, you won't be the first parents, either, who find it hard to sleep, even though you may be absolutely exhausted. It's too tempting to keep admiring your baby and to feel proud that she's here at last—and to keep checking up on her.

After a hospital birth, your discharge will depend on your own and your baby's health, your insurance coverage, and hospital policy. The usual stay is 2 or 3 days, or 3 to 5 following a c-section. If you delivered at home, your midwife will stay for a few hours to make sure you're healthy and assess your baby. She'll also give you a phone number in case you need to contact her. If you have any questions about baby care, your pediatrician (or your own mom) is also just a phone call away. And don't worry whether your question seems trivial or insignificant; your doctor (or the nurse on call) has heard everything before, and the reassurance will give you peace of mind.

babycenter buzz
home sweet home

"The first night at home felt so much better—not a single uncomfortable plastic hospital bed in sight!"—**Abby**

"Our first night home was crazy. Jaden breastfeeds wonderfully, but she was so hungry that night that all she wanted to do was nurse, and I was so tired that all I wanted to do was sleep! Every time she'd fall asleep and the nipple would come out of her mouth, she'd start screaming like crazy. Finally we put her in the swing and she fell asleep, so I was able to get a couple hours of sleep (after literally 3 days without it)."—**Heather**

"I actually found the first night at home much easier than the first night in the noisy hospital. I was a lot more comfortable and had rocking chairs and other things to help distract him when he got fussy."—**Kristen**

"We installed a night-light and a dimmer switch in the baby's room to keep night wakings calm and to differentiate day from night right from the start."—**Anonymous**

Many moms say that it was only when they got home that they felt that their baby was really *theirs*. Of course, it's when you step inside the front door that the full weight of responsibility hits you. Being home with your baby can be relaxing and intimidating at the same time. Don't be surprised if your feelings yo-yo. One moment, you're on a high, delighted to have your baby (and to be finished with pregnancy!). The next, you feel sore, tired, and tearful, not to mention a little apprehensive about feeding and caring for your new baby. It's a big change in your life, and a combination of physical and emotional causes may leave you feeling topsy-turvy.

One of the most common worries, beginning the first night, is SIDS (Sudden Infant Death Syndrome). Follow the guidance on page 118 for putting your baby to sleep safely.

first bath

Bathing is a great opportunity to connect and play with your baby. How often you bathe him depends on your personal preference and your baby's, though a daily bath isn't necessary. Some babies enjoy water right from the start. Others dislike being naked and protest strongly at first. That's okay: A sponge bath—washing your baby's head and face, then the rest of his body, while he's partially covered—is enough to keep him clean.

The first time you bathe your baby is a bit intimidating, so it's not a bad idea to have someone else around, for assistance *and* reassurance. Dads and grandparents often want to join in, anyway. And an extra pair of hands is especially useful if you've forgotten something and your baby is already wet. Your baby's first baths will be sponge baths.

Caution: For safety's sake, never leave your baby unattended in a bath, even an infant tub. Best to close the bathroom door and let the answering machine pick up any messages. If you must leave the tub area, wrap your baby in a towel and take him with you.

giving a sponge bath

You'll need cotton balls, a washcloth, gentle baby soap or cleansing solution, a towel for drying, and a clean diaper.

babycenter buzz
hold the bubbles!

"When my baby was born, I'd place a tub of water next to him on the changing table and give him a sponge bath while keeping the areas I wasn't washing covered with a towel. I was scared to give him a bath, and I felt more comfortable with a sponge bath. The hospital suggested it because newborns don't really get so dirty that they need to be submerged in water."—**Jessey**

"I bathed my newborn after the first week. Just make sure the water isn't too hot—or too cold. The first time I bathed her, the water was too cool, and let me tell you, that was one ticked-off baby. Since that first time, though, she's loved her bath."—**Shauna**

Wrap your baby in a hooded towel with his diaper on. Hold him securely in your lap or lay him on a padded surface with an arm around him. Using a cotton ball dipped in warm (not hot) water (a separate one for each eye), wipe around his eyes, moving from the inside corner out. With another dampened cotton ball, dab around his cheeks, nose, mouth, and chin.

Use a soft, warm washcloth with a few drops of mild soap or baby cleanser to wash the rest of your baby's body: neck, back, chest, and on down to his feet. After washing, rinse each area with a clean washcloth and gently dry him with a towel.

Finally, remove your baby's diaper and clean the genital area and then his bottom with soap or cleanser. For both boys and girls, always clean the genital area from front to back to avoid infection. Also avoid getting soap on a boy's circumcised penis until it's healed.

bath in a tub

Many parents choose to bathe *with* their baby in the big bathtub from the start. Others prefer to use a special infant tub. If you use a baby tub, make sure it's safely on the floor or a counter before you fill it. Some are designed to fit across or inside the family bathtub. A foam wedge or support to rest your baby on can make it easier if you find it nerve-wracking to hold a wriggly baby with one hand and wash him with the other.

You'll need a washcloth or sponge, gentle baby soap or cleansing solution, towels for drying, a clean diaper, and clothes for your baby.

After making sure the room is warm, fill the bath with 2 to 3 inches of water that feels warm but not hot, about 90° to 100°F. Put in the cold water first to avoid scalding. Test the temperature with your elbow or wrist or with a bath thermometer.

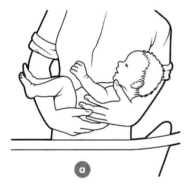

When the bath is ready, undress your baby. Before putting him into the tub, clean his diaper area as you do during a diaper change. The easiest method of getting your baby into the bath is to support his head on your left arm, bringing your left hand beneath his arm and around his chest. Support his lower back with your right arm (a). Lower his body slowly into the water and let him splash around a bit. Pour cupfuls of bath water over your baby regularly during the bath to keep him warm.

Work from top to bottom, front to back. Use moistened cotton balls to clean his eyes and face. If dried mucus has collected in the corner of his nostrils or eyes, dab it several times with a small section of moistened cotton ball to soften it before wiping it out. Wipe from the corner of the eye out toward the nose (b). Because your baby's nose and ears are miraculously self-cleaning, it's unnecessary (and strongly discouraged) to poke cotton swabs into them as you could push dirt in further (and injure your baby).

Wash your baby's scalp with a wet, soapy cloth. To rinse, either do it while he's in the tub with his head tilted back, or remove him from the tub, wrap him in a towel (c), and hold him firmly over the tub as you rinse out the soap.

To wash your baby's hair, dampen it with a washcloth, taking care to keep water away from his eyes. Gently work a little baby shampoo into his scalp with your fingers. Rinse once or twice (again avoiding his eyes) with a cupful of clean, warm water.

Once your baby is clean, wrap him in a fresh towel and pat him dry. If he has diaper rash (see page 435), you can apply a barrier cream after the bath.

umbilical cord care

The umbilical stump will heal itself and fall off naturally after a week or two. Though some doctors still advise putting alcohol on the stump to help it to dry up and heal, this step is no longer part

plain water or bath products?

Using water without mild soap or baby cleanser isn't always enough to keep your baby clean. Baby feces contains up to 4 percent fats, which means that plain water may not be enough to remove the fatty deposits completely.

Nor is water alone always as gentle as you might think. Domestic tap water in hard water areas has been linked to greater incidence of atopic eczema (an itchy skin condition that tends to run in families) than tap water in soft water areas. The solution seems to be to use a small amount of mild, pH-neutral cleanser formulated for babies. Remember: You don't have to bathe your baby every day.

of standard care. It's a normal part of the healing process for a newborn's umbilical cord to look slightly jelly-like, but let your doctor know if the cord has a strong smell, oozes, or bleeds, as these could be the first signs of an infection. (A spot of blood when the cord falls off is normal.)

For live visual instructions on how to give your baby a bath, watch BabyCenter's "Bathing your newborn" video at babycenter.com.

chapter
8

first trip

Ready to head home from the hospital with your baby, or take him for a spin down to the supermarket? You wrap your baby carefully against the elements, strap him securely into his car seat, check and double-check he's safe, and off you go. Never before have you realized just how quickly everyone else in the world drives! Maniacs are overtaking you, driving too close, rushing ahead. Then you notice you're hurtling along at, what, 20 miles per hour? Your new parental instinct to protect your baby from all harm has kicked in.

Channel that instinct productively by always using a car seat, and using it correctly. Choose a rear-facing seat suitable for your baby's weight and age and, if your car's seatbelt configuration allows, position it in the center of the back seat. The car seat should be held tightly in place, with very little sideways movement. Surveys show that the majority of car seats are incorrectly installed, so ideally, have yours checked by an expert. Many hospitals will check your car seat installation before you leave with your newborn. Some police and fire departments also offer this service, and given how many varieties of car seats are available, the peace of mind provided is well worth it.

Take special care if your baby is born more than 3 weeks prematurely; semi-reclining seats may create breathing difficulty. Doctors sometimes recommend a car bed for preemies, but only for the

babycenter buzz
out of the house, into the limelight

"It's all a matter of personal preference. If you feel ready to leave the house, then it's right for you. Same goes for staying at home for however long you feel comfortable. And I don't think anyone should make another person feel guilty about leaving the house. A lady at the mall told me I was crazy for shopping the week after my baby was born. She doesn't know me or my situation."—**Anonymous**

"I take my baby everywhere. When she was 3 days old, I took her grocery shopping. I just don't let strangers touch her. However, when people notice I have a little one, they ask how old and keep their distance. I guess most people realize the rule about newborns and respect the need for distance."—**R. Wolfe**

"My baby and I haven't stayed home since we got out of the hospital. She has loved being around people. We've gone to the mall, the beach, and friends' and families' houses. She loves the attention, and she sleeps through noise very well because of it all. Of course, I'm careful about how she's dressed, and I make sure everyone is in good health before we visit."—**Anonymous**

"I live in China and just had a baby boy. Chinese women don't leave the house, bathe, or do any housework for a month after the birth. So, I was constantly criticized by all the locals when they discovered me out and about after 1 week."—**Suzanne**

"Always, always get your bag ready the night before. I thought I was high maintenance when I went out, but taking a baby out is something else!"
—**Anonymous**

first few weeks. (They're not recommended for general use because they're slightly less safe in a crash.)

To make sure your baby's car seat is properly installed with your car's safety belts, watch BabyCenter's "Securing the seat" video at babycenter.com.

packing a diaper bag

On the first outing with your newborn, your diaper bag may feel
far heavier than your baby! To be prepared, you'll need a few
essentials, including:

- **Diapers:** At least four, even if you're only going to be out for an
  hour. (Better to be safe than sorry.)
- **Wipes:** Buy travel-size packs. Later, they'll come in handy for
  faces, hands, and spills as well as changes.
- **Hand sanitizer:** A small bottle of this can be a lifesaver when
  you're not near a sink for post-poop wash-up. Also helps to
  disinfect your baby after well-meaning older children grab
  his hands.
- **Spare clothes:** Your baby will need them if he produces one of
  "those" diapers. Keep a spare hat and sweater in the bag at all
  times for colder than expected weather. Some moms stow an
  extra T-shirt for themselves, too, in case of untimely upchucks.
- **Burp cloth:** To toss over your shoulder, a cloth diaper or small
  towel works fine.
- **Formula and bottle:** If you are not breastfeeding and will be out
  past a feeding.
- **Pacifier:** If your baby uses one.
- **Spare bib:** Handy for drooling or spit up.

Some diaper bags unfold to give you a portable changing surface,
while others include a separate fold-up mat. Both types provide a
clean and convenient surface for changing your baby.

first
purchases

New parents typically spend between $6,200 and $11,000 on their first babies in just a year. On the other hand, some families cover all the basics for far less, just as there are some who go all out and drop much more.

Babies themselves have pretty simple needs. For parents, however, one person's must-have is another's must-avoid. How much you spend ultimately depends on your tastes and your lifestyle. Borrowing baby gear for the early months can save you big bucks, as some items get very little use. Buying used gear is another way to stretch your budget. The only thing you shouldn't skimp on and buy secondhand is a car seat because there's no way to verify its history, and a seat that's been in even a minor crash is no longer considered safe. Likewise, if you buy a used crib or, later, a second-hand high chair, make sure they're sturdy, have no peeling paint, and that they meet current safety standards.

So what do babies really need?

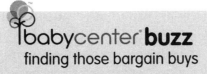

babycenter buzz
finding those bargain buys

"If you're buying online, most companies have a space to enter a promotion or coupon code. This gives you savings of, say, $5 off with an order of $25, or free shipping, etc. If you don't have a coupon, you can usually find one by doing a search online."—**Shara**

"The way we make ends meet is by clipping coupons and surfing coupon Web sites. I can't believe how much money that saves us. I also buy baby clothes on clearance."—**Ali**

"There are actually very few things you absolutely need, like a crib or car seat. Most of the things we tend to buy are nice to have but not necessary. Garage sales and consignment stores are great for bargains."—**Deborah**

"Buy as many onesies as you can but in a size or so too big. Receiving blankets can double as burp cloths."—**Anonymous**

"It's useful to get newborn clothes secondhand from friends or relatives, especially if you're on a budget. Many of our favorite toys were secondhand, and the expensive toys that we bought didn't hold much interest. Sometimes simple is better."—**Malissa**

something to wear

A basic shopping list includes:

- About six all-in-one **sleepers, or coveralls** (Newborns tend to live in these during their first few months and don't really need to wear anything else. Don't buy too many in the newborn size as your baby will quickly outgrow them. A sleep sack, which has no legs, is a handy variation for the first weeks, making middle-of-the-night diaper changes a breeze.)
- About six baby **undershirts, or onesies** (Babies can wear these under sleepers during cold weather. When it's hot, this may be all your baby needs to wear.)

- One or two **button- or snap-front sweaters** to provide an extra layer
- A warm, all-in-one **snow suit** with snaps beneath the legs or an insulated sack with legs to fit in car seat belt (useful if your baby is born in winter or will travel to a cold climate).
- **Hat.** Choose a warm one for a winter birth, as babies lose a lot of heat through their heads. A summer baby needs a **sunhat.**
- **Socks.** Not essential, but they do keep little feet warm. Plan on losing most of them.
- One or two **blankets.** Receiving blankets are a good weight for swaddling. Use a heavier blanket in the stroller outdoors.

Make sure baby clothes are machine washable and dryable and avoid anything that needs ironing.

a change of diapers

There are two kinds of diapers: disposable and reusable. (See page 156 for a decision guide on which to buy.)

buying disposable diapers

A newborn baby will need about 10 to 12 diaper changes a day. You're likely to go through around 150 diapers in the first 2 weeks.

You'll also need:

- **Baby wipes**
- **Barrier cream** to prevent diaper rash
- **Changing mat** or a **changing table**
- **Diaper pail**

buying reusable (cloth) diapers

You'll need at least 18 **diapers.** Choose from two basic types of reusable diapers:

by the numbers

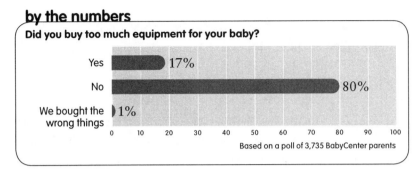

Did you buy too much equipment for your baby?

Yes 17%
No 80%
We bought the wrong things 1%

Based on a poll of 3,735 BabyCenter parents

1. Two-part diapers: These consist of a diaper and a waterproof cover. They come either flat (for folding) or fitted to a baby's bottom. The diaper cover, which may be pull-up or wraparound, goes over it. (You'll need about eight covers.)

2. All-in-one diapers: The inner diaper and the outer waterproof portion are combined. These look like disposables and are usually fastened with Velcro. They tend to be easier to put on but harder to launder (they're slower to dry as they're bulkier and often can't be put in the dryer).

You'll also need:

- **Liners:** the liner catches a bowel movement and the whole thing can be flushed down the toilet
- **Booster pads** for extra-absorbency at night
- Plastic diaper **grips** or diaper **pins:** Some diapers have built-in fasteners or snaps.
- A **diaper pail** with a lid for storing dirty diapers before washing

somewhere to sleep

Many parents choose a **Moses basket, cradle,** or **bassinet** for the first few months, although some mothers and fathers start with their babies sleeping in the same bed as them. You can use a full-size **crib** from the day your baby is born, although newborns look a little lost in a big crib. Baskets (or smaller cradles and bassinets on casters) are more infant-sized and portable so you can move your baby from room to room, but, like cradles, babies outgrow them in a few months. A crib will probably be your baby's bed until he's 2 or 3 years old.

You'll also need:

- A tight-fitting **mattress**, without gaps around the sides. It doesn't matter what kind of mattress you use, as long as it is firm and doesn't sag or show any signs of wear and tear. Unless you know the history of a secondhand mattress, buy a new one.
- A tight-fitting bottom sheet and a baby sleeper or **sleep sack.**
- Waterproof **mattress cover** (optional, but highly recommended if it is tight fitting, such as a cover made for a specific mattress, and is used together with a regular fitted cotton sheet; never use loose-fitting mattress covers or waterproof sheets as these can impair breathing).

A sleep sack or sleeper will keep your baby safe and warm. Some parents still like to use cotton or flannel sheets and cotton blankets as well. Newborns don't need fluffy blankets or quilts, however; if you don't use a sleep sack or swaddle your baby securely, stick to small, lightweight receiving blankets for covering up. Loose, fluffy blankets are considered a SIDS hazard. To avoid tangling (and breathing risks), the AAP recommends "feet to foot" tuck-ins: Place your baby's feet at the bottom (foot) of the crib and tuck in the blanket tightly under the mattress at the sides and foot of the crib.

You'll need about four bottom sheets and two or three blankets to start with. (One of these blankets may later graduate to the exalted role of "lovey" and be dragged around lovingly by your child for years.)

What you shouldn't have in the crib: pillows, sheepskin, soft pillowy bumper pads, or stuffed animals or toys of any kind, which pose a breathing risk in the early months.

Some parents find peace of mind in having an **infant monitor,** available with either audio, video, or both, which allows them to hear and see their babies from another room or another floor.

A **crib light,** a soft light that attaches to your baby's bed, makes middle-of-the-night diaper changes easier by providing just enough illumination to get the job done without letting your baby think it's playtime.

somewhere to get washed

Some parents prefer a special **baby bathtub,** while others use the sink or the regular tub. Using a baby tub means no worries about germs (the kitchen sink is the most bacteria-laden spot in most homes), and it's easy on your back. You'll need a couple of small **towels** (a **hooded towel** is ideal for keeping your baby warm), **baby washcloths,** and some **mild baby soap** or **cleanser** (most double as baby shampoo).

A **sponge bath support** that comfortably helps prop up baby is particularly useful in the early days.

a way to get around

Your baby will need a **car seat.** It's illegal not to use one. Holding your baby on your lap is unsafe, as there's nothing to protect him in the event of an accident, and the force of even a slight impact could wrench him from your arms.

You'll need a **carriage or stroller** that's suitable for newborns (one with a lie-flat position). Comfort and portability are the two key features to consider when buying one. Your choices:

- Traditional carriages, regular strollers, and travel systems (which combine a car seat, a stroller, and a carrier) are sturdy and comfortable for your baby but are heavy and difficult for you to fold up and carry around.
- Lightweight collapsible "umbrella" strollers offer the ultimate in portability but provide a less comfortable ride for your baby. Unless they have a full-recline position, they can't be used until

your baby sits up unsupported. Newborns need a lie-flat setting and a more comfortable padded seat than umbrella strollers usually provide. You'll probably want one, though, when your baby is older.

- Double strollers made for twins come in both heavier and umbrella weights. Look for one that fully reclines.

A **baby sling, carrier,** or **wrap** is a great way to keep your newborn close while enabling you to get other things done because your hands are free. Before buying any baby-wearing gear, test it. Make sure you can actually get your baby into it and the device onto you without assistance. Wear it a little while to see if it's comfortable and agrees with your back. Babies and parents come in all different shapes and sizes, and a carrier that suits your best friend may be the exact wrong fit for you.

For more information about what to look for when buying a sling or carrier, go to babycenter.com. To find out what kind of carrier or sling is the best choice for you and your baby, watch BabyCenter's video at babycenter.com.

a way to get fed

If you're breastfeeding, you'll need very little:

- A **nursing bra** needs to be comfortable and adjustable, give good support, and be easy to open with one hand for feeding.
- A **lanolin-based nipple cream,** such as Lansinoh, may be useful to help heal and soothe cracked or sore nipples.
- **Breast pads** (cloth or disposable) absorb leakage between feedings.

You'll also need a **breast pump** and **bottles** if you plan to express breast milk for your baby. A hand-pump is fine if you're planning to express milk only once or twice a week. A reliable and fast electric breast pump makes more sense if you're going back to work and need to express quickly. Ask a lactation consultant to

by the numbers

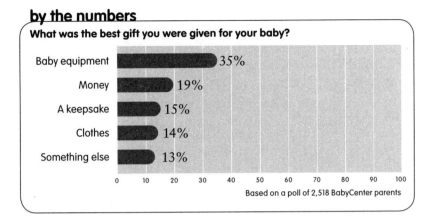

What was the best gift you were given for your baby?

Baby equipment	35%
Money	19%
A keepsake	15%
Clothes	14%
Something else	13%

0 10 20 30 40 50 60 70 80 90 100

Based on a poll of 2,518 BabyCenter parents

help you decide which type will best suit your lifestyle. Renting an electric pump from a hospital or lactation consultant allows you to put one to the test before you decide whether you want to make a potentially expensive purchase.

If you're bottle-feeding, you'll need:

- At least six to eight **bottles:** The smaller 4-ounce bottles are more suitable for newborns, who can take only a little milk at a time. For older babies who can easily manage a large feeding, the larger 8-ounce bottles are better. Experiment to see which shape feels most comfortable and whether you prefer regular bottles or those with disposable liners.
- At least six to eight **nipples:** Buy just a few until you're sure which style your baby prefers, as they come in a variety of shapes and materials.
- **Formula:** Your pediatrician will recommend the best kind for your baby.
- Bottle and nipple **brush**
- **Sterilizing equipment:** You have a choice of three ways to sterilize your baby's bottles and nipples to kill germs: boiling, which requires only an ordinary pot and a set of tongs to get bottles out; sterilizing in a unit made for this purpose; or running everything through the dishwasher on a hot cycle.
- **Bottle warmer** (optional)
- A **drying rack** (optional)

part two
life with a
newborn

birth–3 months

by the numbers
development:
birth to 3 months

When did your baby first grasp a toy?

- Younger than 6 weeks — 7%
- 7 weeks — 6%
- 8 weeks — 11%
- 9 weeks — 12%
- 10 weeks — 17%
- 11 weeks — 11%
- Older than 11 weeks — 32%

Based on a poll of 4,450 BabyCenter parents

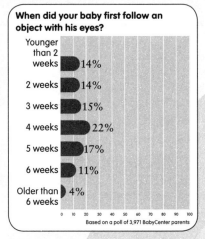

When did your baby first follow an object with his eyes?

- Younger than 2 weeks — 14%
- 2 weeks — 14%
- 3 weeks — 15%
- 4 weeks — 22%
- 5 weeks — 17%
- 6 weeks — 11%
- Older than 6 weeks — 4%

Based on a poll of 3,971 BabyCenter parents

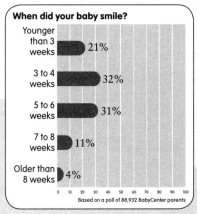

When did your baby smile?

- Younger than 3 weeks — 21%
- 3 to 4 weeks — 32%
- 5 to 6 weeks — 31%
- 7 to 8 weeks — 11%
- Older than 8 weeks — 4%

Based on a poll of 88,932 BabyCenter parents

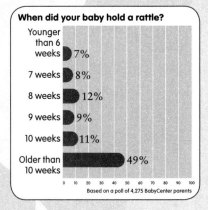

When did your baby hold a rattle?

- Younger than 6 weeks — 7%
- 7 weeks — 8%
- 8 weeks — 12%
- 9 weeks — 9%
- 10 weeks — 11%
- Older than 10 weeks — 49%

Based on a poll of 4,275 BabyCenter parents

the first month:

Are you combining breast and formula feeding?

Yes	26%
No	73%

Based on a poll of 3,006 BabyCenter parents

at 1 month old:

Are you combining breast and formula feeding?

Yes	27%
No	72%

Based on a poll of 4,795 BabyCenter parents

at 3 months old:

Are you combining breast and formula feeding?

Yes	23%
No	76%

Based on a poll of 5,385 BabyCenter parents

by this time, according to the experts . . .

	most babies can . . .	half of babies can . . .	a few babies can . . .
1 month	• Lift head • Respond to sound • Stare at faces	• Follow objects • *Oooh* and *Ahh*	• Smile • Laugh • Hold head at 45-degree angle
2 months	• Vocalize sounds by gurgling and cooing • Follow objects • Hold head up for short periods • Roll from side to back	• Smile, laugh • Hold head at 45-degree angle • Make smooth hand movements	• Hold head steady • Bear weight on legs • Lift head and shoulder (mini-pushup)
3 months	• Laugh • Hold head steady • Recognize your face	• Squeal, gurgle, coo • Do mini-pushups	• Turn toward loud sounds • Bring hands together and may bat at toys • Roll over

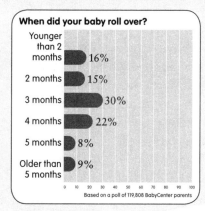

When did your baby roll over?

Younger than 2 months	16%
2 months	15%
3 months	30%
4 months	22%
5 months	8%
Older than 5 months	9%

0 10 20 30 40 50 60 70 80 90 100

Based on a poll of 119,808 BabyCenter parents

the bottom line

Babies develop according to their own schedules. So don't be surprised or concerned when your baby does some things earlier and some things later than others. If your baby was born prematurely, you'll probably find that she needs extra time before she catches up with other babies. Try to enjoy what your baby *can* do, rather than worrying about what she can't.

development—
birth to 3 months

Babies arrive with limbs still curled, pretzel-like. Their movements
are jerky, and they can't control their bodies very well. Learning
control is a gradual process—one your baby will follow at his own
pace. Still, the pattern of development is always the same. Control
moves down through the body. Babies first gain control of their
heads, then their arms, hands, backs, and finally their legs and
feet. Over the next few months, you'll watch your baby stretch
out. His jerky movements will give way to more fluid ones as his
nervous system and muscle control mature, and he'll confidently
reach and grasp a toy if you hold it in your hand.

You'll go through a huge learning curve, too. In the first few
weeks, along with learning the practical skills of parenting, you'll
discover your baby's temperament. This is the general approach to
the world that he's born with. Some babies prefer being with Mom
most of the time. Yours may enjoy being swaddled and handled
gently and quietly. Or, he may wriggle and fight against being
wrapped up, love new faces and places, and delight relatives when
they happily fuss over him. Your baby may sleep for hours and
rarely cry or complain, or he may take catnaps and often seem
unsettled while awake.

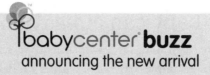

babycenter **buzz**
announcing the new arrival

"My husband and father-in-law made origami bow ties that when pulled open had our baby's name, date, weight, and time of birth. My father-in-law had made a similar announcement for my husband's birth. People loved it!"—**Susan**

"We sent out a mass e-mail to everyone we knew directing them to our Web site. The day my son was born, my husband put his photos up on the site. Everyone could see him the day he was born. We also added our baby's URL to the bottom of our traditional baby announcements, which went out via snail mail to our technophobic friends."—**Kate**

"When my husband was born 32 years ago, his parents had pencils made with his name on them. He's always cherished the leftover pencils. So when our daughter was born, we had ink pens made. We designed our own piece of art and got the pens for about 29 cents each."—**Anonymous**

"I created fill-in-the-blank birth questionnaires for family and friends to work on as they waited at the hospital. The programs provided distraction for those waiting, as well as a keepsake with as little or as much information as they wanted to record. I had my mother fill in one for me while I was in labor."—**Lanette**

Watch how your baby responds to a new experience, such as a toy moved across his line of vision, a new voice, or new face. Does he pay attention, look interested, and wriggle his arms and legs? If so, he may be the kind of baby who goes full speed at the world. Or does he watch carefully but quietly, waiting to decide what's what? Then he may need to proceed slowly before joining in. (For more about your baby's temperament, see page 210.)

You'll learn more about your baby with each passing day. Gradually, you'll get to know what his cries and wriggling mean. Knowing your baby will help you decide how to care for him now and as he grows into a toddler. So take your time. Watch and learn alongside him.

what your baby can already do

Human babies are born with far fewer skills than other creatures. Many animals, for example, can walk within a few hours of being born. Your baby, however, is born with innate reflexes that help her survive. You may notice some of them in your newborn. Not all of these reflexes last for long, and they're gradually replaced by learned behaviors.

Rooting and sucking. Stroke your baby's cheek, and she'll automatically turn her face to the side that you touch, and her lips will purse, ready to suck. If she finds a nipple, or even a finger, she'll suck rhythmically. This is a great help in establishing breastfeeding (see page 73).

Walking. Hold your newborn upright in a standing position, with her feet placed lightly on a hard surface, and she'll lift her legs up and down as if she's marching. This reflex disappears by about 2 months, and your baby won't walk in this way again until around her first birthday.

Grasping. Touch your baby lightly on her hand, and she'll immediately grab whatever touches her and grip hard, a reflex that's thought to be a holdover from our ancient past, when babies kept themselves safe by hanging onto their mothers in much the same way that a baby monkey does. Interestingly, your baby will find letting go harder than grasping. Grasping is a reflex, but letting go requires voluntary control. Around 4 or 5 months, your baby will learn this skill.

Startling. Lay your baby down too quickly, and she'll fling out her arms and legs, then curl them up. She'll probably also cry. She's demonstrating her fear of not having something to hold onto or anyone holding on to her—another example of what's believed to be an ancient reflex from when babies needed to cling to their mothers. It's called the Moro reflex, and it lasts 3 to 4 months.

One of the reasons why humans are born with fewer skills than other animals is because of the way our brains develop. While

what not to worry about

It's unavoidable: With parenthood comes worry. Many concerns stem from unfamiliarity. Here are three common things you're bound to wonder about—but, happily, don't need to worry over:

Racing heartbeat. A baby's heartbeat races faster than an adult's. Because babies are so tiny, they have very little muscle or fat between their hearts and their outer skin, so it's much easier to hear your baby's heartbeat than an adult's. If you heard her heartbeat on the monitor when she was inside you, you noticed how very fast it was then. It will gradually slow to a rate more like yours.

Peeling skin. Your newborn's skin will peel a little in the first few days as it adjusts to life outside the womb. Peeling is usually most visible on the hands and feet.

A squint. Your newborn's eyes appear to squint because of the folds of skin at the inner corners. These folds are normal and become less noticeable after a few weeks.

nearly all of the brain cells—or neurons—your baby will ever use are present at birth, these neurons haven't yet become organized into their specialized functions. Organization develops and is influenced by what your baby experiences. That's why stimulation—which all babies actively seek out—is essential. Your newborn's brain will grow more quickly than any other part of her body. It will triple its volume and reach three-quarters of adult size by her first birthday. The more you interact with your baby, the more you're helping her to learn during this critical first year.

what your baby can see

Your baby isn't born with 20/20 vision, but he certainly isn't blind either, as was once believed. Anything at a distance is blurry, but he sees brightness and movement. He can see most clearly from about 12 to 18 inches away, which is almost precisely the distance from your face when you hold him in your arms. Most newborns will study your face carefully when held, especially if you smile.

Your newborn can follow, or track, objects with his eyes, as long as they're clearly distinguished from the rest of his environment. He'll follow your eyes if you move them from side to side. However, his eye movements are quite jerky because the muscles that control the eyes take a while to become fully coordinated. Some babies seem to squint or have a "wandering" eye, but this is nearly always because of lack of eye-muscle coordination. Your baby will enjoy watching moving objects, such as fans or animals, and following them helps strengthen his eye muscles and develop his sight.

More than anything else, your baby likes looking at human faces. Show him a simple picture of a circle with two eyes, a nose, and a mouth, and he'll look more often and longer at it than at a drawing of random shapes. Babies also like strongly contrasting colors. At least for the first couple of months, they prefer black and white objects (especially in stripes) to pastel shades. Your baby's ability to distinguish where one object finishes and another begins, especially when the objects are similar colors, is very limited at first. By the time your baby is **9 weeks old**, he'll be much better able to distinguish between subtle shades.

what you can do to encourage your baby

Try this experiment: When your baby is **1 week old**, hold a colorful rattle or toy about 8 inches in front of her and move it slowly across her field of vision. Notice how long she tracks the movement. It's usually just a few seconds, and her eye movements may seem slow

eye color

Your baby's eye color at birth may not look the same as it will at age 1. In Caucasian newborns, eyes tend to be gray or blue because they have less melanin (dark brown pigment) than darker-skinned infants. Newborns of Asian, African, Hispanic, or Native American descent are usually born with brown, hazel, or dark gray eyes that may darken further.

by the numbers

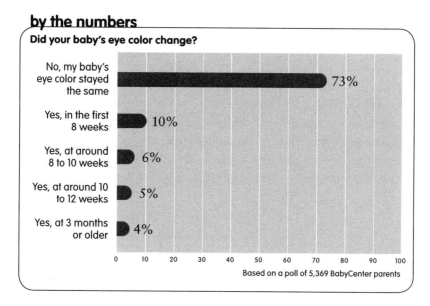

Did your baby's eye color change?

No, my baby's eye color stayed the same	73%
Yes, in the first 8 weeks	10%
Yes, at around 8 to 10 weeks	6%
Yes, at around 10 to 12 weeks	5%
Yes, at 3 months or older	4%

0 10 20 30 40 50 60 70 80 90 100

Based on a poll of 5,369 BabyCenter parents

and jerky. Repeat this game at the end of each week. You'll find that she follows the toy a little longer each time. Her neck muscles grow stronger, too, and she'll soon be able to turn her head as well as track with her eyes. By **2 weeks**, she'll turn her head to follow an object through a very small arc, by a combination of head and eye movements. By around **4 weeks**, she'll follow an object through 90 degrees horizontally and a little way vertically. By **6 weeks**, she may turn her head to search for new objects to look at.

You can help your baby practice focusing by giving her a variety of things to look at: mobiles with high-contrast patterns and picture books with strong line drawings. And shiny or bright household objects will be just as interesting to her as actual "toys," brightly colored rattles, or teethers. But don't forget, your baby prefers looking at a real face than at any other object. Even from **the first days**, your baby searches out faces to study and learn from. So don't be disappointed if you buy her a new toy only to find she ignores it; she'd rather look at you. By **6 weeks**, around half of babies will gaze at a face, exploring it from hairline to chin, always returning to the eyes, and smiling. By about **2 months**, your baby may actively recognize and react differently to you than to strangers, reserving her brightest and best smiles for you alone. By **3 months**, she'll watch you as you move around the room.

what your baby can taste

Even at **a few days old,** babies prefer sweet tastes. Your baby will grimace if given something bitter. In fact, colostrum—the first milk produced by your breasts—is very sweet. Some of the flavors of the food you eat are passed through to your baby before birth and through breast milk, so your baby will be primed to expect them once it's time to start trying solid foods. This is why babies in cultures that eat lots of spicy foods can cope with highly seasoned foods early in life.

what your baby can smell

By **the fifth day** of her life, your baby can recognize you—and probably your partner—by your smell. Even when you aren't there, she recognizes you: A breastfed baby laid between two breast pads, one from her own mother and one from another mom, will turn toward the pad from her own mom.

what your baby can control

Truth is, not much! But two critical things your baby is learning to do are to control her head and to control her hands.

your baby's head control

From **birth,** when you place your baby on her back, you'll notice that she usually turns her head toward one preferred side. Just **a few days after birth,** your baby begins practicing head control. Watch and you'll see her lift her head for just a few seconds when you hold her upright against your shoulder. When she's **a month old,** she'll lift her head very briefly when she's lying on her stomach. She'll also be able to control her head when you hold her upright for a few seconds, as long as you stand very still.

By **6 weeks,** your baby will probably be able to support her head for a minute or two while you remain still, and she may even remain in control as you carry her around. By **8 weeks,** she's

tummy time

Although you should definitely lay your baby on his back to sleep, it's a good idea to give him some "tummy time." Until the "back to sleep" campaign in the early '90s recommending that babies sleep on their backs (to avoid SIDS), they were routinely placed on their bellies. But back-sleeping means they spend less time on their tummies. Even a few waking minutes on your baby's tummy during the day helps him develop and strengthen different muscles that he'll later use for rolling, crawling, and getting around. Varying his position so that he spends some time upright in his bouncy chair, or being carried against your shoulder, helps, too. This may also reduce the chance of a misshapen head (plagiocephaly) and definitely teaches your baby that there are other views of the world than the one he sees when he's lying flat on his back!

gained enough strength in her neck muscles to turn her head from side to side. By **9 weeks**, she may be able to roll from her side onto her back. By **10 weeks**, she'll probably hold her head and neck fairly steady when you carry her around, but you'll still need to keep a supporting hand around her shoulders.

By the end of the third month, your baby will be able to hold her head securely. She'll no longer turn her head to her preferred side all the time. If you put her on her belly, she'll lift her head, chest, and shoulders off the ground, looking up for just a few seconds at first, then gradually longer.

what you can do to encourage your baby

Help your baby exercise the muscles that control his head by holding a toy in front of him. Although he won't be able to reach it or move toward it, he'll want to raise himself to look at it. Your baby won't actually crawl until around 6 months, but these movements help him develop the muscles that enable him to crawl.

your baby's hand control

Your baby's hands will uncurl from tight fists over the first weeks. At around **6 weeks**, you may notice a sudden spurt in his control and coordination. Around now, he'll find one hand with the other by touch and start exploring them. He'll clasp his hands, pull them, and open and shut his fingers. By **8 weeks**, his hands will be open most of the time and will become a source of amusement, as he spends several minutes at a time watching them and figuring out what they can do. By about **3 months**, he'll realize that his hands are actually part of him and begin to explore his hands with his mouth, too. See if he puts his hand in his mouth and then takes it out again to have a look at it.

At first your baby's arms and legs will wave around, but gradually his muscles become strong enough for him to hold them down. During **the second month**, when you put something in your baby's hand, he unclenches his fingers and moves his arm. It's as though he knows he needs to use that arm but isn't coordinated enough to do it. By **the third month**, he starts swiping at and grabbing objects voluntarily. His arm muscles develop before those of his hands, so swiping comes before grasping.

what you can do to encourage your baby

From **the first days**, your baby will grasp your finger if you put it into her loosely closed hand. Around **3 to 4 weeks**, place a light rattle in your baby's hand. (The rattle should be lightweight; because she has no control of her arm movements, she could bop herself on the head with it.) Your baby may be able to hold onto the rattle and even seem to enjoy moving it around. As she waves the rattle, it makes a sound and her eyes follow the sound. This helps her make the connection between her hands and herself: "I see that. I do this. This happens."

If your baby touches something and is rewarded with a jingle or interesting movement, she's encouraged to repeat the gesture. She practices controlling her hands and visually estimating the distance between them and an object she wants. A play gym with plenty of things to watch, swipe at, and listen to allows your baby to practice these skills, as does any mobile or soft toy hung above her bed. She's also learning that her actions have an effect on the world. Lying down suddenly becomes less boring! By the time your

by the numbers

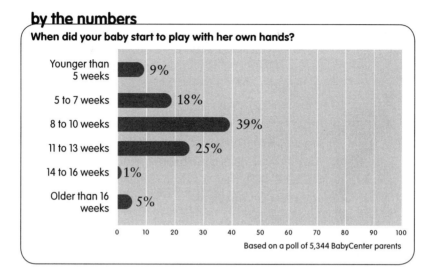

When did your baby start to play with her own hands?

Younger than 5 weeks	9%
5 to 7 weeks	18%
8 to 10 weeks	39%
11 to 13 weeks	25%
14 to 16 weeks	1%
Older than 16 weeks	5%

0   10   20   30   40   50   60   70   80   90   100

Based on a poll of 5,344 BabyCenter parents

baby is **3 months** old, she not only looks at an object but tries to do something about it, usually taking a swipe at it.

You can focus your baby's interest in her hands and feet by reciting "This Little Piggy" and counting her fingers. When you're busy with other things, sit her in a bouncy seat or carrier so that she can see what's going on and feel part of the family. Your baby may also enjoy her newfound physical development more if you allow her time free of restrictive clothing or blankets that impede kicking. In fact, let your baby have some time every day with bare feet so she can exercise her feet and toes. Gently tickle her bare feet and legs to encourage her to flex and stretch her foot muscles.

If you take a step back and look at your 3-month-old, you'll see that she's moving her arms and legs more smoothly. The jerkiness of the early days is giving way to her newfound coordination.

what your baby can hear

From about the 24th week of pregnancy, your baby has listened to the outside world. Even though your voice was slightly muffled, of course, and competing with various internal noises such as your heartbeat, it's familiar to your newborn at birth. The sounds your baby heard while inside you, such as traffic, the vacuum, or your

favorite music (whether Bach or the Red Hot Chili Peppers), are less likely to disturb him than unusual noises. There's no need to keep your home abnormally quiet.

Right from **birth**, your newborn's hearing is almost as sensitive as an adult's, but not quite. That's why your baby sleeps right through a noisy washing machine cycle that would wake you up. On the other hand, your baby will be startled by sudden, loud sounds.

Babies enjoy repetitive, rhythmic sounds, which might include the lullaby you're singing to him or the hum of a car engine. Both are equally soothing. But there's a difference between what your baby hears and what he listens to. What he'll listen to most carefully is the human voice. Experts believe that your baby can recognize your voice from the moment of birth. How can you tell? Although he can't turn toward you to show that he's listening, he may kick his legs and move excitedly when you speak. If he's already kicking when he hears you, he may become still. If he's crying, just the sound of your voice as you approach to pick him up may be enough to calm him.

At birth, your baby can discriminate between all the 150 speech sounds that occur in human language. By the end of his first year, this ability will disappear as his brain tunes in to your native language. Even at **4 days**, your baby can distinguish your mother tongue from another language. If you're bringing up your baby in a bilingual household, he'll lay down pathways in his brain for the sounds needed for both languages.

what you can do to encourage your baby

Let him listen to different noises—wind chimes, a ticking clock, birds, radio voices. Sing songs and nursery rhymes to him. Hold him and move him around to the rhythm of the song. If you don't feel comfortable singing out loud, put on some music and dance

by the numbers

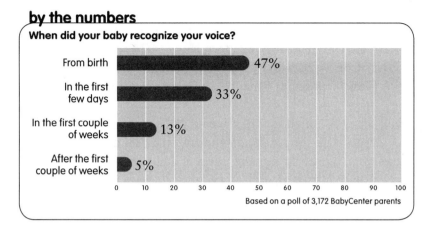

When did your baby recognize your voice?

From birth	47%
In the first few days	33%
In the first couple of weeks	13%
After the first couple of weeks	5%

0 10 20 30 40 50 60 70 80 90 100

Based on a poll of 3,172 BabyCenter parents

around with him in your arms, letting him feel the music through you. And always keep talking to him.

what happens when your baby is born early

Around 12 percent of births in the United States are premature, and this figure is rising rapidly. One reason is the wider use of assisted reproductive techniques. For babies conceived using these techniques, approximately 62 percent of twins and 97 percent of triplets and other higher-order multiples arrive prematurely.

With more preemies being born, the care available for them has become more comprehensive. New techniques and new ways of supporting very tiny babies mean that more survive and thrive than in the past.

understanding the words

If your baby is born preterm, it helps to be familiar with the various terms you'll hear the medical staff use, because babies born at different times will have different needs.

- **Premature baby:** Born before 37 weeks
- **Moderately premature baby:** Born between 35 and 37 weeks

- **Very premature baby:** Born between 29 and 34 weeks
- **Extremely premature baby:** Born between 24 and 28 weeks
- **Low birthweight baby:** Weighs less than 5 pounds, 8 ounces
- **Very low birthweight baby:** Weighs less than 3 pounds, 4 ounces

If your baby is "small for gestational age," she may have had growth problems during the pregnancy. Small for gestational age babies often need help keeping warm and nursing but are less likely to have breathing problems than premature babies because their lungs have had enough time to mature.

If your baby arrives 3 or 4 weeks early but has reached a good weight, she may need to spend only a very short time in special care. The smaller your baby is and the earlier she is born, the more likely she is to need more intensive special care nursing.

Preemies often move immediately into a Special Care Unit or a Neonatal Intensive Care Unit (NICU, or "nick-u"), depending on their needs. Small hospitals tend to have special care units while larger ones are more likely to offer the more high-tech NICUs. If you go into labor early, you may be moved to a large hospital so that your baby can go straight into the NICU if necessary.

Depending on your baby's needs, she may:

- Have continuous monitoring of her respiration or heart rate
- Receive added oxygen
- Receive nasal continuous airway pressure or respiratory support (ventilation)
- Be tube fed or fed intravenously
- Receive phototherapy (treatment for jaundice under special lights)

Having a premature baby can be extremely distressing for you. Your baby may have very red skin, be covered in hair, be very thin, and not look at all like the baby you imagined you'd have. It can take you some time to adapt to having this "unexpected" baby, and these feelings are perfectly normal. Many parents also find the atmosphere of the NICU overwhelming—so many buzzing

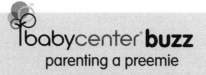

babycenter buzz
parenting a preemie

"Love will give you strength and patience you never ever knew you had. And when you think you can't get through another day, somehow you do. Friends and family say, 'I don't know how you do it.' But you just do. You manage to get through each day in the NICU even though saying goodnight every night and counting another day was for me the hardest thing in the world."—**Tiffany**

"It's the little things that matter most. Most parents would look at changing diapers as a chore, but when my son was in the NICU, I looked forward to diaper changes so much. It was the only time I really got to see him. Every little thing was a huge event that most parents take for granted."—**Angela**

"Ask for help. I always thought I could do it all, but I can't. It doesn't show weakness to ask for help. Plus, family and friends *want* to help."—**Carrie**

"Three things I've learned: (1) that reaching a weight of 4 pounds is a reason to *party!;* (2) that a compassionate healthcare worker is worth his/her weight in gold; (3) that it doesn't matter how much tape is holding your child's NG tube in place, she's the most beautiful creature you've ever seen."—**Rena**

machines, so many people. But just as your baby needs to be gently and gradually introduced to the world, so you can gently and gradually get to know her, and learn how to care for her.

kangaroo care

Kangaroo care is a method of holding a preterm baby skin to skin in an upright position. Your baby will wear just a diaper and a hat and will be held upright on your chest.

This technique started in Colombia in the 1980s, when there weren't enough incubators and there were frequent power outages. To help keep babies warm, they put them in slings between their mother's breasts. It turned out that babies cared for this way were more likely to survive than those in incubators.

Research shows that kangaroo care:

- Reduces breathing difficulties
- Makes a baby's heartbeat more regular
- Reduces a baby's need for oxygen
- Helps control a baby's temperature (Mothers develop thermal synchrony: If the baby is too cold, the mother's body temperature increases; if the baby is too hot, the mother's body temperature decreases.)
- Increases the success rate of breastfeeding and helps with milk production
- Increases weight gain, possibly because babies sleep better this way, which conserves their energy

Because kangaroo care increases the success rate of breastfeeding and leads to better weight gain, it often results in shorter hospital stays. Kangaroo care takes place in short periods at first—around 10 to 30 minutes—building up to 2 or 3 hours a day, and it's done with a baby's monitors and oxygen tubes in place. You usually sit in a chair and the neonatal nurse helps you position the baby on your chest and then covers him with a light blanket.

The suggestion to try kangaroo care can be daunting to you. You'll see the machinery that surrounds your baby as vital to keeping him alive; moving your baby away from what you think of as "safety" can be very alarming. If your baby is very premature, he'll seem very fragile, too, and you'll worry about harming him. But the staff will be close at hand. And you're giving your baby something the machines never can: closeness and bonding. As you become more comfortable with holding and handling your baby, you'll get to know him better, and he'll get to know you.

coming home

Most preemies come home about the time they were due to be born, some a bit before. Release from the hospital depends on your baby no longer needing support, and on his feeding well, gaining weight (around half to one ounce a day and usually weighing about 4 pounds plus), and being healthy.

Some hospitals provide "step down" care—a less high-tech setting that may be an area within the hospital where you gave birth, a special place off-site, or at a hospital nearer your home. Some hospitals provide home visits—a neonatal or pediatric nurse visits you at home. The NICU will supply you with contact numbers for support groups and a helpline number if you're worried.

Occasionally very premature babies come home still needing extra oxygen. Staff will make sure you understand how to use it and will organize regular checkups.

Your baby may find the difference between night and day difficult to sense, especially if he was in a NICU for several weeks. Most units now dim the lights at night to encourage babies to develop a night-day pattern, but there's still some noise and light all the time. To teach your baby about night and day, keep the lights low at night and let him sleep in his (or your) room. During the day, bring your baby into the living area and let him sleep in a crib there. He'll adjust eventually.

It takes time and courage to relax into parenting a premature baby. Talking to the parents of other preemies on the BabyCenter boards can be an invaluable source of support while you make that journey.

your baby's development

You'll have extra follow-up appointments with a pediatrician to check on your baby's progress, especially if your baby had any health problems when he was born.

Premature babies tend to take a while to catch up with full-term babies. It helps to think of your baby in terms of his "corrected age," and anticipate him reaching milestones as measured from the date he was due rather than when he was born. Differences usually disappear by the time a preemie is 2 years old. However, very low birthweight babies are particularly likely to be smaller than their peers for some years. All checkups and vaccinations will be carried out based on your baby's actual age; the hepatitis B vaccine is sometimes deferred until your baby weighs more.

by the numbers
feeding: birth to 3 months

Before your baby was born, did you plan to breastfeed?

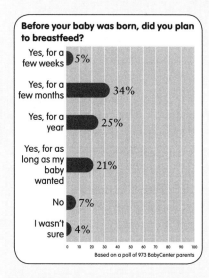

- Yes, for a few weeks — 5%
- Yes, for a few months — 34%
- Yes, for a year — 25%
- Yes, for as long as my baby wanted — 21%
- No — 7%
- I wasn't sure — 4%

Based on a poll of 973 BabyCenter parents

Did you use a lactation consultant?

Yes	62%
No	34%
What's that?	4%

Based on a poll of 7,920 BabyCenter parents

Did your partner support breast-feeding?

Yes	93%
No	7%

Based on a poll of 8,825 BabyCenter parents

the first month:
Breastfeeding—love it, hate it, or somewhere in between?

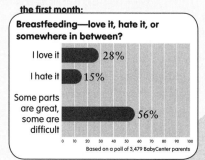

- I love it — 28%
- I hate it — 15%
- Some parts are great, some are difficult — 56%

Based on a poll of 3,479 BabyCenter parents

at 1 month old:
Breastfeeding—love it, hate it, or somewhere in between?

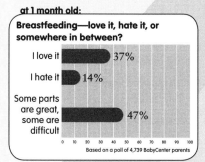

- I love it — 37%
- I hate it — 14%
- Some parts are great, some are difficult — 47%

Based on a poll of 4,739 BabyCenter parents

at 3 months old:
Breastfeeding—love it, hate it, or somewhere in between?

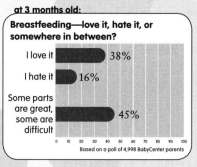

- I love it — 38%
- I hate it — 16%
- Some parts are great, some are difficult — 45%

Based on a poll of 4,998 BabyCenter parents

Which best describes your first week of breastfeeding?

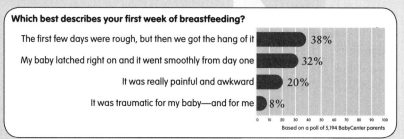

- The first few days were rough, but then we got the hang of it — 38%
- My baby latched right on and it went smoothly from day one — 32%
- It was really painful and awkward — 20%
- It was traumatic for my baby—and for me — 8%

Based on a poll of 5,194 BabyCenter parents

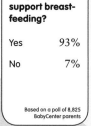

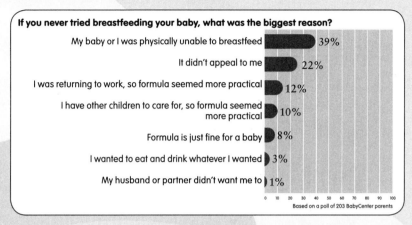

If you never tried breastfeeding your baby, what was the biggest reason?

- My baby or I was physically unable to breastfeed — 39%
- It didn't appeal to me — 22%
- I was returning to work, so formula seemed more practical — 12%
- I have other children to care for, so formula seemed more practical — 10%
- Formula is just fine for a baby — 8%
- I wanted to eat and drink whatever I wanted — 3%
- My husband or partner didn't want me to — 1%

Based on a poll of 203 BabyCenter parents

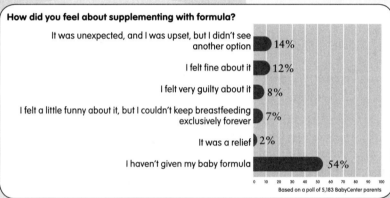

How did you feel about supplementing with formula?

- It was unexpected, and I was upset, but I didn't see another option — 14%
- I felt fine about it — 12%
- I felt very guilty about it — 8%
- I felt a little funny about it, but I couldn't keep breastfeeding exclusively forever — 7%
- It was a relief — 2%
- I haven't given my baby formula — 54%

Based on a poll of 5,183 BabyCenter parents

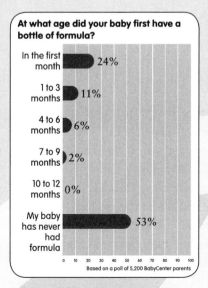

At what age did your baby first have a bottle of formula?

- In the first month — 24%
- 1 to 3 months — 11%
- 4 to 6 months — 6%
- 7 to 9 months — 2%
- 10 to 12 months — 0%
- My baby has never had formula — 53%

Based on a poll of 5,200 BabyCenter parents

the bottom line

Newborns grow very quickly but have very tiny stomachs, so they need to be fed often. After the first 3 to 4 days of life, most babies want to breastfeed 8 to 15 times a day, or every 2 to 3 hours—around the clock—night as well as day. Much of the time your new baby is awake, she'll be feeding. By the end of the first month, she may have developed a feeding and sleeping pattern, or you may not notice any real pattern for months.

chapter
11

feeding— birth to 3 months

If you've ever wondered why parents obsess about what their kids eat, you'll understand completely once your baby is born. Few things about taking care of a newborn are as fraught as the question, "Is he eating enough?" Luckily, once you have the basics down, feeding your baby can become one of the most joyful and fulfilling experiences of new parenthood.

decision guide · · · · · · · · · · · · · · · · ·

BREAST OR BOTTLE?

How to feed your baby? It's one of the first decisions you'll make. Once upon a time, of course, there was little choice. You either breastfed your baby or you gave your baby to someone else to nurse. The development of formula created this feeding option, and it became hugely popular in an era when "modern" automatically meant "better." Today the pendulum in the medical community has swung back to favoring breastfeeding, now that research has identified its many natural benefits. But, given the high quality of today's formulas as well as the wide range of lifestyles and

babycenter buzz
whatever works for you

"I think breastfeeding is the most awesome experience a mother can enjoy! And talk about *convenience*: no bottles to wash, no formula to prepare, none of that extra stuff to tote around on outings, plus breastfed babies are the sweetest-smelling beings on this earth!"—**Bella**

"I didn't even consider breastfeeding when my daughter was born. I want all my family members to enjoy feeding her, and I didn't want the burden of breastfeeding. After a miserable third trimester, I was ready to turn nature off and get back to being a regular person instead of the factory I had become."—**Anonymous**

circumstances in new moms' lives, the way in which a mother feeds her child is ultimately a matter of personal choice.

reasons for breastfeeding

"It's great. It works for me and I like it." Many women find that breastfeeding is easy and straightforward. Perhaps your sister or best friend breastfed and you watched and thought, *Yes, I could do that.*

"That's what breasts are for!" For some women, there's simply no question about how they'll feed their babies.

"It's best for my baby." Breast milk is the ideal food for your baby's physical and mental development. Although formulas try to come close, unlike breast milk they can't adjust to meet the needs of a baby who's born early or becomes ill.

"It may boost my baby's IQ." Some studies show that breastfed babies have higher IQs at age 8 than a similar group of formula-fed babies.

Worry Meter

Q **Will breastfeeding make my breasts sag?**

○ Yes
○ No
● It contributes

Many women worry that if they breastfeed, their breasts will droop and become unattractive. The truth is that life itself takes a toll on women's breasts. Age, weight gain or loss, pregnancy, the effects of gravity, and, yes, breastfeeding all affect the way breasts look. Breastfeeding alone, though, makes little difference.

"It's already prepared." There's no mixing of formula required. Not even in the middle of the night.

"It will protect my baby's health." Babies who are breastfed are less likely to develop several infections or conditions, including:

- Gastrointestinal infection
- Respiratory infections
- Necrotizing enterocolitis (damage to the intestines)
- Urinary tract infections
- Ear infections
- Insulin-dependent diabetes (type 1 diabetes)

"It will help prevent my baby from developing allergies." This is particularly important to women who have allergies themselves or in their families, as breastfeeding helps protect your baby from developing eczema, asthma, and other allergic conditions.

"It's good for me, too." Breastfeeding has surprising benefits for moms. Women who breastfeed have a lower risk of:

- Breast cancer
- Ovarian cancer
- Hip fractures

"It's free." You don't have to pay a penny for it.

"**It's rewarding.**" Not only is there a special relationship between you and your baby, it's very rewarding to know that you're nourishing your baby, just as nature intended.

"**I can stay close after I return to work.**" Many women enjoy knowing that they're continuing to give the best nutrition to their babies even after returning to work. Expressed milk is just as nourishing for your baby as feeding at the breast. When you express milk, dads and other family members can also share in feeding time by bottle-feeding your baby.

reasons for formula-feeding

"**I tried breastfeeding and didn't like it.**" Some women don't enjoy the sensation or the sense that only they can feed their babies.

"**I just don't like the idea of breastfeeding.**" Our society has an ambivalent attitude toward breastfeeding. Women are rarely seen nursing in public, and, culturally, breasts are more associated with sex than nutrition. For this reason, some women feel uncomfortable baring their breasts to feed their babies.

"**I tried breastfeeding and it hurt.**" Problems such as soreness, blocked ducts, and mastitis put off some women. It's estimated that about 25 percent of women who want to breastfeed run into problems that cause them to stop. You're much more likely to overcome problems if you know how breastfeeding works, if you have a supportive partner, and if you enlist the help of a good midwife or lactation consultant.

"**My baby was sick and needed to be in special care.**" Small or sick babies can find it harder to learn how to breastfeed. Many women express their milk and feed it to their babies via tubes or in cups. But sometimes it's all just too much to deal with, especially if you're stressed and worried about your baby.

"**I've done it for the length of time I think is right and now want to change to formula.**" If you breastfeed, how long you do it is entirely up to you and your baby. It may be a day, week, month, or year. Any breast milk you give your baby is good for her, so if you've fed for the time you want to, then give yourself a pat on the back.

"I don't like the idea of breastfeeding in public." How breast-feeding in public is viewed varies from country to country, culture to culture, and even family to family. There's no doubt that it's easier to breastfeed if others are doing the same. If your relatives insist you go to a spare bedroom, or store clerks ask mothers to go into bathrooms or dressing rooms, it's much more difficult to continue breastfeeding.

"I can share feeding my baby with someone else." Many dads enjoy the warmth and closeness of giving their babies bottles. Grandparents, older brothers and sisters, and aunts and uncles can also get involved, and the special closeness of feeding can help them bond with the new family member.

"It takes pressure off me." If you've had a difficult labor and aren't fully recovered, or if your baby is sick, formula feeding enables medical staff to care for your baby when you're not there.

"It makes it easier for me to go back to work." If you have to return to work soon after your baby is born, formula-feeding means that you don't have to go through a transition to mixed feeding or feeding expressed milk. Life will stay just the same for both you and your baby.

"I have more than one baby!" Breastfeeding twins is possible, but it's hard work. Mixing breast- and formula-feeding can help you share the load.

how breastfeeding works

To feed your baby, your milk needs to be "letdown" from your breasts. As your baby nurses, the sucking stimulates your pituitary gland to release the hormones prolactin and oxytocin into your

Worry Meter

Q

Will I produce milk even if I don't want to breastfeed?

● Yes
○ Sometimes
○ Never

Yes. The fact that you've given birth means that your body will make milk. It will take a week or two before your milk dries up completely. If it becomes very uncomfortable, you can express just enough to relieve the discomfort. Take a warm shower and just gently press your breasts until you feel relief. Don't empty your breasts completely, however, because that will stimulate your body to make even more milk. Putting cold packs on your breasts helps ease the discomfort, too.

bloodstream. The prolactin stimulates milk production in the breast tissue from your blood sugar. The oxytocin causes tiny muscles around your milk-filled alveoli (the glands that produce milk) to contract and squeeze. The milk empties into the ducts, which transport it to the milk pools just below the areola. When your baby suckles, she presses the milk from these pools into her mouth.

When your milk lets down, it can cause a tingling sensation or initially even pain in your breasts. While breastfeeding during the first days, you may feel contractions in your abdomen, as well. The oxytocin is helping your uterus to shrink back to its prepregnancy size. The same hormone may also make you feel calm and happy as you breastfeed.

supply and demand

The more you breastfeed, the more milk you produce. Every time your baby nurses, it's a signal to your body to make more milk. The law of supply and demand applies to all moms, including those of twins or more. If you breastfeed each time your baby is hungry, you can trust your body to supply enough milk. A low milk supply can almost always be corrected by feeding more often.

If your baby doesn't feed frequently, your body will make less milk. That's why you need to feed a sleepy newborn more often, and why you need to nurse more often when your baby goes through a growth spurt.

It's important to know that the volume of milk production is low during the first 3 days or so because what's mainly produced is colostrum (see below). Many women quit breastfeeding prematurely because they think their babies are "not getting enough."

what's in breast milk

Breast milk is wonderfully complex. The first milk produced by the breasts is colostrum, a rich and creamy substance. Gradually, over the first few days, this changes to mature milk, which looks thinner. Sometimes women worry it looks too thin. But your body makes the milk your baby needs. The milk you produce varies according to your baby's age, and it adjusts to how thirsty or hungry he is, even if he's sick or born prematurely. It may not look like the jug of milk you buy at the supermarket, but it's just right for your baby.

colostrum

In the first few days, you produce colostrum, which contains antibodies and other protections to help your baby adjust to the outside world. During the first 10 days, there are more white cells (which fight infections) per millileter in your breast milk than there are in blood. If your baby is born early, your body makes milk that provides even more protection.

Colostrum also delivers several *immunoglobulins*, one of which, IgA, helps to coat your baby's intestinal walls and protect the surfaces against harmful bacteria. This action of protecting the "virgin gut" is one of the reasons why exclusive breastfeeding helps prevent allergies such as asthma and eczema. It prevents foreign proteins from leaking across your baby's gut wall and causing his immune system to flare up.

The latest research suggests that if your baby has an infection, during the feeding he may pass on to you some of the germs he's picked up. Your immune system produces antibodies to fight the

babycenter **buzz**
breastfeeding in public

"Practice at home in front of the mirror to see how little of you shows, and what you can do to minimize exposure. Look for ways to start small when you're out and about—isolated corners, nursing rooms, that sort of thing. Once you've done it that first time, it gets easier. I've also found that focusing on the baby takes my mind off passersby; you can't get upset about someone glaring if you're busy looking into your baby's eyes."**—Heather**

"Wink at people who stare. It throws them right off."**—Kathy**

"I was actually asked once at a picnic if I was going to breastfeed my baby in front of everyone. I had to laugh and said, 'Well you just ate in front of her!'"**—Anonymous**

infection, which you then pass back to your baby during feeding. It's a tidy way of using your immune system to protect your baby.

foremilk and hindmilk

Breast milk is mostly fat. This fat contains the enzyme needed for your baby to digest it, so it's rapidly utilized. The long-chain polyunsaturated fatty acids in breast milk play an important role in the development of your baby's retina and visual cortex, and in brain growth.

Fat provides about half the calories your baby needs. The other calories mainly come from lactose, the milk sugar. Lactose also enhances the absorption of calcium and promotes the growth of bacteria, which increase intestinal acidity and reduce the growth of harmful organisms.

At the beginning of a feeding, the **foremilk** gives your baby a high volume of low-fat milk, which is thirst-quenching and easy to digest. As the feeding progresses, the **hindmilk** comes in and the volume of milk decreases, but the proportion of fat increases. It's the fat that makes your baby feel full and helps him gain weight.

Human milk contains small amounts of minerals such as iron, calcium, and zinc. Although commercial formulas have higher levels, the minerals are better absorbed from breast milk. Your baby absorbs only about 10 percent of the iron in formula milk but 70 percent of the iron in breast milk.

a good start to breastfeeding

In the first 6 weeks, as your milk supply adjusts, breastfeeding can feel stressful. Once you and your baby are in sync, though, you'll be able to breastfeed in all sorts of situations: while speaking on the phone, talking to friends over lunch, lying in bed at night half-asleep, or watching TV or reading a book in the evening. Perhaps you've seen other women do this and thought that breastfeeding would be just as easy and relaxed for you. It can be. But it's a rare mother who's this adept from the get-go. Feeding your baby is an art both you and your baby need to learn.

The good news: Because it's a new skill for both of you, you learn together. Bear in mind, though, that you'll both learn much more easily if you give yourselves uninterrupted time and space to practice.

A key skill is to get your baby "latched on," or positioned at your breast correctly. Follow these four simple steps:

1. Touch the edge of your baby's mouth with your finger or nipple to encourage her to turn toward your breast and open her mouth. **Your baby's mouth needs to open very wide.** If she latches on without opening her mouth wide, break the suction by putting your finger into the suction by putting your finger into the corner of her mouth, take her from the breast, and start again. Don't pull your nipple out, as that can cause you pain.

2. Wait until your baby's mouth opens wide, then pull the baby's entire body toward you as you place your nipple and surrounding areola right inside it. **Your baby needs to take a large mouthful of breast**—not just the nipple—into her mouth before she begins to suck. If your baby has to suck or pull your nipple into her mouth, this can cause soreness and pain. If she's just sucking on the nipple, it will probably hurt. So place your breast well into your baby's mouth. Check to see that your baby has a large mouthful of the breast, encircling most, if not the entire, areola. Make sure your baby's lips are positioned correctly. Her lips should be splayed, and her gums should be encircling your nipple. Her lower lip should be turned out.

3. When your baby is finished nursing, insert the tip of your finger in the side of her mouth and gently force her to release suction. Some babies suck in their lower lip along with the breast, and this can cause you pain.

Ask someone to look under your breast while you are feeding. A little bit of the inside of your baby's lip should be visible (which shows that your baby's bottom lip is turned out), and it might be possible to see some tongue movement as your baby moves her tongue in and out to help "milk" the breast. If none of this is visible, then your baby's bottom lip may be sucked in. If this is the case, take your baby from the breast and start again.

As your baby breastfeeds contentedly, hold her close. When nursing as a newborn, her entire front side—from head to toe—should be snug against your body.

a good feeding

Over time, you'll begin to use your senses to develop a sense of what makes for a good feeding. And, of course, your baby will weigh in on the subject as well.

what can you feel?

If your baby is latched on to your breast correctly, your nipple will be up by your baby's soft palate toward the back of her mouth, and her tongue will be underneath your breast. You'll feel her squeezing your breast with her jaw and her tongue pushing forward and back under the breast.

If you can feel gums or your baby's tongue rubbing on your nipple, then she doesn't have enough of your breast in her mouth. Break the suction with your little finger and try bringing her back to the breast. This time, as she latches on, give her a little extra pull toward you, so she takes a bit more breast into her mouth.

what can you see?

A well-latched baby has a steady jaw movement as she squeezes your breast. The muscles that run from her jaw up to her ears will move in time with the jaw movement; even her ears and her eyebrows may move a bit. She'll have plump rounded cheeks, not the pinched-in cheeks that you get with sucking.

what can you hear?

Even if everything looks fine, listen for a few moments. You should hear your baby gulping and swallowing the milk. You shouldn't hear sucking or clicking sounds. These noises indicate that air is getting in as your baby nurses, which means that she isn't latched on correctly. Take your baby off the breast and try again.

Most babies will swallow and gulp quickly at first, then settle into a steady "swallow and rest" pattern. If your baby gulps and swallows almost nonstop, she may be getting too much milk too quickly. Take her off the breast and try again.

positions for feeding

Most women start breastfeeding by cradling their babies across their tummies. However, there are other positions that you may find even more comfortable, so be sure to experiment. It's also a good idea to vary breastfeeding holds to prevent soreness. By changing positions, your baby will put pressure on a different part of your breast, and you may be able to persuade him to take more of the breast into his mouth, so that the soreness doesn't get any worse. Some holds to try:

classic cradle hold

Sit in a chair with supportive armrests or on a bed with lots of pillows. If you're in a chair, rest your feet on a stool to avoid leaning down over your baby. Hold your baby on your lap (or on a pillow on your lap) so that he's lying on his side with his face, stomach, and knees directly facing you. Line up his nose with your nipple.

If he's feeding on the right breast, rest his head in the crook of your right arm. Extend your right forearm and hand down his

back to support his neck, spine, and
bottom. Secure his knees against your
body, across or just below your left
breast. He should lie horizontally, or
at a slight angle.

Some mothers find that this hold
makes it hard to guide their newborn's
mouth to the nipple. You may prefer
to use this position once your baby is
about 1 month old and has stronger neck muscles.

Try experimenting with this position by moving your baby's head
further down your arm, toward your hand. A small adjustment
can often make you both much more comfortable.

crossover hold

This position differs from the
cradle hold in that your arms
switch roles. If you're feeding from
your right breast, use your left
hand and arm to support your
baby. Turn his body so that his
chest and tummy are directly
facing you.

Guide your baby's mouth to your breast using your right thumb
and fingers behind his head and below his ears. Alternately, if you
have large breasts, you can use your right hand to support your
right breast for most accurate positioning, especially until he
masters his latch. Doing so may help you prevent some nipple
chapping.

underarm

Also called the football hold, this position can be comfortable after
a c-section and is also good for nursing twins. Support your baby on

several pillows, with his body along your forearm and his head resting in your palm on the same side from which you're nursing.

Sit well forward on your chair to give your baby room to stretch his legs out behind you, and make sure he is high enough on the pillows that you don't have to bend over him to nurse.

lying down

A particularly comfortable position for night feedings, it's also easier after a Caesarean, although at first you may need someone to help you get in position. You and baby both lie on your sides, facing each other, with his nose level with your nipple. Use your outside arm to draw your baby in close.

If you need them to get really comfortable, put plenty of pillows under your shoulder, inside arm, and head. Have your partner tuck an extra one behind your back, for extra support.

finger test

The easiest way to understand how your baby should attach to your breast is to suck your own finger. Put your finger in your mouth only as far as the first joint. Now move your tongue around. Feel how the tongue can move all around the tip of the finger. If that were your nipple, it would soon get sore. Now put your finger into your mouth up to the second joint. This forces your tongue underneath your finger, and you can't move it around the end of the finger and make it sore. A baby who's latched on well has plenty of the breast in his mouth, with your nipple at the back of his mouth. In that way, your nipple can't get squashed by your baby's gum ridge or aggravated by his tongue.

5 things that help establish breastfeeding

1. **Being relaxed.** Because feedings can last from just a few minutes to almost an hour, get comfortable in a chair or bed. The more relaxed you are, the easier it will be.

2. **Keeping your surroundings calm.** Atmosphere is very important, especially in the early days of breastfeeding when you're still trying to get the hang of it.

3. **Holding your baby in a position that won't leave your arms and back sore.** Add support around you with plenty of cushions.

4. **Ideally, having an expert**—a breastfeeding counselor or nurse—sit with you and watch what's happening when you first begin feeding. Once you know what a good latch and comfortable position feel like for you and your baby, you'll know what to look for in the future.

5. **Watching for signs that your baby is ready to nurse.** Don't wait for the crying to begin. Rather, pay attention to rooting, lip-smacking, and other signs, so that she's not frantic by the time she gets to the breast.

5 things that hinder breastfeeding

1. **Trying to nurse your baby by the clock.** Nurse your baby as often as she needs to feed. If you take this "on demand" approach, your baby's needs and your milk supply will harmonize. You'll soon establish a breastfeeding rhythm that's best for both of you.

2. **Worrying that you can't breastfeed.** Most women can. Throughout most of history, women who couldn't feed (and their babies) failed to survive. So the ability to breastfeed is in your genes. Only about 2 percent of women are physically incapable of producing enough milk for their babies.

3. **Not knowing enough about breastfeeding.** If you grow up in a culture where everyone breastfeeds, you learn about it naturally as a child—literally with your mother's milk. If you don't see it happening, it's hard to know how it works or what to expect. So find out as much as you can, assume you can breastfeed successfully, and plan to get help early on if you need it.

4. **Other people telling you you'd be better off bottle-feeding.** Remind yourself (and them!) of the benefits of breastfeeding.

5. **Thinking your milk supply is low when it's not.** This can happen if you stop feeling a strong letdown reflex or lose the feeling of fullness in your breasts, or if milk stops leaking from your nipples. These are actually natural, common signs that your body has adjusted to your baby's feeding requirements. Rest assured that you're still producing plenty of milk. Also remember that in the first few days, your body is not producing a lot of fluid (it's making colostrum rather than milk), and this is perfectly normal. That's how it's meant to be.

nipple confusion

Babies are born knowing how to suck, but breasts and bottles require different techniques. Some babies happily swap back and forth, while others find it confusing.

by the numbers

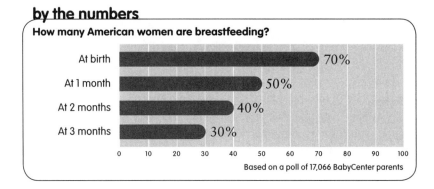

How many American women are breastfeeding?

At birth	70%
At 1 month	50%
At 2 months	40%
At 3 months	30%

Based on a poll of 17,066 BabyCenter parents

Breasts are soft and flexible. Your baby has to open her mouth wide to latch on and engage a range of muscles. The nipples on bottles, on the other hand, are preformed and fairly rigid, so they don't demand much effort from a baby and can even be coaxed into sealed lips. In general, breastfeeding requires more vigorous mouth and tongue movements and greater muscle coordination by your baby.

A bottle-fed baby (especially a newborn) may try to nurse from the breast using the same jaw and mouth motions she used to suck on the bottle, and these aren't usually strong enough to draw milk from the breast. She'll quickly become frustrated and cry, or refuse to breastfeed. As a result, she won't get much milk or feel satisfied. If this happens in the first few weeks after birth, it may be difficult for a baby to learn to breastfeed effectively.

For this reason, it's a good idea to avoid bottles until breastfeeding is well established, especially if your baby has trouble latching on or sucking correctly, or if you're concerned about your milk supply. You may likewise want to delay pacifier use for the first month, according to the American Academy of Pediatrics. (Although pacifiers are associated with a lower risk of SIDS, most SIDS cases happen after the first 4 weeks of life.) If your baby experiences nipple confusion, she may cry and fuss as she goes to the breast, or latch on but give up after a few moments, as she expects milk to flow out quickly like it does from a bottle. She may become upset and refuse to breastfeed, or keep latching on and coming off to cry.

what to do

- Avoid bottles and pacifiers for just the first month
- Breastfeed your baby before she's too hungry. (Look for signs that she's getting hungry, such as turning her head from side to side and making sucking sounds.)
- Express a little breast milk onto your nipple to encourage her to nurse.
- Experiment with different feeding positions.
- Ask your midwife or lactation consultant to check that your baby is well latched on your breast and that she's getting plenty of milk.

feeding checkpoint: how much, how often?

During the first few weeks, your body is still adjusting to your baby's demand for milk, so feedings may be spaced out and predictable one day and frequent and erratic the next. In any case, it's unusual for a breastfed baby to go more than 4 hours between feedings in the first few weeks. Most **newborns** will have around 8 feedings a day, though some will want 10 or more. Two or three of those feedings will likely be during the night for the first month.

Often by the time your baby is **1 month old,** there's only one feeding in the middle of the night with a couple of evening feedings and an early morning session around 4:00 or 5:00 a.m. Often, during **the third month,** you can juggle the evening feeding to be just before you go to bed so you can get one stretch of 5 or 6 hours of sleep during the night.

Gradually, as your baby gets bigger and becomes able to take more milk at a time, he'll reduce the number of feedings to perhaps six to eight a day. But don't worry or be surprised if there are those occasional days when he needs more, as all babies have growth spurts and hungry days.

common questions

At some point in the breastfeeding process, every new mom can't help but worry about one thing or another.

"is my baby getting enough milk?"

We live in a society that measures, weighs, and times everything. Breastfeeding doesn't fit that mold exactly, and that can be hard to accept at first. Newborns normally lose 5 to 10 percent of their birth weight in the first few days, and most take around 2 weeks to regain it. So weighing your baby within that stage isn't a useful way to reassure yourself that your baby is getting enough milk. However, there are some ways to check whether he is.

Answering *yes* to these questions is a good sign that your baby is getting enough milk:

- Is your baby feeding every 2 to 3 hours, or at least eight times in 24 hours during the first 2 to 3 weeks?
- Are your breasts being emptied or feeling softer after feedings?
- Does your baby finish a feeding with a look of sleepy contentment on his face?
- Can you hear your baby swallow while breastfeeding?
- Does your baby wet six to eight diapers in a 24-hour period? (Try putting a small piece of a tissue in the diaper when you change your baby; you can pull it out and check for moistness.)
- Is your baby producing mustardy-yellow stools? Breastfed babies vary as to how often they pass stools; some do so at every feeding, some once a day. However often a stool appears, it should be a bright mustard color and very loose.

Some babies simply become more efficient and therefore faster feeders, giving you the impression that you must not be supplying enough milk, when actually it's just that you've become more efficient at breastfeeding.

There are also definite signs that a baby may *not* be getting enough milk and is becoming dehydrated. Although dehydration in newborns is rare, it's important to know the signs so you can alert your doctor if anything seems amiss. Does your baby's skin bounce right back if pinched? If you gently pinch a small piece of a dehydrated baby's skin, it will briefly stay puckered. Does your baby's activity level seem decreased? Is he uninterested in feedings? Tell your doctor if you notice these things, as well as if your baby's stools are small, hard, or dark, or your baby isn't producing any stools at all. It may just be ordinary constipation or, especially if you notice these other signs as well, your baby may not be getting enough milk to have any excess to excrete.

"I seem to have too much milk. what can I do?"

In the early days, as your body adjusts to making milk for your baby, it can take a while for supply and demand to match up. Some women find they have far too much milk, or a very fast letdown. Some women also leak breast milk in these first few weeks, often in the mornings when milk stores are fullest.

- **If your baby gulps and swallows almost nonstop, then splutters as she starts a feeding,** she may be getting too much milk too quickly. Take her off the breast and try again. You may find it helps to nurse lying down so that she's at the same level as the breast and the milk doesn't squirt quite so quickly into the back of her throat. If your letdown is very fierce, try feeding "uphill" by lying down and putting your baby on top of you so that she's above the breast. As your baby grows, she'll be able to cope better with a quick letdown; this situation also usually resolves itself as supply and demand become more closely matched.
- **If one breast always leaks when your baby is feeding on the other,** put a cloth or breast pad inside your bra before you start to feed. Or use a breast shell to catch the drips. (You can always freeze this milk, too.)
- **If you feel your milk letting down when you don't want it to,** cross your arms and hug yourself, pressing gently against your breasts. This may stop the unexpected flow. Use breast pads but change them at regular intervals to avoid getting damp and sore, or developing thrush.

"what if my baby seems too sleepy to nurse?"

If your baby is very sleepy in the early days, you may need to waken her and encourage her to feed more vigorously, thus stimulating your breasts to produce more milk. To keep her interested, try changing sides frequently, alternating positions, or even undressing her. Some moms play with their babies' feet during feedings to keep them awake. Sleepiness can also be a sign of dehydration, especially if you notice other symptoms as described on page 83.

"why does my baby want to feed all the time?"

Almost all moms wonder at some point whether they can keep up with 24-7 feedings. Handing Dad a bottle of formula can seem awfully tempting. It's true that formula isn't as easily digested as breast milk, so a bottle-fed baby will go longer between feedings simply because his stomach feels fuller. But the benefits of breastfeeding are so pronounced that persevering through a tiring adjustment phase will reward you with an easier feeding system later. The supply and demand system of breastfeeding can't work until your body has worked out how much to supply for your baby's demand. Frequent feeding may be your baby's way of saying "make more milk."

If you can hang in there, the spaces between your baby's feedings will grow longer. (Although you'll find that during times of illness or stress, such as your baby's first immunization, she turns to your breast more often for comfort.) Likewise, feedings could become more closely spaced again at around 6 weeks if your baby goes through a growth spurt. On the whole, however, you and your baby *will* settle into a predictable pattern.

To catch up with a baby who's going through a growth spurt:

- Let her feed as often and for as long as she wants.
- Offer both breasts at each feeding.
- Give your baby only breast milk and not formula, as the more milk she takes from you, the more you'll produce.
- Sleep and relax as much as you can.
- Eat well and keep up your intake of water and other fluids.

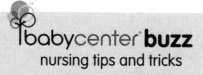

babycenter **buzz**
nursing tips and tricks

"I'm so glad I persevered. The first 7 weeks were very difficult. All the info about breastfeeding says the first few *days* may be a *little* painful. Hah!" **—Anonymous**

"The best advice I can give is to *never* let your baby latch on incorrectly. When you're in the hospital, have the nurses show you the absolute correct way. All it takes is one incorrect latching on for one feeding, and you'll be incredibly sore."**—K.M.**

"Not all babies will latch right after birth. Mine wasn't interested until about 8 hours later, and then she was a little fiend. Don't panic if this is the case. Just watch your baby for cues."**—Mel**

"Something I've relearned again and again: If your little one wakes a lot during the night (more than usual), becomes fussier, is fussy during eating, or is more clingy than usual, then make sure that when you're feeding him, you're paying attention to him and not watching TV, playing on the computer, or talking too much to others."**—S.S.**

eating well while breastfeeding

It's a myth that you need to drink milk to make milk. (If this were true, then cows with their diet of grass wouldn't be able to feed their calves.)

You won't need lots of extra calories, either. (Darn!) Studies show that breastfeeding women have a highly efficient metabolism, allowing them to produce milk from fewer calories each day than you might expect (about 500). Because most new moms are also trying to shed pregnancy weight, there's little benefit to adding calories for breastfeeding. Some women, in fact, claim that breast-feeding helps them lose weight. Better than fixating on calories, focus on the quality of the foods you eat so that you're taking in balanced nutrients, especially proteins and B-vitamins (found in dark leafy greens and fortified wheat products).

Nursing moms are often thirstier than usual; water is the best way to slake thirst. Keep a sports bottle filled with water and carry it with you to sip from during the day, or keep one filled next to the chair where you usually breastfeed. Drinking a sip or two at the start of a nursing session can often help your milk letdown.

Because alcohol can pass through milk in less than an hour, it's best to avoid it. And if you have an occasional glass of beer or wine, time it so you drink it immediately *after* a feeding.

To find out even more about what kinds of foods are good to eat while you're breastfeeding, go to babycenter.com.

breastfeeding problems

Perhaps surprisingly, it's around the end of the first week and into the second that many women often run into problems with breastfeeding. The best way to avoid roadblocks is to get plenty of rest and eat well yourself. The more run-down you are, the more susceptible you become to infections and other problems. Many glitches are easily remedied:

engorgement

About 2 to 3 days after you give birth, your breast milk "comes in." As that happens, more blood flows to your breasts and some of the surrounding tissue swells. The result? Full, swollen, engorged breasts that may feel tender, throb, and seem uncomfortably full. Not every mom experiences true engorgement. Some women's breasts become only slightly full, but others find their breasts have grown astonishingly big and hard, often accompanied by a low-grade fever.

Fortunately, engorgement passes pretty quickly. You can expect it to diminish within 24 to 48 hours. Once the engorgement passes, your breasts will be softer, although still full of milk. Breastfeeding your baby will alleviate the problem. If you're not breastfeeding, the engorgement will probably get worse before it gets better. But it's a temporary, although painful, situation.

To help avoid engorgement, breastfeed your baby immediately after birth, if possible, and often from that point on.

how can I treat it?

First, keep in mind that engorgement is a positive sign: It means you're producing milk to feed your baby. It won't affect your baby, except that you may be even more inclined to feed him as often as you can. You'll soon be producing the right amount of milk he needs.

how can I help myself?

- Nursing frequently during the day—every 2 to 3 hours—even if it means waking your baby. This is especially important because if you don't relieve the engorgement, it can result in a permanent drop in your milk production.
- While your baby's nursing, gently massage the breast your baby is feeding from. This encourages milk to flow and will relieve some of your discomfort.
- Avoid letting your baby latch on and suckle when the areola— the dark area around your nipple—is very firm. To reduce the possibility of nipple damage and to help your baby latch on, you can manually express or pump milk until your areola softens. It may be easier to manually express milk in the shower; the warm water by itself may cause enough leakage to soften your areola.
- Avoid pumping milk except when you need to soften the areola or when your baby is unable to latch on. Too much pumping can lead to overproduction of milk and prolonged engorgement.
- Wear a supportive nursing bra, even during the night. Be sure it doesn't feel too tight.
- To soothe the pain and relieve swelling, apply cold packs to your breasts for a short period after nursing. Crushed ice in a plastic bag works well.

- If you're really in pain, take acetaminophen, ibuprofen, or a mild pain reliever as prescribed by your doctor.
- Don't apply direct heat, such as warm washcloths, heating pads, or hot water bottles to your engorged breasts, unless it's to soften the areola and help your milk letdown. Rather than alleviate the pain, it can stimulate the production of more milk.

Most of all, look ahead: You'll get past this stage and soon be enjoying your breastfeeding relationship with your baby.

sore nipples

Sore nipples are so common in these early days that many breast-feeding mothers think they're just part and parcel of breastfeeding. But they don't have to be. You may feel some tenderness at the beginning of a feeding during the first few days, as your body adjusts to this new sensation, but severe or prolonged pain is neither necessary nor normal. If the pain is intense or lasts longer than a few days, it's a sign that you and your baby need to make some changes. Breastfeeding can and should be a pleasurable experience for both of you.

Frequent feeding *doesn't* cause sore nipples. A baby who isn't latching on well or isn't positioned correctly at the breast is much more likely to be the cause.

how can I treat it?

Get help to improve the way your baby attaches to the breast and her positioning at the breast (see page 76 for more on good positions). Often very minor changes can have major effects on how feeding feels.

how can I help myself?

- Checking your baby's positioning at every feeding
- Rubbing a little expressed breast milk into your nipple after nursing

- Allowing your nipples to air-dry before covering them
- Making sure you have a nursing bra that fits well and is not too tight; there should be no underwires placing pressure on breast tissue; consider being fitted at a maternity store or asking a lactation consultant to check for proper fit

It's very important to solve the underlying problem. A session or two with an expert, such as a lactation consultant, will usually do the trick. Once your baby is feeding properly, the pain will be reduced and eventually disappear as your nipples heal.

cracked nipples

If you have cracked or bleeding nipples, most likely it's because your baby isn't positioned well at the breast. Adjusting your feeding technique often provides substantial relief. However, your nipples may also crack or bleed because of severe dry skin, eczema, or thrush. (See **thrush** on page 92 for an explanation.)

how can I treat it?

Get help quickly. It takes a lot of determination to continue to nurse, as well as excellent support and help with positioning your baby correctly at the breast. If a crack shows no sign of healing, see your doctor.

how can I help myself?

- Checking your baby's positioning at every feeding
- Changing positions at every feeding (This puts the pressure of your baby's gums on a different area of the breast each time.)
- Feeding more frequently, but for shorter periods (Remember, the longer you go between feedings, the hungrier your baby will be—and the harder he'll suck.)
- Rubbing a little breast milk on your nipples after each feeding and letting it air dry
- Not using soap, alcohol, lotions, or perfumes on your nipples (Washing with clear water is all it takes to keep them clean.)

- Taking acetaminophen about 30 minutes before feeding if the
  pain is severe (It's safe for breastfeeding.)

Some women find using a modified lanolin helps. Rubbing a small
amount of the ointment on your nipples relieves pain and allows
the wounds to heal much faster. Your local pharmacist should be
able to help you select a lanolin product made specifically for
breastfeeding.

Babies generally aren't bothered by cracked nipples. Blood in
the milk doesn't hurt them, and they are happy to continue
breastfeeding.

blocked ducts

Blocked milk ducts are just what they sound like. One of the ducts,
or channels, that your milk flows through becomes blocked,
causing inflammation and soreness. You may see a small, hard
lump that's sore to the touch, or a very red or tender spot on your
breast. If you also feel achy, run-down, and feverish, the blocked
duct may have become infected.

how can I treat it?

Feed, feed, feed! Ducts become blocked when milk fails to drain
completely. Frequent breastfeeding is vital to completely emptying
your breast and making you more comfortable and reducing
inflammation. Left untreated, a blocked duct can develop into
mastitis (see opposite page), so don't ignore the symptoms.

how can I help myself?

- Massaging the sore area, starting at the top of the breast and
  working your way down (Try this in the shower with a little
  soap on your hands so you can handle the delicate breast tissue
  gently. The warmth will help, too.)
- Applying warm compresses before feeding (This helps empty
  the breast.)

- Varying your feeding position (Try to position your baby with his chin pointed toward the sore spot so that his sucking will help clear the duct.)
- After nursing, try expressing milk with a breast pump to help clear the duct, too
- Resting (This can be difficult or even impossible with a baby to care for, but it's an important step to healing.)

Even with a blocked duct, you should still breastfeed, as the antibacterial properties of your milk keep your baby safe from any bacteria that may be present. Sometimes your milk flow on the affected breast slows down, so your baby may become fussy when feeding on that side.

To help prevent future blocked ducts, try to avoid long stretches between feedings. A badly fitting bra may also contribute to this problem, so make sure yours isn't too tight. Try arm exercises, too; extend your arm out sideways at a right angle to your shoulder. Now bend your arm at the elbow so your hand is pointing upward. Make circling motions with your arm, moving forward and then backward. This exercises the muscles around the breast, frees up circulation, and helps to prevent blockages.

mastitis

Mastitis is an infection that causes areas of redness, hardness, soreness, or heat in your breast, and swelling of the affected milk duct. Mastitis can have a debilitating effect on you at a time when you need all of your energy; it can feel like the flu. About one in 20 breastfeeding mothers is afflicted. (Some bottle-feeding mothers are, too.) While you can get mastitis more than once, it's very unlikely that both breasts will be affected at the same time.

Usual causes of mastitis are invading germs or a breastfeeding problem, such as a blocked duct or poor positioning of the baby on the breast. Other contributing factors include not completely emptying the breasts of milk and lowered resistance to illness.

(Most new mothers are tired, stressed, and probably not eating all that well.)

Mastitis can occur at any time while you're breastfeeding, but it's most common between about 10 and 28 days after you give birth.

how can I treat it?

If diagnosed early, mastitis is quick and easy to treat, and you won't need to stop feeding from the affected breast. See your doctor, as you may need antibiotics. You may also need bed rest, pain relievers, and ice or hot compresses. When the antibiotics kick in over the next couple of days, you'll start feeling better.

how can I help myself?

- Continuing to breastfeed (In fact, breastfeed frequently to keep the affected breast empty, which may help clear up the infection faster. Although it may be extremely painful at times, this will keep your milk supply flowing and discourage further blockage. Try warm compresses on your breasts for several minutes before nursing, which should help your letdown reflex and make feeding easier.)
- Making sure your baby is positioned properly at the breast
- Trying different feeding positions
- Resting as much as you can (Take your baby to bed with you.)
- Applying warmth to the affected area and gently massaging it

You may feel awful, but mastitis won't affect your baby. The germs that caused the infection probably came from your baby's mouth in the first place, so don't worry about passing the same germs back to him.

thrush

Thrush is a fungal infection in your baby's mouth that can spread to your breasts. Everyone carries the fungus—*Candida albicans*—in their bodies, but it's generally kept in check. Thrush thrives in

babies get thrush, too

Thrush is a mouth infection that happens when yeast, which is part of everybody's digestive system, grows out of proportion to the normal balance. Sometimes oral thrush occurs as a result of hormonal changes right after birth. Breastfeeding moms and babies can pass the infection back and forth. Sucking a pacifier or a bottle may make a baby vulnerable to thrush. Basically thrush is so common an infection that it isn't always known why or how a baby got it. Some children are more susceptible to yeast infection than others.

Oral thrush shows up as white patches on the gums or the tongue. It can look like milk, but if you gently try to wipe a patch of it away with a gauze-covered finger, you can't clear it away easily. If the white patch does come off, the gum or tongue is usually raw and red underneath. Your baby is also apt to cry when nursing or if you touch his mouth; these patches can be painful. In fact, crying and not wanting to feed are often the first signs. On the other hand, thrush doesn't bother other babies at all.

Thrush can lead to a diaper yeast infection, so be alert and tell your doctor if your baby develops a severe diaper rash that doesn't clear.

warm, moist, sugary environments, which is exactly what your baby's mouth is like during breastfeeding, so this is why it gets a chance to grow and spread, sometimes leading to an infection. Thrush can cause your nipples to feel sore and itchy. Other common signs are deep, shooting breast pain during or after feedings and white patches in your baby's mouth.

how can I treat it?

If you suspect thrush, contact your doctor, who will probably prescribe an antifungal medication. Thrush can take up to a few weeks to cure, and you and your baby need to be treated simultaneously.

how can I help myself?

- Washing all toys, pacifiers, and breast pump parts in boiling water after each use, to avoid re-infecting yourself or your baby
- Washing your hands frequently, especially after feedings
- Keeping your nipples as dry as possible, as thrush flourishes in damp conditions

- Taking a mild painkiller, such as acetaminophen, to ease any deep breast pain

You can continue to breastfeed. If you have thrush, the chances are that your baby has it, too, even if you can't see any telltale white spots. She needs treatment just as much as you do—and at the same time, or you can pass the infection back and forth.

A baby with thrush may be fussier than usual during feedings or reluctant to feed because of mouth tenderness. Other babies, however, aren't bothered at all.

To help figure out what's standing in the way of getting your baby to breastfeed, enter your specific symptoms on BabyCenter's "Breastfeeding Problem Solver" at babycenter.com.

special breastfeeding situations

All babies are special, of course, but some require just a bit different care when it comes to breastfeeding.

breastfeeding a premature baby

If your baby needs special care and can't nurse, you need to start pumping as soon as is practical after delivery. It's the stimulation of your breasts that produces milk, so try to pump often—every couple of hours if you can. Aim for six to eight pumping sessions in 24 hours, with one session at night when your milk-making hormone levels are at their highest.

Without your newborn nearby, you may find the experience hard to cope with. Using a pump can feel cold and clinical, and you may be tired and worried about your baby, too, which can reduce your milk production. But even a small amount of breast milk matters to your baby. Remember: Colostrum is highly

Q

Breastfeeding still hurts after 8 weeks. Should I worry?

● Yes
○ Sometimes
○ Never

Breastfeeding isn't meant to hurt. Many women feel sore at first, but this feeling should pass within a few days. If it hurts—and goes on hurting—something isn't right. Ask your doctor or lactation consultant for advice. It may just be a case of improving positioning and attachment. But this problem is unlikely to get better on its own, so it's advisable to get help.

concentrated. Just a little bit contains antibodies and will help your baby.

It can help to massage your breast before pumping to stimulate the nipples, and to have a picture of your baby to look at while you pump. You may prefer to hand express, as this is warmer and softer than a pump; some women begin with hand expressing and then move to the pump once they start to produce milk. Many NICUs have lactation support stations outfitted with hospital-grade pumps for new moms to use; these pumps are very effective and can help you build your milk supply during these trying early days.

Preemies need only a little milk at a time. Try expressing the foremilk into one container, then express the fat-rich hindmilk that's more concentrated. If your baby has the hindmilk first, she'll get the most benefit. If she can take more, then feed her the foremilk.

Preemies are likely to be tube fed at first, which is how your baby will be given your milk. It may also be mixed with formula at first, but as you gradually produce more milk, your milk can replace other supplements.

Moving your baby from tube feeding to breastfeeding can take some time. Preemies tire very easily, but keep trying a couple of times each day. Even if your baby can't nurse, she'll become familiar with the feel and smell of your breast, and you'll both get some bonding time.

breastfeeding more than one baby

Breastfeeding multiples is definitely possible, but it requires determination—and plenty of help. You'll benefit especially from someone to sit with you during feedings and help you latch the babies on if you're feeding two at a time, or someone to look after the other baby (or babies) while you feed another.

simultaneous feeding

Feeding one baby at a time is easier when you (and your babies) are learning how to breastfeed. But this means you'll spend a huge amount of time feeding. It's quicker if you can feed both babies at the same time; however, your babies may not *want* to feed simultaneously. So, when one baby wakes, try waking the other so that gradually they synchronize themselves.

As your babies get stronger and can latch on more easily, you'll find it easier to feed two babies at once. Some mothers choose to "assign" each baby to one breast; others swap them around. Another option: Breastfeed one baby at one feeding and give the other formula, then change over at the next feeding. Don't worry about "running out" of milk; the more you nurse, the more milk your body will supply.

finding the right position

Good positions for feeding depend on whether your babies are happy to nurse in different positions or show a preference for one breast.

Several positions are especially effective for feeding two babies at a time:

- **Football hold.** Tuck one baby under each arm, with plenty of pillows to support them and you
- **Parallel hold.** Hold one baby across your body and the other in the football hold

just for dads

supporting your breastfeeding partner

Dads needn't feel like a third wheel during breast feeding. You play a huge, important role in breastfeeding. Research has shown that if a woman has the wholehearted support of her partner, she's much more likely to enjoy nursing and to breastfeed for longer than if his support is lacking. You can do a lot to build your partner's confidence in her ability to breastfeed. Sharing your pride in her nourishing of your baby is a good place to start. And involving yourself in feeding is a slam-dunk way to show your support.

what you can do to help feed your baby

- In the middle of the night, bring your baby to your partner. After the feeding, settle your baby back to sleep. In fact, you may be more successful at settling your baby than your partner because you don't smell like milk.
- Make snacks and drinks for your partner, bring her a book or a newspaper, pitch in with the housework, cook supper, get the laundry done, or go shopping. Breastfeeding is demanding work. The more you do, the more easily your partner will recover from childbirth *and* feel rested and relaxed for feedings.
- Give your partner a break and take on the responsibility for a feeding if she can express milk. Some women find expressing difficult or uncomfortable, so it's not a good idea to pressure her to do so. But you can certainly encourage her to try or offer to rent a pump for her if she's open to the idea. A decent night of sleep for her will score you serious brownie points!
- Remember: Just because your partner's in charge of feeding doesn't mean you can't play a huge part in your baby's life during these early months. Diaper changing, bathing, taking your baby out for a walk—all of these things will help you build a closer relationship. It doesn't all have to be hard work. Allow yourself time just to hold, cuddle, and play with your baby, too. You're teaching your baby that he can love and be loved without food necessarily being involved.

- **Crossover hold.** Hold each baby in the conventional position, but with their bodies crossing over each other

For those with triplets or more, breastfeeding is possible but time-consuming. And, if your babies need special care, starting and establishing breastfeeding is particularly difficult. Anything you can do to get your babies that precious colostrum is wonderful; beyond that, just do what you can.

breastfeeding after breast surgery

Whether or not you'll be able to breastfeed after surgery depends on such factors as how long ago the surgery took place, how major the surgery was, whether key nerves or the milk ducts were cut, and whether the nipple was moved. Breast reduction and augmentation often require repositioning of the nipple. If you've had an injury or surgery to one breast only, you can probably produce enough milk from your other breast alone.

If you've lost sensation in an area of your breast or around the nipple, it's likely that nerves have been cut and that your milk ducts have been affected. If you're unsure, check with your surgeon, who will be able to describe the process she used.

It's a good idea to talk to a lactation consultant as early as possible. And be aware, too, that it's easy to blame breastfeeding problems on surgery when, in fact, you may be having the exact same problems that other mothers face if their babies aren't positioned correctly at the breast.

expressing breast milk

If you'll be returning to work soon, pumping milk will enable you to continue breastfeeding. Even while you're at home on maternity leave, or if you plan to stay home with your baby, expressing the occasional bottle gives you the opportunity to leave the house—or just get a good night's sleep—while someone else gives your baby breast milk. (For more on expressing milk, see page 221.)

formula-feeding

If you've chosen to bottle-feed, you can learn to interpret your
baby's needs in exactly the same way as if you were breastfeeding.
Be sensitive of your baby's behavior so you can catch on quickly
when he's telling you he's hungry and respond with a bottle of
formula. Don't assume that, because you're bottle-feeding rather
than breastfeeding, your baby will be on a routine within days or
even weeks. Babies' needs change from day to day. In time you
should be able to work out an approximate pattern for feeding, but
in the early weeks, you'll need to offer a bottle every 2 to 3 hours,
or whenever your baby seems hungry. Until your baby reaches
about 10 pounds, he'll probably take 1 to 3 ounces of formula per
feeding session.

types of formula

Most formulas are based on cow's milk, which is modified to
resemble breast milk as closely as possible. Manufacturers modify
cow's milk by adjusting carbohydrate, protein, and fat levels and
adding vitamins and minerals. For most infants, formula with iron
is recommended.

Soy-based formula is made from soybeans fortified with vitamins,
minerals, and nutrients. But soy-based formula should be used
only for babies with an established intolerance to regular formula,
on the advice of your doctor. Other special types of formula are
manufactured for premature babies.

added nutrients

In the past few years, various additions have been made to the
recipe for formula to try to make it even more similar to breast milk.

Long-chain fatty acids (LCFAs). LCFAs are an important component of breast milk and play a key role in brain development
and eyesight, but the jury is still out on whether adding them
to formula is effective. Recent studies show that formulas with

first- and second-stage formulas

Some manufacturers produce two types of formulas: first-stage formula and second-stage formula, which is promoted as being for the older baby. The protein in milk can be broken down into curds (casein) and whey. First-stage formulas are whey dominant, with a ratio of 40:60 (casein to whey), which is about the same ratio as in breast milk. These formulas are suitable for babies at birth because it's believed they're easier to digest. Second-stage formulas are casein dominant, with a ratio of 80:20 (casein to whey). Because these formulas have more protein, they take longer to digest; they also have more iron. First-stage formula (that is, regular formula) is fine for babies up until about a year old—when most babies are ready for whole cow's milk. Many doctors don't believe babies need a special second level of formula, and switching formulas too early can cause constipation. It's a good idea to check with your doctor before making any formula changes.

long-chain fatty acids are safe and that babies tolerate them as well as traditional formulas. But do they have any developmental advantages for your baby? Several studies have come up with no clear answers. Some studies show no effects on neurodevelopment, growth patterns, feeding, or general health. Others show improvements in eyesight and mental development and a positive effect on blood pressure. Currently, it's unclear whether it's worth buying a formula that contains long-chain fatty acids. Formulas with LCFAs are about 25 percent more expensive than those without, and it's not entirely clear what levels of the different LCFAs are most effective.

Nucleotides. Nucleotides are compounds involved in almost all biological processes. Some limited studies of supplementation of formula with nucleotides have shown an enhanced immune response in babies fed these formulas, and improved catch-up growth in babies who are small for their gestational age.

different forms

Along with the ingredients in the formula, the other main choice is the form in which you purchase it. You have three possibilities:

Ready-to-use formula. The most convenient format is also the most expensive and bulky to store. Ready-to-use formula also has a short life span. Once a can is opened, you need to use it all within 48 hours. The water used to make these formulas generally doesn't contain fluoride, a nutrient important for strong teeth (although your tap water, used in formulas that require mixing, probably does). Minor inconvenience: Because this formula often has a darker color than powdered formula, some mothers complain that it's more likely to stain clothes.

Liquid concentrate formula. With concentrate, you mix equal parts water and formula. (But always read the container carefully for specific instructions.) Compared to ready-to-use formula, it's cheaper and takes up less storage space. Compared to powdered formula, it's a little easier to prepare, but it's more expensive and must be used within 48 hours of opening.

Powdered formula. This is the most economical choice, but you have to mix the powder and water together and follow the directions on the can exactly. It takes more time to prepare than other formula varieties, but the powder has a 1-month shelf life after it's opened, which helps prevent waste.

If your baby doesn't seem content with the formula you first started her on, talk to your pediatrician before changing brands or type of formula.

what you'll need

Bottle-feeding equipment comes down to just a few basics.

nipples

Artificial nipples, just like the human kind, come in different shapes and sizes. They come in different materials, too—latex, silicone, and rubber. You won't know which nipple your baby prefers until you try one and see how he responds to it.

by the numbers

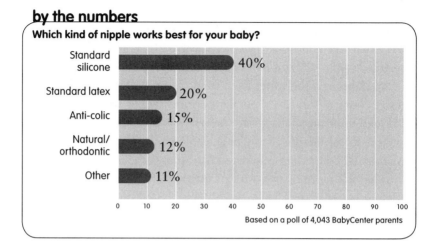

Which kind of nipple works best for your baby?

Standard silicone	40%
Standard latex	20%
Anti-colic	15%
Natural/ orthodontic	12%
Other	11%

0 10 20 30 40 50 60 70 80 90 100

Based on a poll of 4,043 BabyCenter parents

Latex nipples are softer and more flexible than rubber, but they tend not to last as long. Silicone is a little less flexible than latex but more durable. You can also buy anti-colic nipples that aim to reduce the amount of air your baby takes in while feeding. Orthodontic nipples have a flat side and are designed to emulate a human nipple as much as possible. You can even get disposable nipples for single use when you're out and about. Nipples also come in different flow speeds. Start with slow flow for newborns until they get used to bottle-feeding, then switch to a medium flow.

bottles

You'll need to experiment to find out which bottles work best for your baby. In general, wide-necked bottles are easier to fill than traditional narrow-necked ones, plus they're easier to clean. For newborns, start with smaller 4-ounce bottles, since that's as much as your baby will take at a single feeding.

Anti-colic or anti-gas bottles reduce the amount of air a baby takes in. One popular design features a vent that allows air to escape during a feeding, so your baby swallows less air. Also available: Bottles that hold collapsible bags for the milk, which, again, means your baby is less likely to take in air as he drinks. Again, experiment and see what suits you and your baby.

by the numbers

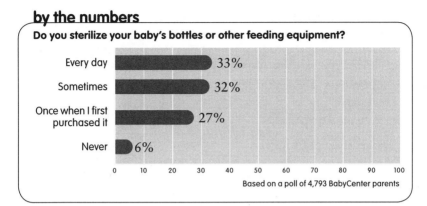

Do you sterilize your baby's bottles or other feeding equipment?

Every day 33%
Sometimes 32%
Once when I first purchased it 27%
Never 6%

Based on a poll of 4,793 BabyCenter parents

sterilizing equipment

You don't need to sterilize equipment other than when you first purchase it, before the first use. (To do this, boil the items— bottles, caps, rings, nipples—in a pot on the stove for 5 minutes and then air-dry on a clean towel.) After that, a pass through the dishwasher or a good cleaning in hot, soapy water is sufficient. Use nipple- and bottle-brushes for a more thorough job.

There's one exception to this rule. If you rely on well water, it's a good idea to sterilize equipment after each use. You can boil the bottles and nipples on the stove in a pot or use a specially made bottle sterilizer.

preparing bottles

Make up powdered formula fresh for each feeding. There's considerable difference of opinion on what kind of water to use. Some doctors say that if the water is safe for adults to drink, it's okay for babies. Others advise using cooled boiled water for the first 3 months. (And still other doctors prefer the first 6 months, or longer if you use well water.) To do this, bring a pot of tap water to a boil for 1 minute and let it cool completely before mixing. Make life easier by boiling enough for the entire day's feedings in the morning; after it cools, store it in a clean empty milk jug or other container. You can also buy presterilized water for babies, but it's expensive. Ordinary bottled water isn't sterile and may not contain fluoride.

by the numbers

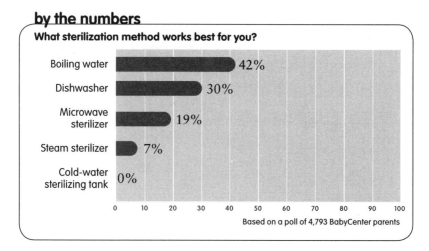

What sterilization method works best for you?

Method	Percentage
Boiling water	42%
Dishwasher	30%
Microwave sterilizer	19%
Steam sterilizer	7%
Cold-water sterilizing tank	0%

Based on a poll of 4,793 BabyCenter parents

If you're making up powdered formula, beware of making the mix too strong. This can make your baby very thirsty and cause him to cry. The typical response is to give him more formula, which makes him even more thirsty. Often babies who are given over-concentrated mixes will throw up the formula, but it can also make them sick.

How to ensure that the formula isn't too strong?

- Pour the required amount of water into the bottle first, *before* adding the powder. Check the measurement on the formula packaging. If you put powder in first, it changes the ratio of water to powder (because the powder takes up the initial space in the bottle) and makes the formula too strong.
- Always use the scoop provided, as it measures just the right amount of powder.
- Measure the powder and level off the scoop using the back of a clean knife.
- Don't pack the powder down.
- Never, ever add extra scoops.

You can also buy packets of premeasured powdered formula for making up one bottle at a time. These are very accurate and convenient but cost more. They're especially handy to keep in your diaper bag when you're away from home.

before you feed your baby

When you're getting ready for a feeding, always:

Check the temperature. If you've warmed the bottle, shake it carefully to ensure that the formula is an even temperature throughout. Test it by shaking a few drops onto the inside of your wrist, where the skin is more sensitive than on your hand. The formula should feel just warm, not hot. If you need to, cool the formula by holding the bottle, with a cap covering the nipple, under cold running water.

Check the flow. Nipples come with various rates of flow. Newborns need a nipple with a small hole. Before each feeding, check the nipple, which should flow at about two or three drops of formula a second.

Get comfortable. Then, when you're ready, settle your baby comfortably onto your lap. Feeding your baby is an opportunity for the two of you to get to know each other better; your baby will prefer maintaining eye contact with you during a feeding. Relax and take your time during feedings, and take the opportunity to just enjoy your baby.

Position correctly. Babies are born with a very strong sucking reflex. Touch the nipple of the bottle to your baby's lips, and she'll open her mouth wide. Hold the bottle firmly as your baby sucks, and tilt it so that the hole in the nipple is always full of formula and not air (which can give her uncomfortable gas). If the nipple collapses, move it gently around her mouth to let the air back into the bottle.

Get the gas out. When your baby seems to be full (after about 10 minutes), she may need burping. Sit her up on your lap or put her over your shoulder and rub her back gently. She may give a good belch or make a soft burp and spit up slightly, and then want more formula.

Q

My baby doesn't finish his bottle. Should I worry?

○ Always
● Hardly ever
○ Never

Not making it to the last drop probably means that your baby's had enough for the moment, that's all. Throw away any that's left over. Never reheat a bottle that your baby has already started because it may be contaminated by bacteria and could make him ill.

feeding checkpoint: how much, how often?

How much formula your baby needs depends on his age as well as his weight. Don't expect a newborn to follow a schedule or mathematical chart. The following amounts are rough guidelines; your pediatrician may make different suggestions for your baby.

Newborns don't have the capacity for large amounts of formula, so they need small, frequent feedings. As a rough guide, most **newborns** require about six feedings a day, each of about 3 ounces. In the past, mothers were encouraged to feed every 4 hours, but this thinking has changed. Sticking to a rigid timetable could lead to your baby becoming hungry and too distressed to feed well.

By the time your baby is **1 month old,** he'll probably be taking around 3 to 4 ounces at each feeding. That's about 20 to 28 ounces a day. You'll soon sense if your baby needs more; he'll finish the feeding quickly and then look around for a second helping.

By **the second month,** he may be taking slightly fewer bottles throughout the day, but more at a time; probably five feedings, each of about 4 to 6 ounces. Let your baby's appetite be your guide and expect it to vary a little from day to day. He'll probably continue to have this much milk until he's **6 months old.** (Now's the time when you may need to switch to larger-size bottles.)

As your baby's digestive system matures, he'll last longer between feedings. Try to let him set the pace. All babies go through growth spurts. They may be hungry for a day or two, demanding extra feedings, and then settle down again.

For formula-fed babies older than 3 to 4 months, offer cooled boiled water (but not more than 4 ounces in a day) to quench his thirst between feedings, especially in hot weather. (Breastfed babies usually need no extra liquids.)

common questions

During—and after—feedings, you're bound to have a number of concerns. Such as:

"can I give my baby room-temperature formula?"

Absolutely. If you feed your baby room temperature formula right from the start, then that's what she'll be used to. You're only likely to run into problems if your baby has become accustomed to warm formula and so may object if you offer a bottle that seems comparatively cold.

However, many parents prefer their babies' bottles to be warm, as that's how breast milk comes out. If you're going to warm your baby's bottles, do so in a pan or bowl of hot—never boiling—water, or buy a bottle warmer. Don't microwave a bottle of breast milk or formula. Because a microwave oven heats unevenly, it can create hot pockets, leading to burns.

Warm a bottle only when your baby is ready to eat. Never carry already warmed-up formula or breast milk in an insulated water bottle or bag. This provides the ideal conditions for bacteria to thrive and could make your baby very ill.

hands-on bottle-feeding

Never leave your baby to nurse unattended by propping up the bottle. Beside the fact that both of you will be missing out on vital time for bonding and snuggling, she could choke.

Nor should you take a bottle from the refrigerator and leave it out on the counter until it reaches room temperature. This, too, invites bacteria; it's better to serve a refrigerated bottle cold (if your baby doesn't protest, it won't hurt him) or to offer it right away after heating it on the stove or in a warmer.

"can I do anything about my baby's gas?"

For some newborns, gassiness is a real problem. They squirm around, apparently in discomfort, unable to burp and swallowing yet more air when they cry to let you know about the problem.

To keep gas to a minimum, try these strategies:

- Feed your baby in a more upright position.
- If you're breastfeeding, make sure your baby is latched on properly before he begins to feed.
- If you're formula-feeding, try a different shape or size of nipple.
- Shift positions mid-feeding. (The movement may cause your baby to burp, giving him more room in his stomach for milk.)
- Keep your baby upright after a feeding and burp him. Hold him over your shoulder, and gently rub or pat his back to encourage him to burp out any air. (You'll usually hear this, and a little spit-up milk may dribble out, too.)

"why does my baby hiccup so much?"

What causes hiccups—sudden contractions of the muscles used for breathing in—has baffled scientists for hundreds of years, not least because hiccupping doesn't seem to serve any useful purpose. They neither cause any health problem nor are they a sign or symptom of a problem.

Babies hiccup frequently, even before they're born. Ultrasound scans reveal 2-month-old fetuses hiccupping in utero, before any breathing movements appear. No one quite knows why this happens, although there are theories: For example, hiccups prepare

Q My baby seems to spit up after every feeding. Should I worry?

○ Always
● Hardly ever
○ Never

After a meal, both breastfed and formula-fed babies may bring up a small amount of milk. Spitting up is perfectly normal, especially after a burping. It looks like a few teaspoons of milk trickling gently down your baby's chin. Keep a tissue or a bib handy to wipe it up; it's also a good idea to drape a towel over your shoulder before burping to catch the dribbles. If your baby regularly brings up large amounts of milk, mention this to your doctor.

a baby's respiratory muscles for breathing once he's born, or that they stop amniotic fluid from entering the lungs.

The latest theory is that hiccups may be linked to the fact that our ancient ancestors lived in the sea. When someone hiccups, just after the respiratory muscles start to move, the glottis (the middle part of the larynx) shuts off the windpipe, producing that characteristic *hic* sound. Some primitive animals close the glottis and squeeze their mouth cavities to push water across their gills in order to breathe. The theory is that the brain's wiring for this breathing action gradually became adapted for nursing. The sequence of movements in a hiccup is very similar to the movements in nursing, with the mouth cavity being squeezed and the glottis closing so that milk doesn't enter a baby's lungs.

It's only a theory and still doesn't entirely explain why your newborn hiccups like crazy. Often feeding or burping your baby will put an end to hiccups. Some babies hiccup a lot and even drop off to sleep while hiccupping. Most babies stop hiccupping as they grow.

babies' weight gain patterns

Breastfed and formula-fed babies grow at basically the same rate in the first few months.

- During the first month, babies gain, on average, 4 to 7 ounces each week.

babycenter buzz
formula-feeding tips

"Formula these days is way too good to feel guilty about using it to feed your baby. Do what you can and what's best for you. An unhappy (and exhausted) mom can't be a good mom."—**Anonymous**

"I found that powder can sometimes get foamy when it's mixed. I get rid of some of the foam by premixing early and storing the bottles in the fridge."—**Lili**

"I tried a bottle warmer, but it never worked well. To heat the bottle, I keep a small Crock-Pot with hot water always on, then mix some formula, and put the bottle in the Crock-Pot. Four ounces of cold formula heats up in about a minute or so."—**Kathy**

- After that, on average babies gain 1 to 2 pounds each month for the first 6 months.
- From 6 months to 1 year, babies average 1 pound each month.
- A healthy 1-year-old weighs from 21 to 26 pounds.

Between 4 and 6 months, formula-fed babies tend to gain weight faster than breastfeeding babies. In one study, breastfeeding babies gained an average of 1 pound less than formula-fed babies during the first 12 months, although growth in length and head circumference were similar in both groups.

Your baby's growth chart will give you a general picture of how your baby is developing physically. By comparing your baby's measurements—weight, length, and head circumference—to national averages for children of the same age and sex, and to measurements from previous checkups, your doctor determines whether your baby is following a healthy overall growth pattern.

Although it's tempting, don't get too hung up on your baby's percentiles. The most important thing is that she's growing at a steady, appropriate rate, not that she's hit some magic number. Patterns of growth are also influenced by genetics; if other members of your family are taller, shorter, bigger-framed, or smaller than other people, your baby may be, too.

by the numbers
sleep: birth to 3 months

When did your baby start sleeping through the night?

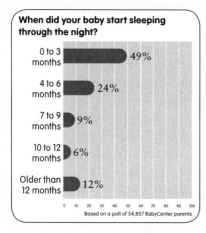

- 0 to 3 months — 49%
- 4 to 6 months — 24%
- 7 to 9 months — 9%
- 10 to 12 months — 6%
- Older than 12 months — 12%

Based on a poll of 54,857 BabyCenter parents

How do you stay awake after you've been up all night with your baby?

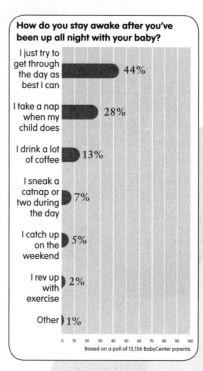

- I just try to get through the day as best I can — 44%
- I take a nap when my child does — 28%
- I drink a lot of coffee — 13%
- I sneak a catnap or two during the day — 7%
- I catch up on the weekend — 5%
- I rev up with exercise — 2%
- Other — 1%

Based on a poll of 13,156 BabyCenter parents

Who gets out of bed in the middle of the night?

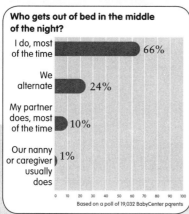

- I do, most of the time — 66%
- We alternate — 24%
- My partner does, most of the time — 10%
- Our nanny or caregiver usually does — 1%

Based on a poll of 19,032 BabyCenter parents

How do you catch up on sleep?

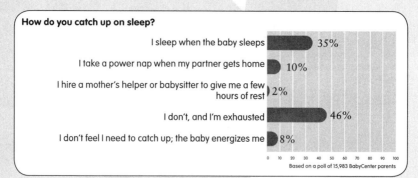

- I sleep when the baby sleeps — 35%
- I take a power nap when my partner gets home — 10%
- I hire a mother's helper or babysitter to give me a few hours of rest — 2%
- I don't, and I'm exhausted — 46%
- I don't feel I need to catch up; the baby energizes me — 8%

Based on a poll of 15,983 BabyCenter parents

How often do you check on your baby at night?

I lose track. Any small noise sets me scurrying to my baby's room — 20%

I steal a peek once or twice a night — 58%

What, and miss out on the blessed quietness? — 23%

Based on a poll of 26,209 BabyCenter parents

during the first week:

How many times did your baby wake you each night?

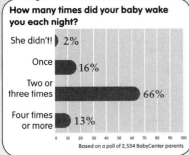

She didn't! — 2%

Once — 16%

Two or three times — 66%

Four times or more — 13%

Based on a poll of 2,534 BabyCenter parents

at 6 weeks old:

How many times did your baby wake you each night?

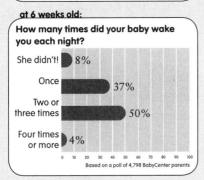

She didn't! — 8%

Once — 37%

Two or three times — 50%

Four times or more — 4%

Based on a poll of 4,798 BabyCenter parents

at 3 months old:

How many times did your baby wake you each night?

She didn't! — 38%

Once — 37%

Two or three times — 22%

Four times or more — 1%

Based on a poll of 5,378 BabyCenter parents

Does your baby sleep with you?

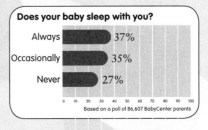

Always — 37%

Occasionally — 35%

Never — 27%

Based on a poll of 86,607 BabyCenter parents

If yes, how many months old is your baby?

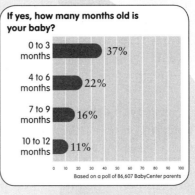

0 to 3 months — 37%

4 to 6 months — 22%

7 to 9 months — 16%

10 to 12 months — 11%

Based on a poll of 86,607 BabyCenter parents

the bottom line

Most newborns sleep for a total of 16 to 18 hours in each 24 hours, with sleep periods of about 2½ to 4 hours at a time. By the end of the first month, your baby may have developed a feeding and sleeping pattern, or you may not notice any real pattern for months.

chapter
12

sleep—
birth to 3 months

A newborn isn't wired to sleep like an adult. Her tummy is tiny, so she has to feed on a very regular basis. She also has to do a great deal of learning. So it's best for her to sleep in shorter bursts, then to wake for food and stimulation, and then to sleep again.

Adults have a definite sleep pattern: During the day, they're awake and alert; at night, they get sleepy, their body temperature drops, and most of their bodily functions slow down. It's unusual for an adult to wake up and feel energetic during the night. Babies haven't adapted to this rhythm and sleep as easily during the day as at night. Your baby's routine, such as it is, is the one best suited to her individual development.

But that doesn't mean it's suited to yours. The first few weeks are very demanding for new parents, and many have never experienced such tiredness before.

It's not just the hours of sleep that differ between a baby and an adult. The type of sleep is different as well. Adults fall into very deep sleep in the first part of the night, then move up into lighter, mostly dreaming sleep (called REM sleep from the rapid eye movements visible during this time). It's easy to wake from this

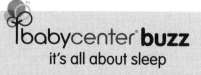

babycenter **buzz**
it's all about sleep

"My baby is 2 weeks old. We usually set bedtime around 10:00 p.m., when we give him a bath and then feed him. Then we put him in his crib wide awake, and he usually falls asleep. He wakes every 2 to 4 hours for a feeding or changing. It's not so bad, given that he's only 2 weeks old."**—Danielle**

"My son is 7 days old and has his days and nights mixed up. He sleeps all day and cries and fusses throughout the night, and by 3:00 a.m. he's ready to party. I get no sleep."**—Rhiannon**

"You can't spoil a 1-week-old baby! It's fine to sleep with him at this age. He's still getting used to life outside. Once he's over the newborn stage and becomes more of a baby, he'll become more settled. Give him 3 or 4 weeks of whatever it takes before you start worrying about anything."**—Jill**

dreaming sleep, but much harder to wake from deep sleep. While adults spend 80 percent of their sleeping time in deep sleep and 20 percent in light REM sleep, it's believed that babies split their sleeping time 50/50.

When your baby first falls asleep, you'll be able to see sucking motions, smiles, frowns, irregular breathing, and the occasional twitching of her arms and legs. She then sinks into quiet sleep (like adults' deep sleep). She'll move very little and have steady rhythmic breathing cycles—sometimes so slow and steady that you worry about the arrival of the next breath! Baby sleep cycles are very short, lasting about 50 to 60 minutes, so every hour or so your baby moves from active sleep to quiet sleep and back again. It's at these transitions that your baby is likely to wake up. That's why young babies have easily disrupted sleep patterns.

As your baby grows, she'll sleep for longer stretches and stay awake for longer periods. Most 2-month-olds have two to four long sleep periods and as many as 10 hours a day when they're awake.

Unfortunately, these hours don't always coincide with your night. Right from the start, however, you can take steps to help both of you get the sleep you need—when you need it. Your baby has no idea that there's a difference between day and night, but you can help her learn.

helping your baby sleep through the night

When other parents boast about their babies sleeping through the night for the past umpteen weeks, it can drive you to despair. Is yours the only baby who doesn't?

Question those parents more closely, however, and you may find that their definition of "through the night" and yours don't exactly coincide. One parent gives a final feeding at midnight and her baby sleeps till 6:00 a.m. Another baby starts the day at dawn. So what *is* "sleeping through the night," and when can you expect it to happen?

Most babies aged 2 or 3 months begin to sleep for longer stretches. However, because their stomachs are still so small, they'll need to wake once or twice during the night to nurse, particularly if they're breastfed. Some babies will continue to demand that nighttime feeding until the age of 5 or 6 months.

But if your baby still wakes in the night at the age of 5 or 6 months, it may no longer be because he *needs* to nurse, but because he's become *accustomed* to it. He may even have come to expect three or four nighttime feedings, which, though comforting, aren't nutritionally necessary. You can try waking him for a late evening feeding, so that he'll sleep longer.

If you're suffering because your nights are broken, then it's worth trying to alter your baby's behavior so that you can get an unbroken 6 to 8 hours sleep. Things to try:

- Save fun for the daylight hours. Your newborn needs to nurse several times during your sleeping hours, but keep the feedings calm and quiet and save the socializing for daytime.
- Keep the room darker at night (which would seem obvious, but during the early days it's tempting to switch the light on so you can admire him all over again).
- Consider putting your baby to sleep in different places: at night in a crib next to your bed or in your bed, during the day in his carriage or a cradle.
- When your baby is alert and awake during the day, play with him. Don't worry about keeping household noises to a minimum during daytime naps, either.
- Increase the size of the last feeding before your baby goes to bed; if your baby falls asleep while nursing, try gently waking him to see if he'll take more milk.
- If you hear your baby stir, give him a chance to fall back to sleep by himself; he may go another 2 to 3 hours. So long as he's not crying, there's no need to pick him up right away. Even if he does cry, you can try holding off for 5 to 10 minutes before you rush in; he may quickly cry himself to sleep. In this way, you can increase the length between night feedings and gradually reduce their number.

You can also help by making sure your baby gets lots of light during the day. A study of premature babies in the hospital found that using brighter lights during the day and dim lights at night encouraged these babies to be more active during the day and sleep longer at night once they went home. Another study found that babies who slept well at 6 weeks were exposed to significantly more light in the early afternoon period—so maybe that daily walk that Grandma advocates has some merit to it!

Try not to let your baby develop sleep associations that will be hard to break later, and give him the chance to fall asleep on his own. Put him down when he's sleepy but still awake. This will give him the experience of falling asleep without feeling your body right next to his. If you always get your baby to fall asleep by breastfeeding, he'll quickly get used to the fact that drifting off is always accompanied by the warmth of your breast and the trickle of warm milk. It's not a "bad" way to get him to sleep—in fact, it may be very comfortable for both of you—but it's unrealistic to then expect your baby to go back to sleep by himself when he wakes up a few hours later in the middle of the night. Along the same lines, if you regularly feed or rock your baby to sleep or drive him around in the car, he'll need the same cue to drop off again during the night.

There's no age at which a baby can be guaranteed to sleep through the night. Just remember that your baby *will* continue to wake several times in the night—everyone does, even adults. The difference is that adults know how to fall back to sleep on their own. In teaching your baby to sleep through the night, you're breaking the association between feeding, or being held by you, and falling asleep. Once you've done this, instead of waking and calling for you, your baby will wake, snuggle down again, and drift back to sleep.

sleep safety

Most new parents can't help but worry about Sudden Infant Death Syndrome (SIDS). Many dislike the feeling of powerlessness that comes with the knowledge that any baby can be affected and it's unknown exactly why it happens. There is, however, a great deal you can do to protect your baby. The rate of SIDS has fallen 75 percent since the advice to put babies to sleep on their backs was introduced in the early '90s.

In fact, SIDS is rare. The rate is about 0.43 per 1,000 births. It's not common in babies less than a month old, but peaks between ages 2 and 4 months, and becomes rare again after the age of 5 months—about the time when babies figure out how to roll over and move a bit. Some 90 percent of SIDS cases are in infants under 6 months old. Premature and low birth-weight babies and babies born to very young mothers are at greater risk, and slightly more boys than girls are affected. African-American and Native-

American infants have a higher-than-average SIDS risk, while Asian babies have a lower-than-average risk. It's believed these differences are due to cultural traditions regarding the position (on her back versus her tummy) a baby is put to sleep in.

SIDS can happen to any family, though it's more frequent in families with smokers. It's very rare for SIDS to occur twice in the same family.

Although researchers still can't identify which specific children are at greatest risk, they now understand that SIDS is linked to abnormalities in the brain stem, where heart rate, breathing, and body temperature are controlled. Normally, nerve cells in the brain are triggered to cause the body to react if a baby breathes in more carbon dioxide and less oxygen, as when he sleeps facedown on a mattress, on a pillow, or with his face covered by a blanket. But for some reason this doesn't happen in the brain stems of a very small minority of babies.

The good news is that this new discovery helps show how to keep all babies safer. The most effective way you can protect your baby is to take care with his sleeping arrangements. Make sure every babysitter knows this, too.

- **Put your baby on his back to sleep**—not on his front or side. SIDS is more common in babies who are put to sleep on their stomachs. (There's no evidence that babies who lie on their backs will choke. This unfounded worry was the reason it used to be common to place babies on their tummies.) When your baby can roll over (about 5 to 6 months), it's safe for him to sleep in whatever position he likes. The risk of SIDS falls sharply at this age. Like adults, he'll toss and turn in his sleep and this is fine.
- **Don't use a pillow,** as your baby risks rolling off or smothering. You should also keep pillowy bumpers, fluffy quilts or blankets, sheepskin pads, and plush toys out of a young baby's crib.
- **Use a firm mattress** that fits well into the crib.

Worry Meter

Q My 3-month-old insists on sleeping on his tummy. Should I worry?

○ Always
● Maybe
○ Never

Not all babies sleep well on their backs, and some prefer to be on their fronts. But back-sleeping is considered the safest position because it lowers the risk of Sudden Infant Death Syndrome. So when you lay your baby down, do your best to keep him settled on his back or his side. Don't put him on his tummy just because you think he likes it better; try to find other ways to comfort him to sleep so you can put him down on his back. A baby this young is still at an elevated SIDS risk.

- **Use a sleep sack instead of a blanket.** Duvets and loose covers are more likely to cover your baby's face. If you do use sheets and blankets, it's better to use several thin layers (such as crib-size top sheets or cotton or flannel receiving blankets) that are securely swaddled around your baby's body or firmly tucked into the mattress at the sides and foot of the crib.

- **Check the temperature.** Babies need to be warm, but not overly warm. Excessive heat increases the risk of SIDS. Keep the room at a temperature that's comfortable for you. If your baby is sweating or feels hot, then she's too warm; lower the room temperature or remove some coverings.

- **Keep your baby's head uncovered.** Periodically check to make sure she hasn't wriggled under the blankets. Never swaddle a baby around the head.

- **Consider sharing a room with your baby** until she's at least 6 months old. Some SIDS prevention groups make this recommendation, although the thinking on whether your baby should actually be in your bed or not is mixed. A "co-sleeper" next to your bed is another option.

- **Create a smoke-free area around your baby.** Research shows that cigarette smoke is a main risk factor for SIDS. Don't let anyone smoke in the same room as your baby.

- **Don't fall asleep on a sofa with your baby,** which increases the risk of SIDS.

- **Offer your baby a pacifier.** The American Academy of Pediatrics recommends a pacifier as its use is associated with a lower risk of SIDS. Wait until your baby is 1 month old if you're breastfeeding, to help establish good feeding (pacifier sucking requires different mouth motions).

decision guide •

CO-SLEEP OR CRIB?

Should you share a bed with your baby? Some studies suggest it's not a good idea for babies less than 8 weeks old because it raises the risk of SIDS, while others suggest that bed sharing helps protect against SIDS. Given the divided evidence on safety, where you choose to put your baby to sleep is ultimately a matter of what feels right to you and your partner.

Remember that whatever sleeping arrangement you choose can always be changed. There's no reason you can't start on one course and try it for a few weeks, then switch if it's not working for you.

reasons for the family bed

"I've read that it helps prevent SIDS." In societies where babies usually co-sleep, SIDS rates tend to be low. It may be that sleeping with your baby allows you to notice more quickly if she's ill. Or it may be that being beside a parent helps regulate the baby's temperature. Many small babies have breathing pauses (apnea). Co-sleeping allows you to be aware of these pauses, even in your sleep. You move or make sounds that bring your baby to a brief arousal so that she can tune into your breathing and join in again at the same pace, without waking fully.

"Breastfeeding at night is so much easier." After nursing, both of you can go right back to sleep, without having to get out of your warm bed. Also, you're more likely to continue breastfeeding your baby if it's quick and easy.

if you do plan to bring your baby into your bed:

- Use a small blanket to cover your baby, not your bedding, which she can slip under and become overheated
- Keep pillows away from your baby
- Use a firm mattress
- Make sure your baby can't slip between the mattress and the wall or the mattress and the headboard

don't share a bed with your baby if:

- You or your partner smokes
- You are very tired or are taking medication that can make you drowsy
- You've taken any alcohol or drugs
- You're sleeping on a sofa, a bean-bag chair or pillow, or a waterbed

"It's the only way to get enough sleep." Disturbed nights are inevitable, so anything that cuts down the time you spend settling your baby is a bonus. You can breastfeed while you're half awake, and many babies learn to help themselves at the breast. Some studies show that babies who co-sleep also cry less overall.

"I get so little time with him that I don't want to put him in a crib." If you work away from your home, nighttime feeding and snuggling can be an important way to spend time together.

"I just can't sleep if she isn't nearby." Some new parents worry if they can't see or hear their babies. Sleeping close to your baby allows you to quickly respond if she cries in the night, too.

"Babies aren't meant to be independent at first." Some parents believe that babies need as much physical contact as possible in the first few months.

reasons for a baby's own bed

"I've heard that not sleeping in my bed helps prevent SIDS." Studies seem to give conflicting messages. Some researchers believe that extra bodies in a bed raises the risk of accidental suffocation, just as excess pillows and blankets do, and that a baby is safer sleeping in his own bed.

"My bed just doesn't feel safe." Many parents find the idea of having a tiny baby in their beds just plain worrying. In addition to the presence of pillows and heavy blankets in a grown-up bed, you may worry about accidentally rolling over onto your baby. The anxiety can interfere with sleep you badly need. If you sleep on a waterbed, you shouldn't bring your baby into your bed.

"Co-sleeping would ruin what little is left of our sex life." Having a baby in bed with you may well inhibit your love life, and this makes many couples ambivalent about trying it.

"I can't sleep without pillows and a duvet." If your baby is in his own crib, you won't have to readjust your bedding or worry about whether he'll suffocate or overheat.

"After a long day I want my own bed for me." Many people find sharing a bed with their partner hard enough some of the time. Three in a bed can be the proverbial straw when all you want is peace and quiet.

"Our baby will get used to being in our bed." Some parents find it hard to move their babies into their own beds eventually, and this transition can take a long time. Also, if your baby gets used to falling asleep next to you, she may have trouble sleeping when you leave her with a relative or babysitter.

"I can't sleep if my baby is in bed with me." Many babies make little snuffly noises and move around in their sleep, and some parents find that this keeps them awake. Bed sharing doesn't work unless both partners are comfortable with the practice.

Here's a middle-ground option: You can buy a "co-sleeper" that attaches to your bed.

what not to worry about

If you wake occasionally in the middle of the night and check whether your baby is still breathing, you're not alone. New moms have plenty of common worries when it comes to baby sleep. Put your mind at rest so you can go back to bed.

Cold hands. Your baby's hands and feet may seem cold to you, even when the rest of his body feels as warm as toast. A better way to ensure your baby really is warm enough is by touching his tummy or the back of his neck. Either should feel warm but not sweaty.

Snuffling noises. Some babies snuffle all the time—even when they're sleeping—because their nasal passages are relatively tiny and easily affected by changes in air temperature. So those little snorts your baby makes while sleeping and feeding are normal.

Startling while asleep. Babies have periods of dreamlike sleep, usually when they first settle in. During this time, your baby suddenly jerks and cries out, then settles down again. This happens in adults as well; it's just more noticeable in babies because they sleep more and have longer periods of dreamlike sleep, during which these actions take place.

swaddling

Swaddling is the age-old practice of wrapping a baby in cloths or blankets so that movement of his limbs is restricted. In some cultures, swaddling babies and putting them on a cradleboard was the only way to keep them warm and out of danger—away from damp weather, wild animals, or just being stepped on—while the mother worked. In other cultures, it was thought to prevent a baby from "growing crooked." But, mostly, babies are swaddled because it seems to reduce crying and helps them to sleep. The latest research backs up these old ideas.

Some small-scale studies have shown that swaddling helps babies sleep better and helps them settle back to sleep if they do wake. It

babycenter buzz
sound sleep solutions

"Our first baby wasn't a sleeper. Some babies just aren't. She was too curious about everything around her."—**Rebecca**

"When my 3-year-old was born, I made everyone keep very quiet when he was asleep, whispering and tiptoeing around. As he grew older, he'd wake at the slightest noise—a floor creak. I didn't do that with my new baby, and she's now 4 months and can sleep through anything."—**Anonymous**

"When my baby cries at night and nothing else works, I take her in my bed, shut my eyes, and breathe deeply close to her face. She listens to me and in 5 to 10 minutes, she's asleep."—**Liana**

"After I would feed my newborn, he'd wake up and cry when I laid him down. I noticed that if I swaddled him first, then fed him, and laid him down that way, he was much more content. Figured out he doesn't like a cold bed!"—**Julie**

"I've come to realize that there's no sleep with twins!"—**Marcos**

"As hard as it is to do sometimes, the best advice is to go to bed when the kids do. My housework is so behind, but my husband and I tackle it on weekends."—**Amanda**

"When I need some sleep, I put my baby on my chest and move my body back and forth. We fall asleep for at least an hour."—**Erika**

can also help a baby to sleep on his back, which reduces the risks of SIDS. In some countries, swaddling is one of several comfort measures doctors and nurses routinely use when carrying out minor procedures in the hospital.

Swaddling gives a baby warmth and security, particularly in the first few days of life. It also keeps him from being disturbed by his own startle reflex. It helps settle your baby down when he's overstimulated or when he just needs to feel something close to the snugness and security of the womb. Fussy babies tend to benefit more from swaddling than naturally calm ones.

how to swaddle your baby

Your baby may love being swaddled. Or he may hate it and fight
the wrap. Try it and see. Be sure the wrap is snug enough to help
him feel secure.

- Check that your baby isn't hungry or wet.
- Place a cotton receiving blanket on a flat surface. Fold down the
  top right corner about 6 inches (a).
- Place your baby on his back with his head on the fold.
- Pull the corner near your baby's left hand across his body. Tuck the
  leading edge under his back, on the right side under the arm (b).
- Pull the bottom corner up under your baby's chin (c).
- Bring the loose corner over your baby's right arm and tuck it
  under the back on his left side (d).

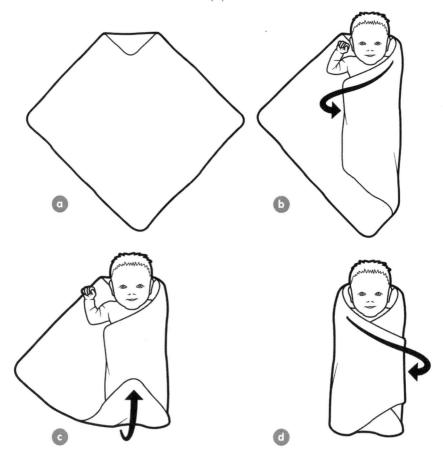

You can also swaddle with your baby's arms at his sides. Some babies prefer to have their arms free, so you can swaddle your baby under the arms, giving him access to his hands and fingers. Others grow more agitated with their arms loose and calm down better when swaddled snuggly, hands in and down. Be aware that babies can overheat when swaddled tightly, so be sure the room isn't too warm.

So take some sensible precautions:

- Use a thin material, such as a cotton crib sheet or a lightweight receiving blanket made of flannel or cotton.
- Leave your baby's head uncovered.
- If the room is already warm, dress your baby in a lightweight onesie, or if you find she doesn't try to wriggle out of the blanket, you can leave her in nothing more than a diaper.
- Use swaddling instead of a blanket, not in addition to one.
- Check that your baby isn't getting hot and sweaty.
- Make sure you lay your baby on her back.

Stop swaddling your baby by the time he's 3 to 4 months old because after that it can interfere with mobility and development. Some babies begin to resist swaddling sooner.

by the numbers
baby care: birth to 3 months

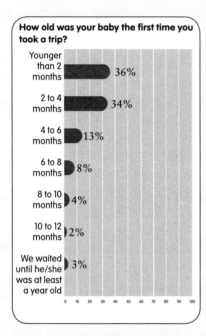

How old was your baby the first time you took a trip?

- Younger than 2 months — 36%
- 2 to 4 months — 34%
- 4 to 6 months — 13%
- 6 to 8 months — 8%
- 8 to 10 months — 4%
- 10 to 12 months — 2%
- We waited until he/she was at least a year old — 3%

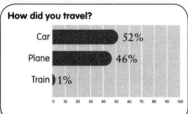

How did you travel?

- Car — 52%
- Plane — 46%
- Train — 1%

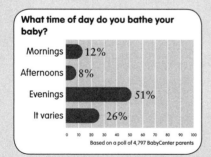

What time of day do you bathe your baby?

- Mornings — 12%
- Afternoons — 8%
- Evenings — 51%
- It varies — 26%

Based on a poll of 4,797 BabyCenter parents

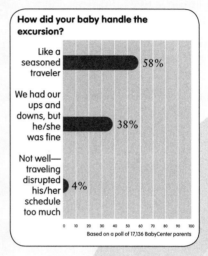

How did your baby handle the excursion?

- Like a seasoned traveler — 58%
- We had our ups and downs, but he/she was fine — 38%
- Not well—traveling disrupted his/her schedule too much — 4%

Based on a poll of 17,136 BabyCenter parents

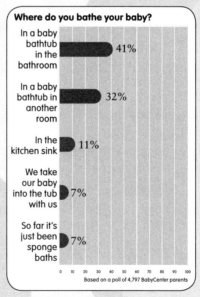

Where do you bathe your baby?

- In a baby bathtub in the bathroom — 41%
- In a baby bathtub in another room — 32%
- In the kitchen sink — 11%
- We take our baby into the tub with us — 7%
- So far it's just been sponge baths — 7%

Based on a poll of 4,797 BabyCenter parents

What kind of diapers will you/did you use?

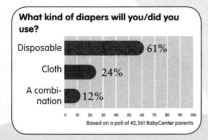

Disposable 61%
Cloth 24%
A combi-nation 12%

0 10 20 30 40 50 60 70 80 90 100

Based on a poll of 42,561 BabyCenter parents

Do you stick to a routine with your baby?

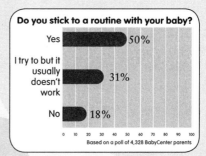

Yes 50%
I try to but it usually doesn't work 31%
No 18%

0 10 20 30 40 50 60 70 80 90 100

Based on a poll of 4,328 BabyCenter parents

Did your baby get diaper rash?

Yes 70%

No 30%

Based on a poll of 4,872 BabyCenter parents

Will you—or do you—let your baby cry it out?

Yes 41%

No 59%

Based on a poll of 148,610 BabyCenter parents

the bottom line

Parenting can only be learned on the job. The learning curve is steep, but you quickly become an old hand at all the practical aspects of caring for your baby. If something doesn't work for you, try something else. Stay flexible and concentrate on enjoying your baby instead of doing every aspect of baby care perfectly. If you're worried, talk to other parents whose babies are at the same stage as yours at babycenter.com.

Did you give your baby a pacifier?

Yes 62%

No 37%

Based on a poll of 9,266 BabyCenter parents

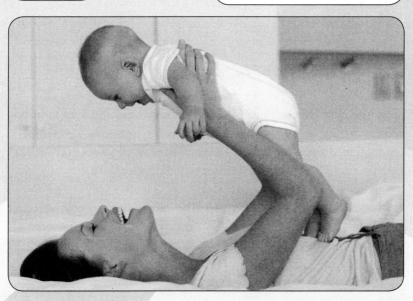

baby care—
birth to 3 months

Baby care is a big, broad area—especially in the beginning stages—and it covers everything from health and safety to your baby's behavior. With the passage of time, much of what you have to think about now will become second nature to you, within just a few weeks or months.

decision guide ·

SCHEDULE OR NOT?

Schedules used to be all the rage in baby care in the 1940s and '50s, and now they're making a comeback. Typically, scheduling centers around feeding your baby at specific intervals, as well as organizing sleep, play, and baby care based on a preset plan. Most new parents either love the idea of scheduling or hate it.

At the other end of the spectrum is the baby-led approach, in which you pay attention to reading your baby's signals and organize your day around what she seems to need at any given time.

babycenter buzz
what's right for you and your baby

"Your baby is a precious gift! Do what feels right for both of you."
—Anonymous

"Let other people help if they're willing. They can do laundry, dishes, cooking, or just help watch your older kids while you take care of the baby. Or let them care for your baby so that you can shower or otherwise take care of yourself. If you have a mom or in-law who's willing to stay with you postpartum, take advantage. You'll really appreciate the help, especially if you have older kids who don't yet really understand why mom can't lift them."**—Anonymous**

There's also a middle-ground option—and for all the attention given to schedules, it's probably the path that the majority of parents wind up taking—and that is to introduce regular routines, where you feed, bathe, play with, and put your baby to sleep at more-or-less the same predictable times every day, without eyeing the clock or worrying too much if you're away from home or your usual daily plan falls apart. It's a more ordered plan for the day than being completely baby-led, while being less rigid than scheduling.

Schedules with hard-and-fast timetables that a baby is expected to conform to are extreme, because babies' needs are so individualized. And simply going-with-the-flow works well in the early weeks, but it can be exhausting for parents as the weeks turn to months. Ask your friends how their experiences with structuring their babies' days went. Many mothers who began with quite a rigid view later ease up. Others who began very laid back gradually bring in a bit of order. How will you start out?

reasons for sticking to a schedule

"It works for us!" If you hold to a routine, you may find that life is pleasant all around—there are few surprises, especially if your baby adapts easily.

"I like being organized." If you're an organized sort of person, the thought of just going with the flow may worry you. Building structure into your baby's life may make you much happier and feel more in control.

"It allows me to know when I need to put time aside for my baby." If life with a baby is new and strange, organizing your days can help you cope.

"I'm going back to work soon." Women often feel that getting their babies on schedules before they return to work will make things easier for them and for whomever is going to be caring for their babies, and make for more continuity in care on evenings and weekends.

"I'm eager to get her sleeping well." Sleep is in very short supply in the early days, and anything that promises more sleep can be attractive.

"In the long term, it makes for better behaved children." You may feel that babies who know what's going to happen, and when, are more likely to grow into better behaved toddlers and children.

reasons for being "baby-led"

"Schedules are cruel." Teaching a baby to follow the clock requires inevitable crying time. Some parents feel strongly that this isn't acceptable.

"Schedules just didn't work for us." Trying to impose a routine on some babies can be stressful for everyone. It means you have to change your social life in order to be at home when your baby is due to sleep, for example.

babycenter **buzz**
running on schedule?

"Several people in my childbirth class tried really rigid routines. Most gave up when they realized they couldn't even go out for lunch or for coffee without upsetting the baby's routine. The one mom who's still doing it has a very placid baby and would probably have gotten into a routine quickly anyway. The rest of us are just muddling along!"—**Zara**

"Babies aren't trains; you can't make them run on time!"—**Anonymous**

"I was completely at sea. I never knew when she'd wake up or feed. My mother-in-law came to stay for a week and imposed some structure, and now everything is going smoothly. Thank goodness for routines!"—**Emma**

"I think it's important to meet my baby's needs." Learning how to read your baby and figure out what he needs takes some time, but once you've tuned in, it makes life easier for both of you.

"Following my baby's cues makes for a confident child." Some child psychologists believe that babies develop confidence by having their needs met.

"I don't want my baby to conform to a textbook." Schedules exist only in societies that have clocks and timetables. In many cultures, life is much more fluid and people develop and live at their own speeds.

"Being rigid doesn't make sense to me." Adults don't sleep, eat, and drink at the exact same times every day, so why should babies?

If you're thinking of introducing a routine, try keeping a diary for a couple of days. You may find your baby already has more of a routine than you imagined; he wakes at about the same time each day, naps for a couple of hours in the morning and another hour in the afternoon, and nurses around about the same times each day. Perhaps it's just one part of the day that you feel is unpredictable, such as the evening, when maybe he nurses on and off all the time. If this is the case, start with the routine you already have and build on it. Put your baby down for naps at about the same time each day, and gradually he'll get used to the idea. Then try putting him in his bed awake but drowsy in the evening instead of letting him fall asleep at the breast. Make each change a small one, and you may develop a routine that suits you both—just don't expect a schedule to establish itself overnight.

decision guide

PACIFIER OR NOT?

Some parents view pacifiers as a lifesaver, while others dislike them and never use them. Although a baby certainly can live and thrive without pacifiers, they can sometimes make life smoother. See if any of these arguments resonate with you:

reasons for using a pacifier

"He just cries and cries without it." Some babies cry more than others, and a pacifier can help reduce or stop crying bouts. For some parents, it's the only way to cope. Often parents-to-be dismiss

pacifiers and SIDS

Some studies have shown that pacifiers lead to a reduced risk of SIDS. It may be that the bulky handle of the pacifier keeps the baby's nose and mouth clear of covers, or that the sucking action helps improve the way the baby controls the upper airway. Thumbsucking appears to have a protective influence as well. (It's important to remember, though, that other factors, such as putting your baby to sleep on his back and not smoking, are critical in preventing SIDS.) If you choose to offer a pacifier, wait until your baby is 1 month old if you're breastfeeding, to eliminate the risk of nipple confusion and get nursing off to a good start. (SIDS risk is low in the first month and much higher from 2 to 4 months.)

pacifiers only to change their minds once their babies are born and they find it impossible to stop the crying.

"She wants to suck all the time. Without a pacifier, I'd spend all day feeding." Some babies need to comfort suck. They aren't hungry but want something to suck on. A pacifier is a convenient alternative to the breast.

"Better a pacifier than a thumb." Stopping thumb sucking can be difficult. Many parents feel they can take a pacifier away at the right time but they can't take away a thumb, so they'd rather start their child on a pacifier.

"He had terrible colic, and it cut down the noise!" Coping with colic is hard work, and a pacifier, even if it doesn't completely curb crying, may just help both of you get through the tough times.

"It helps him settle at night." Some babies prefer to suck as they drop off to sleep, and a pacifier allows them to settle in bed rather than at the breast.

"My baby is a preemie." Premature babies transfer more quickly from tube to bottle-feeding if they're given a pacifier to suck on before being fed. Using a pacifier can result in shorter hospital stays for preterm babies, too.

"I'm worried about SIDS." Introducing a pacifier is associated with a reduced SIDS risk.

reasons against using a pacifier

"I just hate to see babies with pacifiers." Some parents simply don't like the look of one cluttering a baby's face. In some cultures, a pacifier is associated—rightly or wrongly—with poor parenting.

"I'd rather comfort her myself." Checking out why a baby is crying and dealing with the cause is a better alternative for some parents, some of the time. Of course, you can't always find the cause of the crying.

"We ended up waking up whenever he lost the pacifier." A young baby can't find and replace the pacifier when she pushes it out of her mouth. She then wakes and cries for you to come and find it.

"My dentist said it will affect her teeth." Prolonged pacifier use can lead to dental problems. Most kids stop sucking on their own or are easily weaned before problems develop, but if you're concerned you won't be able to break the habit, you may not wish to start it.

"I'm concerned about possible unintended consequences." Using a pacifier on a daily basis can interfere with breastfeeding, and there's a link between pacifier use and middle-ear infections. In the longer term, pacifiers can interfere with babbling—an important step in learning to talk and your baby's language development—although this is mainly seen in babies who have "pacis" in their mouths most of the time.

"My baby is a thumb sucker." By 3 months, some babies find their thumbs, fingers, or hands and suck to comfort themselves. (On ultrasound images, some babies suck their thumbs in utero.) Life may be easier if you take advantage of this built-in pacifier. Thumb sucking is safe until age 3 or 4, and in some children even later, according to the American Dental Association.

pacifier safety

If you decide to use a pacifier, here are some guidelines to use it safely and most effectively:

- Use an orthodontic pacifier.
- Keep the pacifier as clean as possible—wash it in the dishwasher or with hot, soapy water periodically.
- Check the pacifier regularly for cracks, splits, and holes, which can trap germs, and if you see them, replace it with a new pacifier immediately.

- Never dip the pacifier in sweets such as honey, syrup, or orange juice to stop your baby's crying. This can lead to rapid tooth decay. (Additionally, always avoid honey before age 1 because of the risk of it causing infant botulism, plus orange juice and other citrus foods aren't recommended before 6 months because of allergy risk.)
- Try limiting pacifier use to key times, such as during spells of colic or just for settling down.
- Try to wean your baby off the pacifier before 4 to 5 months so the pacifier doesn't become a transitional object for your baby. It's much harder to get rid of a pacifier by the second half of the first year, and after the first birthday it can also interfere with language development.

decision guide

CIRCUMCISE OR NOT?

No doubt you already made this decision during pregnancy, but if you haven't, you may be considering it after your son is born. The American Academy of Pediatrics says that the choice is best left up to parents, who should make an informed decision based on possible health benefits and risks, as well as their cultural, religious, and ethnic traditions.

Circumcision rates are about 60 percent in the United States, down from 85 percent in the 1970s. They vary widely from region to region, however, being highest in the Midwest (81 percent) and lowest in the West (39 percent). These are all higher than in Australia, where 10 to 20 percent of boys are circumcised, or across Europe and much of Asia, where overall rates are even lower. One interesting trend is that the rates of circumcision among white and black American infants are now about the same, after more than 20 years of the rate being higher among Caucasian infants. Studies have shown that Hispanic infants tend to have lower rates of circumcision than blacks or whites.

Only around one in every 100 men needs a circumcision for medical reasons. The main medical indication for circumcision is a
too-small opening of the foreskin. It's normal for the foreskins of
baby boys to be too tight to pull back completely until as late as
age 6. Occasionally, medical circumcision may be carried out as a
result of repeated infection beneath the foreskin or for some other
rare conditions.

reasons for circumcising

"It's part of our religious beliefs." This may be so important to
you that no other argument is necessary.

**"It's good protection against sexually transmitted diseases
(STDs) and other health problems."** Some studies suggest that
circumcision helps to prevent cancer of the penis, a very rare
cancer, and reduces the risk of STDs, including HIV. Circumcised
men also have fewer urinary tract infections.

"We don't think the foreskin is necessary." Some cultures
practice circumcision because they think the foreskin is unhygienic,
is unnecessary, or causes health problems.

"We want our son to look the same as his dad." This is often
an important issue for dads who want to protect their sons from
feeling "different."

"Uncircumcised boys will be made fun of." Anyone who has
ever been made fun of as a child knows how painful it can be; you
may consider the brief pain of the circumcision worth it if this is
the norm where you live. (You'd want to consider the norm among
babies in this case, rather than their fathers, since circumcision
rates are changing from generation to generation.)

"We want to get it over with while he's little." Certainly if you
think your son will regret that you didn't do it, you'll want to go
ahead while he's a baby.

"**We like the way it looks.**" The issue is sometimes an aesthetic one for parents.

reasons for not circumcising

"**It's just wrong!**" Some parents believe boys are born the way they're meant to be, and interfering with that is genital mutilation.

"**It's not medically necessary and a risk we don't want to take.**" Complications are rare, but possible, and you may feel the risks aren't worth taking.

"**We don't want to cause our baby unnecessary pain.**" Although steps can be taken to minimize pain, it's not true, as was once believed, that newborns can't feel or remember trauma.

"**It's not usual in my family.**" It may be your religious or cultural belief *not* to circumcise, or you may want your child to resemble his uncircumcised father.

"**Circumcision is unhealthy.**" While there are some STDs that are more common and more difficult to spot in uncircumcised men, other STDs and urethritis (inflammation of the exit tube from the bladder, usually due to infection) are more common in circumcised men.

"**A foreskin is there for a reason.**" The foreskin is thought to protect the glans from irritation from dirt or feces and to keep it soft and sensitive as nature intended. Some people believe that circumcision interferes with male sexual pleasure. There are more than 1,000 nerve endings in the foreskin.

"**We like the way it looks.**" The issue is sometimes an aesthetic one for parents.

crying

It's perfectly normal for babies to fuss and cry a lot during their first 3 to 4 months. Some babies seem to be perpetual crying machines: They cry more often and, once they get started, they continue longer than other babies. If you think your baby cries a great deal, then you're probably right; parents' perceptions of crying are usually accurate.

why babies cry

Between 12 and 20 percent of moms are upset enough by their baby's persistent crying to seek help. So if you're worried about your baby's crying, you have plenty of company. European studies found a "crying peak" at 2 to 3 weeks. Interestingly, in American and Canadian studies, the peak is at 5 to 6 weeks, which suggests either a cultural difference or that European moms and dads are quicker to seek help with a crying baby.

It's rare for a baby to wail nonstop for hours at a time. Rather, babies who cry a lot spend the majority of their crying time fussing, intermixed with periods of more continuous and intense crying. Your "fussy" baby probably doesn't cry intensely all the time because you spend time soothing and preventing her from crying. It's very common for babies in the early months to have an early evening crying peak, although no one knows for sure what causes it.

Generally, as babies get older, the amount of crying reduces, but this is relative to how much they cry in the first place. Babies who cry and fuss a lot in the early weeks will cry and fuss much less by the time they're 5 months old, but they'll still cry and fuss *more* than many other 5-month-olds.

Chalk up excessive crying just to the way your baby is rather than to your inexperience as a parent. Nor does the way you feed your baby predict how much she'll cry. Although it's true that not knowing what to do as a parent of a new baby can result in greater amounts of crying, babies fuss and cry a lot even when their parents give them highly sensitive and responsive care.

In short, babies do plenty of crying in the first 3 months despite excellent parenting!

Babies who seem especially difficult are often described as high-needs babies. They are prone to crying, require lots of physical contact, want to comfort suck frequently, and generally demand a high level of attention from their parents. If your baby fits this description, remember that he cries to express a *need*, and that the need won't go away if you ignore it. The intense parenting that these babies require is exhausting, and the more resources, support, and help you can call on, the better. If your baby cries for no apparent reason, is impossible to soothe, and is uncontrollable, this can result in you feeling helpless and inadequate—even angry—which can cause anxiety and depression.

Your own response may be a cultural one. For those who live in an affluent society, persistent crying may be viewed negatively and as something to worry about. In an impoverished society, a baby who cries a lot may be viewed as showing positive signs of strength and a will to live. In the past, a crying baby was viewed as healthy. Even now, older relatives may suggest that a baby needs to cry to "exercise his lungs."

But that's little consolation if you can't settle your baby. First try the list below of some actions that may help to reduce crying in young babies. Once you've cleared these, you can move on to more diverse tricks. (See more in **just for dads: crying is a good thing** on page 144 and **crying checklist** on the opposite page.)

Be responsive. Picking up your baby and soothing him quickly can reduce crying in the long term. Research suggests that prompt attention to a crying baby in the first 3 months leads to less crying later in infancy.

Encourage self-soothing. At the same time, other studies have shown that allowing your baby to cry for a short while encourages him to learn how to settle himself. This is, needless to say, controversial: What some parents see as helping their babies learn to soothe themselves, others view as a form of cruelty, so this approach won't suit everyone.

Prevent overtiredness. Babies who have a peak of crying in the early evening tend to have had less sleep than other babies. And babies who sleep well at 6 weeks have usually been exposed to more light during the early afternoon. So helping your baby to settle into a sleep routine may help reduce the tears if his crying is due to being overtired and overstimulated. Some babies are much better than others at cutting off from the world and getting to sleep anywhere. Others need a routine and gentle help to settle themselves down. One study involved a nurse working in partnership with families through an intensive 4-week home visitation program. Parents kept a diary, identified crying periods, and introduced some routines to the day to help prevent their babies from getting overtired and overstimulated. This, along with skin-to-skin contact and holding and rocking the baby during crying spells helped reduce typical crying periods from an average of 3 hours a day to 1.3 hours.

crying checklist

When your baby cries, what's she asking for? Here's a list of the most common things.

"I need food." Hunger is the most common reason a new baby cries. The younger your baby, the more likely it is that she's crying to be nursed. A baby's small stomach can't hold very much, so if your baby cries, try offering to feed her.

"I need to be comfortable." Some babies will very sensibly protest if their clothes are too tight or if a soiled diaper bothers them. Other babies don't seem to mind a little discomfort. But it's worth checking if you can do something to make your baby, and you, feel better.

"I need to be warm, but not too hot or too cold." Check whether your baby is too hot or too cold by feeling her stomach. If she's too hot, remove a blanket, if she's cold, add one. Don't be guided by her hands or feet, as it's normal for them to feel slightly cold. Keep your baby's room temperature around 64°F. A good rule to follow is that your baby needs to wear one more layer of clothing than you do to be comfortable.

"I need to be held." Some babies need a great deal of cuddling and reassurance. Just seeing you in the room or hearing your voice is enough to soothe an older child, but newborns often need close physical contact for comfort. If you've fed your baby and changed her diaper, she may simply want to be held. Some parents worry about spoiling their babies if they hold them too much, but during the first few months of life that's impossible. Although some babies don't seem to need much physical contact, others want to be held almost all the time.

"I need a rest." It's easy to assume that babies will fall asleep whenever they need to, wherever they are, simply because so many

(continued on page 146)

just for dads

crying is a good thing

Few things decimate a dad's confidence faster than a screaming baby. It's simply amazing that something so tiny and so fragile can produce such an unholy racket. But screaming is what babies do, and it's okay if you can't stop it.

Crying, of course, is the most potent weapon in your baby's communication arsenal. Poopy diapers at awkward moments, odd sleep patterns, and the constant need to feed are also in his quiver. The best way to face these threats is head on: Don't hand off your baby. But do give yourself permission not to know everything right from the start. All that matters is that you have the desire and interest to learn.

Even a couple of months from now your baby is going to cry and you'll still feel absolutely clueless. But as you pace the house at night with your unsoothable baby, you'll be sending him signals about security, care, and love that will last well beyond these early days—for both of you.

How you can help soothe the sobs:

- Learn how to comfortably hold your baby. (Many dads find the over-the-shoulder snuggle to be both easy and comfortable.) He'll pick up on your general vibe, so if you're relaxed, he'll relax.
- Don't worry that your partner or anyone else seems to have the magic touch in quieting your baby. The truth is, your partner's probably equally clueless. The trick is to just stick with it. The more you try to comfort, the more your baby will find comfort in your arms.
- Dancing around with your baby is not only soothing, it's fun for you, too. And as you dance, try tapping the floor with your foot and chanting. It doesn't matter what the words are, the

repetition and rhythm coupled with your movement will often lull your baby into blissful silence.

- If you're proficient at making bodily function noises, outlandish facial expressions, or any other radical physical behavior that got laughs from your friends at any time during your life, dust them off now because babies are hard-wired to respond to this foolishness.
- Got one of those front-loading baby carriers? Pull it on, pop your baby in it, and hit the bricks. Your natural movement and warmth can work wonders.
- Sure, you don't have boobs or soft warm skin like mom, but don't sell short your deep voice, fascinatingly scratchy beard, or arrhythmic rocking technique. To your baby, who's spending these 3 months learning about sensations and devouring every new experience, you're pretty cool. And the more you hold, rock, talk, or sing to your baby, the more you'll find out about how to calm him when he's uncomfortable, and you'll also help him learn to focus on the outside world.

of them do. But sometimes they become overstimulated and find it hard to turn the switch off and settle down. Newborns can find it difficult to cope with too much stimulation at once—the lights, the noise, being passed from one adoring relative to the next—and become overwhelmed by it all. If it seems there's no specific reason for your baby's crying, it's possible she's saying, "I've had enough." Take her somewhere calm and quiet, gradually withdrawing the stimulation, and she may express her feelings by crying for a while and then eventually settling to sleep.

"I'm sick." Not usually the case, but this is the reason that often springs into the mind of new parents. It's so hard to tell whether your baby is crying purely because she's unhappy, or whether there's something genuinely wrong. A baby who's ill often cries in a tone different from her usual cry; it may be more urgent or high-pitched. The most important thing to remember is that nobody knows your baby as well as you do.

If you feel that there's something wrong, give your doctor a call. Always contact your doctor if your baby has difficulty breathing through the crying, or if the crying is accompanied by vomiting, diarrhea, or constipation.

"I need something, but I don't know what." Sometimes you'll find it impossible to figure out what's wrong when your baby cries. Many newborns go through patches of fretfulness and aren't easily comforted. The unhappiness can range from a few minutes of hard-to-console crying to several hours at a stretch.

ways to comfort a new baby

If you've worked through the crying checklist and your baby is still inconsolable, try these ways to comfort her:

Wrap up, hold tight. Most newborns show a definite preference for feeling snug and secure, just as they were in utero, so try swaddling your baby in a blanket to see if she likes that. (See page 126 for swaddling instructions.)

Worry Meter

Q **My baby sucks his thumb. Should I worry?**

○ Always
○ Sometimes
● Never

Many babies suck their thumbs, and some are even born with blisters on their lips from sucking their thumbs in utero. Many child psychologists believe that being able to "self comfort" in this way is a good thing. Whenever a baby is distressed, sucking his thumb helps him manage that distress.

You might also find that holding your baby close, especially so that she can hear your heartbeat, or placing her in a baby sling is soothing. Other babies prefer different forms of reassurance such as being rocked or sung to.

Pass the parcel. Often babies cry and fuss simply because they can smell your beloved milk. They don't actually *want* any, but it's nearby and that makes them fuss. Hand your baby over to Dad or Grandma and, with the familiar smell gone, your child may drop off to sleep. Although it can feel undermining if other people can settle your baby when you can't, at least you'll feel reassured that it's just because they don't smell as appealing as you do!

Find soothing sounds. Before birth, your baby could hear the regular beat of your heart. One of the reasons many babies like being held close is because then they can continue to hear it. Other regular, repetitive noises also have a calming effect, including the steady rhythm of a washing machine or dishwasher or the white noise made by a vacuum cleaner or hair dryer. (Note: Never put your baby's infant seat or cradle on top of a washing machine or clothes dryer. Always put her in a seat or cradle on the floor *next* to it.)

Rock-a-bye baby. Gentle rocking is very calming, whether you just walk your baby around the floor or sit with her in a rocking chair. Special baby swings soothe some babies, while others prefer faster motion and drop off to sleep almost as soon as they're driven somewhere in a car. Or put on some soft music, cuddle your baby, and dance with her around the room. Music is a great stress reducer, and it affects you much as it does your baby.

Try a massage. Giving your baby a massage or gently rubbing her back or tummy is a natural soother. If your baby seems to have gas pain, be sure to burp her after each feeding by holding her against your shoulder and caressing her back. Sometimes you can soothe a baby with colic by rubbing her tummy. Massage has been shown to reduce crying, especially when carried out on a regular day-to-day basis.

Let her suck on something. In some newborns, the need to suck is very strong. Sucking a pacifier or your (clean) finger or thumb can provide great comfort. Comfort sucking steadies a baby's heart rate, relaxes her stomach, and helps her settle.

what no one tells you about:
how *you'll* feel when your baby cries

A baby's cry is designed to get your attention. It's the equivalent to a baby animal's distress call. No wonder it has a powerful effect on you. Dads respond, too, but they're typically less overwhelmed because they don't have the biologically driven response that a mother's hormones create. Most women find their baby's cry is enough to make their milk letdown—you can feel your breasts start to tingle and may notice them leaking. If you can't get to your baby or it takes a while for you to pick your baby up, you may grow more and more stressed as his cries intensify. Some women find they can't think straight, can't coordinate well, may get the shakes, and eventually can't do anything but attend to their babies.

That's how nature intends it, of course. Once you pick your baby up and feed or comfort him, his cries die down and you both feel calm again.

What happens if your baby doesn't settle down? Most new moms become very distressed themselves if they can't comfort their babies. A baby who won't go to the breast or who has colic (see page 150) can drive a mom to distraction. Everyone ends up in tears. Many women unable to comfort their babies begin to feel angry. If you reach this stage, it's time for someone else to help

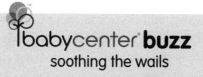

babycenter **buzz**
soothing the wails

"My little guy has this new gritty-sounding cry. The only thing that soothes him is his swing. Some days I feel like pulling my hair out and screaming." —**Melissa**

"Sometimes babies cry and you won't be able to figure out why. If you've gone through your checklist—hungry? cold? hot? wet? dirty?—and can't come up with an answer, it's okay. Your baby isn't broken, and you're not a bad parent. Sometimes they just cry."—**Betsy**

"It's really tough when you have a fussy, high-needs baby. Mine started his crying-fussy-miserable stage at about 6 to 8 weeks. He cried all the time. I always thought there must be something wrong with him but was never able to find anything. He was a pretty unhappy kid until, all of a sudden, the light bulb came on and he suddenly became happy!"—**Tanya**

"I have a swing on my back porch, and when it's nice outside, I take my baby out and lay him on the swing and sing to him; he just loves it and it calms him down every time."—**Sheila**

"When my baby is upset for no apparent reason, I always wrap her in her blanket, sit in the rocking chair with her, and sing very softly in her ear. A lot of times, I'm just repeating her name in a rhythmic manner, but she normally quits crying and starts listening to me until she falls asleep. Another thing to remember: Stay calm! Babies always sense when Mom and Dad are getting frustrated!"—**Anonymous**

"When my baby is crying, I take off everything except his diaper, take my shirt off, and lay him on bare skin with a blanket over him. This tends to calm him down because he dislikes being very hot."—**Anonymous**

"When my 4-month-old is crying and I can't seem to get her to stop, the one thing that always helps is a warm bath. It works wonders and relaxes her."—**Amy**

"Even if it's just for a daily walk, bundle them up, put them in the stroller, and don't think about it too much—otherwise you won't do it."—**Anonymous**

"Things do get easier with time. As you see them getting older and achieving milestones, all the hard work pays off."—**Anonymous**

out. Pass your baby to Dad (or your mom or a friend) while you take some time out. If you're on your own, put your baby safely in his crib and take a few minutes to calm down and then try again.

Nature created a system that ensures new mothers respond to their babies' needs. If you understand that and try to keep it front and center in your mind during your baby's crying jags, you can work with it rather than being alarmed or upset by it.

explained: colic

Any parent who's raised a colicky baby never forgets it. Colic describes a certain sort of crying, and babies afflicted with it have repeated episodes of excessive and inconsolable crying, although they otherwise appear to be healthy and thriving. They seem to suffer misery and apparent pain, often drawing their knees up toward their stomachs, clenching their fists, and screwing up their faces. Doctors are divided as to whether colic truly exists. But if you have a baby who screams uncontrollably every evening, then you might as well call it colic, because you still have to deal with it—whatever it's called.

Colic generally starts when a baby is around 2 to 3 weeks old, and usually stops by about 3 to 4 months. So the good news is that it's a temporary condition, and your baby won't suffer any long-term effects. The bad news is that the weeks between the onset of colic and the time most babies grow out of it are very stressful. It can last for short bursts around the same time each day (often in the evening) or come and go continuously throughout the day. Coping with a colicky baby is exhausting and demoralizing, and it can put a great strain on the whole family. The feelings of helplessness and guilt caused by the unexplained and uncontrollable nature of the crying are enough to make any caring parent feel pretty ineffective.

Between 5 percent and 20 percent of babies suffer from colic—the figures vary from study to study. The underlying cause of colic isn't known and may be due to a combination of factors. The two main theories suggest that either it has to do with a baby's digestive system or that it's behavioral, that is, your baby is easily distressed and slow to settle, perhaps because the central nervous system is slow to mature.

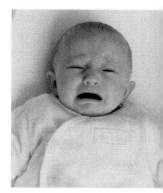

One study points out that 10 percent of babies with colic can't tolerate cow's milk protein and would benefit from elimination of the protein from their, or their mother's, diet. Usually other symptoms accompany the colic, such as vomiting or diarrhea and a strong family history of allergies.

Another study showed that colic is associated with feeding problems, including difficulty coordinating sucking, swallowing, and breathing, and an inability to slow down the sucking rate. So it could be that colicky babies find it hard to feed easily or that the feeding difficulties lead to the colic—no one seems to be sure which comes first.

coping with colic

You won't always be successful, but parents do report occasional or regular success in dealing with colic. First, make sure there isn't some obvious cause for the crying, such as discomfort due to hunger, pain, cold, heat, or itch. Ask a breastfeeding counselor to double-check positioning and attachment. Problems with either of these can reduce the amount of milk your baby takes at each feeding and lead to excessive crying.

If your baby cries for prolonged periods, and you can't see any reason for it, have your baby checked by a doctor. There may be some physical problem causing the crying, and it's essential to rule out the possibility of something more serious. So see your doctor, even if only to assure yourself that it *is* colic and your baby is actually well and healthy. It's unlikely that your doctor will run any tests or take blood if he sees no other obvious symptoms or a problem.

You may feel your doctor isn't doing enough, but he'll have experience with many colicky babies, both during the height of the affliction *and* after the colic has permanently passed, when babies are happy and healthy and showing no aftereffects. So try not to be disappointed that your doctor doesn't have a magic wand to wave. No one does. What you need to find out is that there is nothing wrong—medically or otherwise.

Once you're assured that's the case, it's time to develop your own colic survival plan:

- Think about ways to cope with your baby when she's crying: carrying her around, rocking her, or swaddling her and placing her in her bed. You'll need lots of options. You and your partner may find different tactics easier.
- Organize your day so that you have time during the crying periods to attend to your baby.
- Call in reinforcements. Many parents feel they can't leave their colicky baby with anyone else. Actually, your baby won't mind who's holding him at this stage—as long as *someone* is. If you can force yourself to go out for a while without your baby, it's helpful to be away from the crying and get some perspective on things. Ask relatives and friends to help out. If you can't leave your baby, get people to keep you company during the tough hours each day. Just having someone to hold your hand, make you a warm drink, and tell you it will pass can make you feel a whole lot better.
- Spend time with your baby when she's not crying. It will help to remind you that the colic is temporary and your baby *can* be joyful and happy.
- It's a good idea to check with your doctor before giving your baby any medication, whether natural, over-the-counter, or prescription. In general, avoid home remedies, too. None are proven to be especially effective.

looking for a cure

One respected medical journal carried out a review of all the available treatments for colic and found that very few have been shown to help. Interestingly, just being able to talk with someone

babycenter **buzz**
colic: what worked for us

"One thing that worked for us was the white noise of the vacuum cleaner—in fact, that's all that worked. If your little one is anything like mine, be careful not to let her get overtired. Once she's been up for an hour or two, put her in a quiet place with soothing white noise."—**Maggie**

"My daughter had colic from weeks 2 to 6, when she cried the majority of her waking hours. The things that helped were carrying her around in the Baby Bjorn and the noise of the hair dryer. The hair dryer worked so well that I made a CD with nothing but 60 minutes of continuous hair dryer sound. This was a lifesaver. "—**Anonymous**

"A drive around the neighborhood can put my baby to sleep in seconds."
—**Kate**

about how to cope with a colicky baby seems to provide relief in some cases. Here's a rundown of some common "cures":

- **Reduce stimulation.** One study showed that reduced stimulation (not patting, lifting, or jiggling your baby, and keeping down noise) reduced crying after 7 days in infants under 12 weeks. Swaddling may help some babies (see page 126).
- **Exclude dairy foods from your diet.** If your baby is breastfed, talk to your doctor about a trial of continuing breastfeeding while excluding dairy products from *your* diet. This may be effective, because breast milk contains intact cow's milk proteins.
- **Change feeding equipment.** If your baby is bottle-fed, try a gas-reducing bottle system or a nipple different from the one you've been using.

The traditional techniques for soothing regular crying (such as going for a car ride and increased carrying of your baby) are also worth a try. Even if they don't make any difference, you'll at least feel like you're actively doing something, which can make *you* feel better.

colic sanity savers

Many parents feel desperate about their baby's crying. Often that desperation turns to anger as you try to comfort your baby and nothing works. It can feel like your baby is rejecting your help. In a strange way, the more you love your baby, the angrier you may feel. This is your baby, you gave birth to him, and you *should* be able to make him feel better. It may sound strange to anyone who has not held a screaming, colicky baby for hours on end, but that's the thinking of many parents who face this situation.

You may begin to dread the time of day the crying usually starts and feel desperate both *for* your baby and *with* your baby. Part of you wants to make him feel better; part of you is angry that whatever you do seems to have no effect.

Hang in there. You won't be the only parent who's cried over their crying baby—or felt at the breaking point.

A very real danger when your baby is colicky is inadvertent abuse. Never—ever—shake your baby, yell at your baby, or handle him roughly. Even moderate shaking can damage a baby's brain. If you feel tempted, it's time to hand him over to someone else or just put him safely in his crib and walk away. If you're a single parent, you may need to get advice from your doctor or even hire a visiting nurse or aide to come to your home a few hours a day or week to watch your baby. Or ask a relative or friend to come and stay with you for a few days. When you're feeling so fragile and your baby is so demanding, it's important to have another adult nearby. If there's no one who can physically be with you, make sure you have an understanding ear so you can put your baby to bed, close the door, and talk to someone.

Remind yourself: Nothing you've done or not done is causing the colic. Your baby isn't crying because you did or didn't breastfeed, or because of something you've eaten, or the way you did or didn't pick him up when he cried. Some babies get colic. Some get it very badly. *It's not your fault.*

babycenter **buzz**
overcoming your frustration with colic

"There are times when my daughter is inconsolable and I'm so frustrated and overwhelmed that I've had to leave the room to regain my sanity. When she's calm I look at her and feel so badly for feeling any negative feelings toward her. I finally talked to my doctor about it, and he put me on antidepressants. It was a hard decision for me to go on them, but I know that for everyone's sake it's the best thing to do."—**Anonymous**

"My baby cries inconsolably from 10:00 p.m. until 3:00 a.m. almost every night. There are occasional nights when I really freak, and I have to put him down and sit and cry a bit. Most nights I hold him, rock him, put him in the football hold and swing him, do laps around the house, do squats and lunges—might as well get some exercise!"—**Katie**

"Our twins both had colic. We'd carry them around in front carriers when the crying started, and that often soothed them. Some nights my wife and I would waltz around the darkened living room to music with them in their carriers, just to keep the crying at bay. It was brutal, but then, on their 3-month birthday, the colic just disappeared."—**B. R.**

Do whatever you think helps. If rocking your baby helps him (or you), then go ahead and rock. If massaging your baby's belly or putting him in a sling seems to help, do it. Sometimes it's good to feel that you're doing *something*. Get support from other parents who have been through colic. Find out from friends and family how they coped, and ask other parents for help and suggestions.

Babies with colic grow out of it and are none the worse for that period of their lives. Colic rarely lasts more than 3 months, and many babies stage a miraculous recovery, almost overnight. While you may look back on those dark evenings with despair, your baby won't remember them at all.

For great ideas on how parents deal with their colicky babies, visit the BabyCenter bulletin board about colic at babycenter.com.

diapers

The first few diaper changes may seem awkward; but, like it or not, you'll get plenty of practice. On average, a baby goes through six to eight diapers a day, 7 days a week, 52 weeks a year—and more during the first two weeks. By the end of the first month alone, you'll have changed more than 200 diapers. Some will be quick and easy, some a messy affair that ends up with your baby needing a bath.

decision guide

CLOTH OR DISPOSABLE DIAPERS?

The "green diaper" debate has, for decades now, been one of the hottest in parenting. Environmentalists are concerned about the amount of waste disposable diapers generate as well as the number of trees that need to be cut down to manufacture them. In a household with a new baby, diapers account for up to 50 percent of the weekly garbage.

At the same time, reusable diapers certainly don't come without an environmental cost. With reusables, you'll be running the washing machine and dryer many times in the years ahead, using electricity to heat the water and run the equipment.

There are other factors to consider, too:

reasons for buying disposables

"They're convenient." You can use them and throw them away, so there's no washing or drying involved. You'll need about 10 diapers a day for a newborn (down to six to eight a day by toddlerhood), and that would require a lot of washing. Disposables are available nearly everywhere.

Worry Meter

Q My baby seems to have hardly any wet diapers. Should I worry?

● Yes
○ Sometimes
○ Never

Your very young baby should wet five or six diapers per day. If the diapers aren't wet, there may be a problem with your baby's bladder or kidneys, or she could be dehydrated. Disposable diapers absorb wetness so well that they may feel dry to the touch. The easiest way to tell is to hold a dry diaper just out of the packet in one hand and the one you've taken off your baby in the other. If it's wet, it will feel heavier. If she really isn't having wet diapers, take her to your family doctor immediately.

"We have a busy lifestyle; we're always out and about." This is especially important if you're traveling, on vacation, or leaving your baby in daycare. You don't have to carry wet or dirty diapers home with you.

"My daycare won't use cloth." Some childcare facilities will accept babies only in disposables.

"I don't like the idea of carrying around dirty diapers." Sealable perfumed bags make life sweeter, but there's no getting away from the fact that you need to take dirty cloth diapers home and wash them.

"Life's too short to wash and dry." Sleep-deprived new parents often feel too busy with childcare and other household responsibilities to want the added chore of laundering diapers.

"They look better under clothes; cloth ones are so bulky." Some parents feel this is particularly important when their babies are crawling and walking, as the diaper doesn't bunch up between the babies' legs and provides a more comfortable fit.

"My kids all have sensitive skin and disposables keep them drier." Most disposable diapers are filled with a moisture-absorbing gel that soaks up the urine. This keeps the layer of diaper next to your baby's skin dry, which helps prevent diaper rash.

reasons for buying cloth reusables

"I feel good not contributing to the environmental problems."
Disposables don't degrade easily, so they tend to stay in landfills
for many, many years. To really lessen the environmental impact
of cloth, some groups recommend using flushable liners, always
washing a full load (about 24 diapers and covers), using cloth
wipes, and line-drying.

"I would rather have cotton next to her skin." Soft cotton feels
good against baby skin, and today's reusables come with a range of
fashionable outer covers.

"I don't like the idea of chemicals in disposables." The moisture-
absorbing gel that soaks up the urine does have chemicals in it,
which is a concern to many parents.

"It saves me money." The initial costs are higher, but after that,
you have to take into account only the costs of washing and drying.

"You can use them again for another baby." Reusing cloth
diapers reduces the cost even further.

**"You know when your baby is wet or dirty and can change
her."** Because the mess is less well-absorbed, your baby notices it—
and reacts more quickly. It may mean changing diapers more often,
but it avoids a baby stewing in a wet or dirty diaper.

"It's actually pretty easy." Most parents say they quickly get into
a routine, or they use diaper laundering services. It certainly helps
to have a washing machine and dryer in your home.

Which diapers work better?

Parents are divided. Some feel that disposables leak less and cause
less diaper rash. Others say that today's reusable diapers are much
better than the traditional diaper squares that needed folding and
shaping. Some parents use a combination of cloth and disposables,

using cloth diapers at home and disposables while out. Others start with disposables when their babies are tiny and then swap to cloth diapers once they feel they've managed to get into the swing of parenting.

. . . .

what's in a diaper—colors and contents

It's amazing how much time parents spend inspecting their baby's diapers, trying to figure out whether the frequency, color, and consistency is normal or not. But what's normal today changes tomorrow as your baby grows, and depends on whether your baby is breast- or bottle-fed and whether she's started solids.

There's no rule of thumb about how often your breastfed baby should pass a stool: It could be as often as four times a day or as little as once every 3 days or longer. If a bottle-fed baby urinates normally, then she doesn't need to pass a stool every day to prevent constipation.

For the first few days after her birth, your baby's bowel movement will consist of **meconium**, a sticky, greenish-black substance that built up in her intestines while she was in utero. It's made up of bile, mucus, cells from the bowel wall, secretions, and amniotic fluid.

for boys only . . .

If you have a son, remember that the foreskin can't slide back over the head of the penis in babies. The foreskin starts off attached to the head of the penis, is still in the process of developing at birth, and is often non-retractable up to the age of 3 years. By that time, 90 percent of boys will have a foreskin that slides back. The natural process of separation from the head of the penis doesn't require manipulation; trying to force the foreskin back can cause damage.

Q **My baby has had diaper rash for a week and it's not getting better. Should I worry?**

- ● Yes
- ○ Sometimes
- ○ Never

It could be a yeast infection (see page 93) or a bacterial infection. Both require medical attention. Your doctor can prescribe an antifungal cream or an antibiotic ointment. Combine this treatment with very regular diaper changes, and allow your baby to spend a little time without a diaper on an old towel or a mat so that fresh air gets to her skin. Then watch how quickly it clears up.

The colostrum in your breast milk acts as a laxative, helping to move the meconium out of your baby's system. Once your milk supply becomes established, after about 3 days, your baby's stools will change to a bright or mustard yellow color and be sweet-smelling. They'll be loose but textured, sometimes grainy and at other times curdled.

Green poop can mean your baby isn't getting enough of the rich hindmilk when you breastfeed. Foremilk has lots of milk sugar (lactose) in it. Too much lactose in the gut can cause gas, and the discomfort makes your baby cry more. If your baby nurses very often—every hour or so—and cries a lot and has green poop, check your feeding position. Also try to encourage her to go slightly longer between feedings and stay at the breast for longer so that she gets more hindmilk. It may take 2 to 3 days to improve her feeding technique and for her poop to change to a more usual bright yellow.

If you're bottle-feeding, your baby's stools will be pale yellow or yellowish-brown in color. Remnants of the formula will cause it to look bulkier and more formed than a breastfed baby's, as the formula will not be as completely digested as breast milk. The smell will be fairly pungent, more like an adult's stools.

how often does a baby need changing?

This depends partly on how you're feeding your baby and the sensitivity of her skin. If her diaper causes discomfort, your baby will cry. As a guide, however, expect to go through between 6 and 10 diapers a day in the first weeks. Change the diaper as soon as you smell a poop.

If the diaper is just wet, the urine may be so well absorbed that your baby will be comfortable in it for a couple of hours.

bathing

Your baby may take to his bath like a fish to water, or he may fuss and squirm and cry. How often you bathe your baby is really up to you: Many parents bathe their babies every day, but until your baby is crawling around and getting into things, a bath isn't really necessary more than once or twice a week (and the more preferable route if your baby hates his bath). At other times, you can just wash his face, neck area, and hands frequently and clean his genital area thoroughly after each diaper change. This is sometimes called "topping and tailing."

bathing safety

- Never, ever leave your baby unattended in the bath. If someone knocks at the door or the phone rings and you feel you must answer it, scoop him up in a towel and take him with you.
- Gather *all* your bath supplies before you begin; that way there's no chance you'll be tempted to leave your baby as you grab for a forgotten item.
- Never put your baby into a tub when the water is still running. (The water temperature could change or the depth could become too high.)
- Put cold water in the bath first, then hot. This will reduce the risk of scalding your baby.
- Make sure the bath water is comfortably warm (about 90 to 95°F). Babies generally prefer a cooler bath than you probably do.

cradle cap

Cradle cap, also called seborrhoeic dermatitis, looks like a very bad case of dandruff. It shows up as flaking reddish patches or thick yellowish and greasy scales on your newborn's scalp, but it also appears on the face and around the diaper area. Although unsightly, it's extremely common and nothing at all to worry about. Its cause isn't known for certain; theories include hormonal changes or a fungus.

Treat cradle cap by rubbing a mild baby oil into your baby's scalp to remove the scales, then sponge or gently comb off the flakes afterward. Or rub shampoo into your baby's hair and leave the suds on his head for around 20 minutes (this can be difficult!) and then massage the scalp with a soft baby toothbrush. A dandruff shampoo works even faster and is fine to use. Cradle cap eventually disappears on its own, but it can last through the first year, less often into toddlerhood.

explained: your baby's skin

Newborn skin is quite different from that of an older child or an adult: Almost unbelievably soft, it just begs to be stroked and held.

Exactly how your baby's skin looks and feels differs slightly according to his gestational age—that is, how far into your pregnancy you were when he was born. Premature babies have thin, rather red skin and may be covered with lanugo, a fine, downy hair. Late babies, on the other hand, have a slightly wrinkly appearance and very little, if any, lanugo. Babies born prematurely are also covered with vernix, a cheesy white substance that protects your baby's skin before birth. Full-term and post-mature babies will have only a few traces of vernix in the folds of their skin. Here are a few things you may not know about your baby's skin:

- The skin of full-term babies has a thinner outer layer—the epidermis—than adult skin.

just for dads

why it's nice to be mr. clean

For the first 6 to 8 weeks of your baby's life, you're not going to get much feedback: hardly any smiles, no laughs, not much beyond, well, the crying. It's enough to make you dream of being single again. However, now's the time to strengthen your resolve, because believe it or not, soon those smiles and laughs will come on—big time.

A great way to ensure that you get your fair share of the good stuff is to be a bath giver. Lots of babies love bath time and equate a good soak with fun. Learn how to bathe your baby safely and comfortably now, so that when she's ready to splash, you're ready, too. Many dads find this their favorite job right through the preschool years.

Q **My baby has teary eyes. Should I worry?**

○ Always
○ Sometimes
● Hardly ever

If your baby has teary eyes, or if her eyes seem sticky after she awakens, it's little cause for alarm. About a quarter of babies have undeveloped tear ducts, which means that their tears can't drain away into their noses. One or both ducts may be affected. The problem generally solves itself in the first 6 months. If your baby's eyeballs are white and look healthy, and she's happy, there's no need to worry about wateriness. To clean around your baby's eyes, use a cotton ball dipped into cooled boiled water. Be sure to wash your hands before you start and after you've finished.

- Babies sweat when the temperature is 107°F, whereas adult women sweat at 89°F and adult men at 84°F.
- Babies have deep folds and wrinkles in their skin that trap excess moisture, allowing microbes to multiply and leading to rashes and dermatitis.
- Baby skin can become too moist as the result of being covered in diapers. Wet skin is then more vulnerable to damage.

skin blemishes and rashes

Babies often get blemishes of one kind or another: Just as in adolescence, hormones are often the cause. In the case of a newborn, acne is usually the result of the mother's hormones still circulating in the baby's system. Your baby is unlikely to suffer any pain or discomfort beyond mild itchiness, if that.

Around half of all newborns develop a rash called milia, which tends to appear around 2 weeks after birth. It looks like small white bumps or spots across the tip of the nose, the chin, and elsewhere on the face or on the shoulders; they are small keratin-filled cysts. The spots appear raised, but they are usually smooth and dome-shaped to the touch. The condition usually peaks at around 3 weeks of age.

Seeing a rash on your baby may set off alarm bells, but bear in mind that skin rashes are extremely common. What's more, if it's related to something serious, there will certainly be other symptoms as well.

Most likely, your baby will have a fever, or perhaps be more irritable or fussy or have little appetite.

Left alone, most baby blemishes disappear on their own, and within a month or two your child will have beautiful, clear skin. Avoid touching or squeezing any spots or pimples. And there's no need to apply any lotions or creams; simply wash your baby's face gently a couple of times a day with warm water and pat dry.

heat rash (prickly heat)

A bright, red, pimply rash on your baby's neck, under his arms, or near the edges of his diaper or shirt is almost certainly heat rash, also known as prickly heat. It's caused by sweat on your baby's skin. It's not serious but is a sign that your child is too warm; so take immediate steps to cool him off, because overheating is a potentially dangerous condition in a small baby.

by the numbers
you: birth to 3 months

How has your baby changed your relationship?

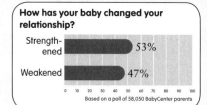

Strength-ened 53%
Weakened 47%

0 10 20 30 40 50 60 70 80 90 100

Based on a poll of 58,050 BabyCenter parents

Did you get stretch marks during your pregnancy?

Yes   69%   No   31%

If so, did any creams or lotions help them shrink or go away?

Yes   33%   No   67%

Based on a poll of 31,684 BabyCenter parents

Do you enjoy being a parent?

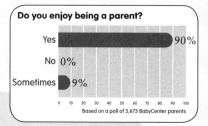

Yes 90%
No 0%
Sometimes 9%

0 10 20 30 40 50 60 70 80 90 100

Based on a poll of 3,673 BabyCenter parents

How long did you wear your maternity clothes after giving birth?

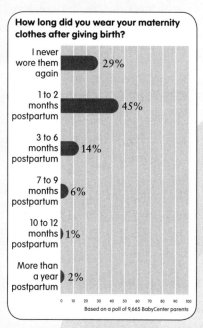

I never wore them again 29%
1 to 2 months postpartum 45%
3 to 6 months postpartum 14%
7 to 9 months postpartum 6%
10 to 12 months postpartum 1%
More than a year postpartum 2%

0 10 20 30 40 50 60 70 80 90 100

Based on a poll of 9,665 BabyCenter parents

Did your spouse give you a gift after you delivered your baby?

No, our baby was the only "reward" I needed 39%
Yes, my spouse gave me jewelry or another keepsake 23%
No, despite the many hints I dropped, he didn't 20%
Yes, he gave me something simple but heartfelt—a framed picture of me with our newborn, a bouquet of flowers, or a note I'll treasure 15%
Yes, he gave me something pampering—a spa visit, a professional massage, or had the house cleaned 2%
We gave each other a gift to mark the occasion; we planted a new tree or treated ourselves to a celebratory dinner 1%

0 10 20 30 40 50 60 70 80 90 100

Based on a poll of 47,670 BabyCenter parents

Did you go back to work after taking maternity leave?

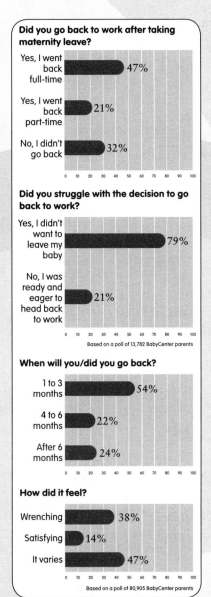

- Yes, I went back full-time — 47%
- Yes, I went back part-time — 21%
- No, I didn't go back — 32%

0 10 20 30 40 50 60 70 80 90 100

Did you struggle with the decision to go back to work?

- Yes, I didn't want to leave my baby — 79%
- No, I was ready and eager to head back to work — 21%

0 10 20 30 40 50 60 70 80 90 100

Based on a poll of 13,782 BabyCenter parents

When will you/did you go back?

- 1 to 3 months — 54%
- 4 to 6 months — 22%
- After 6 months — 24%

0 10 20 30 40 50 60 70 80 90 100

How did it feel?

- Wrenching — 38%
- Satisfying — 14%
- It varies — 47%

0 10 20 30 40 50 60 70 80 90 100

Based on a poll of 80,905 BabyCenter parents

After your baby was born, when did you first have sex?

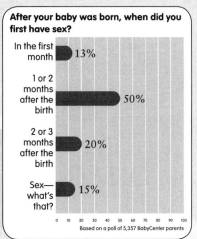

- In the first month — 13%
- 1 or 2 months after the birth — 50%
- 2 or 3 months after the birth — 20%
- Sex—what's that? — 15%

0 10 20 30 40 50 60 70 80 90 100

Based on a poll of 5,357 BabyCenter parents

Feeling weepy and emotional is common in the first few days. Did you get the "baby blues"?

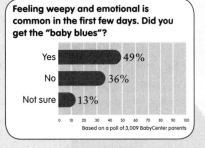

- Yes — 49%
- No — 36%
- Not sure — 13%

0 10 20 30 40 50 60 70 80 90 100

Based on a poll of 3,009 BabyCenter parents

Which would you rather have?

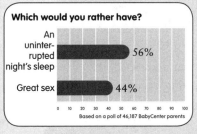

- An uninterrupted night's sleep — 56%
- Great sex — 44%

0 10 20 30 40 50 60 70 80 90 100

Based on a poll of 46,187 BabyCenter parents

the bottom line

Getting used to being a parent takes time, and you'll have moments when you may feel quite overwhelmed. You'll have tough days, and you'll have good days; feeling like you're on an emotional roller coaster is normal.

you—
birth to 3 months

This time in your life is full of new emotions and plenty of decisions. You'll experience the euphoria of bonding with your baby, but you'll also wrestle with such choices as whether or not (or when) to return to work and how to find the right daycare provider.

bonding with your baby

For some parents, a new feeling takes hold within the first few days—or even minutes—of birth. It's the feeling that makes you want to shower your child with love and affection, or to do anything you can to protect her. For other parents, this feeling takes weeks or months to develop. There's no magic formula.

Like other relationships, your relationship with your baby takes time to grow. As you get to know your baby and learn how to soothe her and enjoy watching her grow, your feelings will deepen. And one day—it may be the first time you see her smile—you'll look at your baby and realize you're in love.

If, after a few weeks, you find that you don't feel more attached to and comfortable with your baby than you did right after she was

babycenter buzz
settling in to parenting

"It took us a while to realize that we didn't have to be like our parents or even be the sorts of parents our friends were. Only when we stopped trying to be perfect did we really begin to enjoy our baby and each other again."
—**Caroline**

"At first I felt overwhelmed by being a mom. But gradually the fog of exhaustion has cleared, and I've realized I'm still me. Now we try to go out one night a week, just so we can have some time together as adults rather than parents."—**J. B.**

born, or if you actually feel detached and resentful of your baby, talk to your doctor. These feelings are more common than you think. They don't mean you're a bad mother or that you don't love your child. They just mean that you're a new mother, trying to adjust to a huge change in your life and enormous new responsibilities while you're bone-tired. (See **the baby blues** on page 172.) With a little help and time, you'll get the hang of it and feel closer to your baby. Your doctor can also screen you for postpartum depression, a chemical imbalance that influences your feelings toward your baby but that has nothing to do with your maternal skill or the depth of your love.

To learn a few tips on how your partner can bond with your baby, go to babycenter.com.

bonding and adoption

Bonding takes time for many birth parents, so don't worry, or be surprised, if it doesn't happen instantly after adoption. After all, bonding is neatly bound with caring for your baby—the bathing, soothing, diaper changing, and day-to-day care that you provide. Many birth and adoptive parents say they were doing something

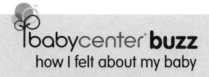

quite ordinary and routine, like changing a diaper or playing with their baby, when they first felt overwhelmed with love. So take the time you and your baby need to fall in love.

To give yourselves the right opportunities, it may help to think of ways you can use all the senses to make your baby feel loved and cared for.

Touch. Some adopted babies find it difficult to be touched. If your baby was in an orphanage where staffing levels were low, she may have been handled only when she was changed and fed. At first, she may tolerate you holding her only for short periods or turn away when she wants to sleep. Try to be consistent and make as much physical contact as your baby will allow. Carry your baby in a sling around the house, as well as when you're out for a walk.

Baby massage helps, too, though it's best to begin very gently; perhaps just by stroking your baby's arms after a diaper change and gradually increasing your touch. If she responds positively, let it become a daily ritual for both of you.

Smell. The sense of smell is very important to newborns. Your home—and you—won't smell familiar at first. It may help if you can bring home some of your baby's blankets with her, so that they still smell "right." If yours is an open adoption, suggest to the birth mother that you send her a T-shirt or some other article of clothing that smells of you (and that hasn't been washed recently) to keep near her after the birth, as a way of establishing your scent early on.

Sight. Some babies find it hard to make eye-to-eye contact. It may take some time before she can relax enough to look at you. You don't need to force the issue. Give your baby the time and space she needs, and remind yourself that she'll one day look you in the eye and smile.

Some babies who've been cared for in orphanages in other countries may have spent long periods in their cribs with little stimulation. Arriving at your brightly colored nursery could cause sensory overload. Reduce surrounding colors and lights and your baby may settle in more easily. Give your baby the safe haven she needs by making sure there's little in her crib to distract her. Then, gradually introduce more color and light into her life.

Sound. If your baby was born in another culture, she may be used to a language very different from yours in pitch and tone, not to mention entirely different background noise. Try making a tape of her familiar daily sounds and play it to her when it's time to sleep.

Taste. Your baby may have been fed a specific formula. For continuity, use the same brand if possible, and then gradually mix it with the formula you plan to use. Over a couple of days, increase the ratio until your baby makes a complete transition.

Looking to the future. Try making a photo collection of your baby's first day with you. Keep it, along with anything your baby brought from her birthplace, and later use it to tell your toddler or preschooler the story of how she came to live with you.

the baby blues

You thought you'd be on cloud nine with your new baby. Instead, you're moody, teary-eyed, exhausted, unable to sleep, and anxious. You might be eating more (or less) than you usually do. You're feeling irritable, nervous, worried about being a mother, or afraid that being a mother will never feel better than it does right now.

Within the first 3 weeks of giving birth (though it typically starts in the first few days), fully 60 to 80 percent of new moms experience a sadness that's so common it has its own name—the "baby blues." The blues are hardly surprising, and they're believed to stem from the one-two-three punch of coping with the dramatic hormonal shifts that occur right after the birth, the emotional adjustments involved in becoming a mom, and the fatigue and discomfort you're feeling as a result of labor and birth and adjusting to round-the-clock baby care.

This emotional upheaval generally passes as quickly as it appeared. If you don't feel better within the first few weeks, or you feel you're getting worse rather than better, then this could be a sign of postpartum depression, which is a different and more serious problem that requires treatment. (See **postpartum depression** on page 175.) And if at *any* time you think you might hurt yourself or your baby, or if you feel incapable of looking after your new baby, call your doctor and tell your partner.

ways to help yourself feel better

During these busy days, you may constantly have to remind yourself to take care of "you," and by doing so both you and your baby will benefit.

Rest. This starts with sleeping when your baby sleeps—day and night and as often as possible.

Take care of yourself. You need to eat, too—skipping meals will only wear you down. Ask your partner to watch your baby in the morning so you can eat breakfast and take a shower, or don't be afraid to set your baby in a bouncy seat positioned in the bathroom. Do anything that helps you feel better. Some women find that living in their sweats or pj's helps. Others feel better when they put on a little makeup and clothes they like to wear.

Get help. You don't win a prize for changing every diaper or soothing every crying spell yourself. Part of being a good mom is knowing when to ask for help. Let friends cook meals, bring groceries, or do the vacuuming. Relatives can entertain your baby. Have your partner, mother, or a trusted friend step in now and then. They'll love the bonding time with your baby, and you'll get a much-needed break.

Ease up. Of course you want to be the world's best mother—and in your baby's eyes, you are. Tune out long lists of expectations for yourself and comparisons to what other moms are doing.

Exercise. Moving around every day not only helps your body recover, but more important, it improves your mood. Generally, if you exercised right up until the birth, you can probably safely get back to it within days afterward, as long as you had a normal vaginal delivery. If you don't feel up to your regular workout, begin with light exercise such as pelvic tilts and stretching.

Expect to wait about 6 to 8 weeks before starting regular exercise if you had a c-section. Your joints and ligaments will be relatively loose for 3 to 5 months after the birth, so you'll need to watch your exercise techniques carefully.

Get out. Put your baby in a stroller or in a soft carrier on your chest and take a walk around the block, or run a short errand. In a pinch, just walk around your home or sit outside for a few minutes. Never underestimate the power of fresh air and sunshine. (Even in winter you can safely bundle your baby and take her outside.)

Don't be alone a lot. Being around other people helps. Find someone you trust and let that person know how you feel. Call a friend, especially someone who's been there herself as a recent new mother. Look for a new mothers' group for support. It's equally important to make sure your partner knows how you're feeling and what you're worried about.

Slow down. Remember to stop occasionally and focus on the good things. The early days with your new baby are a wonderful time in your life, one you and your partner will treasure forever. Don't focus on the practical issues to the exclusion of allowing yourself time to marvel over this miraculous new person who's come into your life. However high the ironing pile grows, and however late supper is going to be, there should always be time to enjoy your baby and share your feelings for her, and your hopes for your future as a family.

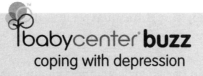

babycenter **buzz**
coping with depression

"I have PPD, and there are days when I don't want to get out of bed in the morning, days when I think that life has no meaning at all. It helps me to try to write down one good thing that has happened each day. It reminds me of the good things in my life, and it helps give me the motivation to face another day."—**Andrea**

"I gave birth 10 days ago. A few days afterward, I started feeling very down and now all I can do is cry all day. I have no interest in anything, not even food. Last night I went to bed without eating dinner. It's so hard to feel like this, especially when you have a newborn and a 20-month-old to look after. My husband is very concerned and calls me often from work and tells me he loves me, and that he's very proud of what I do. But everything seems so hard; I can hardly look at my kids. I feel like a failure and like giving up."
—**Anonymous**

postpartum depression

Postpartum depression (PPD) describes a collection of symptoms that can occur within a few weeks after giving birth or show up anytime within the first year of motherhood. These symptoms range from exhaustion and irritability through persistent low mood, poor sleeping, and lack of appetite. Many women with PPD feel angry and lonely, blaming themselves for not being able to cope as well as other moms seem to. Some also feel angry and resentful toward their babies. On top of everything, many PPD sufferers also feel guilty about feeling depressed at a time when our culture expects them to be happy and joyous.

Postpartum depression affects about one in 10 new moms. It's an illness, not a sign of being a bad mother, or of being a parent who can't cope. PPD isn't a condition you should try to deal with by yourself. It's not likely to "just go away" on its own. Untreated, PPD is a threat to your health as well as to your child. When you're in a depressed state, you're unable to give your baby the positive emotional feedback his development depends upon, and you may find day-to-day baby care difficult as well. A depressed mom may endanger her baby by being more likely to ignore or strike her child.

Talk to your ob-gyn or pediatrician and explain how you feel. No one will think less of you—tens of thousands of women suffer from PPD every year. Treatment typically includes talk therapy, medication, and added household or babycare support, and, fortunately, it is highly effective.

If you're feeling anxious or down, and want to chat with other moms going through a similar phase, visit the anxiety and depression bulletin boards at babycenter.com.

your relationship

Having a baby changes your relationship with your partner forever. In the long term, most couples find that having children strengthens rather than diminishes the bond between them. But in the early weeks and months while you're both adjusting to your new roles as parents, it's normal to find you have more areas of conflict than you did in the past. The important thing about any conflict is, first, to recognize that it's to be expected and, second, to work out how you're going to deal with it. Agree on how you'll disagree: Arguing effectively (which is what you should be aiming to do) means making rules about how to do it. So, in a calm moment, talk about how you're going to handle disagreements. Maybe you'll agree that you'll never go to bed angry, or that you'll have a walk together to talk things through when the going gets tough, or that you'll never argue in front of your baby.

expectations

Much of the conflict between a couple with a new baby springs from different expectations about their new roles. In the past, getting married or setting up house together was the change that brought new roles for a couple. Today, it's far more likely to be the

babycenter buzz
how the relationship changes

"My husband has repeatedly told me that he's jealous of the baby because she takes up time that we used to have alone together. He gets very angry over seemingly small things and snaps at me in front of the baby and even directly at her. I thought he'd be so happy to be a father, and it's hard to learn to balance being a mom *and* wife."—**Wendy**

"My relationship with my husband has blossomed in the year since we had our first child. It was difficult at first; we had to learn to balance our relationship with our new role as parents. Being a parent means making sacrifices. Once we accepted the need to sacrifice, we were rewarded by the dimension and meaning that having children has brought to our life."
—**Katherine**

"I've tried very hard to be supportive of my wife and help with our son, but I feel like I give and give and still experience what seems like neglect at best from my wife, who seems to be concerned only with the baby. She was wonderfully attentive and supportive of me before motherhood, and now her resentful attitude makes me feel like I've been replaced in her affections by our son."—**Sam**

moment when a first baby arrives that really changes the way you live. Even if you're going back to work, every new mom gets at least some time off work after giving birth, and being at home, and probably on a reduced income, causes stress.

Expectations about what's involved in being a father or a mother spring from an individual's own experience of being parented, so it's important to sit down with your partner and talk through how your own parents did things. You may discover that you want to follow a familiar pattern, or you may feel very strongly that you want to do things very differently. The point is that subconsciously you'll each have ideas about who does what in your family based on what your own father and mother did, and sharing your experiences will help you better understand each other.

finding your own way

Good communication is the key to how you're going to organize your family life, so regularly talk about how you'd like your partnership and your life as parents to work.

Think about where new responsibilities are going to lie. Will one partner be chiefly in charge of babycare, or will you care for your baby jointly—and how? How will you split up household chores now—the same as before or differently? This is a particular topic of concern during a maternity leave or if one of you stays home with the baby permanently. There isn't a right and a wrong answer to these questions: Some couples decide to organize themselves in a "traditional" model, while others decide on a more equitable arrangement than their parents'. What matters is that you discuss these things and agree on your roles and responsibilities, so that resentments don't creep in at a time when you're both going to be under more stress than usual.

sharing your feelings

It's very common for a new mom to feel she has very little left to give to her partner in the weeks after childbirth: The demands of a new baby are so all-encompassing and so emotionally charged that she often feels both psychologically and physically exhausted much of the time. What helps most is simply being there for one another. Try to empathize, as much as you can, with your partner: Recognize that, while you may be going through a trying time, so is your partner.

sex

There are no rules about resuming your sex life after you've had a baby. Right now, sex is probably the last thing you want to think about. If that's the case, don't think about it—and certainly don't start worrying that you should be doing it already. There's no right and wrong about how quickly you start having sex, and some couples wait months before having intercourse again.

just for dads

it's a family affair

Before "you two" became "you three" (or more), you and your partner lived for each other and your relationship. Now everything is about the baby. When you're not knocked out for the few hours of sleep you're getting, chances are you're feeding, cleaning, or trying to calm your baby. And yet, life isn't over.

If you can carve out a few minutes a day to talk with your partner, start there. Be sure to tell her she looks great (because there's no woman alive who feels like a million bucks during the newborn months). And it's worth trying to talk about more than just the baby, which helps you to remember having something in common besides midnight feedings. Classic kindnesses like flowers and cooking dinner (or ordering take-out) are also great gestures.

As for sex, you'll probably want to take the bases slowly. The normal rule is a minimum of 6 weeks of abstention after the birth. Of course, even then the massive hormonal changes your partner experienced, as well as the physical effects of her pregnancy, will keep the heat from rising.

Once you get to that point, a sure way to get your partner in the mood, or at least to look at you like she might consider it, is to take care of the baby, which, to a new mom, is sexy, sexy, sexy (and gives your partner the chance to sleep and recharge her batteries). After the 6-week mark, consider bringing in a baby-sitter, a close friend, or a grandmother and heading out for dinner and an evening at a hotel—a nice hotel.

Here's how to keep the love alive:

- Take the baby and give your partner time just for herself.
- Go out together as a family. Hold your partner's hand. Carry your baby in the baby carrier.
- Buy her gifts, and not just on her birthday.
- Do not—under any circumstances—complain about the absence of sex in your lives.

what's normal?

Almost anything is normal. Some couples resume intercourse in
the early weeks after the birth, though it's more common to find
your libido is low. This is especially true for the woman, whose
perineum is likely to be sore for a few weeks if she's had stitches to
repair a vaginal tear or an episiotomy. Breastfeeding can also
affect your libido. But having a reduced sex drive is also quite
likely to be true for the man, who's coming to terms with a whole
new way of life while sharing sleep deprivation, and who may
easily have other priorities than his sex life.

For both of you, tiredness will be a big factor. When you get into
bed, chances are what you'll most want to do is go to sleep.

staying close

Even if you're not having sex for a while, you need to stay close.
Remember that kind words and cuddling go a long way toward
making sure you both feel loved and cared for. Sex doesn't have to
mean full penetration. Before you're ready for that, you may prefer
to simply hold one another close and gradually get used to being
touched in a sexual way again.

Sex therapists often suggest building up to penetrative sex over a
period of several love-making sessions after giving birth. They say
that touching can give a mother time to heal, and the orgasms she
experiences from this kind of stimulation will help her feel like a
sexual being again and give her more confidence about progressing
to full intercourse.

have treats as a couple

As soon as you feel you're getting the hang of your new life as
parents, try to set aside some time for the two of you as a couple
as well. Many parents find they gain a lot from having a parents-
only date once every week or two, even if it's only to a dinner or a
movie for a couple of hours between feedings.

babycenter buzz
changes in your sex life

"I've found that I enjoy sex a *lot* more than I used to. I don't know if having a baby moved things around inside of me or what, but it feels so much better than before. It's hard to find the time for it, though."—**Dana**

"Before I had my baby 5 months ago, my sex life was great. I've just resumed having sex, but I can't seem to bring myself to enjoy it or to bring my libido back up to where it was."—**Anonymous**

"My baby is 5 months old now. My husband and I have probably had sex seven times since I had my baby. It hurts! I love the idea of having sex, but I don't have the desire. My husband seems understanding, but I feel guilty all the time. I used lube, which made it better painwise, but I still had no interest."—**Ruby**

"My doctor described it well. Before giving birth, the wall of your vagina can be compared to a feather bed, soft and moveable. After the baby, it's like an army cot. But don't fear! Sex will get better. Just keep the lubricant handy."—**Amy**

"Once in a while we drop our daughter off at Grandma's house for the day and go to a hotel with day rates and a Jacuzzi tub in the room. We order take-out food and enjoy our day in the hotel! When we come back to pick up our daughter, our love life is recharged and refreshed."—**Anonymous**

"We do date swaps or babysitting trades with another couple. On alternating weeks, we have a date while our friends watch our kids, and the next week their two kids come over to play."—**Anonymous**

In the early weeks, going out with your baby can be especially easy because newborns sleep so much; your baby may snooze in her infant seat during an entire meal. If that seems like too much, you can still set aside couple-time at home—perhaps a favorite take-out meal and a glass of wine. Some people find the presence of a baby interferes with the process of reconnecting with their partner in a sexual way, even if they're not aiming for full intercourse. If

(continued on page 184)

test yourself contraception quiz

1. When do you think about contraception?
   a. I don't need to. I got this organized years ago.
   b. At least an hour before it might be needed. It's important to be prepared.
   c. Damn, I knew there was something I forgot last night!

2. Are you squeamish?
   a. Come on, I've given birth, you can't be squeamish after that!
   b. I can normally hide my embarrassment, if my partner promises to look away.
   c. Like a 14-year-old girl in a biology class.

3. Are you comfortable taking the pill?
   a. My body is a temple. Nothing short of wheatgrass passes these lips. I'm a breastfeeding mom.
   b. I'm happy to do it for a while, but I'm concerned about the long-term effects.
   c. Anything, as long as it protects me against another nine months!

4. When you go to the doctor for your shots, you...
   a. Don't blink an eye. They're just part of everyday life.
   b. Leave bruise marks on the nurse's knee as she injects me.
   c. Faint at the mere sight of a needle.

5. Do you want more children?
   a. No way. I've had enough of smelly diapers, 3:00 a.m. feedings, and worrying about how long my baby has nursed on either side.
   b. Maybe. Just wait until I have this one potty trained.
   c. Of course. Both my partner and I want a big family.

6. Are you detail oriented?
   a. Wait! I can fit this quiz into my schedule between our morning feeding at 6:42 a.m. and my morning coffee at 6:54 a.m.
   b. Enough to get through the day without putting the darks and whites through the wash together.
   c. Does wearing the same color socks count?

ANSWERS

Mostly a's

You are organized, can deal with mess and bodily functions, and want a reliable form of contraception that you can control. The diaphragm or condoms could be your short-term solution. Longer term, if you're sure your family is complete, you may feel ready to consider something permanent.

Mostly b's

You can be organized and can cope with internal examinations and bodily functions when you need to. You're not too excited about injections or implants. Think about using the mini-pill in the short- to medium-term, or consider being fitted for a diaphragm.

Mostly c's

Go for reliable contraception that doesn't require you to remember to use something or take something. Opt for long-term choices so you can get it resolved and then forget about it. Try an injectable contraceptive or an implant. Even a coil may be right for you; it's not 100 percent effective, but at least it's always there!

babycenter buzz
frustrated about sex

"Two weeks after our son was born, my wife was back in school. I admire her for this, but our relationship has suffered severely. We haven't had any kind of intimacy or physical contact in almost 6 months. Most days it feels like I have a child with a friend, not a lover."**—Hendrik**

"Having sex after having children can be an adventure. Just look at it as trying to sneak around and have sex without being caught by your parents; it's really about the same. And it can be fun. And spice up a relationship. You'll have fun just flirting with your spouse again."**—Andre**

"My wife and I are still waiting to take the plunge into sex again nearly 3 months after our baby son's birth. I'm beginning to become very frustrated at the lack of physical love in our relationship, and it's starting to cause arguments."**—Bob**

"Assume the baby will wake up crying at exactly the wrong time. My suggestion: Let your baby fall into her schedule before you plan any uninterrupted intimate time together."**—Anonymous**

this is a problem for you, move your baby's bed away from yours temporarily. You'll still be able to hear her if she needs you.

practical tips

When you decide to have intercourse again, there are several ways of making it as comfortable as possible:

- Use a lubricant (and lots of it), as your perineal area will be feeling sensitive. In the early weeks after childbirth and while breastfeeding, you're likely to experience more vaginal dryness than usual, so a lubricant is a real help.
- Choose a position for intercourse that doesn't put too much pressure on wherever you're feeling sensitive. This may or may not be your favorite pre-baby position.
- If tiredness is your biggest problem, try making love during

your baby's naptime, or after an early-morning feeding, rather than at bedtime.

- Becoming aroused sexually may cause your breasts to leak. The hormones involved in arousal are closely related to the hormones involved in the let-down process of milk production. As time goes on, the tendency to leak milk while making love will lessen.

Don't forget that if you're bottle-feeding, your fertility is likely to return much sooner than if you're breastfeeding. And, contrary to some popular wisdom, you can conceive even if you're nursing. There's no way to know when your first postpartum ovulation will occur, so unless you want very closely spaced children, it's wise to use contraception. Ask your doctor about contraception plans at the postpartum checkup. You may need or want to use a different form than you did before pregnancy. The IUD, for example, is recommended as a better choice for women who have given birth than those who haven't. If you used a diaphragm before, it will need to be refitted. If you prefer hormonal birth control, your doctor can prescribe a type compatible with breastfeeding.

decision guide · · · · · · · · · · · · · · · · ·

BACK TO WORK OR STAY AT HOME?

Going back to work may not be a bona fide choice for you. You may need a job to put food on the table for your family; or there may be no work options open to you, which means you'll be staying at home. But, for many women with options, the question of whether to continue working after having a baby can be difficult, even wrenching. Every family has its own calculus, based on factors both practical and emotional. (See **balancing work and family: how you feel** on page 265 for more thoughts on this topic.)

You've no doubt gone through this decision process during pregnancy, but feelings can change once a baby arrives. It's more

common than you'd think to change your mind after giving birth—
whether you were certain you wanted to stay home but now miss
your job, or at the end of your maternity leave you discover you
aren't ready to return to your workplace. No decision is irrevers-
ible, if you can find a way to make the situation work for you.

reasons for going back to work

"We need the money." Not being able to pay the bills creates
tremendous stress. Two incomes may be vital for your household.
Single parents rarely have the luxury of a choice. Be sure to factor
childcare costs into your decision; they can eat up a large portion of
one income.

"I make more money than my partner." Some couples find it
more logical to have a stay-at-home dad and a working mom.
Sometimes the mother has a better insurance plan, for instance.

"I like work and being a parent. It makes me a better mom."
Getting the best of both worlds may make you happier, which
positively affects your mood around your baby.

"If I step off the career ladder, there's no going back." In many
jobs and professions, it's very hard to step back onto the path to the
top once you've taken a few years off.

"I'm a better part-time mom than full-time mom." Many women
feel they need outside stimulation and interests in order to give
their child their best at home. Especially if your baby is difficult or
high needs, working at least part-time can provide a healthy break
for you. Some couples split shifts in order to allow both parents to
work while providing hands-on parental care.

"My friends all work." Society encourages mothers to return to
work, and often doesn't value mothers who stay at home as much.
You may decide to work simply because it's the norm where you live.

"I can't cope with not earning." Giving up your own income is a big step, and not all women want to do it.

"Work is 'me' time." Many women like being with adults and having a break from parenting.

reasons for staying home

"I don't want to miss out on the early years." It can be hard, if not impossible, to hand over your baby to someone else to look after. Many parents simply prefer to do it themselves.

"I think it's important for my child's well-being and development." Some parents simply feel that parental care is in their child's best interests.

"My mom was a career mom. I refuse to do the same." You may want to give your children the same sort of upbringing you had—or the opposite.

"Where I live, there's not much choice." If you can't find the right childcare or a job that's compatible with motherhood, staying home may be the better or more economical option.

"Working doesn't make economic sense." If your income is roughly the equivalent of childcare, especially when you also factor in transportation costs, lunches, and a work wardrobe, a job may be a wash, making it an easier choice to stay home. Moms of twins especially sometimes find paying for infant daycare times two doesn't make economic sense for their families.

"My partner is hardly ever here." If one of you works long hours, travels frequently, or comes home stressed, perhaps both of you working would be too much to cope with.

"It's less stressful." Even if your partner works regular hours, managing a two-worker household and a child can be hectic and hard on everybody.

"I'm looking forward to a break from work for a few years."
For some women, parenting comes as a relief after time spent in
a high-stress job and an opportunity to unwind for several years
before returning to the work force.

Whatever choice you make about working or staying home, it
helps to think of it as temporary. You can, and should, continually
re-evaluate how your choice is working out. Think about it often
as your child grows and circumstances change. It might suit you to
work while you have one baby but stop when a second arrives, for
example. It may be preferable to stay home for the first few years
and then go back once your children start school. Part-time work
schedules may be feasible for you and your partner. Or you may
discover a way to work from home, by starting a business or
working freelance. Ask your friends, and you'll find parents in an
array of work scenarios: telecommuting, freelance, temporary
work, or working for themselves. Figuring out what to do is never
simple, but on the plus side, there have never been as many choices
for mothers and fathers.

choosing infant daycare

Just thinking about who will look after your baby when you go
back to work is stressful. Some moms try to avoid the topic as long
as possible. But actually, the sooner you start your search for
childcare, the better you'll feel because it will benefit both you and
your baby. What ultimately works for your family may be different
from what works for your best friend. With so many different
kinds of childcare, it helps to approach the question with an open
mind so that you don't overlook any possibilities.

Bear in mind that babies under 1 year old have different needs
from older children, and so what's ideal in infant daycare is not
the same as what's best in a toddler or preschooler setting.

Here's a way to approach your search:

consider the options

There are three basic types of childcare:

- **In-your-home care.** Caregivers may be a babysitter or nanny who comes to your home every day, or an au pair, nanny, or relative who lives with you.
- **Home-based daycare.** You bring your child to someone else's home. The caregiver may be a professional with years of experience, a kindly neighbor, or a relative. Your baby may be the only child there, or there may be many children.
- **Daycare center.** A commercial site that can be independent, part of a chain, or connected with a church, employer, or community organization.

Any of these formats can provide effective, appropriate care for an infant. Within each of these types of care, though, the range of quality can be significant, so it's best not to base your choice on type alone.

think about your preferences and needs

What are your priorities? First, of course, you'll want to base your considerations on suitability for your baby. Here are some other things to consider:

- How close to your home or workplace, or your partner's, should care be? What's your maximum distance from home? Some people choose sites along their commutes; others prefer to have the care provided as close to their workplaces as possible.
- How much care do you need? Will you be working part-time or full-time? Will you and your partner be working the same hours or different ones? What kind of hours? Will you travel for your job?
- What can you afford? Costs vary considerably, with in-home nanny care being the most expensive and, generally, home-based

care outside your home being least expensive. But there are many variations. Consider hours and vacation availability, too.

identify possibilities

Next you'll want to draw up a list of people and places that might meet your needs. Cast as wide a net as possible. Among the resources you should check out:

- **Word of mouth.** Ask your friends, colleagues, or relatives with young children for referrals. Other sources include your pediatrician, playgroup, local mother's groups, local parenting chat groups online, university child development programs, or your workplace human resources department.
- **Agencies.** ChildCare Aware has a hotline (800-424-2246) that can point you to licensed local facilities. Two major accrediting groups include the National Association for the Education of Young Children (NAEYC) and the National Association of Family Child Care (NAFCC); check their databases via their Web sites. For a fee, local nanny placement agencies prescreen candidates. (Check your phone book for listings.)
- **The Internet.** In addition to the Web resources listed above, don't overlook nanny and au pair networks found online, and chat groups for local moms where you can post questions about specific centers or where to find a reliable babysitter.

visit and interview

You'll need to put in a fair amount of legwork in the form of site visits and in-person interviews with prospective caregivers. (This is another good reason to start your search early.) Narrow your list down to your top four or five possibilities to make the task more manageable. (You can always go back to add more candidates.) Always get referrals, whether you're investigating a person or a place, and follow up on them.

Here are some things to look for that can help you gauge whether the caregiver and setting are suitable for a baby:

- **A low ratio of caregivers to babies.** The nonprofit early child-hood advocacy group Zero to Three recommends one caregiver for every three babies under 18 months old. It further recommends a total group size no larger than six, and in settings with mixed ages (such as nanny care or family-run daycare), no more than two children under age 2 in a single group. The National Association for the Education of Young Children recommends a maximum of six to eight infants per group.
- **One primary caregiver.** Even if there's a team approach, one person should be assigned as the main caregiver to each baby.
- **Minimal staff turnover.** It's best for a baby to have continuous care.
- **Lots of interaction.** Spend an hour or more observing if you can. Watch how often babies are picked up and held.
- **How babies are put to sleep.** You'll want to make sure caregivers are up-to-date on SIDS prevention measures.
- **Experience caring for babies.** This is a big plus, especially the younger your baby is. Training in early childhood education is also beneficial, though not essential.
- **Flexibility on feeding and sleeping schedules.** With a young baby, the schedule should suit his needs, not the caregiver's.
- **An environment that's safe for exploration.** Look for evidence of childproofing so that eventually your baby can move around.
- **A stimulating environment.** It doesn't need to have all the latest, newest gadgets, but there should be safe, age-appropriate toys (you can also supply these) and music.
- **A sanitary environment.** Caregivers should wash their hands and clean the changing area after changing diapers.
- **An inviting environment.** Consider whether or not you are free to drop in unannounced at any time. Ask yourself if you would want to spend time in this place.

Your baby doesn't have to be present for an initial interview, but if you like what you see enough for a second interview, be sure your baby is a part of it. Notice how the caregiver responds to your child. (At a center or family daycare, make certain the person who will be in charge of your child is present, not just the center director.)

Does she seem to be comfortable around children? Does she address your child with warmth and confidence? (Don't worry if your child doesn't seem to like her at first, since stranger anxiety can flare up at certain ages.)

For a printable daycare interview sheet to take with you on visits, go to babycenter.com.

what no one tells you: when someone else cares for your baby

The rational thoughts you had before your baby was born can transform into raw emotion once you're thinking about childcare for your baby. Can anybody look after your baby as well as you can? How will your baby cope without you? What if the crying goes on all day? Will your baby ever forgive you? Will you ever forgive yourself?

Once you're back at work and your baby is settled with her caregiver, it's not uncommon to experience a sense of jealousy. Someone else is spending time with your baby and enjoying her company. That can cause you to judge your caregiver rather harshly at times. You might also feel slightly guilty when you realize that you're actually enjoying being at work.

These conflicting emotions can cause feelings of insecurity about your choice. Give it time. Most women gradually find that they reach a point where they know that what they are doing is right for their family, or they realize that it isn't and figure out a way to make changes.

Preparation is key to your peace of mind and a calm transition. Here are some steps to take.

- **Be sure of your childcare**. Returning to work can be difficult if you aren't convinced that your baby is in the best hands. Allow yourself enough time to find reliable good-quality childcare.

babycenter buzz
leaving your baby

"I say good-bye; then I leave calmly but quietly without further ado."— **Anonymous**

"In my experience, sneaking out while my son's attention is diverted by his caregiver is the only way to avoid a meltdown. He stays happy as long as he doesn't see Mommy leave."—**Suzanna**

"I decided on a home daycare for my children because they receive very personalized care there. A home provider tends to get more attached to the children she cares for and ends up having a loving interest in the children as opposed to a financial one."—**Kimberly**

"My baby has been in daycare since she was 4 months old. I was devastated when I had to drop her off that first day, but I knew that she'd be fine. While I was pregnant, I researched numerous daycares in our area, paying close attention to inspections by the state department. I felt comfortable with the one that I chose and she's still there. Just build a good relationship with the teachers and always go with your instinct if something doesn't feel right."—**Anonymous**

- **Make back-up arrangements.** Have contingency plans in place for when your baby or your caregiver is sick. An emergency isn't the best time to make emergency plans.
- **Gradually introduce your caregiver.** Allow enough time for your baby to be introduced slowly to the new arrangements. Most facilities encourage you to stay for the first couple of sessions. You might like to try leaving for a short time, then extend the length of time you're apart. If possible, arrange to go back to work at reduced hours for the first week to transition your baby into childcare.
- **Send familiar objects with your baby.** Your child will recognize them and feel more secure.
- **Most of all, stay patient.** Your baby may behave beautifully all day, then seem to "take it out on you" when it's time to go home, though this may be nothing more than end-of-day

fussiness. Your baby isn't physically capable yet of manipulating your feelings by showing revenge.

- **For twins, find a caregiver used to more than one.** If you're the mom of twins, look for someone to care for your babies who'll truly understand their needs. If possible, try the arrangement a few times before actually returning to your job so that you can make changes if necessary.

the best advice my mother ever gave me

Here, a miscellany of good ideas BabyCenter moms heard from *their* own moms:

"Everyone will have advice for you. If you love your baby and have her best interests at heart, there is very little that you can actually do 'wrong.' There are things you may *wish* you'd done differently, but this is a live-and-learn proposition. There are no *wrong* choices, only choices that may or may not be right for you. Even the experts don't agree on everything."—**Betsy**

"The breathing technique you learn isn't for the birthing process. It's really for raising the child. That's when you will need it the most. Patience, patience, patience—that's the key."—**Anonymous**

"If you get too upset with your baby, there's nothing wrong with putting him in his crib, shutting the door, and taking a breather as long as you can still hear him. But only for a few minutes. If it doesn't work, call someone to give you a break."—**Anonymous**

"You aren't Superwoman. So quit trying to be. Don't be too proud to ask for help or advice."—**Wendi**

"When you start to think 'Why did I have a baby? I'm crazy. She's ruining my life,' you're normal. You *will* eventually get more time for yourself, and it will happen sooner than you think. The first few months are a blur."—**Anonymous**

"If your baby is driving you crazy and you think you need to get away from it all, what you may really need is to forget everything else and focus on the baby. Take your baby for a walk in the sling or just snuggle with her. Often what frustrates us is not the baby, but the fact that we think that the baby is keeping us from doing what we need to do. The *baby* is what we need to do. Let the housework wait."
—**Anonymous**

"Don't pay one iota of attention to anyone who tells you your baby is developing a bad habit or manipulating you. Babies just want to have their needs met. Meet them, and even though you may have a baby who wants a lot of attention, if you give her that attention, you'll have a happy toddler."
—**Anonymous**

"Babies who are held more cry less."—**Anonymous**

part three
settling
in
4–6 months

by the numbers
development:
4 to 6 months

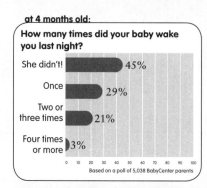

at 4 months old:

How many times did your baby wake you last night?

- She didn't! — 45%
- Once — 29%
- Two or three times — 21%
- Four times or more — 3%

Based on a poll of 5,038 BabyCenter parents

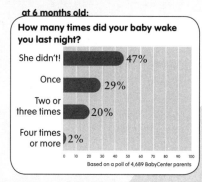

at 6 months old:

How many times did your baby wake you last night?

- She didn't! — 47%
- Once — 29%
- Two or three times — 20%
- Four times or more — 2%

Based on a poll of 4,689 BabyCenter parents

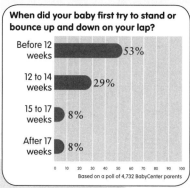

When did your baby first try to stand or bounce up and down on your lap?

- Before 12 weeks — 53%
- 12 to 14 weeks — 29%
- 15 to 17 weeks — 8%
- After 17 weeks — 8%

Based on a poll of 4,732 BabyCenter parents

When did your baby do mini-pushups?

- Before 8 weeks — 19%
- 8 to 10 weeks — 23%
- 11 to 13 weeks — 27%
- 14 to 16 weeks — 18%
- After 16 weeks — 10%

Based on a poll of 5,281 BabyCenter parents

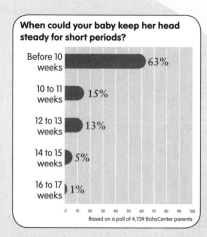

When could your baby keep her head steady for short periods?

- Before 10 weeks — 63%
- 10 to 11 weeks — 15%
- 12 to 13 weeks — 13%
- 14 to 15 weeks — 5%
- 16 to 17 weeks — 1%

Based on a poll of 4,739 BabyCenter parents

How old was your baby when he sat up for the first time?

- Younger than 5 months — 21%
- 5 months — 36%
- 6 months — 27%
- 7 months — 9%
- 8 months — 3%
- Older than 8 months — 4%

Based on a poll of 89,951 BabyCenter parents

by this time, according to the experts . . .

	most babies can . . .	half of babies can . . .	a few babies can . . .
4 months	• Do mini-pushups • Hold head steady for short periods • Bring hands together • Coo back at you when you talk • Bear weight on legs • Roll from side to back	• Roll over • Bat at toys • Reach out for an object	• Imitate speech sounds: *baba, dada* • Reach out and grasp an object
5 months	• Roll over • Amuse themselves by playing with hands and feet	• Turn toward new sounds and voices • Recognize own name	• Sit momentarily without support • Mouth objects • Identify strangers and be anxious about them
6 months	• Turn toward new sounds and voices • Imitate sounds • Blow bubbles • Roll in both directions • Sit with support	• Reach for objects and put them in their mouths • Drag objects toward themselves	• Lunge forward or start crawling • Babble or combine syllables • Sit without support

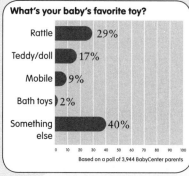

What's your baby's favorite toy?

Rattle	29%
Teddy/doll	17%
Mobile	9%
Bath toys	2%
Something else	40%

Based on a poll of 3,944 BabyCenter parents

the bottom line

Between 4 and 6 months, the age at which babies do certain things varies enormously. However, the sequence in which babies develop is almost always the same. So look at what your baby can already do in order to judge what he might do next.

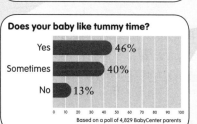

Does your baby like tummy time?

Yes	46%
Sometimes	40%
No	13%

Based on a poll of 4,829 BabyCenter parents

development— 4 to 6 months

Your baby uses all of his senses to learn about the world. If he sees something new, he'll stare at it, as if trying to take in all the details. By **4 months**, your baby prefers to look at new things rather than objects he's seen before, still choosing to focus on the most complex and patterned visuals. He'll prefer people to toys or objects, and you to any other person. If he grabs a toy, he'll put it in his mouth so he can taste it. If he hears a new sound, he'll listen intently. And just watch as he responds to new textures.

the power of touch

Touch is a powerful sense, and the feel of everything from a gentle breeze to being carried on your hip or kissed on the nose will interest your baby. You can stimulate his sense of touch with a variety of materials—felt, terry cloth, cotton, silk, wool.

Your skin touching your baby's provides one of the best tactile sensations. Try a simple baby massage, and don't worry about special strokes: He'll simply enjoy your touch. Find a warm, flat surface to lay your baby on—a blanket on the floor is fine. Pour a little baby oil or vegetable oil in your palms. Rub your hands together to warm them and the oil. Look into your baby's eyes, and sing or talk as you massage him.

If your baby isn't enjoying the massage, try a lighter or heavier touch, or simply stop. If he likes it, think of it as a bonus for you: Babies who are regularly massaged tend to sleep better.

tummy time

Being on his belly helps your baby strengthen important muscles that he'll use to push up, roll over, sit up, crawl, and, eventually, pull himself to a standing position. If he has some neck strength and head control at around **4 months,** but isn't yet strong enough to lift himself up on his forearms, try placing a rolled-up towel or pillow under his chest and armpits, with his arms in front of it. When he can raise himself on his forearms, you can take the towel or pillow away.

Of course, your baby may protest when you put him on his tummy. He's not used to it, and it's actually hard work for him to keep his head up, especially if he can't see much from that position. That's where you can help.

what you can do to encourage your baby

When your baby isn't hungry or tired but ready for play, join him on the floor. Talk with him, shake a rattle, make funny faces, show him a new toy. Start slowly—perhaps just a minute at a time—and gradually increase play time as he gets used to it, and as he gets stronger. Many babies become happier on their tummies once they can roll over—then it's their choice!

rolling over

At **4 months** of age, your baby will wave her arms and kick her legs. As her hip and knee joints become more flexible, her kicks will grow stronger. If you hold her upright with her feet on the floor, you'll feel her push down. Once she's learned to roll from her side to her back, she'll soon figure out how to roll from her stomach to her back. A few weeks later, she'll roll from her back to her stomach.

By around **5 to 6 months,** she can lie on her back and bend her feet up to play with them. It's often this action that helps her roll over: She holds onto those interesting toes, wriggles her bottom, and the next thing she knows she's rolled onto her belly and the world looks completely different.

what you can do to keep your baby safe

You never know when your baby is going to accomplish that first rollover. Don't risk leaving her alone on a bed or a changing table, as it might just happen while your eyes are off her that she decides she's ready to roll—right onto the floor.

ready to crawl

When you place your **4-month-old** on her tummy, she'll probably be able to lift up her whole chest as well as her head and hold this

photo ready?

As your baby grows, keep a camera on hand to capture each of his tiny milestones. If you're the parent of twins or triplets, take photographs of each child separately. (Put your babies' names on the back of each picture to avoid confusion in later years.)

position for several minutes. A few 4-month-olds can shift their weight from their forearms to their hands, raising themselves even higher. You'll notice that she pulls her legs up beneath her so that her bottom is in the air, and she may even push up with her feet.

By **5 months**, she can push her head and bottom up, but not together. She'll see-saw rather than be able to get on all-fours. She may even see-saw her way across the floor, but few babies manage a true crawl by 5 months.

If you hold her in a standing position on your lap, she'll practice holding her weight on her feet, pushing down on her toes, and straightening her knees. By **4 to 5 months**, she'll do this rhythmically, and prefer this action to sitting still.

To get a live-action look demonstrating the different ways babies crawl, see BabyCenter's video at babycenter.com.

how your baby learns to sit

By **4 months**, your baby will try to pull himself up to sitting if you hold his hands while he's lying on his back. By **6 months**, he'll sit up under his own power, just using your hands for balance, and try to sit up completely on his own. By this stage, he needs less support for sitting, as control of his back has vastly improved. Wedge a pillow behind his bottom to help keep him upright. At 6 months, his balance while sitting isn't reliable, and he'll easily keel over when he's trying to turn his head or use his hands.

hand control

From **4 months,** your baby can bring both her hands together, open and close her fingers, and raise both hands toward an object. Between **4 and 5 months,** she'll stare at her hand, then the object she wants, then at her hand again, as if working out the distance between the two. At **5 months,** your baby will really concentrate on her hands, first moving her hands out of view and then back in again, then moving her head to follow where her hand has gone, and following her hand as she brings it back. By **6 months,** she can reach out directly for things and pick them up, though she'll usually do this with both hands and grasp objects in her palm, not yet between finger and thumb. Anything within your baby's reach is fair game now! Once she moves on from holding objects in her palm to holding them with her fingers curled around them, she'll learn how to move objects from one hand to the other as well as to her mouth.

Around **6 months,** your baby will transfer her fascination from her hands to her feet, and make a big effort to grab them. It's not easy: If she lifts her head and shoulders, her feet move out of reach; if she lifts up her feet, her shoulders go down. It takes muscle power and ability to grasp that foot and successfully stick it in her mouth.

what you can do to encourage your baby

Hold out a toy to see if she'll reach for it. This encourages her eye-hand coordination. While she's busy learning to grab things, give your baby safe, interesting objects to hold. She's hungry to see, feel, and hold as many different things as possible. Try lightweight rattles, plastic or rubber rings, squeaky toys, or small stuffed animals. At 6 months old, though, your baby can cope with only one thing at a time. Offer her a new toy and she'll drop the one she's holding, but she can't yet deliberately let go or hand a toy back to you.

Your baby's attention span varies a lot now, depending on her mood. You'll know she loves your interaction when she turns toward you, smiling or laughing. But if she squirms away from

Q **My baby puts everything in his mouth. Should I worry?**

○ Always
○ Sometimes
● Almost Never

Your baby explores the world, in part, by using his mouth. He's not trying to eat everything, just assess its shape, texture, feel, and weight with his very sensitive mouth. It's a perfectly normal behavior, one your baby will continue for several months. Just be extra careful that he can't get a hold of small items—coins, chunks of food, paper clips, and so on—that he might choke on or things that are dirty. It's a good idea to wash all the toys every now and then, as well, if only to get his drool off them!

you, looks away, or cries, it's time to change the activity. Some babies are easily overstimulated. If yours starts to cry during playtime, don't despair. Switch to calmer activities such as cuddling, looking at picture books, or singing soft songs.

communicating with you

The range of sounds your baby makes begins to increase at around **4 months**. He'll squeal, gurgle, laugh and coo when you talk to him, making noises like *ooooh* and *aaaah*. He'll start to add consonants so that his noises imitate speech sounds, such as *baa baa, maa maa,* and *paa paa.* By **6 months**, his babble is part of his wider social interaction. Notice how he responds to you when you move out of his sight. He'll smile, wave, and "talk" all at once. He'll recognize familiar words at this stage and respond when you say, "Where's Daddy?" by turning his head and looking for him. He may also understand when you tell him it's time for a feeding.

By **6 months**, your baby can express his feelings more clearly, too. He'll cling tightly to you while staring at someone or something new. He knows he's safe with you and wants to find out more but still feels scared. He'll fuss and whine when tired, or if you're doing something he doesn't like, such as washing his face and hands. He'll close his lips and turn his face away if he doesn't want to eat some puréed food, or he may eat it and then scrunch his face up as he experiences a new flavor. If he likes it, he may open his mouth and shake his arms and legs to let you know he wants more.

by the numbers

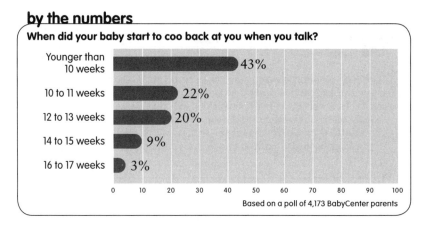

When did your baby start to coo back at you when you talk?

Younger than 10 weeks	43%
10 to 11 weeks	22%
12 to 13 weeks	20%
14 to 15 weeks	9%
16 to 17 weeks	3%

0   10   20   30   40   50   60   70   80   90   100

Based on a poll of 4,173 BabyCenter parents

what you can do to encourage your baby

Talk and sing to your baby throughout the day. Varying your tone and rhythm will hold her attention. Talk about what you see during a stroll. Tell her the names of things: at the grocery store, the park, the doctor's office. Hearing those words over and over helps her learn what's in her world. Your baby can't repeat these words yet, but she's storing all the information in her developing memory.

When your baby begins to make noises directed at you, reply to her. This will both delight her and teach her how to take turns and carry on a conversation. Give her a chance to talk back before you continue.

Songs and rhymes your baby might enjoy are—well, anything you enjoy. She'll also like songs with movements, such as "Itsy Bitsy Spider," "The Wheels on the Bus," "This Little Piggy," "Row, Row, Row Your Boat," and "Head, Shoulders, Knees, and Toes."

If you feel self-conscious singing at first, you'll soon begin to enjoy it as you see how well your baby responds. Branch out into songs with sounds or animal noises in them, too, such as "Old MacDonald Had a Farm" or "How Much Is That Doggie in the Window?"

Feeling particularly inventive? Watch your baby's reaction when you sing a song in a low gravelly voice and then in a high squeaky tone.

by the numbers

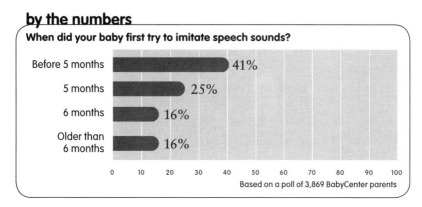

When did your baby first try to imitate speech sounds?

Before 5 months — 41%
5 months — 25%
6 months — 16%
Older than 6 months — 16%

0 10 20 30 40 50 60 70 80 90 100

Based on a poll of 3,869 BabyCenter parents

Try singing the song softly into your baby's ear, or use a hand puppet (or a napkin or sock willing to play the part of a hand puppet).

Don't hesitate to read simple books to your baby. She won't follow the story line yet, but she loves sitting close to you and listening to your voice. She'll be drawn to the bright pictures, as color differences become clearer to your baby at this stage of development. Books with different textures, like *Pat the Bunny,* that make reading a tactile experience are a big hit, too.

Can't remember the words? Look for your favorite lullaby lyrics on babycenter.com.

understanding the world

The world is beginning to make sense to your baby at **4 months**. He knows where his body stops and the rest of the world begins. He's starting to anticipate events, too. He recognizes the signs that you're about to feed him and stops crying in anticipation. He kicks his feet and wriggles his body when you approach him, as if to say, "Great, here comes someone to play with." By **5 months,** he lifts his arms to show you he wants to be held. His memory is improving, too. When you play a game he's played before, he anticipates the end results and looks forward to them. If you blow raspberries on his tummy, he'll giggle as you lift up his shirt, and again as you

pretend to blow the raspberry, and then again when you really do it.

He still has a long way to go before he understands cause and effect, though. If he splashes water in the bath, he looks startled when the water makes a noise and wets his face. He cries when he accidentally bops himself on the head with the rattle he's holding—and may even give you an accusing look!

One of the big changes in your baby's understanding of the world occurs over these months. He learns to expect certain sounds, expressions, and actions from the people close to him and becomes wary of anything new or strange. At **4 months**, your baby will, usually, still happily go to anyone. By around **5 months**, he's developed a pretty clear idea about his world, knowing what's familiar and "his," and what's strange. Instead of being happy to be picked up by anyone, he begins to take a long, cool look at other people before deciding whether they're acceptable or not. He turns and hides his face when you're talking to someone else and cries if someone he doesn't know gets too close to him or wants to play too energetically. He giggles when you play with him but remains still and looks puzzled when someone new talks to him.

Often by **6 months** or soon after, your baby will object to strangers and fusses and cries when you leave him. Previously, once you were out of sight, you were out of mind. Now, he knows that you're somewhere—and it's not with him! He'll greet your return with excited cries and move his arms and legs around as if to say, "See, I knew you were nearby."

Sudden loud noises, which your baby ignored before, make him cry or look worried now. He needs the reassurance of your voice to know that it's not a cause for alarm when the doorbell rings or the dog barks. He's much more wary of strange places, too, and wants to be held closely or hold onto a favorite toy when he goes somewhere new. This behavior can last for several months.

Your baby finds it much harder to fall asleep in strange places, as well. Although he settles happily in his own crib, he wants you to hold or rock him to sleep if you're out and about when he needs a nap.

As your baby's short-term memory develops, he'll look toward the door waiting for you to return when you leave the room, or turn toward the front door when he hears the doorbell, or toward the phone when it rings. He begins to remember people, too. When Grandma or a friend he's met before visits, your baby adjusts to them and relaxes more quickly than with someone he's never seen before. Soon after that he'll recognize and remember the most frequent visitors, which means that if he's in daycare and a familiar caregiver greets him, he's likely to settle quickly. But if an unfamiliar person is there to take him, he'll be far less happy.

your baby's temperament

As any parent of more than one child will tell you, babies have their own personalities right from the start. At times you'll wonder, "What did I do to cause *that* behavior?" In fact, much of your baby's personality develops from within.

Some babies are placid from day 1, happy to be handled, quick to sleep, and content to gaze at the world from their cribs. Others seem generally unimpressed with the world, preferring to fuss, and quick to cry. Some babies are sleepy, others wakeful; some resilient, others sensitive. You can blame yourself only as far as you're responsible for the genes you've passed along to your baby, for it appears that babies' personalities have much more to do with nature than nurture.

What you can do is get to know your baby's temperament and learn how to structure his (and your) environment in ways that make it easiest for him to interact enjoyably with his surroundings.

adapting your parenting style to your baby's personality

Several key traits make up personality, with a wide range of behaviors within each trait. A baby can fall in the middle of the scale of some traits but be high or low on others. Knowing where your baby needs extra stimulation or special attention will help you both find the right balance.

activity-energy level

Low: Your baby doesn't move much, and he barely notices when you read to him, change his diaper, or strap him in the car seat.

What you can do: A placid baby means it's easy to pop him into the playpen while you fold the laundry. Just don't overuse this strategy; it's also important for your baby to play and learn, so leave the laundry, get down on the floor with him, and roll around.

High: Dressing your baby is a challenge because he squirms constantly—all over the bed, the floor, and your lap.

What you can do: Let go of the hope that your baby will just lie there quietly while you catch up on housework. Give him plenty of time to wriggle around on the floor. And babyproof! He'll be scaling the furniture before you know it.

openness to novelty

Low: Your baby eyes a brand-new toy or caregiver with suspicion and tends to fuss whenever you introduce something new.

What you can do: Don't rush your baby into unfamiliar situations. Introduce new foods slowly, give him extra time to warm up to a new sitter, and go slowly introducing new games.

High: He's happy to play "pass the baby" at a party, and is very interested in new toys, books, and games. A new babysitter doesn't faze him a bit.

What you can do: If you're on the shy side, start expanding your own horizons to satisfy your baby's need for variety—and curb your tendency to be overprotective as he explores.

intensity

Low: Not only do your neighbors never hear a peep out of your baby—often you don't either. He's more likely to smile than to laugh and to fuss mildly than to wail at full volume.

What you can do: Pay close attention to his needs, since he won't make a big deal about them.

High: If your baby's not sleeping, he's usually laughing or crying—at the top of his lungs.

What you can do: Take it easy: Just because everything's a drama for him doesn't mean it has to be for you, too.

sensitivity

Low: Your baby is oblivious to soaking diapers, scratchy labels, and funny smells, and could happily nap next to a marching band.

What you can do: He may not let you know when he's hot or cold, hungry or wet, or overtired, so be extra vigilant about checking him.

High: Your baby's unable to put up with even minor discomforts, such as a slightly wet diaper or unusual noises.

What you can do: Respect the fact that his senses are working overtime. Cut out labels from clothing, use plenty of fabric softener (fragrance free), and expect your baby to be emotionally sensitive, too.

regularity

Low: You have a hard time planning your day because there's no tracking his schedule; it's all over the place.

What you can do: Go with the flow. When you do introduce a routine, take it gently and don't force it.

High: You can set your watch by his first yawn of the morning or snack of the afternoon.

What you can do: Wrap your mind around the idea that you'll need to arrange your life around your baby's naps and mealtimes. If you're the seat-of-your-pants type, remind yourself that he really needs the predictability.

adaptability

Low: Your baby has a hard time abandoning one activity to start another, even if it's to do something he loves.

What you can do: Help your baby learn to shift gears by providing gradual transitions. If he's playing with a toy and you need to go out, for example, take the toy with you.

High: When you head out for a walk, your baby can't wait to get going. When you arrive at the playground, he's practically out of the stroller. When it's time to go home, he's back in.

What you can do: Try not to take advantage of your baby's flexibility; even these non-protesters benefit from a little transition time between activities.

distractibility

Low: When he's occupied with something, it's as if nothing and no one else exists.

What you can do: Enjoy your baby's long attention span; it means you can catch up on e-mail and chores while he plays.

High: Your baby's attention flits like a butterfly. If someone walks in when you're feeding him, mealtime is as good as over.

What you can do: Minimize chaos in his immediate environment to allow him to focus. This trait also has a major upside: All he needs to snap out of a fussy spell is a change of toy.

persistence

Low: Your baby becomes easily upset by anything he finds difficult, like trying to sit up or roll over, and isn't a big fan of tummy time.

What you can do: Recognize that your baby gets frustrated easily and needs a prompt response from you. Gradually, you can show him that persistence pays off.

High: Your baby puzzles over a toy or skill until he gets the hang of it.

What you can do: Highly persistent babies will plug away until they figure something out, but they also have trouble giving up anything before they're finished. Have patience; your baby can't help being stubborn.

overall mood

Positive: Your baby is quick to giggle at a game of peekaboo and lights up when he sees someone or something he likes. When he cries, it means he really does need something—a diaper change, a feeding, or comfort.

What you can do: Lucky you! Your baby will quickly recover from any upsets.

Negative: Your baby is more likely to cry or frown than to smile and laugh. He'll often fuss even when he's well fed and rested, clean and comfortable.

What you can do: Recognize this for what it is: an inborn tendency.

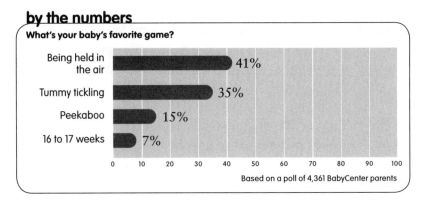

What's your baby's favorite game?

Being held in the air	41%
Tummy tickling	35%
Peekaboo	15%
16 to 17 weeks	7%

Based on a poll of 4,361 BabyCenter parents

competitive parenting

Comparing your baby to others is hard to resist. It's also hard to avoid hearing other parents drawing comparisons to your child or your parenting choices, in ways both veiled and blunt. You'll even hear this in the first week, when another mom looks at the dark circles under your eyes and says, "Baby not sleeping through the night yet? Poor thing. I was so lucky with mine."

Resist the temptation to measure your baby against milestone charts and other external yardsticks and instead focus on her individual feats. You won't be the first mom to wish that her baby would hurry up and reach the next milestone—sitting, crawling, standing, and so on. But early sitting, for example, is neither a sign of superior intelligence nor a hallmark of better parenting. It simply means that this is a baby who sits early.

Sometimes parents worry that their baby is doing things later than all the other babies they know. But the normal range at which babies reach each milestone is amazingly wide. If you're concerned, ask your own parents, and your partner's parents, at what ages each of you reached milestones, as patterns often run in families. If you crawled late or never crawled, then your baby may do the same.

If your baby is adopted, you won't necessarily have a family history to inform your parenting. But this is an added reason to make notes on the milestones your baby reaches, so that you have them to hand down when those grandchildren arrive.

Even though normal development covers a broad range of time, your intuition is as useful an assessment tool as a milestone chart. Always see your doctor if you suspect your baby has a developmental delay.

And what about other parents who want to compare notes? Sometimes people just want to gauge what to expect. But often, even well-intentioned comparison can lead to anxiety. Best not to get sucked into these kinds of conversations. Comparing notes to marvel or exchange tips is one thing; being made to feel badly is something else. Focus on what your baby *can* do and how wonderful it is; when the stroller gang starts getting snarky, though, change the subject to something more benign, like baby clothes, or head home.

Once you relax and accept that baby development isn't a race— absent of winners and losers—and that all babies develop at their own paces, then you'll enjoy these "baby days" for the special and fleeting time that they are. And if you can manage to do that, *you* deserve a gold medal.

by the numbers
feeding: 4 to 6 months

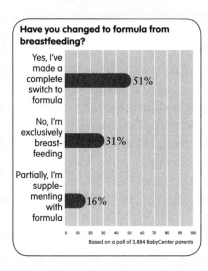

Have you changed to formula from breastfeeding?

- Yes, I've made a complete switch to formula — **51%**
- No, I'm exclusively breast-feeding — **31%**
- Partially, I'm supplementing with formula — **16%**

Based on a poll of 3,884 BabyCenter parents

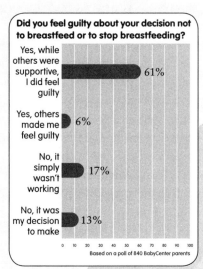

Did you feel guilty about your decision not to breastfeed or to stop breastfeeding?

- Yes, while others were supportive, I did feel guilty — **61%**
- Yes, others made me feel guilty — **6%**
- No, it simply wasn't working — **17%**
- No, it was my decision to make — **13%**

Based on a poll of 840 BabyCenter parents

Have you used a breast pump?

Yes	95%
No	5%

Based on a poll of 4,795 BabyCenter parents

Did you use a manual or an electric pump?

Electric	64%
Manual	36%

Based on a poll of 20,763 BabyCenter parents

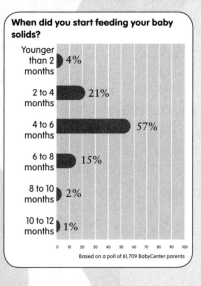

When did you start feeding your baby solids?

- Younger than 2 months — **4%**
- 2 to 4 months — **21%**
- 4 to 6 months — **57%**
- 6 to 8 months — **15%**
- 8 to 10 months — **2%**
- 10 to 12 months — **1%**

Based on a poll of 61,709 BabyCenter parents

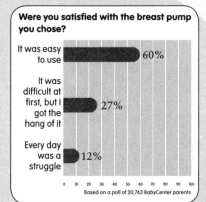
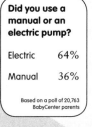

Were you satisfied with the breast pump you chose?

- It was easy to use — **60%**
- It was difficult at first, but I got the hang of it — **27%**
- Every day was a struggle — **12%**

Based on a poll of 20,763 BabyCenter parents

If you started breastfeeding, what was the main reason you stopped?

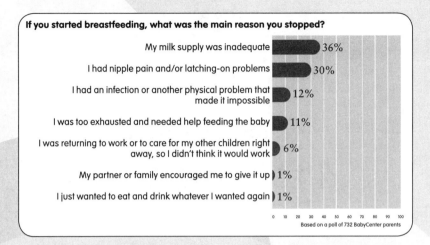

My milk supply was inadequate	36%
I had nipple pain and/or latching-on problems	30%
I had an infection or another physical problem that made it impossible	12%
I was too exhausted and needed help feeding the baby	11%
I was returning to work or to care for my other children right away, so I didn't think it would work	6%
My partner or family encouraged me to give it up	1%
I just wanted to eat and drink whatever I wanted again	1%

Based on a poll of 732 BabyCenter parents

Would you breastfeed in public?

Yes   81%

No   19%

Based on a poll of 71,764 BabyCenter parents

Do you think it's okay to have a drink while breastfeeding?

Yes   50%

No   50%

Based on a poll of 31,444 BabyCenter parents

Did breastfeeding help you lose weight after your pregnancy?

Yes   60%

No   40%

Based on a poll of 53,929 BabyCenter parents

the bottom line

Your baby has a larger stomach now, so he won't need to feed as often as he did in the early days. You'll also find that he's easily distracted during feedings—stopping if he hears an interesting noise or the arrival of a favorite person. Your baby has probably doubled his birth weight by now, with lots more growth ahead.

feeding—
4 to 6 months

Just as you and your baby have turned feedings into an almost-science, it will be time to start introducing solids—a new milestone for your baby, and a new challenge for you.

feeding checkpoint: how much milk?

if you're breastfeeding

Is your baby breastfeeding exclusively? If so, he'll nurse about five to eight times a day at **4 months old.** This includes one feeding during the night, an early morning feeding, and another three to six sessions during the day.

By **6 months,** feedings are likely to reduce to four or five a day; usually one in early morning, one late at night, and two or three spaced out during the day.

if you're formula-feeding

From the age of **4 months** up to **6 months,** your baby should take 4 to 6 ounces at each feeding, and he'll consume from 23 to 35

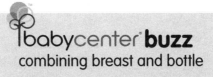

babycenter buzz
combining breast and bottle

"I'm a nursing mom and supplementing with formula. My son has one bottle of formula on most days. I use that bottle-feeding as a time for me to do chores or spend play time with my 2-year-old. Or I'll express my milk during his bottle-feeding to keep my milk supply up and going."—**Shannon**

"I found my manual breast pump very easy to use. I first started to practice with it when my daughter was near me. I pumped a little to begin with, and then slowly increased the amount—1 to 2 ounces at the beginning, and I worked up to 6 to 8 ounces. I pump only for about 5 to 10 minutes on either breast. It's handy to have milk on hand for times when I don't know if I can feed in a public place, or those nighttime feedings when I'm just too tired."
—**Schell**

"Here's a trick that might help avoid nipple confusion when you use bottles: Try using different bottles and nipples so that your baby won't get used to one nipple."—**Sarah**

"I breastfeed my son most of the time, but his dad gives him one bottle of formula at bedtime. I've tried pumping, but the pump just doesn't get much milk out. My lactation consultant told me that's the case for some women."—**Becca**

ounces a day. Just as with breastfed babies, he'll take the bottle between five to eight times a day: one in early morning, three to six during the day, one in early evening, and one in late evening—around the time you go to bed. Perhaps you'll also give a bottle during the night.

Once your baby reaches **6 months**, you can feed him from 6 to 8 ounces at each feeding, and his total formula intake will be roughly 32 ounces a day. After you've introduced solids (see page 225), his daily formula consumption will gradually decrease to about 24 ounces.

Your baby's weight gain slows down around 6 months. Until now, he's gained about 1 to 2 pounds each month. From 6 months until the first birthday, babies typically gain 1 pound each month. Bear in mind that these are only rough guidelines, and your baby will let you know if he needs more or less formula. If you aren't sure, talk with your doctor.

biting babies

Some moms wean their babies from the breast when they think teeth are about to come in, but you don't need to if you don't want to. Although the first tooth typically comes in at around 6 months, your baby's nutritional needs will be met primarily by breast milk or formula for at least the first year. Many breastfed babies have teeth, and the vast majority never bite while they're feeding.

In fact, it's impossible for your baby to bite with the first two bottom teeth that emerge, as his tongue covers his lower gums while he's feeding. To bite, he'd need to pull his tongue back to expose his teeth, which he can't do while he's latched on.

When he has more teeth, though, it's possible for your baby to bite. New teeth are sharp. If they fasten onto your breast, chances are you'll shout! Your strong reaction could shock your baby so much he won't do it again. But if your reaction piques his curiosity, he could try it again to see how you respond—a bit like experimenting with a rattle to see if it will make the same noise. If this happens, try to stay calm and quiet. Pull your baby in toward your breast so that his nose is covered with breast tissue and he has to let go of your breast to breathe. Stop feeding him, make eye contact, and tell him a firm "no." He needs to associate biting with losing the breast. Most babies will dislike this separation. If he persists, put him on the floor for a short time immediately after he bites. You can also try not feeding him unless he's really hungry, because then he'll concentrate on his food rather than experimenting with bites.

If you think your baby is biting because he's trying to relieve his sore gums as his teeth come through, give him a cold teething ring to chew on before you feed him. Some babies bite at the end of a feeding when they're falling asleep. If this is the case, watch for the slowing down and weakening of his jaw movements and remove him before he dozes off. Another cause of biting: Offering your breast when your baby doesn't really want it. Time to take the hint and drop a feeding!

expressing breast milk

When you squeeze milk from your breasts, either by hand or with a manual or electric pump, you're expressing. It's the only way, apart from breastfeeding itself, to release milk from your breasts. You can store the expressed milk to feed to your baby at a later date.

Some women say expressing milk makes them feel like a cow, so if you've had this thought, don't think you're the only one. However, if you're going to be away from your baby (for either a few hours or a whole day), you can express and store some breast milk beforehand. That way, your baby still gets the benefits of your milk even though someone else is feeding him.

hand expressing

If you need to express milk only every once in a while, you can probably get by with expressing by hand. This is the cheapest way to do it because it requires no equipment, but it's time-consuming and takes practice. Some women find it simple while many find it cumbersome; try it and see what you think.

Wash your hands before you start. Place a sterilized, wide-rimmed bowl beneath your breast to collect the milk. Place your thumb about 1½ to 2 inches away from your nipple and your fingers below so they form a "C" around the areola. Squeeze your fingers and thumb together, pushing your hand back into the breast tissue. If your fingers and thumb are too close to your nipple, the "squeeze" will hurt and won't work. If your fingers and thumb are further back, above the milk that's held in the breast, it won't hurt and milk will flow. It may take a couple of minutes to get started. Sometimes it helps to look at your baby, or a picture of your baby, and think about her feeding to help your body begin to release milk. Continue the process in a circular motion around your areola. Most women can express only a little milk at a time; so don't expect to fill a bottle in one try. It's likely you'll have to collect and store milk over a day or two to have enough for a single feeding.

breast pumps

A breast pump makes the job go faster. There are two kinds of pumps: electric and manual. Good breast pumps try to mimic the sucking action of a baby, stimulating your letdown reflex. On average, it takes 15 minutes (electric) to 45 minutes (manual) to express milk from both breasts.

To use an electric pump, put the suction cup over your breast, turn the machine on, and let it do the work of extracting your milk into the attached, sterilized container. The best hospital-grade electric pumps allow you to double-pump simultaneously; less powerful battery-powered models usually work on only one breast at a time. Manual pumps also use a suction cup, but you extract the milk through a squeezing mechanism rather than by relying on electric power.

Knowing which breast pump is right for you depends on how often you plan to use one and how much time you can spare for expressing. If you work full-time and have to find time to pump during a busy day, choose an ultrafast hospital-grade electric pump. These are expensive to buy but can be rented. Many working moms find a high-grade personal electric pump worth the investment, as these combine the efficiency of hospital-grade pumps with lightweight portability and a lower price tag.

The Federal Drug Administration frowns on borrowing a friend's pump because of the risk of viruses such as hepatitis B or HIV being transmitted; rental pumps are designed to avoid this risk.

On the other hand, if you need to express only occasionally so your partner can feed the baby when you're out, an inexpensive manual pump may be sufficient. Most women find they have personal preferences based on need, ease of use, and comfort level.

You'll also need an insulated storage bag if you're transporting milk from your workplace, as well as a place to pump and store milk at work.

storing breast milk

It's best to store expressed breast milk in plastic baby bottles with secure tops to seal in freshness. You can also use disposable bottle liners or plastic bags made especially for storing milk. Store only about 2 to 4 ounces per bottle depending on how much you think your baby will take. Write the date you expressed on a label on the bottle or bag before putting it in the refrigerator or freezer, so you'll know how fresh it is.

Keep expressed milk at the back of the refrigerator, away from the door, at a temperature of 39°F or lower. Use refrigerated milk within 3 to 5 days. You can also freeze the milk. The process of freezing destroys some of the milk's antibodies, so don't freeze milk that you plan to use in the next few days. But frozen breast milk is still healthier and offers more protection from disease than formula does. Frozen milk lasts 3 to 6 months.

To thaw frozen milk, place the bottle or bag in a bowl of warm water, run it under warm tap water, or defrost it in the refrigerator overnight. Never leave it out on the counter to defrost. Defrosted breast milk can look very thin with creamier bits in it; just shake it up before using. After thawing, frozen milk lasts up to 12 hours in the refrigerator. If your baby drinks a partial bottle, don't save the remainder for later use as bacteria can grow in the milk and make your baby sick.

ways to persuade your baby to take a bottle

Some babies become so accustomed to breastfeeding that it's difficult to transition them to a bottle. Plan well ahead if you're going back to work. Introduce a bottle at least 2 to 3 weeks before you need to leave your baby, and expect the transition from breast to bottle to take a while.

If your baby balks at the bottle, you can try the following:

- Get someone else—Dad or Grandma, perhaps—to offer the bottle. If you're the one to try, your baby will know that breast milk is available.
- Give expressed breast milk rather than formula so that the taste is the same.
- Use latex nipples; they're softer and more like the real thing.
- Massage the nipple to make it really soft and put some breast milk on the outside to tempt your baby further.
- Experiment with nipple sizes and the size of the hole. The rate of flow, compared to breastfeeding, can overwhelm your baby, in which case try a nipple with a smaller hole.
- Experiment with the temperature of the milk; your baby may prefer it cooler or warmer.
- Use a bottle with an airflow system that prevents taking in air with the milk.
- Hold your baby in a position different from the one you usually

babycenter **buzz**
getting your baby on the bottle

"We tried everything to get Grace to take the bottle, but it became so stressful that I think she picked up on it and it became a real drama. In the end, it was my mom who got her to take it. I think that because she wasn't so anxious about it, Grace felt calmer, too."—**Nicky**

"We tried different bottles and cups, but in the end he took a bottle with a latex nipple rather than silicone, and I think that helped as well. It's much softer."—**Sara**

use for breastfeeding, so she gets the signal that this feeding will be different.

- Offer your baby a bottle when she's at her most alert and before she's really hungry; if she's tired or starving, she won't deal as well with the new experience.
- Some moms find that they can begin a feeding by nursing and then, once their baby is no longer very hungry and getting sleepy, finish with a bottle of formula.

If your baby completely refuses a bottle, offer a cup with a soft spout and fine holes.

starting solids

Breast milk or formula provides all the nutrients a baby needs for healthy development in the first 6 months of life. At around 6 months, your baby begins to get teeth, has the strength to hold her head up well, and sits up better unsupported, all of which make eating easier. So 6 months is a good time to introduce and then gradually increase the amount of solid foods you give your baby. Many pediatricians still recommend starting solids earlier, between 4 and 6 months, which used to be the universal norm.

babycenter buzz
expressing yourself

"I'm a full-time working mom who pumped while at work and nursed while at home. I'd advise anyone who wants to do it to get a good pump, some quiet time, and a picture of your sweet little one."—**Jennifer**

"I felt badly taking the 15 minutes to pump and store my milk. Then I said to myself, 'How many times do people use the restroom at work in a day and take 15 minutes, or go for a smoke, or get a coffee?' Why should pumping time be any different? If guilt is what's keeping you from taking time away, let it go. You're justified in taking a few minutes."—**Anonymous**

"I have an 8-month-old and have been pumping at work since she was 3 months old, and it's working great. My teammates and manager know that at 10:00 a.m. and 2:00 p.m. every day I pump. I have set times so everyone knows the schedule. Just keep to the schedule to maintain your milk supply. Your co-workers will come to see that pumping doesn't interfere with your productivity at work."—**Terry**

Is my baby ready for solids? The American Academy of Pediatrics now recommends exclusive breastfeeding for the first 6 months of life, but also says some babies may need complementary foods (solids) as early as 4 months, while other babies may not be ready until 8 months.

It's believed that waiting until 6 months to introduce solid foods into your baby's diet will minimize the risk of her developing adverse reactions to foods and allergies. So if you have a family history of allergies, this is something to consider.

Here are other signs that your baby is ready for more than milk:

• She can hold her head up by herself and has lost the tongue-thrust extrusion reflex that causes her to push food out of her mouth (which means she can now learn to take more than just liquid food).

- She becomes hungry again soon after a feeding.
- She starts showing an interest in your food, casting a curious eye on your meals and possibly reaching for your plate.

Not that this means your baby's ready for a knife and fork. A baby's first solid foods aren't solid at all. In fact, first foods should be semi-liquid, as eating is a skill babies learn gradually. The consistency and variety of baby food changes over the coming months, and by 12 months solid foods will be the main part of what she eats, with breast or formula milk making up the balance. (Cow's milk isn't suitable for babies under a year old because a baby's digestive system can't process cow's milk proteins; it also contains too much salt and potassium and not enough iron and other nutrients to meet your baby's needs.)

All babies are different. Some welcome solid foods earlier, some later. Some take to change quickly and with relish, some are more hesitant and take longer. Some are picky eaters, others seem to like everything you put in front of them. Whether your baby is eager or curious, introducing your baby to solids should take place in stages.

stage 1: tiny teaspoons

So what should you start with? The most often recommended first food is iron-fortified rice cereal. Babies digest it easily, and the grain is the least likely to trigger an allergic reaction. However, there's no reason why you can't try vegetable or fruit purées first. Mix a teaspoon of the cereal or purée with 4 to 5 teaspoons of your baby's usual milk (breast or formula) or water. Offer this to your baby before or after one of your usual milk feedings, or in the middle of a feeding, if that works better.

Most parents use a plastic-tipped baby-feeding spoon, but your clean finger is just fine for the first introductions. Simply dip your fingertip into the cereal mixture and offer it to your baby. Don't expect her to eat very much at a time. Tiny stomachs need tiny portions, and most of her nutrition will continue to come from breast milk or formula for months to come. It takes a while for most babies to learn how to eat food from a spoon. Be patient and be prepared for some mess. You'll need to throw away any of the heated food that your baby doesn't eat, as it's not safe to reheat previously warmed food.

At 6 months, you can also offer your baby some of these foods:

- Smooth vegetable purée, such as carrots, peas, green beans, butternut squash, cauliflower, zucchini, potatoes, sweet potatoes, or yams
- Fruit purée, such as bananas, cooked apple (or unsweetened applesauce), papaya, pear, or mango
- Non-wheat-based cereal such as baby rice, oatmeal, or barley, mixed with your baby's usual breast milk or formula

Always introduce one food at a time so that you can tell if your baby reacts adversely, although this is rarely a problem with first cereals and vegetables. If she tolerates a food well after a day or two, you can mix baby rice with, say, apple or carrot purée. Offer your baby savory as well as sweet foods at this stage, so she gets used to both.

Go at your baby's pace. Allow plenty of time for first tastes, especially at the beginning. Your baby needs to learn to move solid food from the front of her tongue to the back, to taste it, and then swallow it. The food tastes and feels different from milk, so it may take her time to get used to it.

stage 2: a little more

Once your baby is happily eating from a spoon, you can increase the range of foods you offer to include:

- Purées of lean meat or poultry
- Purées of lentils or split peas
- Purées of mixed vegetables with potatoes or rice
- Purées that include green vegetables, such as peas, cabbage, spinach, or broccoli

Try to limit the number of sweet or cereal purées to one a day and always include a vegetable purée once each day. Gradually make the food a thicker consistency.

Spoon out the amount you think your baby will eat and heat it up, rather than heating a large amount that then goes to waste. As in stage 1, for safety's sake, get rid of any of the heated food that your baby doesn't eat. If you prepare larger quantities than you need, freeze small portions for later use, for example in an ice cube tray.

You can move gradually from solid food at one feeding a day to serving it at two and then three meals.

To get a complete list of solid feeding supplies your baby will need, go to babycenter.com.

what not to introduce

Some foods are definitely off-limits for your baby for the entire first year:

- **Cow's milk.** Not before 12 months
- **Shellfish.** Can cause an allergic reaction. Some other types of fish (shark, marlin, tuna, and swordfish, or certain fish caught in local waters) may contain relatively high levels of methyl mercury, which can affect the nervous system.
- **Whole and chopped nuts or peanuts.** Both tree nuts and peanuts present a choking danger and an allergy risk in some children.
- **Honey.** Very occasionally, honey contains a type of bacteria that causes botulism in an infant. After your baby is a year old, the intestines mature and the bacteria can't grow.
- **Egg whites.** The yolk is usually okay (well-cooked), but the whites present an allergy risk, especially if allergies run in your family. Uncommonly, some kids have allergies to proteins in the yolk.
- **Fatty foods.** This includes foods such as hot dogs and processed meat dishes. Babies find it hard to digest fats.
- **Tea (hot or iced).** The tannin in tea prevents iron absorption.

- **Carbonated drinks and drinks high in sugar, including fruit juice.** Babies need breast milk and formula to drink, and water. (You no longer need to sterilize the water, unless you have well water.)
- **Instant foods.** Foods such as sauces and soups intended for adults are often high in salt content.
- **High-fiber foods.** Babies don't need fiber in the way adults do, and too much fiber can prevent your baby from absorbing nutrients from other foods.
- **Salt.** Don't add salt to baby food because your baby's kidneys can't cope with it.
- **Sugar.** The limited calories a baby needs are better spent on nutrient-rich foods, so don't feed sweets (like cookies) or add sugar to baby food.
- **Small, hard foods.** To avoid choking, babies this age need relatively soft food served in a mushy state or in small bits.

It's also a good idea to delay introducing certain foods, especially if there's a history of allergies or asthma in your family. The American Academy of Pediatrics recommends that infants with a family history of allergies (inherited conditions such as asthma, eczema, and hay fever) or food sensitivities shouldn't have:

- Cow's milk until 1 year of age
- Eggs until 2 years of age
- Peanuts, nuts, and fish until 3 years of age

Some researchers believe that wheat-based foods served before 6 months are associated with allergies, while a recent study showed that babies in whom wheat is delayed are actually three times more likely to develop wheat allergy than those who were exposed to the grain sooner. It's thought that introducing grains between 4 and 6 months can lessen allergies by exposing the developing immune system.

Also, if other family members have intolerances to any of the following foods, it's a good idea to delay introducing them until your baby is older:

- Wheat, rye, oats, and barley
- Eggs, especially the whites
- Sesame seeds
- Nuts
- Soy
- Citrus fruits
- Cow's milk and foods made from it
- Shellfish
- Seeded fruits such as strawberries

common questions about feeding

Once your baby begins eating solids, initially you'll find that you're just as concerned about what comes out as you are about what goes in.

"what's that in the diaper?"

Don't be surprised if your baby's stools change color and smell as soon as he starts eating even small amounts of solid food. This is normal. If your baby's stools seem too firm, introduce more fruits and vegetables and oatmeal or barley cereal. (Rice cereal and bananas can be constipating.)

"can't I introduce solids before 6 months?"

If your baby seems constantly hungry, of course you're going to worry that she isn't getting enough food from breast milk or formula alone. But there may be several reasons why she's hungry:

- She may be having a growth spurt. These often occur at around 2, 3, and 6 months of age. If so, she'll soon settle down again to an increased interval between feedings.
- If your baby is formula fed, she may be ready for a "second-stage" casein-based formula (as opposed to a first-stage whey-based milk). Always ask your doctor before changing your baby's formula.

babycenter **buzz**
starting solids

"I've had 3 days of attempting to feed my 4-month-old cereal, and she simply doesn't like it. Once she sees the spoon, she shuts her mouth and waits for me to give her a bottle. She's such a good baby in every way that I hate 'punishing' her with cereal, so I'll wait it out. When she's ready, she'll let me know."—**Gaby**

"I think people should realize that every baby is different, and just because you feed your baby cereal at 6 months doesn't mean that the mother feeding her baby cereal at 3 months is a bad mother. Everyone should do what they think is right for their child. Go with your instincts; no one knows your child better than you."—**Anonymous**

"I have four daughters: One ate at 4 months, one at 6, one at 8, and now the fourth has had cereal since 5 months and veggies, too. Each one showed signs of readiness and of not being ready, too! I nursed all for at least 15 months, and they're healthy and wonderful. Watch for signs of readiness, and do what works for your family."—**Anonymous**

- Some babies need to "comfort suck." If so, your baby's apparent demand for a feeding could be satisfied by simply cuddling her or responding in other ways.

If you feel your baby needs to start solids before 6 months, discuss it with your doctor. This is particularly important with premature babies, whose kidneys may be too immature to cope with solids. Many full-term babies who seem ready do perfectly well eating solids after 4 months.

why shouldn't I wait much longer than 6 months?

It won't give your baby any extra benefits if you carry on exclusive breastfeeding beyond the age of 6 months. In fact, there are good reasons why you definitely should introduce solid foods around this time:

- Your baby's energy needs increase. You could satisfy this growing need with lots more breast milk, but milk is a bulky food and there comes a point where a baby would have to feed very often to get enough energy from milk alone. Solid foods are denser and give more energy in a more concentrated form.
- In developed countries, babies typically get about 400 calories from breast milk at 6 months, 370 at 9 months, and 340 at 12 months.
- Breast milk alone can't always supply enough micronutrients, especially iron, zinc, and vitamin B_6. The micronutrients in breast milk are more easily absorbed than those in formula, but even allowing for this fact, the levels of some micronutrients in breast milk are low. A more varied range of foods helps your baby's diet get enough micronutrients.
- There's some evidence of a window of opportunity for introducing lumpy solid foods. If you delay introducing these beyond 10 months of age, it can increase the risk of feeding difficulties later on. Interestingly, the muscles that develop with eating semisolid foods and solid foods are the same ones that your baby needs to use when she begins speaking.

To find out how to make your own baby food, visit babycenter.com.

by the numbers
sleep: 4 to 6 months

What time does your baby wake up in the morning?

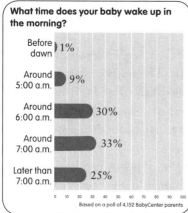

Before dawn	1%
Around 5:00 a.m.	9%
Around 6:00 a.m.	30%
Around 7:00 a.m.	33%
Later than 7:00 a.m.	25%

Based on a poll of 4,152 BabyCenter parents

Where does your baby sleep?

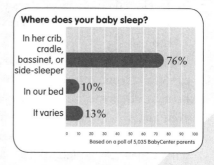

In her crib, cradle, bassinet, or side-sleeper	76%
In our bed	10%
It varies	13%

Based on a poll of 5,035 BabyCenter parents

Does your baby have a comfort object?

Yes	54%
No	46%

Based on a poll of 11,973 BabyCenter parents

Does your baby have a bedtime routine?

Yes	86%
No	13%

Based on a poll of 4,198 BabyCenter parents

Have you tried sleep training?

Yes	36%
No	63%

Based on a poll of 4,794 BabyCenter parents

the bottom line

Most babies are likely to be sleeping for around 10 hours at night now. But if your baby isn't sleeping through the night yet, you've got plenty of company: Some babies take until age 6 months or longer. Even a baby who usually sleeps well can have his sleep pattern changed by illness or a major change in routine such as vacation. Sometimes busy days like holidays tire out a baby so much that he wakes in the night.

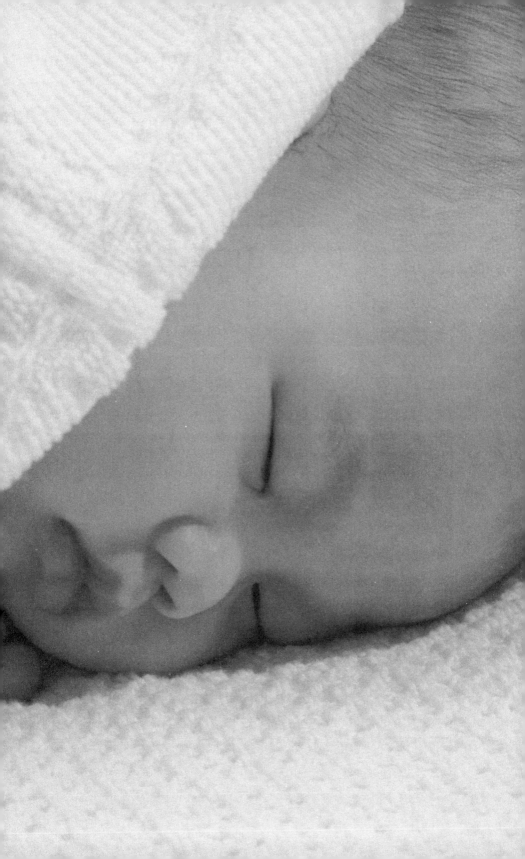

sleep—
4 to 6 months

As your baby gets older, her sleep patterns become more predictable. By the time she reaches **4 months** of age, she'll sleep around 15 hours daily, 10 of these at night and the other 5 divided among three daytime naps. She won't wake every couple of hours during the night anymore, but her nighttime sleep (and yours) may still be interrupted by at least one feeding, and possibly two.

Many 4-month-olds sleep for a 6-hour or longer stretch through the night. As your baby's sleep pattern starts to settle down, you'll feel more rested, too.

By **6 months** of age, your baby will be sleeping a little less— around 14 hours in every 24, with 11 of those during the night. Most babies still manage at least an unbroken 6-hour stretch or so in the night. Some might need to wake for one nighttime feeding but then go back to sleep again.

Between 4 and 6 months, your baby will probably drop one of the daytime naps and have two 1½- or 2-hour naps each day, one each morning and one each afternoon.

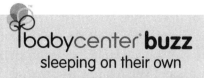

babycenter buzz
sleeping on their own

"There's no set rule about when to switch to the crib. Just do what works best for your baby. The only thing to keep in mind is the weight limit on the cradle. Because our daughter is quickly approaching the limit, we're trying to start transitioning into her crib. She's been taking a nap in there a couple times a week, but she won't sleep for long periods of time. We may just move the crib into our room for a while and see if that helps."—**Anonymous**

"I wouldn't let my baby cry it out before 4 months or so. Just make daytime bright, noisy, and stimulating and make nighttime quiet and subdued. Don't talk or play with your baby and make feeding and changing time quick and all business. I never let my babies sleep longer than a 2-hour stretch during the day. I wake them to eat or play, and then they learn that the long stretch should be at night."—**Wendy**

"It's tough to get through the first 4 days of doing this! Your precious one will cry 45 minutes to an hour the first night! Each night it gets shorter and shorter, and by the fourth night—give or take a couple of days—you'll have a sweet, lovable baby who goes down quietly."—**Anonymous**

"I never let my daughter cry longer than 15 minutes. Sometimes I pick her up and we play for 20 minutes, and she happily goes to sleep once I put her down again. However, I usually listen to the type of crying that she's doing. If it's just complaining (albeit very loudly!), I don't pick her up. A true wailing cry is answered promptly after the 15 minutes. Most of the time this only happens if she's ill."—**Anonymous**

sleep worries

If your baby's sleeping is still erratic, and you're still being woken several times a night, you can take steps to encourage good habits that really make a difference.

Learn the signs that mean your baby's tired: Is he rubbing his eyes, pulling on his ear, or developing faint dark circles under his eyes? If you spot these or any other signs of sleepiness, put him down in his bed. You'll soon develop a sixth sense about your baby's daily rhythms and patterns, and you'll know instinctively when he's ready for a nap.

settling down for the night

It's important to be consistent with your messages about sleep: No baby learns instantly that nighttime is for sleeping and that daytime is for fun. But nothing will get the message about sleep across to your baby as much as sticking to a series of cues and keeping to a pattern that eventually imposes itself on your child's life.

One of the most important cues to establish is a bedtime routine. Even if you like to live moment-to-moment, you'll find life much easier if this becomes the one-and-only routine you do stick to (most of the time, anyway). What's more, many experts believe that babies feel happier and more comfortable if they know what's coming next in their lives, at least some of the time.

What you include in the routine is up to you. The most usual pattern is to start with a bath, put on pajamas, read a story while you snuggle, give a bottle or breastfeeding, and finally settle your baby down in his bed. You can start the routine in the bathroom or the living room, but definitely aim to finish in your baby's bedroom.

The idea is to make your baby's bedtime routine something you both look forward to: a pleasant time that underlines how much you love your child and how important you are to one another. At this point in the day, you want to devote yourself completely to your baby, as a way of signaling to him that it's a time to look forward to and enjoy. Some couples divide the bedtime routine. Maybe Dad does the bath and story while Mom nurses and settles him, for example.

Put your baby in his bed when he's drowsy but not fully asleep. If he gets upset as you're putting him down, you can try:

- **The "don't look back" approach.** Say goodnight to your baby, leave the room, and don't turn back. Most babies will cry for up to 30 minutes on the first night, before they realize they're not getting anywhere, then fall asleep. Usually, after 3 or 4 nights of unchecked crying, your baby will start going to sleep by himself. This approach is appropriate if you feel that going back into the room to check on your baby simply upsets rather than reassures him. On the other hand, you might find it impossible to ignore his cries completely and find this approach upsetting.

- **The "gradual leaving" approach.** Say goodnight and leave as described above. If your baby cries, go back into his room. Pat him gently and tell him everything is fine but that it's time to go to sleep. Don't turn on the lights, linger, pick him up, or cuddle him. Be gentle but firm. Leave. Wait a few minutes, then check again. Do this repeatedly until your baby falls asleep, extending the time between each visit. The first night you might wait 5 minutes before returning, the second night 10 minutes, and so on. Eventually, your baby will learn to fall asleep on his own. It might take a while, but this approach teaches him that he won't be ignored *and* that you won't pick him up. This can be a difficult approach for many parents. You need to be committed to making it work because if you give up, all you'll have taught your baby is that he needs to cry for longer before you'll come.

- **The "stay near" approach.** Put your baby down awake and stay with him, reassuring him that you're present but that he can fall asleep by himself. If Dad shares the comforting duties, your baby will learn to be comforted by his presence and more quickly adapt to not needing anyone because it's clear that at bedtime there's no more food coming. On the other hand, as long as you're nearby, your baby may not sleep, and this approach can be time-consuming.

- **The "go with it" approach.** Some parents believe that if they leave their baby while he's crying, he'll feel abandoned. If that's the case with you, pick him up, rock him, or pace the floor with him until he sleeps, and then place him gently back in his crib. If this approach doesn't work and he stays awake—and you can't cope with the broken sleep—you'll need to try a different technique.

Many experts believe that it helps if you don't nurse or rock your baby to sleep. After all, if you're used to sleeping with a blanket over you, and you wake in the night to find it gone, you'll get up, look for it, and get upset if you can't find it. You'd find it hard to go back to sleep without the blanket. It's the same for your baby. If he's used to falling asleep while nursing, being rocked, or hearing a lullaby, he'll find it hard to settle to sleep *without* such soothing. And this is the case not just when he settles to sleep in the evenings, but when he wakes in the middle of the night, too.

Learning how to sleep is like learning to crawl: If you always carry your baby, he'll never have a chance to discover crawling, since he won't be on the floor long enough to figure it out. Likewise, if you always feed or rock your baby to sleep, he'll never have a chance to learn how to soothe himself to sleep.

No one approach is "right." It's simply a question of what seems best to you, and what you're willing to stick to and follow through on. Decide what *you* want, and then go for it. You're more likely to stick with a plan that feels right for you than one that deep down you're unhappy with.

Once you begin a course of action, consistency is important. For example, if you decide that you're going to place your baby in his crib sleepy but awake and return every 5 or 10 minutes, don't give in after 45 minutes and then rock him to sleep. All you'll have done is teach your baby that it's worthwhile to persist for as long as possible.

Give your plan time to work—at least a week or two. It will confuse your baby if you keep changing. Ideally, pick a 2- or 3-week period that's free from any added stress such as changing jobs, moving to a new house, or going on vacation.

Teaching your baby to sleep through the night can be a stressful time. Listening to your baby cry, you may feel as if your heart is going to break. Partners need to be in agreement about the approach they choose, as consistency is key to getting the message across. So be prepared to support one another through this time. You'll all be happier at the end of it.

decision guide · · · · · · · · · · · · · · · · · · ·

SLEEP TRAINING OR NOT?

When people refer to sleep training, they mean one of the many systematic approaches to teaching a baby to sleep. Every expert seems to offer a method, the best-known of which is "Ferberizing," after Dr. Richard Ferber, who described a graduated series of withdrawals from a baby's room in his best-selling book. Basically, they are all variations of the approaches for settling a baby described by the techniques on page 238 and involve varying degrees of letting your baby cry. If your baby isn't sleeping well by 4 to 6 months and you aren't happy about it, you may be ready to explore one of these options, although be forewarned: Parents have different levels of tolerance for "crying it out."

reasons for sleep training

"It works!" Learning to sleep through the night can take days, or it can happen in a single night. For many families, "crying it out" finally cracks the problem of lack of sleep. Babies usually seem no worse for the experience of a few nights of extra crying.

"We finally have our evenings back." Getting your baby to sleep at a reasonable hour and through the night means that you have some free time with your partner and the rest of your family again. That alone provides plenty of incentive for trying.

"Her daytime behavior is better." Tired, grumpy babies and tired, grumpy parents are a recipe for tough days. If your baby sleeps better, you will, too, and you can enjoy the day together.

"It's part of learning to have a routine." A set sleep schedule may be part-and-parcel of your overall planned routine.

"We have other kids; the baby has to fit in." In larger families, getting your baby to bed in the early evening is vital if you want to spend time with your older children.

reasons for not sleep training

"It's cruel! When my baby cries, I want to comfort him." Letting your baby cry may not be your style of parenting. Some experts and many parents think that letting a baby cry is harmful.

"We tried it and it just made our baby throw up." Sleep training doesn't always work, and it can make you all feel worse if you try it and it fails.

"My partner wanted to try it, but I just hated doing it." You both need to agree on how you're going to approach sleep training and for how long.

"I was so tired I couldn't cope with it." Sleep training can be easier during a holiday, when you can share the process with your partner and catch up on sleep the next day.

"Bedtime routines are kinder than letting a baby cry it out." Many parents find that introducing a routine helps their babies go to sleep at the same time each day, and to settle quickly and easily.

. . . .

coping with interrupted sleep

If you're still suffering through night wakings, it can take quite a toll on you. In contrast to surfacing naturally from light sleep, being woken from a deeper sleep is truly unpleasant. It leaves you feeling groggy and disoriented the next day, especially if you're interrupted during dream sleep.

Your baby wakes naturally at the top of his sleep cycle about five times a night. Because your baby is more likely to wake up as dawn approaches, that's when your sleep will be disturbed as well, which is when adults spend a greater proportion of their 90-to-100-minute sleep cycles in REM sleep. That's why your baby is bouncy the next day and you feel jet-lagged, even though you've both woken up the same amount of times.

Being deprived of sleep, especially REM sleep, is serious. It can leave you disoriented, confused, and irritable, and affect your speech and decision-making. You're more apt to feel depressed and bicker with your partner. Losing your temper comes more easily, as do angry feelings toward your baby because you blame her for your lack of sleep. Some parents admit to plopping their babies in the crib a bit too roughly, or even being tempted to hit or shake their babies.

Deprived of sleep for too long, you may fall asleep while caring for your baby, which is risky. Most new moms report feeling notice-ably better as their babies get older and as their babies sleep far more reliably for long stretches at night. In the meantime, though, the feeling of bone-tiredness can take away some of the joy you feel toward your baby.

So what can you do to help yourself cope with broken sleep?

5 things that help

1. **Power naps.** A 15-to-20-minute nap during the day improves alertness, sharpens memory, and reduces your feelings of tiredness. It can be very hard to sleep while your baby naps, especially if you are a single parent and feel that there's so much that has to get done, but resting will give you more energy than simply soldiering on. If you find sleep impossible, at least put your feet up and close your eyes.

2. **Exercise.** It may be the last thing on your mind when you're asleep on your feet, but it helps. Take your baby out for a walk. The exercise helps you feel less tired, and the fresh air and movement lets you both sleep better at night.

3. **A bedtime routine.** Once you've established one for your baby, do the same for yourself. It's easy to lie in bed tossing and turning, wondering when your baby will wake, instead of being able to drift off easily. Give yourself a warm bath, a glass of milk or cup of herbal tea, and an early lights-out.

4. **Shift work.** Split the night with your partner. You go to bed early and sleep well for the first half of the night, say 10:00 p.m. until 2:00 a.m. Then you deal with any baby wake-ups and your partner gets a few hours of sleep. Don't rule out one of you sleeping in a spare room for a few nights to avoid disturbing each other.

5. **Support.** Remember that you're not the only one coping with a sleepless baby. Talking to friends, relatives, and other new moms about life with a baby can help you realize that you're not struggling alone. Visit the BabyCenter bulletin boards to talk directly to other moms who've survived this phase.

5 things that hinder

1. **Too much caffeine.** Allow yourself a caffeinated drink early in the groggy mornings, but avoid a caffeine boost after midday, as it can keep you awake at night.

2. **Too much junk food.** Sugar provides a quick high, but then your energy levels drop dramatically. It's better to eat a balanced range of foods rich in fruits, vegetables, and whole grains to keep your energy up. Now isn't the time to cut calories or crash diet. Food is your fuel.

3. **Getting dehydrated.** If you feel thirsty, you're already dehydrated, and that can cause you to feel very sleepy. Get into the habit of drinking plenty of water and other liquids during the day.

4. **Trying to cope alone.** Bring in reinforcements. Accept all offers for help with cooking, cleaning, childcare, errands, and the like. If you aren't receiving offers, ask for help. Your friends and family *want* to help and most will feel honored you asked.

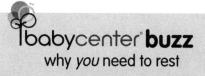

babycenter buzz
why *you* need to rest

"I was so tired and just needed a shower to wake myself up. As I was showering, I shaved my armpits, finished, and got dressed. Later that evening, I still felt stubs of hair in my underarm, and when I looked, it appeared that I hadn't shaved at all. Later I looked inside my shower and realized that I had tried to shave with my toothbrush. I think it was at that point that I realized how lack of sleep can really make a person go a little crazy."—**Rachel**

"When my son was about 3 months old, I changed his diaper and put his sleeper back on for a nap, and it wasn't until after his nap that I realized I never actually put a diaper on him. Needless to say, he was a soggy mess."—**Christine**

"I went shopping alone when my baby was around 8 weeks old, even though the dark circles under my eyes were as bad as a panda's. I picked out a really sweet pink skirt for her and proceeded to put it in my bag and half an hour later left the store—without paying for it! So I returned it to the store the next day. Thank God I wasn't caught."—**Joanna**

"When my first son was about 2 months old, I cleaned out my closet and carried two huge bags out to my car—one for the drycleaner and one for Goodwill. My son, who hated being in the car, screamed all the way to the Goodwill drop-off. By the time we got to Goodwill, I was exhausted, my nerves were fried, and I was almost in tears. I left the bag and drove off. Turns out I left my good winter clothes there."—**Anonymous**

Consider temporarily hiring a babysitter to help you for a few hours a week.

5. **Being house-proud.** Does it matter if crumbs nestle under the toaster—or on your kitchen floor, for that matter? Nope. Spend your time taking it easy and marveling at your new baby, not doing loads of laundry or keeping everything perfectly tidy.

If you find that you can't sleep, have lost interest in doing anything, and feel despairing, see your doctor. There's tiredness and there's the baby blues, but there's also postpartum depression. The sooner you get help with depression, the sooner you'll get well.

out of your bed and into his own

If your baby's been sharing your bed, he's definitely taking up more room now (and kicking you more). Is it time to move him into his own bed? Generally speaking, the younger your baby, the easier this transition will be. It may take from a few days to several months, depending on your baby's age.

To ease the transition, try moving your baby to a Moses basket or portable crib first, rather than a big crib. Or place your baby's crib near your bed. Move the crib gradually away from the bed and eventually into your baby's own room.

Another way to make the move is by putting your baby in the crib for naps. Or start with bedtime, letting him fall asleep on his own and in his own room but bringing him into your bed when he wakes in the night. After a couple of weeks, take the final step to having him sleep in his own room all night.

Give your baby plenty of comfort, but try not to bring him back to your bed or back into your room. This will confuse him and send the message that he'll be rewarded if he cries long and hard enough.

Once your baby is old enough to begin moving around in his bed during sleep, it's hard to keep him in a back- or side-sleeping position. If he's rolling over, that means that he's probably capable of holding his head up and turning it from side to side, which reduces the chances of him getting into breathing difficulties when he moves onto his belly. Babies often learn to roll onto their stomachs first, but usually they also quickly learn to roll back again.

Remember that a sleeping position is just one factor in safe sleeping. To help keep your baby safe:

- Make sure his bed has a firm mattress. A softer mattress can allow your baby to sink in and have trouble breathing.
- Keep your baby's room at a comfortable temperature, and not too hot. If the temperature in your house seems comfortable to you, it should be just right for your baby.
- Continue to keep pillows, stuffed animals, and extra blankets out of the crib.

by the numbers
baby care: 4 to 6 months

How old was your baby when she cut her first tooth?

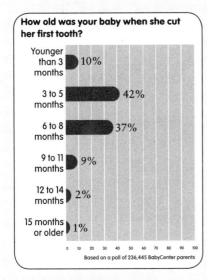

- Younger than 3 months: 10%
- 3 to 5 months: 42%
- 6 to 8 months: 37%
- 9 to 11 months: 9%
- 12 to 14 months: 2%
- 15 months or older: 1%

Based on a poll of 236,445 BabyCenter parents

Will you use childcare during your baby's first year?

Yes 72%
No 28%

Based on a poll of 8,404 BabyCenter parents

When did you start actively looking at childcare options?

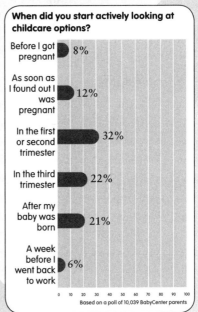

- Before I got pregnant: 8%
- As soon as I found out I was pregnant: 12%
- In the first or second trimester: 32%
- In the third trimester: 22%
- After my baby was born: 21%
- A week before I went back to work: 6%

Based on a poll of 10,039 BabyCenter parents

Which kind of childcare will you use?

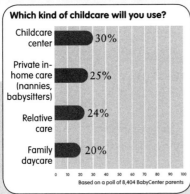

- Childcare center: 30%
- Private in-home care (nannies, babysitters): 25%
- Relative care: 24%
- Family daycare: 20%

Based on a poll of 8,404 BabyCenter parents

How long did it take you to find your childcare provider?

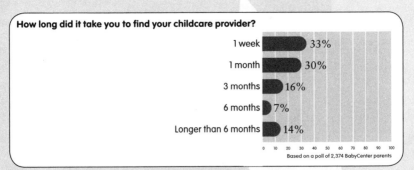

- 1 week: 33%
- 1 month: 30%
- 3 months: 16%
- 6 months: 7%
- Longer than 6 months: 14%

Based on a poll of 2,374 BabyCenter parents

How many weeks of maternity leave did you take?

- 4 weeks or less — 8%
- 4 to 6 weeks — 8%
- 6 to 8 weeks — 16%
- 8 to 10 weeks — 10%
- 10 to 12 weeks — 16%
- 12 to 14 weeks — 13%
- 14 to 16 weeks — 7%
- More than 16 weeks — 23%

Based on a poll of 19,836 BabyCenter parents

How much of that leave did your company pay for?

- None—I took it as sick time or as unpaid leave — 26%
- Less than 2 weeks — 4%
- 2 to 4 weeks — 5%
- 4 to 6 weeks — 17%
- 6 to 8 weeks — 20%
- 8 to 10 weeks — 7%
- 10 to 12 weeks — 7%
- 12 to 14 weeks — 4%
- 14 to 16 weeks — 2%
- More than 16 weeks — 7%

Based on a poll of 19,836 BabyCenter parents

Have you ever disagreed with your pediatrician?

Yes   85%

No   15%

Who won the argument?

I did   86%

The doctor did   14%

Have you ever changed pediatricians over a disagreement?

Yes   39%

No   61%

Based on a poll of 4,282 BabyCenter parents

the bottom line

Being a parent and caring for your baby usually gets easier around now. You can do most of the basics, such as diapering and feeding, without a second thought, and you feel much more confident about most things. If you've been doing everything "by the book" so far, you'll probably find you can relax and do it your way now.

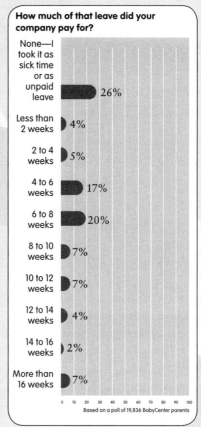

baby care—
4 to 6 months

Changes in the way you care for your baby are more gradual than dramatic during this period. Of course, now that your baby is alert more of the time, you'll take on more of a role as an entertainer.

is it teething?

Any day now, your baby will cut his first tooth. The average age is 5 or 6 months, though it can happen as early as 3 months or as late as 1 year. The first tooth to appear is usually one of the bottom middle teeth. Next, you can expect to see the top two middle teeth, then the ones along the sides and back. Teething is a relatively long process; it's not until about age 3 that your baby will have a full set of 20 baby teeth. They won't fall out until your child's permanent teeth are ready to come in around age 6.

Although some babies' teeth appear as if by magic, other children seem to struggle through the experience. You'll notice your baby drooling, and the wetness can cause a rash around his mouth. Other symptoms include irritability, refusing to eat, biting on things, and waking in the night.

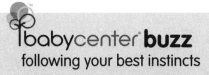

babycenter **buzz**
following your best instincts

"Everyone—nieces, nephews, grandparents—wants to hold the baby. Put them to work! As long as your baby is old enough, they can hold her or give her a bottle while you take a shower or get something else done."—**Callie**

"My son is 5 months old, and his personality is really starting to show. He's so much fun to play with now, and I love how he's showing me his affection!"—**Anonymous**

"When the world gets too hectic, I stop whatever I'm doing and just sit down and play with my daughter. It's amazing how much clearer my head is afterward, and I don't feel so pressured to get everything else done. The laundry and cleaning will be there the next day, but what you do with your child today will be a lasting memory for both of you."—**Anonymous**

"One thing I never mess around with is high fevers. We were just in the ER this weekend with a fever of 103°F. The doctor tried to tell me it might be teething, but I knew better: Teething doesn't cause high fevers. They couldn't see anything wrong with him, and he developed a rash today; turns out he has roseola."—**Jennifer**

"I'll be having a moms' group over in a few weeks. I'm going to put the plush toys away when the playgroup is there and put out plenty of plastics that can be chewed on and then washed in the sink."—**Lani**

Experts don't agree about whether teething causes other problems, such as diarrhea, fever, rashes, and vomiting. If your baby has symptoms that worry you, don't just chalk it up to teething; check with your doctor to make sure there isn't something else going on.

what you can do to help

Teething babies love something to gnaw on, such as a firm rubber teething ring. Simply rubbing a clean finger gently but firmly over your baby's sore gums is soothing, too. Once your baby is eating

Q

My baby shows no signs of teething yet. Should I worry?

○ Always
○ Sometimes
● Not at all

The age at which teeth come through varies greatly. Many babies celebrate their first birthdays completely toothless. Some babies appear to be teething for weeks before a tooth finally cuts through—then several arrive at once. Talk to your doctor or dentist if there are no signs of teeth by around 14 to 16 months.

solids, cold foods such as yogurt help relieve soreness. Another trick: Give him a hard, unsweetened teething cracker to get his gums around.

A small dose of children's pain reliever can help if your baby seems very unhappy (though always check with your doctor before giving your baby any medication). You can also rub your baby's gums with a small amount of topical over-the-counter teething gel. If the drool causes a rash on your baby's face, smooth some petroleum jelly on his chin before a nap or bedtime. This protects his skin from the wetness.

teeth cleaning

As soon as that first tooth erupts, it needs cleaning. Start early to get your baby used to having his teeth cleaned, which helps to avoid future problems with brushing.

Cradle your baby in your arms (as though you're feeding him a bottle) to reach his teeth more easily. You don't need to use any toothpaste until age 2 because it tends to get swallowed and can lead to excessive fluoride intake. Simply brush with a wet soft-bristled brush. Use small, gentle, circular movements, concentrating on the area where the teeth and gums meet. Remember, though: While your baby is teething, his gums will feel especially tender, so don't be too vigorous with the brushing. Your dentist or dental hygienist will be happy to show you how to do the brushing if you need more guidance.

Brush your baby's teeth at least once a day. It's particularly worth doing this after a feeding as the breast milk or formula collects and lingers around your baby's gums.

For more unique tips on how parents helped soothed their baby's tender teething gums, go to babycenter.com.

managing your baby's day

In the early days, your baby slept much of the day, with wakeful periods to nurse. Gradually, one or more of the feedings turns into a time when she's ready to be entertained. By **4 months,** your baby is likely to have two or three wakeful periods each day, and these gradually get longer. She'll probably go back to sleep after her early feeding, have a morning wakeful time, and follow this with a longish sleep after lunch. Then she'll wake to nurse and play in the early afternoon, sleep again, and then wake to nurse and have playtime again in the early evening.

Between **5 months** and **6 months,** this pattern often reverses itself. Your baby stays awake and alert for most of the day and has two or three naps that can last from about ½ hour to 2 hours. It depends on your baby: Some are wakeful and need little sleep, others need more.

Until now, your baby probably just fell asleep when she needed to. But by around **6 months,** she can stay awake even if she's tired. That

triplets

A study by the Australian Multiple Births Association showed that it took 197 hours per week to care for baby triplets and to do the household chores. Unfortunately, there are only 168 hours in a week!

So if you're one of the 7,000 or so families in the United States who have triplets each year—that's why you're feeling so extraordinarily tired.

can lead to periods of grumpiness when she refuses to entertain herself or let you entertain her. You can teach her how to settle down for a daytime nap. Put her in bed shortly after eating, or hold her and sing to her for a little while to encourage her to wind down and sleep.

boredom breakers

Babies need entertaining, just like the rest of us. They can't spend the whole day tucked up in a bouncy seat. And some like a lot of entertainment. Here are 10 great ideas for things to do with a baby who can't yet walk, crawl, talk, or even sit.

1. Buy or borrow a baby gym. While your baby entertains herself with the gym, you do something else, like getting dressed.

2. Take your baby for a dip in a pool.

3. Make use of your extended family—grandparents, stepfamilies, friends—to entertain your baby before separation anxiety kicks in. Your baby is a social creature.

4. Take her for a walk and point out interesting things.

5. Bring your baby in with the rest of the family for mealtimes so she can see what's going on.

6. Give her a mobile. You don't need to buy one; you can easily make your own. Tie or tape some ribbons, fabric, or other interesting streamers onto a wooden spoon and dangle them gently over and in front of your baby's face. Or just take a lightweight scarf and fling it into the air, letting it settle on your baby's head.

7. Blow bubbles. There's something magical about them, whatever your child's age.

8. Turn on some music and dance. Put your baby in a sling or hold her in your arms and either do some soulful swaying or rock out if you need a lift.

9. Open the kitchen cupboard. Look at what's in there! Smell heaven. Although you're familiar with the scent of vanilla, your baby isn't. There's also peppermint, cumin, cloves, nutmeg, and more.

10. Sing your lungs out. Your voice is terrible? Your baby doesn't have a clue.

crying

By the age of 4 or 5 months, most babies cry a lot less than they did as newborns. By this time, too, you're probably beginning to understand which cries mean "feed me" and which say "I'm bored" or "I need to sleep."

Many babies at this age are still prone to crying. Some just cry more than others. It seems to take them a little longer than others simply to get used to the world. They can be nervous, clingy, and not inclined to smile. And they need plenty of love and reassurance to feel that the world is a safe place. Moms sometimes call them "Velcro" babies because it seems they don't want to be unpeeled from you. If your baby needs to be held, investing in a carrier or sling that keeps him close to you (but leaves your hands free to do other things) can make life bearable for both of you.

It's wearying to cope with a baby who seems pretty miserable to be here and who rewards your every effort to comfort or care for him by wailing. Remember: Babies aren't capable of being manipulative in the ways that toddlers can. They don't think to themselves, "If I just cry a little bit louder, then she'll *have* to come." Babies don't cry because they're demanding. They simply cry because they *need* something, and their tears are the only way they can let you know it.

As babies grow older and gain more independence, some of the day-to-day frustrations of babyhood disappear, and so does the crying.

new baby stuff

As your baby gets older, you'll probably need to invest in a new set of equipment that matches her development.

stroller

Lightweight umbrella strollers (so named because they fold up into a long thin shape like an umbrella) are easy to collapse and reopen, even with one hand. They're very portable, so you can toss one in the trunk or take it on a bus instead of a bulkier regular stroller or travel system.

Because umbrella strollers don't have any suspension, they make for a bumpier ride, so they're best for short outings when your baby won't need to lie down and sleep in comfort.

highchair

A highchair becomes a necessity when your baby begins to sit up on her own. Most parents choose either a traditional-style wooden chair (with all the modern safety features) or a contemporary metal-and-plastic highchair.

Your baby will spend lots of time in her highchair so make sure it's durable and stable. Look for a wide base (that's hard to tip over), an easily removable tray (for after-meal cleanup) with tall edges (to catch spills), and a safety restraint (one that fits around the waist and between the legs provides more security than a plain waist belt). Some models adjust at the seat, tray, or footrest as your baby grows—another plus.

For more information on picking the right highchair for your baby, visit babycenter.com.

utensils

When your baby starts to feed herself, buy spoons with wide or looped handles that are easy for small hands to grasp. It will be a

few more months, though, before her coordination develops
enough to get food from bowl to mouth with a utensil.

playtime equipment

Many babies welcome spending time in an activity center or
exersaucer, where they can sit and bounce while playing with
attached toys or toys you put out on the surrounding tray. Some
babies prefer swings, jumpers, or bouncers, all of which provide an
exciting sense of motion.

by the numbers
you: 4 to 6 months

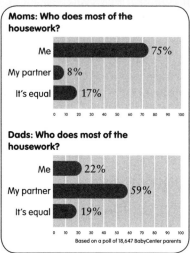

Moms: Who does most of the housework?

- Me — 75%
- My partner — 8%
- It's equal — 17%

Dads: Who does most of the housework?

- Me — 22%
- My partner — 59%
- It's equal — 19%

Based on a poll of 18,647 BabyCenter parents

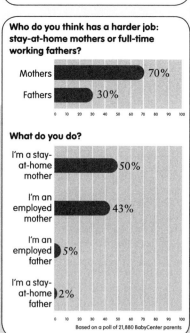

Who do you think has a harder job: stay-at-home mothers or full-time working fathers?

- Mothers — 70%
- Fathers — 30%

What do you do?

- I'm a stay-at-home mother — 50%
- I'm an employed mother — 43%
- I'm an employed father — 5%
- I'm a stay-at-home father — 2%

Based on a poll of 21,880 BabyCenter parents

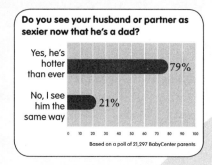

Do you see your husband or partner as sexier now that he's a dad?

- Yes, he's hotter than ever — 79%
- No, I see him the same way — 21%

Based on a poll of 21,297 BabyCenter parents

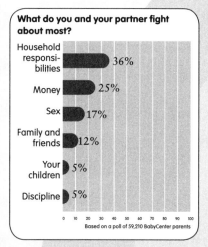

What do you and your partner fight about most?

- Household responsibilities — 36%
- Money — 25%
- Sex — 17%
- Family and friends — 12%
- Your children — 5%
- Discipline — 5%

Based on a poll of 59,210 BabyCenter parents

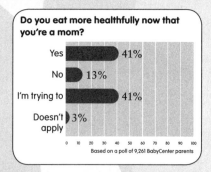

Do you eat more healthfully now that you're a mom?

- Yes — 41%
- No — 13%
- I'm trying to — 41%
- Doesn't apply — 3%

Based on a poll of 9,261 BabyCenter parents

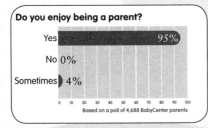

Do you enjoy being a parent?

Yes ████████████████ 95%

No 0%

Sometimes ▶ 4%

0 10 20 30 40 50 60 70 80 90 100
Based on a poll of 4,688 BabyCenter parents

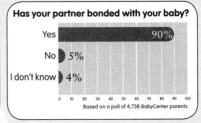

Has your partner bonded with your baby?

Yes ███████████████ 90%

No ▶ 5%

I don't know ▶ 4%

0 10 20 30 40 50 60 70 80 90 100
Based on a poll of 4,738 BabyCenter parents

the bottom line

Has becoming parents changed your relationship more than you expected? Think about how you split the baby care and other household tasks. Are you both happy with it? Or do you need to take a step back and think about who does what? Taking care of a baby consumes 8 to 10 hours a day on basic cleaning, feeding, and caring tasks. How has that fit into your life and what have you given up to squeeze it all in? Is there any space now to get back some "me time?" And how can you find some "couple time?"

you—
4 to 6 months

Soon you'll be feeling like it's time to "get back to normal,"
whatever that means! Issues of work, play (for you and your baby),
body image, and maintaining your energy are paramount now.

body image

Your body has changed. Forever. Just as your life has changed.
Forever.

If you're a little disappointed in your post-baby body, you can take
the common view of many moms: It took your body 9 months to
get like this, and it could take 9 months (or more) to get back to
where you were.

Even if you get back to the weight you were before you had your
baby, or you regain your prepregnancy fitness levels, it's likely
you'll have to live with a changed body image. Your body has
been tried and tested by pregnancy and giving birth. You may
show stretch marks or simply feel different, perhaps slower or
less toned.

babycenter buzz
take good care of yourself, too

"When I was pregnant, I loved how my profile looked. I was so used to my big belly. What I didn't love so much afterward was my stomach. From the front, it was so flabby! However, I was so done with my maternity clothes. I bought a great jeans jacket and wore it all the time. It disguised my stomach until I lost the weight."—**Anonymous**

"Taking good care of yourself by buying a few cute trendy outfits, some great makeup, and taking exercise classes will give you a feeling of well-being and help you look your best!"—**Sonee**

What society defines as beautiful varies from culture to culture. In societies where food is scarce, well-rounded bodies are loved and cherished. In our society, where food is largely plentiful, we value thinness. That's one reason many moms find adjusting to their new shape so difficult.

On the plus side, remind yourself:

- You've delivered a baby.
- You've nurtured your baby and given him the best possible start.
- Your body is more womanly, perhaps more rounded and softer, but this is what women's bodies are *meant* to be like.

You can work at losing weight, getting fit, and toning your muscles—all good for your physical health. Accepting your changed body, and your changed role as a mother, can be more difficult, but doing so can be good for your mental health.

As to what your partner thinks about your changed body, see the fascinating insights from the BabyCenter survey on page 340.

Read feel-and-look-good tips from other new moms at babycenter.com.

connecting with other moms

If you're on your own every day—just you and your baby—it's likely you'll have times when you feel down. This doesn't mean you don't love your baby or that you're a bad mom. It doesn't even mean you're selfish. It simply says that you need other people to make you a whole, rounded, functioning human being. Your baby needs you to meet her needs. You're doing that. But you have other needs, too, and that's what friends are for.

If you're one of the first in your circle to have a baby, it's easy to feel isolated. In fact, it's often hard to keep in touch with non-parent friends as your life becomes so different. Many moms say that even if you're busy and working away from home, you need other mom friends as well as non-mom friends. If you didn't know any before, then now's the time to go out and find them. Who else is going to have an interest in mashed-up carrots or baby poop?

Accept that you'll need two groups of friends—moms and non-moms—and that you'll interact with them differently. Your family will also become more important to you after you've had a baby, especially if you have relatives with a baby, too.

When it comes to finding mom friends in your community, a lot depends on where you live. In some cities, it's easy to connect with other parents through groups advertised in local parenting publications or Web sites.

In other places, you'll have to actively seek out a group. If you have special needs or concerns, try contacting organizations that cater to your situation, whether you're parenting multiples, suffering from postpartum depression, raising a child on your own, or caring for a preemie. They will refer you to a specialized mothers' group. Once you have a list of groups you're interested in, the only foolproof way to make your final decision is to start visiting them. You'll know in an hour whether you feel connected to the women or not.

babycenter **buzz**
adjusting to your new shape

"If a man makes a negative comment about your body, tell him he can chastise you about your weight only after he's been pregnant for 40 weeks, experienced childbirth, bled for 6, and had a little mouth contort his nipple into an ungodly shape."—**Anonymous**

"I've struggled with my body image all of my life, but during my first pregnancy, I started looking at my body in a different way. It's curvy and carries babies very well. After giving birth, it took time getting used to my new squishiness. But my children love to cuddle up to my soft breasts and belly, and I love being able to show them that I'm not ashamed of my body. I've lost all of my baby weight since my second baby was born, and for the first time in my life I'm proud of my body!"—**Kate**

"I have a terrible body now! I gained only 27 pounds and lost it all, but my body is just different. It makes me totally depressed. I can't find time to work out. I work full-time, and when I'm not there I spend time entertaining my daughter, cleaning, and cooking. I hardly find time for sleep."—**Anonymous**

Find new mom friends through:

- Babycenter.com bulletin boards
- Postnatal exercise classes
- Daycare centers
- Universities
- Libraries
- Religious and community groups
- Local book clubs

Preserve your non-mom friends through:

- Phone calls once your baby is settled for the evening (which means resisting the temptation to just fall asleep yourself)
- Planned meetings at times that suit you; not after work when you're putting your baby to bed but perhaps a Saturday morning coffee while your partner looks after the baby

beating the tiredness battle

When you're exhausted—which is, no doubt, much of the time—you can't help but wonder if there's an easier way of doing things. Here are some of the ways BabyCenter parents have cut down the grind, saved time and energy, and come out smiling.

"I try to remember that the world isn't going to end if dinner isn't at a certain time, or if the house isn't completely clean, or if the laundry isn't done."—**Jennifer**

"I use laundry baskets for everything, especially to pick up toys around the house. When I don't have time to clean and company's coming over, I throw everything in a laundry basket and put it in a closet."—**Molly**

"I write a 'to do' list for the week on a dry-erase board. Having everything written down, and crossing things out once they've been done, keeps me from feeling overwhelmed. It also gives my hubby an opportunity to help without having to ask *me* what to do."—**Natasha**

"Cook and purée batches of fruit or veggies and freeze them in ice cube trays. When frozen, pop them out and save them in labeled self-sealing baggies in the freezer. Each cube is about an ounce of food—easy to heat up and easy to measure!"—**Amee**

"When I do find time to fix a meal, I make huge amounts and freeze the extra in freezer bags, ready to be heated up when I don't have time to cook. Many foods lend themselves well to freezing, including soups, stews, pasta sauces, and bean and rice dishes."—**Margarita**

"I've stopped buying anything that needs ironing. Those days are gone."—**Jill**

"When my daughter is down for the night, I usually don't have energy for much, so I pick one thing to do, usually the dishes, and wait until the next day to do the rest without feeling guilty."—**Ryan**

"I purchase all the 'quicker-picker-uppers,' like sanitizing wipes and dusting cloths, and keep them handy in any room that needs cleaning. As I walk through the room, I grab one and clean my way through. It's more expensive, but it saves time."—**Catherine**

"My husband gives our 4-month-old a bath every night. Our son loves it, and it makes him sleepy, so it's easier for my husband to feed him and put him to bed. It's great father-and-son bonding, and it gives me time to myself after a full day caring for our baby."—**Callie**

balancing work and family: how you feel

Our society encourages mothers to return to paid work and gives less value to mothers who stay at home. The fact that running a home and caring for children is far harder work than many other jobs—with no promotions, time off, or financial reward—is often overlooked. This can make employment an attractive option, and around half of all mothers return to work by the time their child reaches the age of 2. Another attraction of employment is that some women prefer not to depend on their partner's income. They need to feel financially independent.

Deciding whether and when to go back to paid work, and managing that process, aren't just financial considerations. Work may mean more than money to you. If you've always defined yourself by your job, it's difficult knowing who you are if you're not that dental hygienist, computer programmer, managing director, or salesperson any more. Giving up your career prospects is difficult. Although many companies offer family-friendly policies, such as part-time hours, you may feel that in order to advance in the workplace, colleagues have to perceive you as being committed, first and foremost, to your job.

But once you've made the decision to return to the workplace, making the adjustment can be harder than you expected. It's as if you can't win, whatever you do. Or that you can't do your job as well as you want to, and that you're not giving your baby your best either. And if you simply have to go back to work because of money, that can cause resentment, too. It feels like a lose-lose situation.

Every working mom has days when she thinks she's made the wrong decision. But so does every stay-at-home mom.

Whichever route you choose, here's how you can turn it into a winning situation:

- Accept that life isn't the same as before your baby was born. It can't be and it won't be.
- Cut yourself some slack. You don't have to be the best employee ever *and* the best mom. At your job, try to focus on the most vital aspects and the areas you enjoy most and get those done. At home, concentrate on the really important aspects of parenting, such as feeding your baby and spending time with both your baby and partner.
- Take shortcuts where you can and accept that they're necessary. If you can't prepare soup from scratch anymore, buy the best you can afford. If you can't get the laundry done today, ask yourself: "Can't it wait until tomorrow?"
- Pay for whatever help you need and can afford.
- Be deaf to other people's opinions. Your relative who thinks you should stay home doesn't have to live *your* life.

Above all, don't beat yourself up. Your baby loves you more than anyone else in the world.

To find out how to create a family-friendly work arrangement, go to babycenter.com.

traveling with a baby

Heading out with a baby can be a wonderful experience as long as you do two contradictory things: plan the outing like a military campaign before you leave, and go with the flow when you get there. It's impossible to come up with an exhaustive list of everything you should think about when you're planning a trip, but here are the essentials.

deciding where to go

Too many new sights and sounds at once can overstimulate your baby. Tourist destinations and places without shade pose an added challenge when you have a baby in tow. You'll be able to relax better at a destination that's used to accommodating babies. Try a lazy beach retreat, family camp, nature resort, or similar kid-friendly place.

If your baby sleeps in a crib, reserve one when you make your room reservation, or you could be out of luck when you arrive.

packing for a trip

What to include?

- Enough diapers for the time you'll be in transit (restock once you arrive), diaper wipes, diaper rash ointment, and plastic bags for dirty diapers
- Infant pain reliever, if recommended by your doctor, in case of fever
- Sun protection for your baby: hats, clothing, sunscreen
- If you aren't breastfeeding, formula you can mix as needed or travel-size packs of ready-made formula
- Baby food, if you're traveling somewhere exotic
- Plastic bib

traveling by car

When traveling by car, your baby should always be in a rear-facing car seat in the back seat. Make sure the car seat is installed properly and that the harness fits your baby snugly and securely. Bring removable window shades to shield your baby from the bright sun.

(continued on page 271)

days and nig
is "wrong" v
doing things
time to adjus

If your partr
be the first n
am I going to
back to norn

Then you rea
and the just-
you had wit
dynamic. Bu
baby *will* sle
your partner
attention an
needs of you
women need

Of course, ju
to handle. O
how to comm
understands
hit by a crisi
comfort or s
true that wh
baby's needs
those needs
care, she'll f

the primary caregiver, a working mom sometimes feels like the "third-wheel.")

A common reason some new dads feel awkward about taking on some of the practical day-to-day care is that they don't remember *their* dad doing these things. You may remember your father being very dedicated to you, but he expressed it by going to work and providing for the family. Certainly, the role of dad as "breadwinner" has been the dominant role model for fatherhood throughout most of the past 50 years. A dad's "success" was often judged by the house, car, material goods, or vacations he provided for his family. But that's changing. Now that most moms work, dads are playing a greater role in the nurturing and care of young children. This isn't just because they have to, but because they want to. Many dads today say they wish their own fathers had been more involved with them. And so they want to provide that involvement to their own children.

Your partner may find day-to-day parenthood less of a challenge in this way. While you're doing things your own father never did, it's likely she's involved with your baby in much the way her own mother was with her.

As if there wasn't enough to tackle, one more fly in the ointment that may be making itself known is the dawning realization that you and your baby's mother have different ideas about how to parent. That's not surprising, partly because you grew up in different families, each with its own habits and approaches. But this is your family—the one you're making together. You'll want to be on the same page, so set aside time to talk about your differences if they're causing tension between you.

By the end of your first half-year of parenthood, your on-the-job

(continued)

parent

new wa

down.

hands

- Show
  worl
  out
  pers
- See
  mon
  the
- Play
  inex
- Talk
  appr
  you'
  ask
  like-
  enjo
  shar
  way
- If yo
  indi
  refer
  exar

Break up the trip by stopping frequently along the way. Pick out parks and rest stops on your route. Bring a bag containing a few of your baby's favorite toys, plus a couple of new ones. Try to end the driving day early so all of you have time to unwind.

To get a feel for what works when you're on the road, lead up to a big trip with some short day trips or weekend getaways. These trial runs can provide key insights about what supplies you should pack, how long your child "lasts" in a car seat, and which toys keep your baby happy (or drive you nuts!).

in the air

Although children under age 2 can usually fly free, the safest place for your baby to sit is in his own car seat, secured with the airplane seat belt. Both the Federal Aviation Administration and the American Academy of Pediatrics recommend buying a separate seat for your child on the plane; when buying tickets, be sure to ask about a discount (typically 50 percent of your ticket price) when reserving an airplane seat for a baby. (Most infant car seats made today are FAA-approved; check the label on the seat or the manufacturer's Web site.)

If you bring a stroller, you can use it to transport the car seat to the gate. Check it at the gate and pick it up when you exit the plane.

Check with your airline about what's acceptable to carry on board. If allowed, bring a supply of water or formula, as well as a bag of snacks if your baby is eating solids. Feed your baby on take-off and landing, if possible, because swallowing will help ease ear pain.

A goody bag is even more important on a plane than on car trips. Take more toys than you think you'll need. Wrap some of them before you leave, and unearth a surprise every once in a while to recapture your baby's interest. Start building your toy cache a few weeks before the trip. Also take some board books for quiet reading time with you.

test yourself) **how are you feeling?**

Tired? Euphoric? Fed up? How are you *really* feeling?

1. Looking back on the last week or two, how would you rate your life?

  a. Hard work but fun; I enjoy looking after our little one, and my baby always makes me laugh.

  b. The lack of sleep is getting to me, but once I do get some shut-eye, life is fine.

  c. It's tough. I can't remember when I last laughed or enjoyed anything.

2. Being a mom means looking after your baby and making decisions about her health. How easy have you found this?

  a. Instinct kicks in and you just know what to do.

  b. Most of the time it's just a case of learning as you go. If you get it wrong this time, you get it right next time.

  c. I haven't a clue what to do most of the time. I end up worrying and panicking.

3. We all feel emotional after we have babies and cry at sad movies and even over items on the news. But sometimes this sadness takes over.

  a. I always take a box of tissues into a good tear-jerker film, but, hey, it's only entertainment!

  b. Sad stories or pictures of sick babies make me want to cry and hug my baby.

  c. I feel like crying most of the time, even though I have no reason to.

4. Sleep is precious when you have a baby. Many new moms never get enough of it. What do you do when you get up in the night?

  a. I'm on automatic. I can just about feed and change my baby, get back into bed, and drop off instantly.

  b. I'm so tired, but I get everything done. I'd sleep most of the day if I could.

  c. When I get up and feed my baby, I just can't get back to sleep. I lie there worrying about the next time I'm going to have to wake up.

5. Thinking back to the birth, how do you feel?

  a. It was really tough, but I'm just so amazed that I could do that—grow a baby and give birth.

  b. At the time I said never again, but now we plan to have another, and I'll know better how to cope.

  c. I can't think back to the birth without having nightmares.

6. How has having a baby changed your relationship?

a. It's made us so much closer. I can't express the love I have for my baby and my partner.

b. It's been rocky. We've both been tired and snippy, but underneath that we're enjoying being parents.

c. It's tough. I can't seem to talk with my partner, and he doesn't want to deal with it when I try.

7. As new parents, how much help did you get?

a. Everyone pitched in. They came to visit, delivered presents, and helped us out in every way they could.

b. Lots of people visited in the first few days, but it's taken me a while to get out and meet other moms.

c. People rushed in to see the new baby, but after that they've disappeared and I rarely get to see anyone now.

8. Are you the sort of mom you thought you'd be?

a. I'm good enough. My baby smiles at me in a way she doesn't at anyone else, except her dad.

b. Not sure I had a clear picture, but I'm muddling through.

c. I thought I'd be really good at it. You know—clean baby gurgling in a pretty nursery. But, in fact, my baby cries a lot, and I never seem to catch up with the cleaning and washing.

ANSWERS

Mostly a's

You seem to be enjoying life. Long may it continue! Get out there and give your support to someone less confident.

Mostly b's

You're doing fine and learning as you go. That's great! Your baby loves you even if you aren't the perfect Mom. You know how to relax and enjoy life with your baby.

Mostly c's

It looks and feels like life is challenging at the moment and you could use some help. You don't have to do it all on your own. Talk to your partner, doctor, a friend, or a relative. There's an African proverb—it takes a village to raise a child—and you can't be a village all by yourself. Life will be much more fun for you and your baby if you get some help and seek out some friends.

when you get there

If your baby is under 6 months, avoid the sun. If he's between
6 months and a year, allow only limited exposure, especially
between 11:00 a.m. and 3:00 p.m. on hot days.

Don't expect your baby to sit still in a stroller and sightsee for long
periods of time. By limiting outings to one activity a day, you'll
find it much easier to make last-minute adjustments if he gets tired
or just wants to spend time splashing in the wading pool.

At a loss about where to travel with your baby? BabyCenter
surveyed readers to collect local information about 50 family-
friendly vacation spots. Find out what other parents recommend
at babycenter.com.

being you again

There comes a time in every mom's life when being a parent seems
all-consuming. You no longer feel like a teacher-nurse-truck driver
or whatever it is you do or did. Sometimes you need to take time
and recharge your batteries. It can be difficult when you have a
baby to care for and little free time or money. But there are ways
to do it, and over the years, BabyCenter parents say they've come
up with the following ways to stay refreshed:

Take a long bubble bath with candles, music, and a good book.
Lock the door and delegate your partner to hold down the fort
while you spend an hour or so on your own. Try to make it a
once-a-week event.

Schedule a massage, manicure, pedicure, facial, or new hairdo.
You'll feel and look better. If your budget is tight, sneak hints for
a birthday or holiday present.

Have a "date" with Dad. This will give you both a break and a
chance to get reacquainted. You may need to call in favors from
friends and relatives to babysit, but you can always offer to help

out with their kids. Agree with Dad that you won't mention babies after the first 30 minutes.

Arrange to see a friend for coffee—without your baby. Adults-only conversation is good for you, though challenging if you haven't thought about much except diapers or sleep problems for weeks. It provides a change of pace, a new perspective, a fresh experience, and reminds you that you're a grown-up, too.

Get out and about with a walk in the fresh air, bike ride, run on the beach, or swim. Almost anything that you can do at a fast and furious pace will make you feel good.

Sleep in. Take turns sleeping late on the weekend to catch up on your sleep debt. Or get someone to do duty for you while you take an afternoon nap.

Go on a shopping spree. A new outfit does wonders for the soul. Like a mini-makeover, it will help you feel renewed.

Brush off the cobwebs on your old hobby and enjoy your hard-won skills. Doing something well is not only rewarding but reminds you that you have other talents in life.

Take time alone to read a book—or just a magazine—all the way through, which is no small feat when you're a mother!

For information about foods that boost your mood and energy levels, go to babycenter.com.

part four

on the
move

7–9 months

7 to 9 months

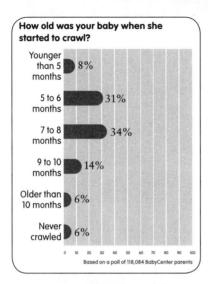

How old was your baby when she started to crawl?

- Younger than 5 months: 8%
- 5 to 6 months: 31%
- 7 to 8 months: 34%
- 9 to 10 months: 14%
- Older than 10 months: 6%
- Never crawled: 6%

Based on a poll of 118,084 BabyCenter parents

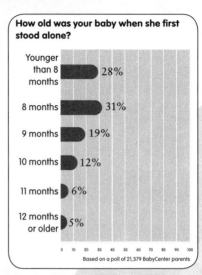

How old was your baby when she first stood alone?

- Younger than 8 months: 28%
- 8 months: 31%
- 9 months: 19%
- 10 months: 12%
- 11 months: 6%
- 12 months or older: 5%

Based on a poll of 21,379 BabyCenter parents

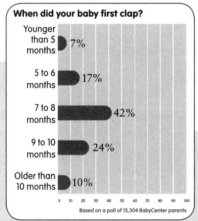

When did your baby first clap?

- Younger than 5 months: 7%
- 5 to 6 months: 17%
- 7 to 8 months: 42%
- 9 to 10 months: 24%
- Older than 10 months: 10%

Based on a poll of 15,304 BabyCenter parents

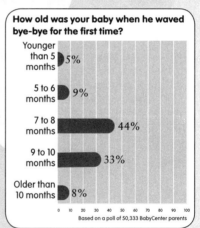

How old was your baby when he waved bye-bye for the first time?

- Younger than 5 months: 5%
- 5 to 6 months: 9%
- 7 to 8 months: 44%
- 9 to 10 months: 33%
- Older than 10 months: 8%

Based on a poll of 50,333 BabyCenter parents

by this time, according to the experts . . .

	most babies can . . .	half of babies can . . .	a few babies can . . .
7 months	• Sit without support • Reach for things with a sweeping motion • Imitate speech sounds (babble)	• Combine syllables into word-like sounds • Crawl or lunge forward	• Stand while holding onto something • Wave good-bye • Bang objects together
8 months	• Say *dada* and *mama* to both parents (isn't specific) • Crawl • Pass object from hand to hand	• Stand while holding onto something • Crawl well • Point at objects	• Pull themselves to standing position, cruise • Pick things up with thumb-finger "pincer" grasp • Indicate wants with gestures
9 months	• Combine syllables into word-like sounds • Stand while holding onto something	• Use pincer grasp to pick up objects • Cruise while holding onto furniture • Say *dada* and *mama* to the right parent (is specific)	• Play patty-cake • Sit and hold toys at the same time • Stand alone

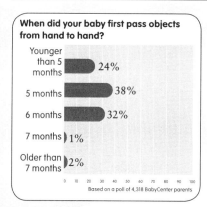

When did your baby first pass objects from hand to hand?

- Younger than 5 months: 24%
- 5 months: 38%
- 6 months: 32%
- 7 months: 1%
- Older than 7 months: 2%

Based on a poll of 4,318 BabyCenter parents

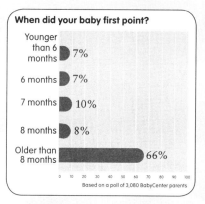

When did your baby first point?

- Younger than 6 months: 7%
- 6 months: 7%
- 7 months: 10%
- 8 months: 8%
- Older than 8 months: 66%

Based on a poll of 3,080 BabyCenter parents

the bottom line

Your baby grows less rapidly now than in previous months, but the excitement of his growing mobility more than makes up for it. Many babies can actively play now and often will amuse themselves for—oh, 5 minutes at a time!

development—
7 to 9 months

Babies follow the sequence of development at their own pace, some quickly and others more slowly. Some babies sit up by themselves at 5 months, and they continue to develop at the same rapid pace, even walking independently before 9 months. Others progress at a slower pace. Try not to get hung up on a specific timetable and focus instead on the order in which development unfolds, so you know what to expect next.

sitting

Between **5 and 7 months**, your baby probably can sit on the floor but not for long, losing his balance and keeling over sideways. So he'll still need support from a pillow or a helping hand. By **6 or 7 months**, some babies figure out that they can keep their balance by leaning forward and putting a hand on the floor; however, they can't see very much from this position and their hands aren't free for playing. By **8 months**, though, your baby will probably be able to sit on the floor and hold toys at the same time—a great achievement! By **9 months**, don't be surprised if your baby can pull himself to a sitting position using the bars of his crib or a handy piece of furniture.

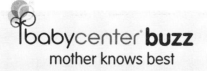

what you can do to encourage your baby

Use pillows to support your baby until he gains the balancing skills required to stay in a steady position. Also, sit on the floor with your baby in front of and facing away from you but supported by you. This is a great position for reading and playing with toys.

crawling

Soon after your baby is able to sit well without support (usually by the time he's 6 or 7 months old), your baby will probably start crawling. At this point, he can hold his head up to look around, and his arm, leg, and back muscles are strong enough to keep him from falling on the floor when he gets up on his hands and knees.

At **7 months**, your baby *wants* to crawl if he hasn't already. You'll see him look at something and then figure out if he can get to it. Even if he can't quite crawl yet, he'll try to reach it—rolling, squirming on his stomach, turning around.

By **8 months**, he'll probably succeed in crawling—backwards. The reason? He's pushing harder with his hands and arms than with his knees and feet. Because he'll become frustrated at actually moving farther away from what he wants than nearer to it, he'll very shortly learn how to move in the right direction.

Once your baby crawls, he'll gradually (over a couple of months) learn to move confidently from a sitting position to being on all fours and soon realize he can rock back and forth when his limbs are straight and his trunk is parallel to the floor.

Sometime around **9 or 10 months**, your baby will figure out that pushing off with his knees gives him just the boost he needs to go mobile. As he gains proficiency, he'll learn to go from a crawling position back into a sitting position. He might also master "cross-crawling"—moving one arm and the opposite leg together when he moves forward, rather than using an arm and a leg from the same side. After that, practice makes perfect.

what you can do to encourage your baby

The best way to encourage crawling—just as with reaching and grabbing—is to place toys and other desirable objects (even yourself) just beyond your baby's reach. If she cries because she can't quite get there, keep giving her relaxed encouragement but not the toy. She is just venting frustration and quickly will become more physically confident if you don't make everything too easy for her. After a few tries, she'll be able to lean forward to grab it and then straighten herself again. And then she'll figure out another way to get it if you place the toy just a bit farther away.

Using pillows, boxes, and sofa cushions, you can create an obstacle course for your crawling baby to negotiate. This will help improve her confidence, speed, and agility. Just don't leave her alone on the assault course.

As your baby starts becoming more active, you can enhance her newfound freedom by dressing her in comfortable clothes. Loose, stretchy, and breathable clothes won't chafe and will provide plenty of room for moving legs; long pants protect the knees better.

standing

When your **7-month-old** stands on your lap, you'll notice him gradually change from jumping with both feet at once to putting his weight first on one foot, then the other. He may even stand on one foot, but he still needs you to hold him, as he can't bear his full weight yet. At about **9 months**, he'll probably put one foot in front of the other and will enjoy these wobbly first steps with you holding him. He's likely to be **10 months** old, however, before he can stand squarely on his own two feet. A few babies try to take their first steps by this age. If he's ready to walk, you'll have to keep a careful eye on him.

what you can do to encourage your baby

Standing won't harm your baby's development if he's doing it of his own accord. In fact, it's difficult to stop him once he's ready.

Worry Meter

Q My baby stands but looks bowlegged. Should I worry?

○ Always
● Probably not
○ Never

Most babies look a bit strange when they first stand alone. It's a complex business getting from all fours onto your feet. Before your baby can stand up straight, he has to learn how to extend his hips and lock his knees. Then he can put his shoulders back and his head up. His legs will be quite chubby at first, and the muscles at the top of his legs need to gradually get stronger so that he can pull his legs straight and make his feet sit flat on the ground. The muscles get stronger as your baby uses them; so it won't be until he begins to walk that his legs appear straighter.

If bowleggedness persists as your baby stands more and more, mention it to your doctor. This is an age when the condition becomes more obvious in kids who truly are bowlegged.

However, it's best not to hurry your baby to independent standing before it's clear he's happy about doing it. The coordination your baby needs for standing also depends on his confidence and motivation. One fall too many can make him fearful of trying again for a while.

hand control

At **7 months**, your baby may still drop the toy she's holding when you offer her another to hold. However, once she can "do" something with an object—bang it, rattle it—she becomes capable of holding a toy in each hand. At **8 months**, though, she still won't use them together. By **9 months**, she probably will. She may bring the two toys close to compare them or bang them together to see if they make a noise. And she can probably let go of a toy by putting it down on a flat surface, but she'll find it difficult to release her grip if you ask her to give something to you.

what you can do to encourage your baby

Before **8 months**, your baby had to learn about an object by handling it himself. From around that age, he'll learn about something if you show him what it can do. You can pull a toy toward you on a string, for example, and then he'll try to do it himself. He'll probably want to do this over and over—just because he can.

The best toys for a baby between 7 and 9 months are those that aren't completely different from something he's already familiar with. It's subtle differences that interest babies of this age, such as blocks or balls of different sizes and colors. Roll a soft ball toward your baby and watch him grab and squeeze it. Roll a harder ball and see how he reacts, or bounce balls of different bounciness on the floor.

Repetition is important at this age. Some games won't work the first time you play them, but if you keep up your efforts, your baby will eventually work out what to expect and enjoy it.

Want to test yourself on how much you know about your baby's development? Take a quiz at babycenter.com.

communicating with you

During these months, your baby learns to imitate and reciprocate behaviors and emotions, which helps to shape his own identity and personality. At **7 months**, your baby discovers ways to let you know how he feels and what he wants. He may put his arms out to be picked up when he's bored, or drop a toy when he's had enough of it—all the while looking to you for a response. When it comes to talking, your baby likes to repeat two-syllable sounds over and over—*ala, ama, lala, looloo*—even when he's alone, as if he's practicing.

By **8 months**, you'll hear more sounds (*mimi, aja*) and he'll start to join them in longer phrases—*la-la-la-la-la*. He'll make short explosive consonant sounds, such as *bbb* or *mmm*, too, and clearly enjoy these new noises. Early in the morning, when he's lying in his bed, you'll hear him babbling away to his toys or just experimenting with making a whole range of sounds from squeaks and cries to real shouts. He'll also start to copy some of the sounds you make, such as kissing noises. Blow a raspberry on his tummy, and he'll make wet blowing sounds as he tries to copy you. Click your tongue at him, and he'll try copying the noise. He'll also make a real effort to copy your actions, such as waving bye-bye or making a funny face. He's saying, "I'm like you!"

By **9 months**, when your baby is playing with his toys, you'll hear a very complex babble, with rising and falling tones. It sounds just like real talk, although there are no recognizable words in it. But the real words aren't far behind. Your baby doesn't want to talk strictly to himself, though. He'll listen when you talk and try to join in conversation. He'll even interrupt you with a shout. Babies understand many words before they try to say them. He'll lift up his arms when you ask him if he wants to get down from the highchair, for instance, and he'll use actions to tell you what he wants—reaching for a cup that's just out of reach and making urgent *uh-uh-uh* sounds to show you that he wants it.

what you can do to encourage your baby

As always, the best way of helping your baby learn to communicate is by communicating with her. When she talks, talk back. If she babbles a recognizable syllable, babble it right back at her and make a game of it ("The sheep says, *baaa*" or "The goat says, *maaa*").

Looking at books together will improve your baby's language skills and help her develop a lifelong love of reading. Board books are colorful and hard-wearing, useful because many babies see chewing as an essential part of the reading experience at this age. Books that have pop-up pictures or textured illustrations delight babies this age (but try not to let her grab the pop-ups). So do picture books that encourage you to make lots of animal noises. Few babies won't be amused by you imitating a dog, then a cat, then a horse.

Your baby won't have the hand control to open a book or turn pages until she's between about 9 and 12 months, nor will she have the patience to sit still while you read her a story, but don't give up. No matter what your child's age, reading provides a great opportunity for cuddling and spending time together.

Worry Meter

Q My baby understands us but makes no attempt to talk. Should I worry?

○ Always
○ Sometimes
● Hardly ever

Babies understand and make sense of the world for some weeks and months before they begin speaking. Understanding that sounds represent specific things and actions is the first step. Getting his mouth, tongue, and lips around words is actually very difficult. The first words come very slowly. By around a year, most babies can say 3 to 5 words. By 18 months, it's closer to 20, and by his second birthday he's likely to have well over 200 words in his vocabulary. Keep on talking and listening to your baby, and the words will come when he is ready. More than a few great scientists and philosophers were extremely late talkers, so if that's the case with your baby, perhaps it portends a brilliant future!

To introduce your baby to different sounds, show her some musical toys. Don't be surprised if she starts to sing in response. Give her objects that make interesting sounds, too, such as hollow containers, metal measuring spoons, and bells.

5 things that help your baby talk

1. Keep your sentences short and simple.

2. Talk about what you're doing and what you see.

3. Repeat things: "Let's get your teddy, okay? You love it when teddy comes, too."

4. Read board books to your baby. He'll begin to gain familiarity with the rhythm of the sentences.

5. Sing songs and nursery rhymes to him.

5 things that hinder

1. Background noise—turn the television or radio off.

2. Using complex language all the time. Simple language works well for babies.

3. Talking over his head (literally). Bend down and talk to him.

4. Not talking to him. He needs to hear you and interact with you. Even if you feel silly, he'll love it when you make the effort to talk with him.

5. Using a pacifier after the first year. This is a good reason to start weaning your baby from the paci now, if he still uses one.

understanding the world

Your **7-month-old** begins to anticipate things. She now knows that running water means a bath, and kicks and shouts enthusiastically at the prospect. Likewise, some things don't appeal to her. She moves her head back and away when you approach with a spoonful of medicine or a tissue to wipe her nose.

She's gaining a lot more physical control and, when she's bouncing up and down on your lap, treats your body as if it's an extension of her own—clambering up you, holding onto your hair, poking your eye, grabbing your ear. But hand her off to a less familiar person, say, Grandma or a friend, and at first she'll sit still on the person's lap, eyeing her carefully. If your baby is shy, don't be surprised if she starts to cry, especially if she's feeling tired or sick, and wants to go back to your familiar arms. If your baby is more extroverted, she may decide, after a while, that this person is acceptable to play with and start to interact.

Around now, your baby becomes interested in other children. She kicks and wriggles with excitement if you're out and about and she sees and hears other children playing. (She'll get just as excited if you go to the park to feed the ducks.)

If you're with other moms and babies, your baby will look at the other children sitting on their moms' laps and reach out to them, or copy them. If the other baby is bouncing up and down, your baby joins in, or starts to make similar sounds, so you end up with a baby-shouting contest. Your baby cries if another baby cries or laughs in response to another baby's laugh, and she's easily entertained by a slightly older child who talks to her and makes silly faces. Sit two babies side by side, and they'll touch and examine each other quietly, until one happens to pull the other's hair, of course.

Separation anxiety often sets in around **9 months**. Your baby now knows which are "her" people and which are strangers. She feels safe and secure with just a few key people and objects to others, even when held safely in your arms. She actively clings to you when you try to leave her with someone else, and you're the only one who can comfort her when she's hurt or upset. (Read more about separation anxiety on page 313.)

At this age, your baby also learns about emotions. She reacts to signs of disapproval from you and even bursts into tears if you shout or scowl or use a warning tone. She understands when you say no and relates it to her own behavior. Sometimes, you can almost see her thought processes as she reaches for something, you say *no*, and she reaches out again while watching your face. She's no longer simply observing the world; now she realizes that she can change it, too. And she's learning that her behaviors, both the ones you like and the ones you don't, draw your attention. From now on, and for years to come, she'll do just about *anything* to get your attention.

Because your baby now has a clearer idea of what she wants and doesn't want, she gets angry and frustrated when she can't have it. She turns her face away when she doesn't want to eat, arches her back when she doesn't want to go in her car seat, or cries when you put her in her stroller because she wants to stay right where she is.

Your secret weapon right now is that your baby is easily distracted. You can often anticipate her reaction and nip it in the bud. For example, if the car seat is often a source of disagreement, put a toy she hasn't seen for a while in the seat before carrying her out to the car. With luck, as soon as she starts to complain, she'll spot the toy

lefty or righty?

Your baby will use one hand then switch to the other, but you won't be able to tell whether she's right-handed or left-handed until she's about 2 or 3 years old. A little more than one-third of identical twins are left-handed, double the rate in the general population.

Q There's nothing I can put my finger on, but my baby just doesn't seem right. Should I worry?

○ Yes
○ Sometimes
○ Never

If your instincts are telling you your baby is sick or that there's something wrong, listen to them. It may be nothing, but your baby could be developing an illness or problem. Visit your baby's doctor. Doctors are used to parents worrying about their babies, but they also know that parental instinct is often right.

and be curious enough to play with it while you buckle her into the seat. If she doesn't want food offered on a spoon, place a few interesting bits of food on her highchair tray and let her look at them, pick them up, explore them—and maybe even eat them. If she wants to stay and play and you need to put her in her stroller and go home, turn the stroller ride into a game. Add colorful ribbons to the side of the stroller or a noisy toy that she can play with as you walk, or just give her a high-speed stroller ride with the wind blowing in her face. The quicker you find something new to distract her, the more likely she is to stop protesting.

As your baby gets older, she's more apt to get into mischief just to provoke a reaction from you. But give her positive feedback when she's being good, too, because she'll love that.

now you see it . . .

As far as your newborn was concerned, when an object disappeared from his field of vision, it fell off the edge of the earth. It simply didn't exist anymore.

Between 7 and 9 months, your baby begins to get the idea of "object permanence." He realizes that just because he can't see something anymore, it doesn't stop existing. That's why games such as peekaboo are such a favorite. It's as if your baby has to convince himself that things really do come back. That's why he'll smile every time you come out from behind those hands. Yes, you still exist!

Here's a game your baby doesn't easily tire of, and offers plenty of room for variation:

- Hold up a towel between your face and your baby's and let it drop, or move it from side to side.
- Hide behind a door so your baby has to push it open to see you.
- Hide behind a chair and pop out first from above then from the sides.
- Get behind a towel with another person and alternate who jumps out and says "Boo!"
- Keep a selection of hats behind the towel and pop up wearing a different one each time. Put a hat on your head and covering your eyes; let your baby take it off, saying "Oh!" in surprise each time he does it.
- Hide objects under blankets for your baby to discover.

by the numbers
feeding: 7 to 9 months

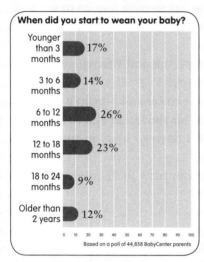

When did you start to wean your baby?

- Younger than 3 months: 17%
- 3 to 6 months: 14%
- 6 to 12 months: 26%
- 12 to 18 months: 23%
- 18 to 24 months: 9%
- Older than 2 years: 12%

Based on a poll of 44,858 BabyCenter parents

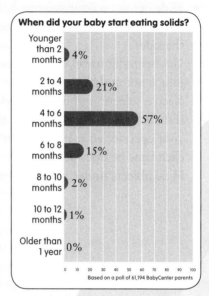

When did your baby start eating solids?

- Younger than 2 months: 4%
- 2 to 4 months: 21%
- 4 to 6 months: 57%
- 6 to 8 months: 15%
- 8 to 10 months: 2%
- 10 to 12 months: 1%
- Older than 1 year: 0%

Based on a poll of 61,194 BabyCenter parents

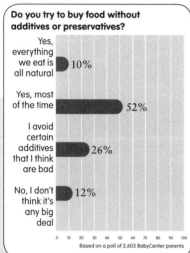

Do you try to buy food without additives or preservatives?

- Yes, everything we eat is all natural: 10%
- Yes, most of the time: 52%
- I avoid certain additives that I think are bad: 26%
- No, I don't think it's any big deal: 12%

Based on a poll of 2,603 BabyCenter parents

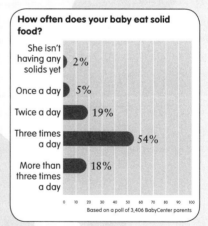

How often does your baby eat solid food?

- She isn't having any solids yet: 2%
- Once a day: 5%
- Twice a day: 19%
- Three times a day: 54%
- More than three times a day: 18%

Based on a poll of 3,406 BabyCenter parents

When did your baby first sit in a high-chair and join you for family meals?

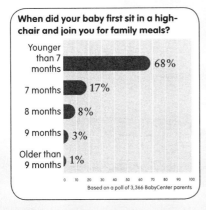

Younger than 7 months 68%
7 months 17%
8 months 8%
9 months 3%
Older than 9 months 1%

Based on a poll of 3,366 BabyCenter parents

When did your baby first eat finger food?

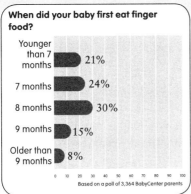

Younger than 7 months 21%
7 months 24%
8 months 30%
9 months 15%
Older than 9 months 8%

Based on a poll of 3,364 BabyCenter parents

Do you buy organic produce for your family?

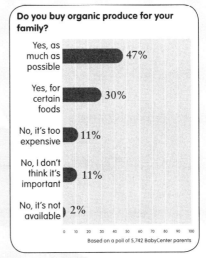

Yes, as much as possible 47%
Yes, for certain foods 30%
No, it's too expensive 11%
No, I don't think it's important 11%
No, it's not available 2%

Based on a poll of 5,742 BabyCenter parents

Do you let your baby drink juice?

Yes 51%
No 48%

Based on a poll of 4,053 BabyCenter parents

Does your baby have a food intolerance?

Yes 15%
No 84%

Based on a poll of 3,347 BabyCenter parents

the bottom line

Breast milk or formula is still very important for your baby. It provides a nutritional safety net, but other foods will gradually make up a growing part of what he eats every day. Your child's expanding diet is a good opportunity to think about how your whole family eats and to make healthy eating a priority for everyone.

feeding—
7 to 9 months

Get ready for an exciting—and delightfully messy—new episode in feeding, as your baby moves more and more into eating solids and feeding himself. Try to stay patient as you watch equal amounts of your baby's food end up in his mouth and on the floor.

feeding checkpoint:
how much breast milk or formula?

if you're breastfeeding

As solid foods become more important, your baby will drop nursing sessions during the 7-to-9-month period. Often he'll sleep longer after the going-to-bed feeding and possibly even sleep through to an early morning feeding. If you nurse after a feeding of solid food, your baby will take much less milk than he used to and will gradually drop breastfeeding around the main daytime meal. Try offering your baby other drinks, such as water or well-diluted juice with the meal instead of breastfeeding, though it's still too early to begin offering cow's milk. At **7 months** he'll nurse four or five times a day, and often by **9 months** this declines to just a morning and evening feeding.

babycenter buzz
something to chew on

"I feed my baby table foods if they're mushy enough, but it's mostly just for the taste. He doesn't eat enough to get much sustenance from it. He still prefers baby food."—**Jessy**

"We give our 8-month-old a bagel, which he loves to chew on, and in between bites, we dip it into whatever mushy food we want him to eat! He won't take the same food from a spoon but will gladly slurp it off the bagel."—**Audrey**

"I introduced solids to my daughter at 6 months. She loved it at first, but now, at 8 months, she refuses to eat from a spoon. However, she loves table food and has no problem grabbing it and feeding herself. So, I pretty much gave up on spoon-feeding and offer her little chunks of tofu, banana, Cheerios, and so on. And we're starting to experiment with more veggies and fruits."—**Anonymous**

By dropping feedings gradually, you'll minimize any discomfort and fullness in your breasts. Once your baby decides to drop a feeding, it's likely that he's already been taking less and less milk at these times anyway. Although your breasts are still a little heavy and full, it should take only a couple of days for your body to adjust.

if you're formula-feeding

Once your baby is established on solids, he should be having approximately 17 to 20 ounces, or 1 pint, of formula per day. As long as he's eating a wide range of solid foods, this diet is fine until he's a year old. After the age of 1, he's ready to move from drinking formula to regular, full-fat cow's milk.

"Follow-up" formulas have higher calcium, protein, and mineral content than ordinary formula. They're suitable for babies older than 6 months, although you don't need to make the switch. Most

babies' increasing nutritional needs can be met with standard
formula and solid foods that contain calcium and iron. Follow-up
formulas are sometimes recommended for babies at risk for
allergies or who have slow-growth histories.

introducing solids

Your baby's tastes are expanding, and he's ready to pick up the pace
on solids. Variety is about to become the spice of life. (For a refresher
on introducing solids, see stages 1 and 2 beginning on page 227.)

stage 3: a wide variety

You're just about ready for family sit-down dinners, as your baby's
ability to join grown-up meals increases enormously between 7 and
9 months. When you offer a wide range of foods, he'll get the
nutrition he needs, while becoming familiar with different flavors
(which might help to avoid picky eating later on). Your baby's also
learning about texture, color, and smell, which is another good
reason to offer a variety of foods. Try starting with mashed or
minced food, rather than purées, to encourage him to learn to
chew and manage small pieces of food, even if he doesn't have any
teeth yet.

Now's a good time to introduce:

- A wider range of starchy food, such as bread, couscous, pasta,
  zwieback or teething crackers made for babies, breakfast
  cereals, oats, potatoes, rice, quinoa, and barley
- Well-cooked egg yolks (but delay until age 2 if you have a
  family history of allergies)
- Fish; lean red meat, such as beef, lamb, and pork; and other
  protein-rich foods, such as chicken and lentils (but delay fish
  until age 3 if you have a family history of allergies)
- Dairy products: cottage cheese, yogurt, and cheese. Although
  you should wait until 1 year to introduce cow's milk as a drink,

you can use it in your baby's breakfast cereal, or in cooking (for example, if you make a cheese sauce to add to vegetables or pasta). Fat is an important source of energy for your baby, so full-fat dairy products are better for him than fat-free and low-fat milk or reduced-fat cheeses.

- Nut butters. They're fine for babies who don't have a family history of allergies (if you do, delay all nuts until age 3). Use unsalted smooth versions, and spread them very thinly to avoid a choking hazard.

Aim for one daily portion of protein-rich food and two to three portions of starchy foods. Offer a wide variety of choices, either jarred baby foods or mashed-up family food, to get your baby used to eating what you eat.

If you've decided not to give your baby meat or fish, he'll need two servings a day of tofu or legumes (such as lentils, beans, or chickpeas). This helps him get all the energy and nutrients he needs.

Avoid foods that carry a risk of food poisoning, such as liver pâté, any raw or undercooked meat, and soft-boiled eggs.

Skip the cookies and cakes, which will fill up your baby without providing the right nutrients. They can also encourage a sweet tooth. Teething biscuits are a better alternative.

Between 7 and 9 months of age, the stores of iron that your baby is born with begin to decrease. This is a good time to introduce foods that are particularly rich in iron, including:

- Beef, turkey, and the dark meat of chicken
- Beans and lentils
- Breakfast cereals, which are often fortified with iron, and the "baby" version almost certainly will be
- Vegetables such as broccoli, cauliflower, and spinach

Serve these iron-rich foods in the company of foods rich in vitamin C (such as fruits or well-diluted fruit juices), as the vitamin C helps your baby absorb the iron.

learning to self-feed

Don't push your baby to eat. Most babies know when they've had enough. If you spend a lot of time persuading your baby to take food, she'll soon learn that refusing food is a great way of getting your attention. If she really doesn't want any more food, just stop and wait until next time. Once your baby begins to crawl, her appetite will probably grow and you'll gradually need to increase the amount of food you offer.

From about 9 months, your baby knows how to grab a spoon, and how to use it. Encourage her to help with the feeding by giving her a spoon to hold while you feed her most of the meal with another spoon. It will be messy at first, but it's all for a good cause.

If you're introducing solid foods to twins or multiples, you have several choices to make. Many moms sit their babies side by side and feed them at the same time, using one spoon and bowl (except when one of the babies is sick) for convenience and speed. Some moms prefer alternating spoonfuls, while others like to feed the hungriest baby first (with the other ready to go in the highchair, but occupied with toys) before starting with the next one. Don't expect that your babies will always like the same foods; as they get

food safety

To avoid the risk of choking, never leave your baby unattended when he's eating solid food. Always dice round fruits such as grapes or blueberries. Beware of anything hard that your baby can bite a bit off and choke on. New teeth are sharp and can easily grate off small chunks of food.

Grate raw fruits such as apples and vegetables (like carrots) at first. Serve only the insides of hard-crusted breads or bagels. Avoid altogether popcorn, raisins, dates, marshmallows, jelly beans, and tree nuts and peanuts, including nut pieces.

Worry Meter

Q **My baby just doesn't seem interested in any solid foods. Should I worry?**

○ Always
○ Sometimes
● Hardly ever

Most babies will try solid foods when they're ready, and that's usually around the 6-month mark. Some babies won't bother until they can pick up the food themselves, around 8 to 9 months. Keep offering a variety of foods at different times of day. Even if your baby doesn't go for solids, as long as she's getting breast milk or formula, she'll be fine.

older, you'll probably have to abandon the "one bowl" approach because one baby likes spinach and the other cauliflower.

finger fun

Finger foods are great once your baby can hold things. They allow her some control over the food she eats, too, which she'll enjoy. Try putting four or five pieces of finger food onto your baby's highchair tray or an unbreakable plate and let her choose.

Here are some popular finger food choices:

• Steamed or cooked (and cooled) carrots, green beans, peas, zucchini, potato, or sweet potato
• Thin cheese strips or string cheese
• Small cubes of tofu
• Toast, bread, breadsticks, pita bread, mini rice cakes, or chapatti
• Well-cooked pasta spiral shapes
• Peeled grated apple, slices of ripe banana or soft pear, or other soft fruits such as mango, plum, peach, cantaloupe, or seedless watermelon, as well as cut-up seedless grapes, pitted cherries, and blueberries

second tastes

Babies seem programmed to need to try new tastes several times before they accept them. This may have been a protective mechanism in primitive times to prevent children from eating poisonous berries and fruits. So if your baby spits out a new food, don't fault your own culinary skills. She's doing it because the food is

babycenter buzz
thriving on veggies

"My son is a year old, and he's a fifth-generation vegetarian, and we have never had any health problems in our family. You have to make sure you're eating a variety of foods to get all the nutrients you need, plus plenty of beans, tofu, and vegetable protein to make sure you're getting enough protein."—**Anonymous**

"I've been a vegetarian for 12 years and am raising my 9-month-old daughter as one. Unfortunately, people wait until they become sick to start eating a more healthy diet, but if you start your child out early, you give her a wonderful head start in life."—**Barbara**

new to her. Keep on offering the new food alongside more familiar ones. It may take 5, 10, or even 20 exposures before she becomes a convert.

baby drinks

An ideal drink for babies this age is water from a cup with a soft spout. This is in addition to her daily breast milk or formula (or follow-up formula). You no longer need to boil water unless you use well water; straight from the tap is fine.

Fruit juices are a good source of vitamin C now, although a baby doesn't "need" juice at all. (Real fruit serves up vitamin C, too.) Some pediatricians say to hold off on OJ until after 9 to 12 months if your baby has a family history of allergies. One problem with giving your baby juice is that it will reduce the amount of breast milk or formula she drinks, and she still needs milk for nutrition. Fruit juice also contains sugars, which are present naturally, and these can cause tooth decay and set a child up for later obesity, if routinely drunk in excess. Fruit juice is acidic as well. If you choose to give your baby fruit juice, limit it to mealtimes only, and never before bedtime. Dilute one part 100 percent pasteurized juice to 10 parts water, and serve it in a cup, rather than a bottle.

Keeping juice to mealtimes helps your baby absorb iron without increasing the risk of damage to her emerging teeth. The American Academy of Pediatrics (AAP) recommends no more than 4 to 6 ounces of fruit juice per day for children 6 months to 6 years of age.

Never give soda or diet drinks to your baby. Artificial sweeteners aren't suitable for young children. Other no-no's: coffee and tea (hot or iced).

introducing a cup

From about 7 months of age, the sucking action at the breast or bottle isn't as necessary to your baby as it was when she was younger. She can take most of her milk and other drinks from a cup with a soft spout. If you wean your baby from the breast when she's 6 months old or more, you may be able to bypass bottles completely. Some babies, however, still prefer to have a bottle or be nursed at night for comfort.

If you start with a spill-proof ("sippy") cup, you can change over time to a hard spout and then an open lidded cup with handles. Most babies make the transition easily. If you're returning to work, it's wise to introduce the cup beforehand to allow your baby at least a couple of weeks to get used to the idea.

To find out more sippy cup do's and don'ts, visit babycenter.com.

weaning

Weaning is the process by which you gradually stop breastfeeding your baby. It often begins at the same time as you introduce solid foods (see page 225). As your baby takes more solids, he depends less on you for all his nutrition.

That's not to say that as soon as your baby takes that first spoon of baby rice, you should stop breastfeeding. It often takes 6 months or more from fully breastfeeding your baby to not breastfeeding at

babycenter **buzz**
when it's time to wean

"The key thing with weaning is to feel comfortable about when you do it and not to let outsiders tell you it's too early or too late. If nursing is becoming a hassle for both of you, or if you work and are spending more time pumping than with your baby, then you may decide it's time to wean."—**Anonymous**

"I feel like I'm being forced to wean my 4-month-old son because I went back to work. My job allows me only 20 minutes in an 8-hour shift to pump, and this has drastically cut my milk supply."—**Alison**

"I was so sad to stop nursing. I miss those long leisurely times together."
—**Anonymous**

"I was relieved: Weeks of struggling with breastfeeding were over and my baby was more settled. But I also felt really guilty at not breastfeeding, and that's hard to deal with."—**Emma**

all. Many mom-and-baby pairs choose to nurse once a day well into the second year (and the AAP recommends nursing for the first full year). It's good to take weaning slowly. You can do it quickly, in a single weekend away from your baby, for example, but that can be an uncomfortable way to end the breastfeeding relationship. It can leave your breasts engorged or give you mastitis, a breast infection, and can be traumatic for your baby if he's not used to the bottle or a cup.

Weaning can happen gradually and naturally as your baby gets more mobile and becomes more interested in the world away from you. The AAP recommends breastfeeding exclusively for the first 6 months, then gradually introducing solid foods while continuing to breastfeed for at least 6 more months (to age 1) and after that for as long as you and your baby both want to. The World Health Organization recommends breastfeeding for at least 2 years. The longer you can breastfeed, the greater the benefits.

Some moms find weaning to be a sad time and miss the special closeness that breastfeeding provided, which is more apt to be the case when you don't feel quite ready but your baby is, or circumstances dictate the need. Other women find relief in no longer being tethered to their babies (or a pump). In some circles, moms feel pressure to keep breastfeeding into toddlerhood, while earlier weaning is often the norm in others. It takes a little courage to buck others' expectations and do what feels right for you and your baby.

cutting back on feedings

For a first step, offer your baby solids and drinks instead of nursing. By reducing feedings one at a time over a period of weeks, your baby will have time to adjust to the changes. Your milk supply also gradually diminishes.

In addition, cut the length of time your baby is actually on the breast. If he usually breastfeeds for 10 minutes, try limiting the time to 7 minutes. Once you've introduced solids, follow the feeding with solid food or a cup of breast milk or formula (though babies younger than 6 months may not be ready for solids.) Bedtime feedings are usually the last to go.

by the numbers
sleep: 7 to 9 months

What time does your baby go to bed in the evening?

- Before 6:00 p.m. 0%
- 6:00 p.m. 1%
- 7:00 p.m. 18%
- 8:00 p.m. 38%
- 9:00 p.m. 29%
- 10:00 p.m. or later 11%

Based on a poll of 4,278 BabyCenter parents

How many naps a day does your baby take?

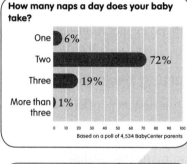

- One 6%
- Two 72%
- Three 19%
- More than three 1%

Based on a poll of 4,534 BabyCenter parents

Where does your baby sleep?

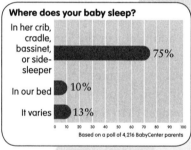

- In her crib, cradle, bassinet, or side-sleeper 75%
- In our bed 10%
- It varies 13%

Based on a poll of 4,216 BabyCenter parents

Do you think your baby has dreams?

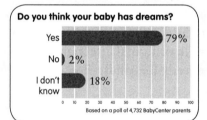

- Yes 79%
- No 2%
- I don't know 18%

Based on a poll of 4,732 BabyCenter parents

Have you tried sleep training?

Yes	35%
No	64%

Based on a poll of 4,232 BabyCenter parents

Does your baby have a favorite bedtime book?

Yes	17%
No	82%

Based on a poll of 3,498 BabyCenter parents

Does your baby have a bedtime routine?

Yes	88%
No	11%

Based on a poll of 3,104 BabyCenter parents

the bottom line

By the time your baby is 9 months old, he'll probably need around 11 hours of sleep at night, and an additional 3 hours during the day, probably divided into two naps—one in the morning and one in the afternoon. But there is also a lot of variability in sleep needs at this age.

sleep—
7 to 9 months

Right about the time you think you have your nighttime routines down pat—and both you and your baby are enjoying longer periods of uninterrupted sleep—is when something causes your baby's sleep patterns to fall out of whack. Fortunately, such inconveniences are often short-lived, and when they occur, there are effective techniques for dealing with them.

sleep problems

At some stage, almost every parent has what they perceive to be "a problem" with their child's sleeping pattern. Sleep problems are predominantly a concern of Western culture. Many other cultures don't expect babies to sleep on their own and, as a result, report few sleep difficulties. But the fact remains that if you have a baby who doesn't sleep well, life is tough.

Remember that your baby is a much smaller person than you are, with a great deal still to learn in life. He isn't deliberately choosing to be awake at a time that isn't convenient to you, and he isn't "misbehaving" by waking in the night and thinking it's a perfect time for play.

babycenter buzz
how older babies sleep

"My son is 7 months old, and I let him lie in bed with me until he gets sleepy. Then I lay him in his crib and rub his back and talk softly to him until he falls asleep. It works for us. We just go to bed earlier so we don't have to stay up late getting him to sleep."—**Hazel**

"I've rocked my 7-month-old to sleep since he was born. It's my time of the day to cuddle with him and be alone with him. Recently, he decided that he just wants to fall asleep on his own in his bed."—**Anonymous**

The key to any sleep problem is to remember that sleeping is a behavior we *learn* how to do. Through your bedtime routine and the procedure you follow when your baby wakes in the night, he learns the steps by which he can fall asleep or return to sleep at different times in the night. If your baby relies on you in any way to fall sleep—being breastfed, rocked, sung to, or walked around the bedroom—then this can become a sleep association that he'll always demand, as that's how he's learned how to fall asleep.

You can solve sleep problems by introducing your baby to new routines and associations.

settling your baby to sleep

Look for what some experts describe as "sleep windows." Just as active sleep is followed by quiet sleep, so your baby has active and drowsy cycles during the day as well. (If you've ever noticed your energy flag at 2:00 or 3:00 p.m., you can see how these circadian rhythms work in grown-ups, too.) By watching for signs that your baby is tired and putting her to bed then, it will be easier for her to fall asleep. Go through your baby's usual bedtime routine while she's still in an active cycle, and she'll probably move into a drowsy phase by the end of it and be happy to doze off.

early waking

Many parents say that their babies wake up too early. But the real question is: Does your baby wake without getting enough sleep, or does she get enough sleep but wake up too early for your liking?

To decide whether your baby is waking up before getting enough sleep, look at her behavior during the day. Does she seem sleepy? Does she take a nap an hour or two after her early morning awakening? Did she sleep for about 10 hours that night?

If your baby wakes up before getting a full night's sleep, check to see whether something's waking her, and then see if it's fixable. For example, if sunlight streams in her window at 5:00 a.m., fit her windows with blackout lining curtains to keep the room dark.

If your baby wakes early in the morning and you think she needs more rest, make sure she knows how to settle herself back to sleep. A baby who's grown accustomed to your presence to fall asleep at bedtime may need your assistance in the morning, too. To teach your baby how to settle herself to sleep, see page 241.

A baby who gets up raring to go at 5:30 or 6:00 a.m. may be doing so because she's going to bed at 7:00 or 7:30 p.m. Remember, your baby can sleep only for a certain number of hours. If an early wakeup isn't working for you, consider a later bedtime for your baby.

nighttime waking

Babies continue to wake at night, but most learn to turn over and go back to sleep quietly. However, periodically your baby will wake at night (and wake you) even if she's previously been sleeping all the way through—even if you have a really good, consistent bedtime routine in place. It becomes a problem when the occasional middle-of-the-night wakeup becomes a pattern. Chronic sleep disturbance adversely affects your baby, you, your parenting, and the whole family.

From 7 months, night feedings become less necessary. Most babies start sleeping between the hours of midnight and 5:00 in the morning around this period, if they haven't already. If your baby wakes and can't get back to sleep without you breastfeeding her, she hasn't yet learned to fall asleep unaided.

Trying suddenly to change her sleeping and feeding patterns in the middle of the night can be upsetting. A gentler approach: Begin to reprogram her during the day. Put her down for her daytime naps just *before* she drops off while nursing. To do this, slide the tip of your little finger gently between her gums to loosen her sucking, and put her right into her bed. This helps her get used to the idea of falling asleep independently.

comfort objects

Many babies develop a fondness for a particular blanket, stuffed toy, or pacifier around 6 months or later. Give your baby something she can have nearby while falling asleep to comfort and reassure her if she wakes in the night. Always start nursing her while she's holding the same blanket, for example. But think twice before offering a pacifier as a way of soothing your baby to sleep; when she finds it missing in her crib in the middle of the night, your baby will let you know it.

Never put your baby to bed with a bottle. A propped bottle is a choking risk. Giving a bottle, even filled with water, raises the likelihood it will become her comfort object of choice. This is a bad habit as, later on, she'll want it filled with milk or juice, and you'll want to stop giving her a bottle around 12 months anyway (whereas a "blankie" can be carried for years). Also, dozing off with a bottle of formula in the bed sets your baby up for tooth decay, called "baby bottle mouth."

by the numbers
baby care: 7 to 9 months

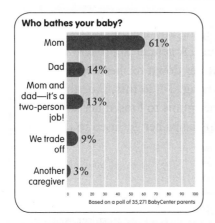

Who bathes your baby?

Mom — 61%
Dad — 14%
Mom and dad—it's a two-person job! — 13%
We trade off — 9%
Another caregiver — 3%

Based on a poll of 35,271 BabyCenter parents

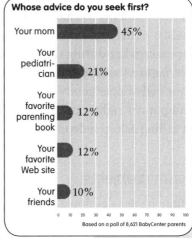

Whose advice do you seek first?

Your mom — 45%
Your pediatrician — 21%
Your favorite parenting book — 12%
Your favorite Web site — 12%
Your friends — 10%

Based on a poll of 8,621 BabyCenter parents

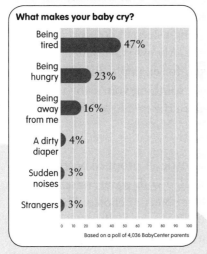

What makes your baby cry?

Being tired — 47%
Being hungry — 23%
Being away from me — 16%
A dirty diaper — 4%
Sudden noises — 3%
Strangers — 3%

Based on a poll of 4,036 BabyCenter parents

Does your baby have a routine?

Yes 85%
No 14%

Based on a poll of 4,319 BabyCenter parents

Does your baby have separation anxiety?

Yes 50%
No 50%

Based on a poll of 4,526 BabyCenter parents

the bottom line

Once your baby is mobile, keeping him safe becomes a priority. Some babies always manage to find (and chew on) the piece of apple that fell under the chair a month ago, or attempt to munch on the potting soil surrounding your favorite houseplant. This leads to another discovery: Crawling babies can get pretty dirty! Many families find, at this point, that it helps to include a bath as part of their baby's daily bedtime routine.

baby care—
7 to 9 months

Active babies demand alert parents—to keep them entertained,
comfortable, and safe. Vigilance during this period will help
ensure your baby's continued happy, healthy development.

managing your baby's day

Your baby is now old enough to know night from day and to
anticipate events, so you can introduce a daily routine if you want
to, and it's a good way to maintain your sanity! Some parents
believe that living their lives by the clock is the only way to bring
up young children. They map feeding, sleeping, baths, and playtime into a timetable—so their baby knows what to expect all day
long. Although this works for some families, others like to react to
their baby's needs on a day-to-day or hour-to-hour basis.

Around **7 months,** your baby is probably ready to move from three
daytime naps to two. You can help him by gradually moving his
day around. If he has one morning nap and two afternoon naps,
you can move his morning nap back a little, say 10 minutes each
day for a week, so that he has one good nap in the middle of the
day and then manages with only one afternoon nap. Or you can

babycenter buzz
revising your baby's schedule

"By keeping track of what time your baby does things, you'll probably find that your baby is on *a* schedule, just not on *your* schedule. The dilemma many of us face when raising our infants is trying to fit them into our schedules."—**Marissa**

"My baby has slept through the night since I went back to work from maternity leave, at about 8 weeks. She started rolling over at 3 months, she crawls, stands, attempts to walk, and just turned 7 months. But she doesn't have a single tooth in her head! You win some, you lose some!"—**Amanda**

plan a walk in the fresh air just after lunch to help your baby stay awake a bit longer. A 20-minute trip to the park will give him plenty of stimulation and tire him out.

explained: separation anxiety

A baby's sense of self takes years to develop. At first, she thinks the two of you are one and the same. As you've probably discovered, by **3 months** most (and by 5 months all) babies clearly recognize and prefer you to a stranger. By about **4 months**, your baby began to behave differently with you than with someone else. She saved her best smiles for you, treated your body as if it were her own, and was confident with you and more restrained with strangers.

Then at around **6 months,** she started to realize that she's separate from you. To her, this also means that you could leave her alone, which leads to a fear of abandonment known as separation anxiety. From around this age, you're the only one who can comfort your baby and, once she's mobile, she'll follow you everywhere.

For babies who are used to other caregivers, the problem is more likely to be a minor one, but if your baby is used to you looking

babycenter **buzz**
when separation anxiety kicks in

"My baby boy just turned 9 months today. He wants only me to hold him and nobody else, and it's really hard when you want to get things done. What I do is put him in his room with toys that he absolutely loves to play with and facing the opposite direction from the door; then I run out of the room. That pretty much keeps him occupied until he crawls into the other room to find me."—**Anonymous**

"One of my twins screams whenever I'm out of sight, and even if she stops for a moment, when I come back and she hears me, she cries again. I feel like I'm constantly picking her up, and I feel badly for my other twin."
—**Sarah**

"I can't stand for people (usually just family does this) to not let my daughter come to me when she's reaching out for me or crying for me. They say 'She has you all the time' or 'She sees you all the time.' I just want to grab my baby, but you can't do that with family."—**Anonymous**

after her all the time, she'll become upset when you leave her. Separation anxiety usually peaks at **9 months**. Your baby's reluctance to be separated from you can be both a delight and a source of frustration at times. In either case, it might help to load a basket with her toys and move it—and her—from room to room so you can get the housework done while enjoying each other's company. Luckily, at this age, your baby also gets better at self-comforting. Does she have a toy or blankie that goes everywhere with her? At **9 months**, such an object offers comfort in unfamiliar places. By around **11 or 12 months**, she's happy to have a comfort object nearby and grabs it only when she needs it; for instance, when she's tired or with strangers.

Separation anxiety often lasts well into a baby's second year. But once your baby becomes more social and more confident that you will, in fact, come back for her when you leave her at daycare or with a babysitter, she'll be able to move forward and forge her own identity. By the toddler years, her budding independence will give you something to occasionally worry about!

Stranger anxiety is related to separation anxiety, and it usually begins by **8 to 10 months** and peaks at **12 to 15 months**. Before this age, your baby may have cheerfully gone to anyone without a fuss. Now, she's not only suspicious of strangers but actually frightened by them. This, too, is a normal developmental stage, one that's usually outgrown. Stranger anxiety develops with your baby's awareness that not everyone is the same and that she prefers you above everyone else.

This form of anxiety can be especially distressing for grandparents, who perhaps live far away and can't visit very often. They arrive bearing gifts, only to find that their darling grandchild cries and tries to hide from them.

Don't try to pressure your baby into smiling and being sociable. Allow her to go at her own pace, getting accustomed to people. Pushing her forward just causes more anxiety. Let grandparents— and anyone else who might get hurt feelings—know that they shouldn't take your baby's behavior personally. Gradually, as she gets to know them, she'll warm up.

If your baby is very anxious about strangers, then take this into account if you're introducing her to new caregivers or babysitters. Ideally, let your baby meet new sitters before leaving her in their care.

do babies need discipline?

We've all seen them: the toddler hitting other children in the park, the 3-year-old whining for candy in the supermarket, the 7-year-old yelling, "No! No! No!" in the restaurant. And we tell ourselves, "My child will never grow up to behave like that!"

Worry Meter

Q I pick my baby up when she cries, but my friend says I'm spoiling her. Should I worry?

○ Always
○ Sometimes
● No

In fact, the opposite is true: By giving your baby as much love and attention as you can now, you help her become a well-adjusted and well-behaved person. It's easy to worry when you're soothing your crying baby for what seems like the 19th time in an hour. But, when she cries, she's telling you she needs something, even if you don't know what it is. Even if *she* doesn't know what it is. Even if all that she needs is to be held.

By meeting her needs, you teach her that she can trust you to respond to her. Having your trust means that in the long run your child will feel more secure and less anxious, knowing that you take her wants and needs seriously. She'll have confidence in you later, too, when it's time to set boundaries and lay down rules, and she'll understand that you love her even when you correct her.

But when should discipline begin? Sooner than you might think!

At around 7 to 9 months, your baby learns to follow basic directions such as, "Give me the teddy." But he realizes he could choose *not* to follow your commands, too. He also learns to understand when you say *no*. In fact, as he gets older, he already knows and remembers that something isn't allowed. For example, he'll reach for the CDs in the rack but at the same time turn to look at you as if thinking, "Now, last time I pulled these onto the floor, she said 'no' and took them all away." When he's a bit older, the decision to ignore the *no* becomes a conscious one, even though he knows what your response will be.

So what should you do? For starters, bear in mind that one kind of discipline your baby *doesn't* need—and certainly won't understand at this age—is spanking.

Negatively disciplining a 7-to-9-month-old won't have much effect or make much of a difference in his behavior. Babies this young aren't really capable of manipulation or consciously being "bad." The mental focus for a baby of this age is learning about cause and effect. He's learning that his bowl falls when he drops it from the highchair, that the CDs make an exciting clatter when he tips the rack. He's curious to see what will happen—that's all. There's a world of difference (if only a matter of months!) between a baby who playfully throws a bowl to the floor and a toddler who *knows* he's creating a mess for Mom or Dad to clean up.

That said, you don't have to stand by while your baby does something you don't like (and you definitely don't want to stand by if your baby grabs for a dangerous object). At this age, and up to about 12 months, all you need to do is take away whatever is causing the problem or physically remove your baby from the situation. Then provide a safe, less messy, or less destructive alternative. In simple words, explain to him what you're doing. Even if he's too young to really understand, you're still teaching a fundamental rule: that some behaviors simply aren't acceptable.

If your baby likes pulling the CDs off the rack because they make a rewarding noise, try putting something on the rack that will satisfy his need for noise and adventure but won't drive you crazy. Move the CDs and fill the rack with board books or plastic tub lids. "I don't want you to break the CDs, but these lids are fine for making a noise with." When your baby's bowl of food goes on the floor, take the bowl away and give him something he can drop from his high-chair. "It's not okay to throw food, but you can throw this sock."

Another behavior that drives many moms crazy is their baby's constant need for attention, like when you're on the telephone and your baby whines and crawls to you. When you try to leave him, he clings to your leg as you attempt to walk away. Over the next couple of months, this behavior turns into pulling your clothes to try to physically hold you back. He's not doing this to annoy you but, rather, because he wants you. If you give your baby attention, he'll feel more secure and less anxious in the long run, giving him the courage to explore the world on his own. Once he understands that you take his cries seriously, he's less likely to cry for no reason. In the long run, responding quickly to your baby's needs will make him less clingy and demanding, not more.

This is a very frustrating phase for parents, though, and it's easy to lose your temper sometimes. Remind yourself that it *is* a phase—and that it will pass.

Another thing you can do, even at this early age, is reward behavior you *do* like with your attention. It's easy—and common—to fall into the habit of paying the most attention to your 7-to-9-month-old when he's whining or clingy. Once he starts yelling, you have no choice but to pick him up and calm him, and that guarantees that he has your attention. But try to pay attention to him *before* the yelling begins. When he's playing quietly, putting toys in his mouth or looking at a mobile, give him lots of brief, nonverbal physical attention, whether it's a kiss on the head, a rub on the back, or a gentle squeeze of his hand.

Even at this young age, your baby learns to see a direct link between his actions and your responses. You're teaching him that there are acceptable and non-acceptable ways to behave, and this is the essence of discipline.

babyproofing for a crawling baby

A crawling baby is a recipe for "trouble." Once your baby is on the move, it's time to get all the way down on the floor and examine your house from his point of view. You'll immediately recognize some quick fixes that will make it a safer place for an inquisitive explorer, whether it's the dangling cord of a lamp, a heavy object on a shelf that your baby could easily pull off, or a drawer that slides open.

Even if you've pooh-poohed safety-proofing devices before, now's a good time to reevaluate: A single latch can save a thousand "no's!" Tried-and-true measures include:

- **Stairway gates.** Stairs are a magnet to crawling babies.
- **Cupboard latches.** These prevent small hands from getting into kitchen cupboards that house potentially harmful products. Consider keeping one cupboard in the kitchen safe for your baby to open. After all, baby-friendly pots and pans can serve as drums and cymbals.
- **Drawer latches.** For kitchen and bedroom use. Some parents like the added peace of mind of having toilet-lid latches, too.

- **Electrical socket covers.** These prevent little fingers from exploring.
- **Rounded covers.** Soften sharp corners of tables.
- **Colorful stickers.** Placed on large areas of glass, such as sliding doors, stickers prevent them from becoming "invisible."
- **Window locks.** Fit windows with locks to prevent your baby from opening them from the bottom. Lock lower windows so that they don't open more than 5 inches. As additional window safety, move furniture and other potential climbing structures away from windows and always open sash windows from the top.

It's impossible to cover up every hard surface in your house, but by dealing with the obvious dangers, you allow your baby to explore with as much freedom as possible.

Don't overlook your baby's bed. Once your child can climb up on his hands and knees, remove crib gyms and hanging mobiles from his crib. Strings and ties pose a choking risk.

For a printable baby-safety checklist, go to babycenter.com.

toy safety

It's hard to believe that anything so innocent-looking as a child's toy could be lethal. But even toys that are entirely safe for older children can be harmful to your baby. For example, a marble can cause choking, the long string on a pull-toy can get wrapped around a small neck, and toys that fold can trap tiny fingers.

The law sets minimum safety standards for toys. They must:

- Be flame resistant
- Not contain any poisonous paint, lacquer, or varnish
- Not have any sharp edges or spikes

Any electric toys must conform to safety rules, and all packaging should be such that a child can't suffocate from plastic bags.

Although systems are in place to protect your baby, your role doesn't end there.

Here are the most important questions to ask yourself about toys, especially while your baby is under 3 years old:

1. **What are the toy's recommended ages?** These notices are safety warnings, not guidelines as to whether the toy is suitable for your child's developmental stage. Toys that aren't suitable for children under 3 should never be given to your baby. They often contain small parts that can be inhaled, cause choking, or be put into ears and noses.

2. **Are there any small parts?** In your baby's first years, he is likely to put everything in his mouth. That's why toy parts should be bigger than the child's mouth up to age 3 to avoid the chance of choking. To determine if a toy is a potential choking hazard, try fitting it through a toilet paper roll. If a toy or part of a toy can fit inside this cylinder, then it's not safe.

3. **Is the toy heavy?** Could your baby be harmed if the toy falls on him? If so, pass.

4. **Is the stuffed animal secure?** Make sure tails are securely sewn on and seams are reinforced; fillings in soft toys can choke young children. Stuffed animals should also be free of buttons, yarn, ribbons, and anything else your child could pull off and pop in his mouth.

5. **Does it look like food?** Your baby is more likely to put something in his mouth if he thinks he can eat it.

6. **Is the toy broken?** A broken toy isn't safe if it has sharp or rough edges, points or splinters, safety locks that no longer lock, or internal workings exposed. Nor should it have holes or gaps into which a baby can put his fingers and be hurt by mechanical parts inside.

7. **Is the toy in good condition?** Used toys passed down from older relatives or siblings or bought at yard sales can be worn, frayed, or have peeling paint. Check all used toys for buttons, batteries,

ribbons, eyes, beads, or plastic appendages that can easily be chewed or snapped off.

8. **Is there a string or cord on the toy longer than 12 inches?** A cord can easily be wrapped around a young child's neck, causing strangulation.

9. **Have you read the instructions?** Always read and follow all warnings and instructions. Don't throw them away; misused toys can be dangerous.

Toy safety isn't something you need to worry about just at the point of purchase. Each day when you're picking up toys and putting them away, check them for signs of wear or danger.

If your baby has a sibling, explain to your older child the importance of keeping small toys away from his younger brother or sister. Giving an older child a space where he's free to play with his blocks and your baby isn't allowed to trespass will give him a chance to indulge himself without his latest creation being destroyed—and keep your baby safe.

babies and books

One of the many side benefits of having kids is rediscovering the delight babies experience when exposed to some very wonderful new things. Reading with your baby is one of the best of these opportunities, a precious and important activity you can share. Children who are read to regularly from an early age have better language development than those who aren't, and they go on to become better readers.

You can feel as if you're not accomplishing very much when you settle down to look for Spot in *Where's Spot?*—yet again. One day your baby sits still for 5 minutes, or 3, another day she just wants to bite or tear the pages. But by spending time with her in this way, you're teaching her far more than the fact that Spot is under the rug.

Reading with your baby has lots of benefits:

A quiet time together. Reading is a safe and calm interlude with one-on-one attention. Make sure there's no background noise such as the radio or TV to distract either of you.

Wind-down time. Reading is an essential part of the going-to-bed routine, and it's soothing when your baby is upset.

A lesson in how books work. Your baby learns that books have pages. That the pages have an order and go from left to right. That books have a right way up. That books have words *and* pictures. That books can tell a story. That each time you look at a familiar book, it tells the *same* story. Your baby even learns what a book *is*—a DVD in its case or a package of tissues might look remarkably similar to a book, but they're not the same when she tries to open them. The simplest board books are the perfect starter library, and they're easy for her to hold and carry as she gets bigger.

An easy introduction to logical progression. That is, your baby learns that a story has a beginning, middle, and end. Through stories, she learns how the world is ordered and begins to understand it. It may seem like a big step from a book to "the rest of the world," but all journeys are made up of lots of little steps; and reading is one of them for your baby.

A way of developing your baby's memory. Doing the same things time and again is essential to help your baby's memory develop. Reading the same book over and over may bore you, but it helps your baby remember, recognize familiar things, and gradually develop the ability to anticipate and plan ahead.

Comfort. Your baby knows that reading time feels warm and safe, and she looks forward to it. Eventually, she'll use it herself as a way of asking for comfort and reassurance. If you suggest a story to help her calm down when she's upset, then one day when she's tired or grumpy, she'll hand you a book (or pick one up for herself)—her way of saying, "I need comforting."

Fun lessons in how language works. At first, language is just a stream of sound to your baby. The more you talk to her, the more she'll understand. One of the first steps is identifying the beginning and end of sentences. Your baby picks up the stops and starts and the changes in inflection as you read to her. You'll find that when you read her favorite books, she begins to move her body in time to the rhythm of the words as you say them. She begins to anticipate the end of a sentence and makes a small sound like *ha* when you get there. Later, she begins to identify key words. If you mention Spot the Dog, she'll look toward the book on the nightstand, or show you by excitedly kicking her legs and moving her arms that yes, she wants to read *Where's Spot?* Your baby will learn to match the word with the image, pointing to Spot on the page, at first very vaguely and then, as her fine motor control improves, more accurately.

An opportunity for tactile development. Books your baby can touch stimulate her tactile senses. Pages with furry and silky inlays, ridges, and rough and smooth sections enhance the story and encourage her to explore the story with her fingers. No child can resist poking an exploratory finger through the little holes in the pages of *The Very Hungry Caterpillar* or playing along with *Pat the Bunny*. Some books have sections to push and pages that make noises, pieces that you pull to make actions happen, and even see-through pages. As your baby's fine motor control increases, she'll enjoy exploring them more and more.

Find out more ways to start your baby on the path to becoming a bookworm by visiting babycenter.com.

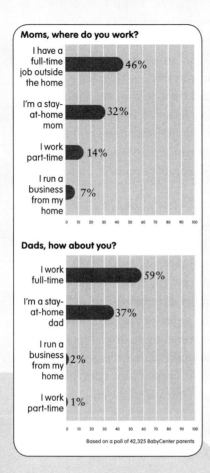

Moms, where do you work?

- I have a full-time job outside the home — **46%**
- I'm a stay-at-home mom — **32%**
- I work part-time — **14%**
- I run a business from my home — **7%**

Dads, how about you?

- I work full-time — **59%**
- I'm a stay-at-home dad — **37%**
- I run a business from my home — **2%**
- I work part-time — **1%**

Based on a poll of 42,325 BabyCenter parents

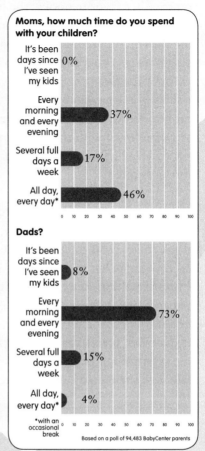

Moms, how much time do you spend with your children?

- It's been days since I've seen my kids — **0%**
- Every morning and every evening — **37%**
- Several full days a week — **17%**
- All day, every day* — **46%**

Dads?

- It's been days since I've seen my kids — **8%**
- Every morning and every evening — **73%**
- Several full days a week — **15%**
- All day, every day* — **4%**

*with an occasional break

Based on a poll of 94,483 BabyCenter parents

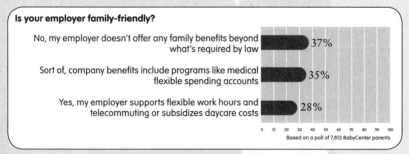

Is your employer family-friendly?

- No, my employer doesn't offer any family benefits beyond what's required by law — **37%**
- Sort of, company benefits include programs like medical flexible spending accounts — **35%**
- Yes, my employer supports flexible work hours and telecommuting or subsidizes daycare costs — **28%**

Based on a poll of 7,813 BabyCenter parents

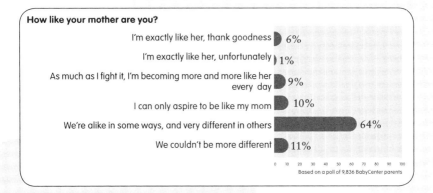

How like your mother are you?

I'm exactly like her, thank goodness — 6%

I'm exactly like her, unfortunately — 1%

As much as I fight it, I'm becoming more and more like her every day — 9%

I can only aspire to be like my mom — 10%

We're alike in some ways, and very different in others — 64%

We couldn't be more different — 11%

Based on a poll of 9,836 BabyCenter parents

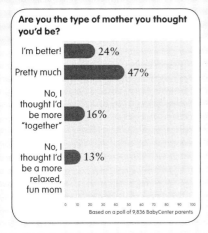

Are you the type of mother you thought you'd be?

I'm better! — 24%

Pretty much — 47%

No, I thought I'd be more "together" — 16%

No, I thought I'd be a more relaxed, fun mom — 13%

Based on a poll of 9,836 BabyCenter parents

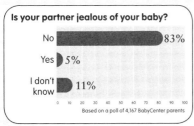

Is your partner jealous of your baby?

No — 83%

Yes — 5%

I don't know — 11%

Based on a poll of 4,167 BabyCenter parents

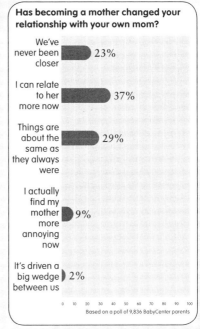

Has becoming a mother changed your relationship with your own mom?

We've never been closer — 23%

I can relate to her more now — 37%

Things are about the same as they always were — 29%

I actually find my mother more annoying now — 9%

It's driven a big wedge between us — 2%

Based on a poll of 9,836 BabyCenter parents

the bottom line

Without even realizing it, you're finding your groove as a parent. Basic childcare that required careful planning and thought is now second nature to you. This is a good time to think about yourself and your relationship as well.

you—
7 to 9 months

Now's a good time to think about your style of parenting. You know enough to make your own decisions rather than automatically follow the advice of your own parents or friends. To make the most of parenthood, think about what suits you, your partner, and your baby.

Everyone seems to know how to be a parent, and everyone seems all too ready to give you their "two cents" about what you should be doing. Experts all have their views. Grandparents and other relatives can't help chiming in. Even childless friends have their say. Often the advice is contradictory. The net result is an illusion that there's some magical parenting standard you'll never quite achieve.

being a "good enough" parent

We all have our standards. Maybe it's to have a baby who nurses well, or who sleeps through the night, or plays happily all the time, or is happy around other people. Maybe it's all of these things. By trying to be the perfect parent of our imaginations, we put ourselves

babycenter **buzz**
when life begins to fall into place—again

"I'm the mother of an 8-month-old boy and work full-time. I feel that I've become more motivated and efficient than I was before I had him."
—Anonymous

"Once a week my husband and I go dancing. It really helps us to spend time as a couple, and it's a great way to help burn those post-baby pounds. Needless to say, our baby benefits all around because he's asleep with my mom while we're gone and wakes up to a very happy momma and papa."**—Leslie-Anne**

under great pressure. The reality is that no one is perfect all the time. In fact, your baby doesn't need you to be perfect. He just wants you to be "good enough"—good enough to make him feel safe and loved, good enough to relax and enjoy life, and good enough to have some fun.

Relaxed parents tend to make for relaxed babies. Important elements of being a confident parent include making sure you get some time to yourself, that you do some of the things that you want to do, that you have some time with your partner, and that you have a support network of other parents to help you out. So ask yourself: "Am I enjoying being a parent? If not, what can I do to make sure I do enjoy it?"

What parts of the parenting job do you like? What areas of parenting cause you stress? How can you rearrange things so that you experience more of the good and less of the stressful parts?

Think about what is "good enough" for you. Babies don't judge. They're just delighted when you pick them up, play with them, feed them, and rock them. To your baby, you're already the perfect parent.

finding the old you

Many women find that when their babies are around 7 to 9 months old, they're ready to spend some time focusing on their own well-being. It's easy to go for an entire 6 months thinking about nothing but your baby and then realize that you're still not happy with your own post-baby body, that you haven't been eating well, and so on. For example, now that your baby is exploring solid foods, it's an ideal opportunity to review your own eating priorities and make sure the whole family is getting the best nutrition possible.

easy ways to eat well

As a basis for your own healthy eating plan, each day aim to eat:

- Six or more servings of grains or starches, including at least three whole grains
- Three or more fruits
- Three or more vegetables (including at least one vitamin C–rich and one vitamin A–rich fruit or vegetable each day)
- 4 to 6 ounces of protein from a variety of sources (such as fish, meat, eggs, and nuts)
- Three or more servings of dairy or calcium-rich foods (such as milk, cheese, and yogurt)
- Three teaspoons of vegetable fat from canola oil or olive oil or products made with these. (Avoid trans fat, the "bad" fat found in many fried, processed, and fast foods.)

If you decide that now is the time to lose weight *and* eat well, don't go on a sudden crash diet. Women tend to need a minimum of 1,200 calories a day to stay healthy, and you need to be at the top of your game to look after your baby! Make a realistic plan for your weight loss. It's likely to take a few months to eliminate excess weight and get your body into the shape you want it to be. A realistic plan is to lose 1 to 2 pounds a week, which allows you to eat healthily and keep the weight off. Consider these simple strategies that will help improve your nutrition automatically.

Get a better breakfast. In the morning do you reach for a plain bagel, a bowl of sugary cereal, or a piece of white toast? They're all simple carbohydrates that cause your blood sugar to spike and then crash, leaving you feeling sleepy—and hungry again.

Complex carbs give you longer-lasting energy and keep you feeling full because they take longer to digest. They also offer more nutrition in the form of vitamins and minerals. So try complex carbs and proteins for breakfast: a yogurt-and-fruit smoothie, a bowl of oatmeal or whole grain cereal, or scrambled eggs and whole wheat toast.

Eat small meals, but more of them. Rather than eating three large meals, aim to eat five smaller ones throughout the day. This keeps your energy levels on an even keel the whole day long, rather than seesawing between hunger and fullness.

Pack a good snack. Carrot sticks aren't the only healthy snacks. Research shows that drinking milk and eating whole grains helps in your weight-loss effort. So try:

- Whole wheat bagels or toast with peanut butter
- Hummus on pita bread
- Cheese and crackers
- Trail mix with nuts and dried fruit
- Yogurt with fruit
- Fruit smoothies
- A glass of milk

Also drink plenty of water. It's important for everyone and especially if you're breastfeeding.

getting back in shape

Remember that diet and exercise together are far more effective for losing weight than either alone. Don't despair if your schedule doesn't allow for marathon swimming sessions or cross-country hikes. Just 10 minutes here and there is better than nothing and

provides an energy boost while burning calories. Find an activity that you enjoy so that you'll look forward to doing it.

Try these 10-minute wonders:

- **Go swimming with another mom and her baby.** Take turns watching both babies while the other mom has a 10-minute swim.
- **Build lots of short bursts of exercise into your day.** Park on the far side of the parking lot and walk briskly across to the supermarket, run up the stairs instead of taking the elevator, or jog briskly up the stairs in your home.
- **Try to do everything more quickly.** Time your walk to the park and see if you can cut a few seconds off it each day, for example.
- **Put your baby in the stroller** and let her watch you from a safe distance while you energetically mow the lawn or do the weeding.
- **Start cleaning!** Housework burns calories, so vacuum, wipe windows, or make beds with vigor.

Once you've gotten used to being on the move again, gradually increase your active time with more sustained exercise.

- **Put your baby in the stroller and go for a walk.** Now that your baby is over 6 months old, you can put him in a jogging stroller and go for a run.
- **Ask your partner to take over parenting duties** for 30 minutes or so after work so you can go for a walk around the neighborhood.
- **If you can manage it, start the day with exercise** by getting up an hour earlier than usual. Consider investing in some home exercise equipment that you can use when your baby naps or in bad weather. A library of exercise DVDs offers a fun and convenient way to squeeze exercise into your day.
- **Check out local health clubs or yoga studios.** Many offer postpartum exercise classes where babies are welcome. If a postpartum class isn't on the roster at your gym, hunt for a low-impact class that has a decent warmup period—at least 10 minutes—and that also includes some stretching and toning.

making it happen

It's easy to find excuses *not* to exercise. Here's what to keep in mind once you decide to get moving.

5 things that help

1. **Easing into exercise.** If you haven't exercised since giving birth, start by doing gentle stretches and picking up the pace as you do household chores or shopping.

2. **Setting realistic goals for yourself.** You're not going to be running a marathon by the end of the week.

3. **Putting your baby in the stroller and going out for a brisk walk.** He'll enjoy the ride while you get a workout.

4. **Finding a buddy.** Someone to work out with you is a great motivator and keeps you focused on your fitness goals.

5. **Eating a good diet.** Remember to eat whole grains and cereals, fresh fruits and vegetables, and foods that provide plenty of protein, calcium, and iron.

5 things that hinder

1. **Expecting your body to bounce back during the first year.** A few lucky women are flat-tummied and back in their regular clothing within weeks of delivery. For mere mortals, though, it takes much longer.

2. **Trying to lose weight too quickly when you're breastfeeding.** Rapid weight loss releases toxins—normally stored in your body fat—into your bloodstream, increasing the amount of these contaminants that wind up in your milk. Aim for a slow and steady weight loss, about 1 to 2 pounds a week.

3. **Inadvertently overeating.** While you may have heard that breastfeeding moms need 500 extra calories a day, that's outdated advice. Recent research indicates that caloric needs while breastfeeding are highly individualized and depend on

your current weight and activity level. Most breastfeeding moms—especially those still trying to lose baby weight at this point—don't need those bonus calories.

4. **Feeling badly that you can't get into your pre-pregnancy clothes.** If you're sick of wearing loose, forgiving clothes—maybe even leftover maternity pants—go ahead and treat yourself to some new clothes that flatter your new shape.

5. **Pushing yourself too fast and too far.** Don't exercise to exhaustion; you still need energy for baby care, especially as your child gets more mobile. Pacing yourself will boost your energy, rather than deplete it.

Every woman loses her pregnancy weight at a different speed. Go to BabyCenter's "Post-Baby Weight-Loss Calculator" (babycenter.com) to see how many calories you should be consuming in order to drop your postpartum pounds. And if you're in the market for home exercise equipment, see babycenter.com to find out which basic machines will best fit your needs.

protect your back

Back pain is a common post-pregnancy ailment. Why? During pregnancy, hormones soften the ligaments that hold your pelvis in place, allowing the joints to move and slip out of line, which can cause lower back pain or pain at the front of the pelvis. Extra weight during pregnancy (and afterward) also puts a strain on your muscles and ligaments. Also, during delivery your pelvis has to open and move to accommodate your baby, and it doesn't always align properly afterward.

Caring for a baby means more bending, lifting, carrying, and twisting: bending over to change diapers, lifting your baby in and out of the tub, carrying him upstairs, and twisting to attend to him in the car seat. Most likely, you're also less fit than before, which means your core body muscles aren't so good at supporting your body and put more strain on your joints.

what you can do about it

Nature and baby care needs may be working against your physical self at this point, but by taking care of your body, you can avoid injury.

Posture is important. Slouching puts more strain on your muscles. So stand straight and tuck in your bottom. Sit up straight when you're driving or using a computer. When you're sitting, ensure that your back is well supported. Try placing a small rolled towel in the hollow of your back. Sitting upright in a dining-type chair will help your back more than sitting in a soft chair or on a sofa.

Breastfeed wisely. Avoid slouching over to nurse your baby. Bring your baby to your breast, not your breast to your baby. Use pillows to bring your baby up to the right height for you. Try using a U-shaped pillow behind your shoulders to support your upper back. If you have lower back pain, raise your feet on a footstool, pillow, or even a telephone book while you're sitting and feeding.

Exercise. Strengthen your core muscles, which will support your back better. Try swimming, yoga, Pilates, and cycling.

Lose weight. But do it gradually.

Avoid heavy lifting. When you need to lift, keep the weight close to your body. Bend your knees rather than leaning over using your back. Avoid twisting actions, which put a strain on your lower

pelvic tilts

To prevent and combat back pain, try this exercise. Stand with your back against a wall. Position your feet a few inches away from the wall and allow your knees to bend very slightly. Slide your hand into the hollow of your back and tilt your pelvis backward so that your back squashes your hand. Now tilt your pelvis the opposite way so that you remove the pressure from your back off your hand. Continue to tilt forward and backward in a rhythmical fashion. Once you are confident with this exercise, you can perform it away from the wall.

babycenter buzz
what about *my* time?

"Before we had our daughter, I was terrified, afraid that I was going to lose my free time, my hobbies, my friends, my sleep—and I was right. I've lost many of those things, or had to cut them back sharply. The funny thing is, I don't mind. Hanging with our baby is one of the best things I've ever done. One day I'll find time to read a good book, but right now I'm busy being Dad and that's just fine with me."—**Anonymous**

"I love being a dad, and believe it or not I'm now looking forward to my mother-in-law's visits. That way I can let her take care of the baby one night while we go mountain biking. It's funny how your perspective can change so fast!"—**Anonymous**

back joints and muscles. When shopping, divide your purchases into two equal loads and carry one bag in each hand.

Go low. Wear flat shoes or ones with low heels, not high heels, and make sure they're comfortable.

If back pain occurs, seek medical help or physical therapy. Exercises and stretching often help, especially early on while your back joints are still soft.

five reasons motherhood benefits you

Are you at the point where you're feeling tired, fed-up, struggling to get back into shape, wondering if you'll ever have a conversation again that doesn't include the words "sleep" or "solids," and generally wondering why you feel like you've aged 6 years in 6 months?

To cheer you up, we've collected five little-known reasons why motherhood is actually good for you.

1. **You may be smarter.** You may not feel smarter when you're coping with sleepless nights and trying to learn the ins and

outs of baby care. But research suggests that mothers are more motivated, fearless, and cope with stress better than non-mothers, and that they have a better ability to multitask. Other research shows, for rats at least, that they're smarter once they become mothers, especially in their ability to learn and remember. What's more, they keep that competitive edge until they're of an age equivalent to 80 in humans. Maybe the motivation is the need to feed their young and keep them safe.

2. **You reduce the risk of some diseases.** Giving birth between the ages of 18 and 25 reduces your risk of breast cancer. Breast-feeding for several months reduces the risk still further in women of all ages. Mothers also reduce their risk of endometrial and ovarian cancers. Having a baby improves outcomes for disorders such as endometriosis, uterine fibroids, and polycystic ovaries.

3. **You take better care of yourself.** A BabyCenter poll of more than 4,000 moms found that most new mothers made lifestyle changes that would improve their health in the long term.

   - 81% said they eat more healthfully or are trying to improve their diets

   - 65% keep a closer watch on their mental health, or are trying to

   - 65% drive more carefully

   - 64% exercise more, or intend to

   - 58% are more likely to wear their seat belts

   - 55% are more likely to see their doctors more often or make an appointment if something seems wrong

4. **You're more likely to be happy.** A study of more than 1,000 women showed that those with children rated the highest on a number of psychological measures, from self-esteem to personal and professional satisfaction. Another large-scale survey showed that parents were more "socially integrated"—meaning surrounded by friends, family, and community—than non-parents, and that married mothers in particular had lower rates of depression than their childless counterparts.

(continued on page 340)

the tao of dad

If you still feel anxio
baby into her car sea
through the day, it c
an excuse to withdra
ence for many dads a
see themselves as the
supporting role—rel
because they're over
moms don't realize t
crazy. What to do? '
own way of doing th
experience, and gair

Although many cou
partners in both wo
that way. By 7 to 9 r
assigned roles in you
ship of the baby care
financial matters.

Trying to balance w
culture in many wor
enough to see your b
Sometimes an impor
partner is sick and c
night before that me
to be comforted, and
are grinding you do
you're making? How
lems—even though
them. Guilt and clas
every new dad faces

Some men forgo career advancement for more time with their families, especially in the early years of their children's lives. Others actually spend more time at work than they used to, feeling that the most important contribution they can make to their families is financial. There are no right or wrong choices. What matters, though, is that you and your partner support each other in the choices you make. Talk with your partner about what you feel are the biggest adjustments you're making in your lives as parents, and what additional changes you'd both like.

One thing that also hits home around now is the sheer lack of spontaneity in your life. Everything has to be planned. The impromptu, solo beers with your pals are out. And if you and your partner want to go to see friends, there's a mountain of baby equipment to pack first. Even then the journey has to be scheduled around naps, feedings, and whether or not there'll be somewhere to change a diaper when you get there. What's devastating about feeling like your life's not your own any more is that right after you feel rotten for being boxed in by your baby, you feel guilty for being so selfish.

Of course, for every moment you feel like it's a no-win situation, along comes a smile that rocks your world. And these days your baby can interact with you much more than before. And the excitement of seeing the smile or hearing the laugh that's reserved just for you is enough to make it all worthwhile.

practical tasks for dads

- Once your baby begins eating solid foods, you can get more

(continued)

Just for dads (cont.)

involved in his day-to-day feeding than ever before. Mashing carrots doesn't take Cordon Bleu culinary skills, but getting that carrot into your baby's mouth is the far greater challenge. Feeding your baby and watching him grow is one of the most rewarding experiences of this first year.

- As your baby gets mobile, he'll appreciate the particular sense of fun that Dad brings to the adventure. Construct a commando course of pillows for your crawling baby, and he'll have fun while you're on hand to shout support (and make sure he's safe).

- It doesn't have to be all action as a dad. If you've been at work all day, then take part in your baby's bedtime routine with sleepy songs and stories. That way, your baby will come to associate you with emotional support as much as physical fun.

- If you're the dad of twins or more, take time to develop a special one-on-one relationship with each baby. Look for the different activities each baby enjoys most so you'll have something that's special just for the two of you.

- Tell your baby how much you love him. Many men are so wrapped up in logic and action that it takes them by surprise when they have a chance to experience the emotional side of life. If you want your child to be able to tell you how he feels when he's older, to talk to you when he's a teenager, you need to teach him that men can communicate and understand emotions. And now is the best time to start.

test yourself **do you see eye-to-eye?**

What are (or, as your child grows, will be) the key rules in your house? And does everyone agree on them? Ask your partner and take this quick quiz yourself.

1. Sweets?

    a. Never.

    b. Sometimes.

    c. Why not?

2. TV?

    a. Never.

    b. Sometimes.

    c. Why not?

3. Please and thank you?

    a. Never.

    b. Sometimes.

    c. Why not?

4. Church?

    a. Never.

    b. Sometimes.

    c. Why not?

5. Toy guns?

    a. Never.

    b. Sometimes.

    c. Why not?

6. Baby bedtime firmly at 7:00 p.m.?

    a. Never.

    b. Sometimes.

    c. Why not?

It doesn't matter so much here which numbers you circle; more important is whether you and your partner both circle the same ones. Being clear about house rules can help you better understand the areas where your parenting styles may clash. If you agree in advance which rules you will *both* abide by— all the time—your baby will enjoy the security that comes from consistency in your family's parenting dynamic.

5. **Your sex life gets better.** Some experts subscribe to the view that the process of pregnancy and birth helps many women get in touch with their bodies and increases their sexuality. It may not feel like that while you're still not getting much sleep or are struggling to shed those post-baby pounds, but most women relate to the feeling of amazement at the body's ability to change and grow and recover from childbirth. Some women experience orgasms only once they've had babies. And many parents say that although sex is less frequent after having a baby, they enjoy it more.

your relationship

Life is probably beginning to settle down a bit now: You've become used to being parents and your life is mostly back on track. This is a good time to think about your time together as a couple, maybe as part of the whole process of thinking about what you want out of life, including having some "me" time: seeing friends, getting back into shape, and rebuilding your own life.

It's not uncommon for sex to still be the victim of tiredness and lack of libido. Although it's easy to think that other parents are having passionate sex all the time, that's not what the BabyCenter sex-after-baby survey showed. Twenty thousand BabyCenter users answered (17,000 moms, 3,000 dads):

- 2 months after their babies were born, most couples were having sex two to three times a month
- 6 months after their babies were born, most couples were having sex three to five times a month
- 60% said their sex lives had improved or stayed the same
- 40% said their sex lives got worse

More on the topic of quality:

- 30% said they never seem to want sex at the same time now
- 23% said they're too exhausted for sex

- 19% want it but never seem to get it
- 27% either say it's the same as before or that sex is better

If parents aren't having sex as much as they used to, what's the main reason?

- 40%—I'm too tired to have sex
- 23%—My sex drive has gone the way of the dinosaur
- 21%—I feel like I have no time for sex
- 16%—I'm more self-conscious about my body.

So, we asked: If you could have only one of the following, what would it be?

Women:
- 69%—I want my pre-baby body back
- 31%—I want my pre-baby sex life back.

Men:
- 71%—I want our pre-baby sex life back
- 29%—I want my wife's pre-baby body back.

Breastfeeding moms may experience vaginal dryness due to fluctuating hormone levels, and sex can be uncomfortable. If this affects you, consider using a lubricant. It's reassuring to know that dryness is just a side effect of breastfeeding and won't last forever.

For more eye-opening insights from the BabyCenter sex survey, visit babycenter.com.

part five

first steps,
first words

10–12 months

development:
10 to 12 months

How old was your baby when he started to walk?

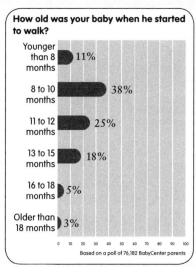

Younger than 8 months — 11%
8 to 10 months — 38%
11 to 12 months — 25%
13 to 15 months — 18%
16 to 18 months — 5%
Older than 18 months — 3%

Based on a poll of 76,182 BabyCenter parents

When did your baby start running?

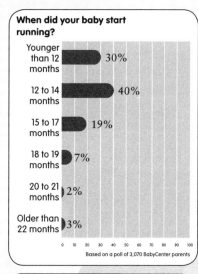

Younger than 12 months — 30%
12 to 14 months — 40%
15 to 17 months — 19%
18 to 19 months — 7%
20 to 21 months — 2%
Older than 22 months — 3%

Based on a poll of 3,070 BabyCenter parents

When did your baby first cruise?

Younger than 9 months — 27%
9 months — 21%
10 months — 25%
11 months — 13%
12 months — 1%
Older than 12 months — 10%

Based on a poll of 3,106 BabyCenter parents

When did your baby first understand "no"?

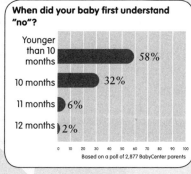

Younger than 10 months — 58%
10 months — 32%
11 months — 6%
12 months — 2%

Based on a poll of 2,877 BabyCenter parents

When did your baby first respond to his name?

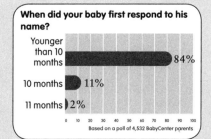

Younger than 10 months — 84%
10 months — 11%
11 months — 2%

Based on a poll of 4,532 BabyCenter parents

When did your baby first scribble with a crayon?

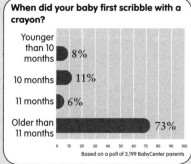

Younger than 10 months — 8%
10 months — 11%
11 months — 6%
Older than 11 months — 73%

Based on a poll of 3,199 BabyCenter parents

by this time, according to the experts . . .

	most babies can . . .	half of babies can . . .	a few babies can . . .
10 months	• Wave goodbye • Pick things up with pincer grasp • Crawl well • Cruise around the furniture	• Say *dada* and *mama* to the right parent (is specific) • Respond to name and understand *no* • Indicate wants with gestures	• Drink from a cup • Stand alone for a couple of seconds • Put objects into a container
11 months	• Say *dada* and *mama* to the right parent (is specific) • Play patty-cake • Stand alone for a couple of seconds	• Imitate others' activities • Put objects into a container • Understand simple instructions	• Say one word besides *dada* and *mama* • Stoop from standing position
12 months	• Imitate others' activities • Jabber word-like sounds • Indicate wants with gestures	• Say one word besides *dada* and *mama* • Take a few steps • Understand and respond to simple instructions	• Scribble with a crayon • Walk well • Say two words besides *dada* and *mama*

How old was your baby when he first said *mama* or *dada*?

Younger than 5 months — 14%
5 months — 16%
6 months — 19%
7 months — 16%
8 months — 12%
Older than 9 months — 24%

0 10 20 30 40 50 60 70 80 90 100

Based on a poll of 106,980 BabyCenter parents

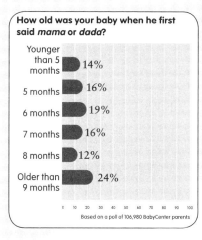

the bottom line

The ages and the sequence in which babies become mobile isn't cast in concrete. Some babies skip crawling altogether. Others don't crawl but find another way of moving around, such as rolling, squirming forward on their front (and dragging their legs behind), walking on all fours on hands and feet, or bottom shuffling around the room in a sitting position. Don't worry about your baby's individual style; it's going mobile that's important, no matter how she does it.

development— 10 to 12 months

Motor skills are developed when the brain, nervous system, and muscles work together. Gross motor skills control the bigger movements—such as running and jumping—that use the large muscles in your baby's arms, legs, body, and feet. Fine motor skills control the small movements—such as picking up something with thumb and forefinger—that use the small muscles of your baby's fingers, toes, wrists, lips, and tongue.

Between **10 and 12 months**, your baby's gross motor skills are improving, but she's also working on the fine motor skills.

crawling, standing, and walking

If your baby already crawls, then during these 3 months she'll begin to crawl well—and even crawl up stairs. Don't be in a hurry to move your baby from crawling to standing. Crawling is good for her improving coordination, and it's believed that it develops connections between the right and left hemispheres of the brain.

At around **10 to 11 months**, once your baby can support her own weight, she will probably stand while steadying herself, though it

babycenter buzz
all in good time

"At our kids' age, it's not really about *what* you do with them, it's about *spending time* with them and just letting them know you're there and you love them. So no matter what you do, even if it's the same thing every day, as long as she knows you love her, it doesn't really matter."—**Jill**

"Too many parents are obsessed with their child's abilities or inabilities. They'll all catch up to each other when they start school. Don't worry too much about the little stuff. Everyone wants an intelligent child, but they all develop at a different pace."—**Angie**

will take several more weeks before she bends her knees and sits back down again without help. Once she stands steady, she'll learn to stoop, which is harder than it sounds. She'll also find ways to pull herself upright using the furniture. From then on it's a matter of gaining confidence and balance.

Usually 2 to 3 weeks after a baby can get herself upright, she learns to "cruise"—to move around the room while holding onto the furniture. She moves sideways at first, but as her confidence grows, she cruises from one item to the next, using them for balance. Once she can do that, she'll be able to stand alone for a couple of seconds. Next, she'll take some steps if you hold her in a walking position. And then, she starts to walk. Most babies take their first steps sometime between **9 and 12 months** and are walking well by the time they're **14 to 15 months old**. Don't worry if yours takes a little longer, though, since many babies don't walk until they're **16 to 17 months old.**

what you can do to encourage your baby

Once your baby is on her feet, she'll probably start trying to pull herself up to a stand whenever she can, so try to make sure everything in her path is sturdy enough to provide support. Encourage her cruising by placing a favorite toy at the far end of the sofa. You can put one of your own toys, such as your mobile phone, a distance away and "cruise" on your knees toward it. If your baby finds this amusing, she'll cruise over to join you.

Introduce some new (or old) push toys and large empty boxes now, which suddenly take on a new lease on life when your baby can push them around the room.

One play option to avoid is the traditional baby walker. More accidents and injuries happen in baby walkers than with any other type of baby equipment because walkers give babies extra speed (a baby can cover up to 3 feet per second in one zoom), extra height, and access to multiple hazards. Walkers won't help your baby learn to walk, and in fact, using one too much can even delay her development slightly. A baby needs to roll, crawl, sit, and play on the floor in order to reach her developmental milestones. If you want a safe, confined play spot for your baby to stay in at times when you need to get something done, consider a stationary walker (no wheels), a playpen, or an exersaucer-type seat.

To see if your baby is showing signs that she's reading to start walking, check out BabyCenter's video at babycenter.com.

hand control

Playing gets easier for your baby now. By **10 months**, she can probably sit unsupported, leaning forward to reach for a toy when she wants it, still maintaining her balance. Also at this age, your baby starts to use her fingers and thumbs instead of her whole hand and begins to coordinate her index finger and thumb in readiness to pick up small objects. As she becomes more skillful, she'll also learn to let go of something deliberately and pick it up again. And she figures out how to drop objects on purpose for someone (probably you) to pick up.

By **11 months**, she can put objects into a container, push and pull things, throw something away, and move after it deliberately. By **12 months**, her fine motor skills improve enough for her to use the pincer grasp of finger against thumb to pick up something as small as a single raisin. As her motor skills develop, she'll find more things to do and gain freedom in her play.

what you can do to encourage your baby

Babies this age love making the connection between cause and effect: "I do this, and that happens." Activity centers present lots of different experiments in one plaything. A good one has knobs to turn, buttons to push, dials to twist, and noises to make.

Your baby is still perfecting her accuracy in letting go, a skill she needs, for example, to build a tower of bricks. So she'll enjoy games that let her practice picking up and letting go: stacking games, building games, and filling up and emptying containers with smaller objects.

Give your baby a box that's easy to open (like a shoe box) and show her how to put things inside and take them out. Offer her some cups and show her how to pour sand or beans from one to the other, or into a larger container.

Water is another wonderful thing to pour. Your baby probably doesn't sit very still in the bath these days. She wants to stand up, splash, grab your hair, pat the shower curtain, and so on. Encourage her to sit still longer by providing bath toys. They don't have to be actual toys. Plenty of household items can be filled, drained, poured from or into, and floated: plastic cups, small buckets, colanders, and squeeze bottles.

communicating with you

By **10 months**, your baby may be able to say one clear word and give a definite shake of his head for no. He'll also understand when you say no. By **12 months**, his vocabulary increases to about three words, and he clearly understands many words and phrases that you say.

Even if your baby doesn't begin speaking until later, his communication skills are nevertheless growing. If at **9 months** or so you ask him, "Where's your teddy?" he'll turn to look at it. By **10 to 11 months**, he'll pick up the teddy or hold it. By around **12 months**, he'll just point to it.

Your baby knows what he likes and what he doesn't like and is much better at "asking" for what he wants. He can point to things that he's interested in, such as the pictures in a nursery-rhyme book. He'll hold a book out to you in hopes that you'll read to him, or wriggle and turn away if you read to him when he doesn't want you to. Instead of just closing his mouth when you try to feed him something he doesn't want, by around **10 months** he actively pushes the spoon away with his hand. He'll turn away a cup of water if he wants juice, and by **11 or 12 months** will even throw it rather than push it away.

Distraction doesn't work quite as well now as it did when your baby was younger, but humor is a good substitute. Amuse him with silly faces or do something unexpected. For example, take his food and eat it yourself (with much appreciation), and he may just decide he wants it after all. Get his teddy dressed for a walk in your baby's jacket and strap teddy in the stroller, and your baby will let you know he'd rather you take him out than teddy.

And because your baby can understand more and more of what you say, he'll be able to demonstrate that, too. Ask him to give you a toy, and he can do it. Say *shoe,* and he'll hold out his foot. As he learns what some things are used for, he'll communicate by letting you know that, too. For example, he'll hold out his arms when you dress him, or follow you around the house and imitate you as you dust, fold the laundry, or tend the garden. He can both imitate and repeat actions he knows, which means he's ready to play clapping games, put his hands over his eyes when you suggest a round of peekaboo, and join in with action rhymes. Suddenly, playing with your baby gets more fun.

At around this age, the differences in the development of twins (or triplets or more) become more apparent. Of course it's difficult, but try not to compare them. Make a point of focusing on what each baby can do best, whether that's learning to stand, to stack boxes, or to talk. Praise each baby for the skills that he has, rather than pointing out what a sibling is suddenly excelling at. Some twins begin to talk to each other in a language only they can understand. Twin talk is a sign of the special bond between them, but they'll eventually outgrow this unique language, so allow them to enjoy it while they can (and try to preserve it on video, if possible).

what you can do to encourage your baby

One of the best ways to help develop language skills is to continue to talk with your baby. Sharing books is a great way to spend time together, too, and you can ask her to point to familiar objects pictured in the book. You'll be amazed by how many she knows. To help your baby develop memory, re-read her favorite bedtime stories so she anticipates and remembers the experience.

understanding the world

Your baby's memory is improving, as is her ability to make inferences. At around **10 months,** she heads toward her highchair when she sees you cooking or crawls toward the door if the bell rings. She not only remembers what things are for but where they are as well. Watch as she tries to buckle the straps in her car seat when you put her in it. If you say it's time to go to the park, she'll bring you her coat or gloves to show that she's ready.

By about **11 months,** most babies recover from their shyness and again show pleasure in attention from other people. What's more, your baby knows that by making faces and noises, she can attract the attention of other people. So your shy baby has become a real flirt!

By **12 months**, she gets angry if you don't pay enough attention to her, pulling at your clothes, perhaps, while you're talking to someone else. She greets people she likes but hasn't seen for a while, such as grandparents, with excited squeals and hugs.

Your baby also wants to know how *you* feel about things. If she falls and bumps herself, watch for a short pause as she looks at you before deciding to cry. If you respond with a calm comment, she's likely to ignore the bump. (Of course that doesn't work if she's really hurt.) If Grandma or someone else picks her up when she cries, she'll turn toward you and squirm and wriggle to get to you instead.

Toward the end of the first year, your baby begins to imitate behavior and indulges in pretend play. She cuddles and pats her teddy just as you do to her, or picks up a cup from a tea set and pretends to drink. She knows there's nothing in the cup, but she's also aware that cups are for drinking from and she's letting you know that *she* understands. Her thinking is moving from the specific to the general: Her cup holds drinks, so *all* cups are for drinking. This way of thinking is an important step as it allows your toddler-to-be to order her world.

Everyone needs some generalizations to help them think. Without being able to make them, everything would constantly have to be learned anew. By categorizing the world, we can, for example, create a category called "things we can drink from" and put related objects in it—glasses, cups, mugs, bottles. These skills enable humans to handle the huge amounts of information they have to process every day. Your nearly 1-year-old is coming to grips with all these important ideas through play.

object permanence revisited

Not long ago your baby was just beginning to learn about object permanence—the fact that things continue to exist even when they're out of his sight. Now, improvements in your baby's memory mean that he can find a toy you've hidden even if he can't see it. Hide his teddy in a towel, and he'll unwrap it to find the toy. Just a few weeks ago, he'd have needed to see part of the teddy bear first, before looking for it. Before that, he'd have forgotten about the bear as soon as it disappeared from view.

Your baby will also remember where things *usually* are. At around **9 months**, he can locate his coat by the door. If it's not there, he'll be disappointed, but he won't be able to look somewhere else for it. At around **10 to 11 months**, with some help from you, he learns to look in other places. You can say, "Well, I wonder where your coat has gone? Is it on the chair? No? Is it on the stroller? Oh, look, it's on the stairs." Your baby realizes it's still his coat, even if it wasn't where he expected it to be.

When your baby is **11 months old**, try this game. Show him a small toy, place it under a plastic cup, then remove the cup and let him get it. Do this two more times. Now take the toy and place it under a different object, such as a little box. Watch what he does. He may still look for the toy under the cup because he's associated the toy with the familiar covering. Although this doesn't seem like a sign of budding intelligence to you, it's definitely an important step toward logical thought!

At around **12 months**, your baby will actively look for something he wants, even if it's not where he thought it would be. He'll be able to hold onto the thought for only a few minutes at first— something else will easily distract him. Before he can consciously look hard for something, he'll have to be much older.

That first *no* you uttered—did you really, really mean it? And what about that second one? And if your baby actually goes ahead and does that forbidden thing, will there be a third *no?* And do you really mean that as well?

If your baby loves testing limits, more power to him. You've raised a confident child who knows there *are* limits to behavior. And when he behaves like this, he's learning by testing those limits. That doesn't mean your baby's naughty; rather, it means he genuinely wants to know if he can dump a bucket of sand here, or here, or here; or bite this, or this, or that; or touch this, or this, or that.

Around **10 months**, your baby is ready to learn the first clues about what's right and what's wrong. Before this time, his memory wouldn't have lasted long enough for him to remember from one day to the next. Now, you can start to teach him both by what you do, and what you tell him to do—or not to do. He's learning self-control, your rules, and how to keep himself safe.

say what you mean, mean what you say

Babies need—and want—limits. Limits set a boundary, a safe space in the world. With too many limits, your baby won't have the space to explore and learn. With not enough, he'll grow up selfish and overindulged. Just because he's a baby doesn't mean he has the right to bite his sibling, deliberately upend his juice on the floor, or scribble on the papers on your desk. Your baby needs to learn which limits you're setting. Those limits will depend on your priorities, but once you've decided them—always keep your crayons in the kitchen, never hit the dog—it's your job to enforce those limits consistently.

And that's *not* easy. When your baby bursts into tears because he wants to take his crayons into the living room, it's tempting to give in. Who likes to see an unhappy child? And a baby can be very disarming; he'll carry the crayons boldly toward the living room with such a charming grin that you melt with adoration (and don't have the heart to say no). But if crayons are allowed in the living room today, then why aren't they tomorrow? And if hitting the dog doesn't warrant a warning today, maybe the dog will get a bigger swat tomorrow. Make sure you focus on the behavior and not your baby's innate character: Hitting the dog is bad, your baby is not bad; poking fingers into the electrical outlet is bad, your baby is not bad.

Be prepared to reinforce your messages repeatedly, because you can't expect your baby to remember every lesson the first time it's taught. Be prepared to follow through, to say that first *no,* and the second, and the third. Be prepared for tears and tantrums. Learning to live with limits is an essential life skill. If your baby learns that limits can be broken, it will make life more difficult for both of you in the long run. But teach him that *no* really does mean no, and he'll accept your limits as a matter of fact and move on.

tantrums

Although toddlers are notorious for tantrums—hence the common phrase "the terrible twos"—they're not unusual in babies as young as 9 months. A tantrum can make *you* want to hold your breath, scream, and kick something, so just imagine the powerful emotions your baby must be feeling to behave in this way.

Not every show of anger is a tantrum. Your baby may run away, yell, even stamp his feet or go so stiff that you can't bend him into his car seat, but that's not a tantrum. That's just plain anger. A full-blown tantrum is an expression of complete rage, frustration, and helplessness—the emotional equivalent of a blown fuse.

It's hard to predict how a tantrum will manifest itself, although your baby will probably behave similarly almost every time. And it can be a shock. That little angel who only a short time ago looked so incredibly cute in her bouncy chair screams hysterically until she makes herself hoarse; and, if she's mobile, flings herself around the place with abandon and writhing, as if she's fighting with invisible demons. She may make herself throw up or turn blue in the face.

what to do when your baby has a tantrum

The most important thing to remember is that your baby is no longer in control of her actions or feelings. This means she *can't* stop. No matter how much you shout, plead, or hope, she's lost to the world, and your messages don't have a prayer of getting through. All you can do is keep her safe and wait for the tantrum to run its course.

Make sure your baby doesn't hurt herself, or anyone or anything. If you don't protect her, she can crash into solid walls and furniture. If you can, move anything that happens to be in her path, or she'll knock it over. If you get within range, you're likely to be kicked—so be careful if you try to pick her up. If your baby comes out of a tantrum to find you hurt, she'll see the damage as proof of her own terrible powers and evidence that when she can't control herself, you can't control her and keep her safe, either.

It's easiest to keep your baby safe if you hold her, although some babies can't bear to be touched. Stay nearby. As your baby calms down, she'll find herself close to you and—surprise!—discover that the world is undamaged by her storm.

However difficult a tantrum is for you to deal with, remember that it's much worse for your baby. She becomes overwhelmed by violent feelings of rage and frustration and can't even put these feelings into words yet. She doesn't understand what's happened, but you do.

Breath-holding tantrums are the most alarming of all for parents to watch. Your baby goes without breathing for so long that her face looks either pale or blue and she can lose consciousness and go limp. (Babies don't usually deliberately hold their breaths; this can also happen involuntarily if your baby takes a sharp intake of breath before a loud scream for a reason other than a tantrum.)

It's impossible for her actually to damage herself in this way. Her body's reflexes will force air back into her lungs long before she's in any danger.

what to do when the tantrum is over

First and foremost, it's comfort time. After that, act as if the tantrum never happened. Don't let your baby feel either rewarded or punished for the tantrum. You want to teach her that tantrums change nothing, either for or against her. If she had a tantrum because you wouldn't let her have a cookie, don't change your mind and give it to her now. If you were heading out before she had the tantrum, take her out now. If you change your mind, she'll learn that this explosion delivers the desired effect.

avoiding tantrums

It's always worth avoiding tantrums if you can, without compromising your standards, because they don't benefit either you or your baby. You may be able to prevent many tantrums by organizing your baby's life so that she can tolerate any frustrations most of the time. When you have to force her to do something unpleasant or forbid something she enjoys, try doing it as tactfully as you can. If she's getting angry or upset about something, try to make it easier for her to accept. Of course she can't eat another cookie if that's what you've told her, but perhaps a slice of bread? Try not to back your baby into corners from which both of you can only explode in rage. Leave a dignified escape route on both sides.

As your baby grows, she will get bigger, stronger, and more capable of controlling events, which means that she'll meet less extreme frustration in her everyday life—and triggers for tantrums will be less common.

In time, your baby will also be able to talk to you more about what she wants and doesn't want. In short, she'll turn into someone you can reason with, and when reason enters the picture, tantrums disappear.

by the numbers
feeding: 10 to 12 months

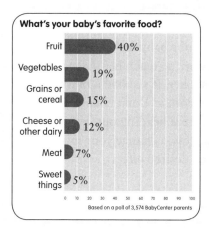

What's your baby's favorite food?

- Fruit — 40%
- Vegetables — 19%
- Grains or cereal — 15%
- Cheese or other dairy — 12%
- Meat — 7%
- Sweet things — 5%

Based on a poll of 3,574 BabyCenter parents

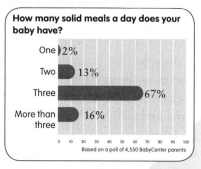

How many solid meals a day does your baby have?

- One — 2%
- Two — 13%
- Three — 67%
- More than three — 16%

Based on a poll of 4,550 BabyCenter parents

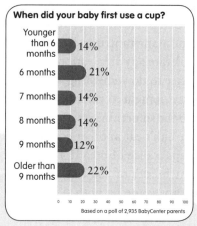

When did your baby first use a cup?

- Younger than 6 months — 14%
- 6 months — 21%
- 7 months — 14%
- 8 months — 14%
- 9 months — 12%
- Older than 9 months — 22%

Based on a poll of 2,935 BabyCenter parents

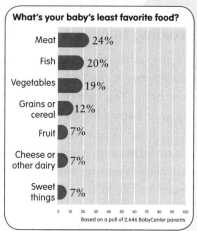

What's your baby's least favorite food?

- Meat — 24%
- Fish — 20%
- Vegetables — 19%
- Grains or cereal — 12%
- Fruit — 7%
- Cheese or other dairy — 7%
- Sweet things — 7%

Based on a poll of 2,646 BabyCenter parents

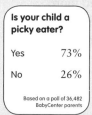

Is your child a picky eater?

Yes — 73%

No — 26%

Based on a poll of 36,482 BabyCenter parents

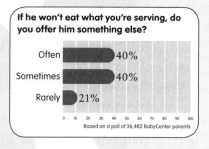

If he won't eat what you're serving, do you offer him something else?

- Often — 40%
- Sometimes — 40%
- Rarely — 21%

Based on a poll of 36,482 BabyCenter parents

the bottom line

Your baby's feeding patterns now become closer to your own. He'll still need extra meals because he can't eat a lot at one time, but some of his meals will coincide with yours. It's a good time to sit him up at the table and let him enjoy family mealtimes. He'll gradually learn how you behave, and as he grows older, mealtimes will become a valuable time to talk and catch up with each other.

chapter
26

feeding—
10 to 12 months

The balance of breast milk or formula to solid foods is beginning to tilt more toward solids. Your baby has some definite likes and dislikes in foods, and you'll find both of those change over time. As always, patience is of the essence when introducing new foods.

feeding checkpoint: how much milk?

if you're breastfeeding

Breast milk should play a part in your baby's nutrition until he's a year old (at which time it's safe to introduce cow's milk). Breastfed babies may be down to just two feedings a day—morning and evening—and often drop the early morning feeding between **10 and 12 months**. Many babies (and their moms) like to keep the going-to-bed feeding as a peaceful end to the day. Some babies choose to keep this feeding for many more months, while others decide for themselves that they don't need any more breast milk. It can come as a surprise and be oddly disappointing if your baby refuses the breast. It feels as if he's telling you he's not a baby anymore.

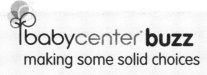

babycenter **buzz**
making some solid choices

"We couldn't get our son to eat rice cereal from a spoon. He'd grab the spoon and try to do it himself, but he couldn't get any food in. When I tried, he'd shut his mouth. Then I started making his food thick and letting him use his hands, and he liked that. It's messy but he's eating, and we're having a good time."—**Catherine**

"One of my biggest obstacles to giving up breastfeeding is that my daughter has been slow with solids. She's really not all that interested in food, so she's still getting a huge percentage of her nutrition from milk and formula. And I don't want to replace breastfeeding at home with a bottle, so I'm trying to get the sippy cup going."—**Julie Ann**

if you're formula-feeding

Your baby should be taking approximately 17 to 20 ounces of formula each day. As long as he's eating a wide range of solid foods, he can continue with this amount until he's a year old. After the age of 1, it's time to move from formula to full-fat cow's milk.

Health professionals recommend that babies be gradually weaned off bottles by the end of their first year. Liquids flow very slowly through a nipple, which slows down the drinking process and causes the liquid to stay in touch with the teeth longer. The unfortunate result is often tooth decay, especially if the drinks are sugary and or acidic.

If you haven't already introduced your baby to a lidded training cup or sippy cup (which you can do any time after 6 or 7 months), allow plenty of time for this process so he can be weaned from the bottle gradually. Start with a soft spout, or bottle-to-cup training cup, which feels more familiar to your baby than a hard plastic spout.

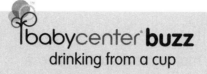

babycenter buzz
drinking from a cup

"If your toddler really doesn't like using sippy cups, you could be brave and try a regular cup, filling it with a little bit of liquid so that if it's spilled, it won't make a huge mess. You could also try a straw."—**Emma**

"If your toddler doesn't like cups, try a water bottle with a sports lid. Or a different brand or type of cup. If your baby is struggling to get the liquid out, move to a more 'free flow' cup for older babies. Experiment with different types until you find one that your baby likes."—**Susie**

"Take a drink from the cup yourself and encourage your toddler to copy you. Put a tiny bit of fluid on the mouthpiece so that your baby gets a taste and realizes that there's a drink in there."—**Christine**

"I used to let my daughter play with plastic cups so she could get used to the feel of them."—**Grace**

Show your baby how to raise the cup to his mouth and tip it up to drink from it. Next, move on to a cup with a hard spout, and from there to an open cup with handles. Training cups with non-spill valves make drinking less messy, but they demand more work to get at the drink. So it may be worth putting up with some mess at first, until he's gotten the hang of how to drink from a cup. Some babies take to the cup more readily than others.

solid foods

With a diet based on solids, it's time to start thinking about balancing your baby's meals. What your baby eats now and how you eat as a family set the pattern for the future.

stage 4: family mealtimes

Encourage your baby to follow a two-or-three meal a day pattern along with one or two snacks and 17 to 20 ounces of breast milk or formula. Chop her food rather than mashing it and keep offering a wide variety of foods, too.

At this stage, each day your baby should be eating:

- ⅓ cup dairy (or ½ ounce cheese)
- ¼ to ½ cup iron-fortified cereal
- ¼ to ½ cup fruit
- ¼ to ½ cup vegetables
- ⅛ to ¼ cup combo foods
- ⅛ to ¼ cup protein foods
- 3 to 4 ounces non-citrus juices

Continue to keep your child off sugar, honey, and foods with artificial sweeteners. For a snack between meals, serve fresh fruit such as a banana or diced grapes, dried cereal your baby can pick up, or baby crackers. (To recheck what can be served during stages 1 through 3, see chapters 16 and 21.)

feeding a reluctant eater

It's going to be incredibly frustrating when your baby rejects each new food you've carefully selected for her. What's the best way to deal with a reluctant eater?

5 things that help

1. **Keeping it low key.** If you allow mealtimes to turn into a battle, your baby will pick up on that and could become even more reluctant. Refusing food sometimes has more to do with your baby seeking attention than not wanting to eat. Try praising her for all the things she's doing well, including her eating, and ignore the food refusal. Offer your baby food, and if she still refuses it, just take it away.

2. **Offering plenty of variety.** Eventually something will interest your baby; she'll try it and like it. What your baby eats over several days matters more than her consuming the right number of nutrients in a single day.

3. **Changing the time of day you offer food.** Maybe she's just not hungry in the middle of the day but will be in the early evening. Experiment and see.

4. **Introducing solid food between two batches of milk.** Your baby may be too hungry and impatient to cope with food. A bit of milk will take the edge off her hunger, so she can slow down and try the food. Finish with some more milk so you know she's had plenty of nutrients.

5. **Not giving up on rejected foods.** Nutritionists say it can take 10 or more exposures to a new food before a baby will consent to trying it. What seems like pickiness may simply be a slow courtship.

5 things that hinder

1. **Insisting your baby stay in her highchair** until she's finished everything. You can put a baby in a highchair, but you can't make her eat.

2. **Cutting down on formula.** It won't make her eat more food and could reduce her nutrient intake.

3. **Forcing your baby to eat.** Even if you push the food into her mouth, she'll spit it out. The scene is then set for a daily mealtime battle. If your baby drinks plenty of formula or breast milk—a nutritional safety net—she'll be fine.

4. **Expecting your baby to eat the same amount every day.** Babies grow in fits and starts; if she's not hungry today, she probably will be tomorrow. Your baby will also be hungrier once she starts crawling or walking as she expends more energy.

5. **Not giving your baby any choice.** Try putting a selection of finger foods on a tray and let your baby pick what she wants. That way, she's in control of what she eats.

Keep in mind that babies are naturally fussy eaters—and with good reasons. Once you understand those reasons, you can use that knowledge to help her become a more adventurous eater.

introducing new foods

Reluctance to try new foods may be a survival mechanism. Our ancient ancestors had to discover by trial and error which foods were safe and which were dangerous. That same primitive instinct protects babies in several ways. First, they naturally have a sweet tooth, so they reject foods that are bitter or sour, and most poisons contain elements that give them bitter or sour flavors. Second, anything a baby has safely eaten before isn't likely to harm him, so that's a good reason why a baby will prefer familiar foods and be suspicious of new ones.

Despite the research suggesting that parents should offer an individual food up to 10 times before a baby will eat it, about half of parents offer a food only two or three times before giving up on it altogether.

Persist! Keep offering new kinds of foods, and re-offering them. It's not that your baby doesn't like a particular food, it's just that it's completely new to her. As a food becomes more familiar, she's more apt to try it.

Vary shapes and colors. If your baby's initial diet of solids consists primarily of cereal, it's possible she'll expect all foods to be mush-like and reject servings of a different color or shape. Likewise, she might swoon over mashed peas but reject whole peas or eat carrot purée but be suspicious of the same vegetable, grated.

Tactic: Offer your baby a variety of shapes, colors, and textures as well as flavors when you first introduce solids, and her picture of what foods *should* look like will be wide, not narrow.

Don't delay introducing lumpy foods. Waiting to introduce lumpier textured foods can contribute to fussy eating habits. One study found that in a group of babies who weren't given lumpy foods until they were 10 months or older, one in five were fussy eaters by the age of 15 months.

Keep broadening the range of textures served. Babies who were served lumpier textures from 6 to 9 months tended to be less fussy eaters by 10 months, research has shown. All the more reason to keep introducing variety now, as your child can handle firmer textures.

Tactic: Buy pasta or crackers in a variety of different shapes and colors so your toddler doesn't get stuck in a rut of always expecting the same thing. Likewise, potatoes, for example, can be served mashed, as hash browns, or baked and cut up. Offer both white and sweet potatoes. Serve both soft and hard cereals.

Be adventurous with tastes. Before birth, your baby swallowed amniotic fluid, and experts now believe it carries flavor from the foods you eat. The same is true of the milk your breastfed baby consumes, which differs in taste from feeding to feeding, depending on your diet. In cultures where spicy foods are the norm, babies taste spices early on. Formula, on the other hand, tastes the same every time, so formula-fed babies may be more reluctant to try new foods.

Tactic: Experiment with different foods to see which flavors your baby likes.

Consider skipping baby food. Some moms choose not to offer baby food at all. They simply breastfeed until their baby reaches out for family food and then let him try anything that catches his eye (and that's safe to eat), in mashed, ground, or chopped form if necessary. In primitive cultures, the process would have been much the same. There's no rule that says babies have to eat commercial baby food.

Tactic: Be especially vigilant about choking if you try this route, and offer foods that don't present a choking hazard. If you take this approach, your baby may continue getting most of his nutrition from breast milk, so keep an eye on his growth as well.

babycenter buzz
food battles: how to win the war

"I have to distract my son by giving him new things to explore while I'm feeding him baby food. If the battle isn't too bad, I try my best not to show any frustration and be patient. If it is bad, and no matter what I do he refuses to eat, then I stop and figure that he'll eat next meal."—**Yasmin**

"We have a rule in our house that worked great with our older daughters and so we're doing it again with our baby: As soon as they start throwing food, they're removed from the high chair. They go off to play with their toys instead of playing with their food. It really shows that they're not interested in eating, so I'd take that cue and just stop feeding."—**Anonymous**

"We usually give our son a bottle about 30 minutes to an hour before going to a restaurant so he's not starving, and just give him Cheerios at the restaurant. If he spills, I don't stress too much about it, babies pick up on that."—**Kelly**

"What I do is give finger foods one at a time. So for breakfast I'll start off with some Cheerios, and when she starts to slow down on that, I'll give some cut-up fruit, then toast, then a different fruit. I just keep going through foods, which seems to keep her interested."—**Jamie**

"My daughter is a slow eater. To distract her, I turn on *Sesame Street,* and as soon as she gets caught up in the action, I tell her to open her mouth and I slip in a spoonful of food or a slice of fruit. She doesn't even realize she's eating."—**K. B.**

Don't be a fussy eater yourself! Children learn behaviors from their parents. Research indicates that 27 percent of toddlers are fussy eaters—and that 22 percent of them have parents who admit to being fussy eaters themselves.

Tactic: When your baby sees you enjoying a wide range of foods, he'll be willing to try a variety, too.

food allergies and intolerance

Babies sometimes develop allergies to foods, most commonly peanuts, wheat, eggs, milk, soy products, tree nuts, shellfish, fish, and citrus fruit. The symptoms of a true food allergy, such as a rash or wheezing, or swelling of the lips and tongue, generally appear within an hour of eating.

Babies can also develop intolerances to some foods, which are different from true allergies. Symptoms of food intolerance are more likely to affect your baby's digestive system, and reactions include tummy pain, bloating, gas, diarrhea, and sometimes vomiting.

If you're worried about a food intolerance, call your doctor, who may refer you and your baby to a dietitian. To help to identify which foods are causing the problem, the dietitian may suggest keeping a food diary or putting your baby on an exclusion diet, which removes suspect foods from her diet and then slowly reintroduces them.

finger food safety

With your baby's expanding palate come a few new guidelines to prevent choking.

- Feeding in a highchair is safer than in a car seat or stroller (and reinforces that it's the place for eating).
- Never leave your child unattended when she's self-feeding.
- Make sure she's upright (not slouched in her chair or lying down).
- Mash or grind food if it's not already soft enough to gum or chew.
- Wait to give peanut butter (unless spread very thinly), raw carrots, uncooked peas, raisins, and hot dogs (even in small pieces) until at least age 4.
- Never force-feed.

If you haven't already taken a class on infant CPR, now is a good time to do so. Check at local community centers, hospitals, or doctors' offices to find out where such courses are offered.

To view an illustrated first aid guide about choking, go to babycenter.com.

by the numbers
sleep: 10 to 12 months

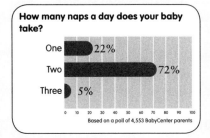

How many naps a day does your baby take?

One — 22%
Two — 72%
Three — 5%

Based on a poll of 4,553 BabyCenter parents

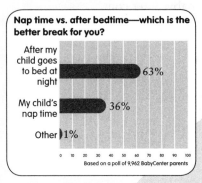

Nap time vs. after bedtime—which is the better break for you?

After my child goes to bed at night — 63%
My child's nap time — 36%
Other — 1%

Based on a poll of 9,962 BabyCenter parents

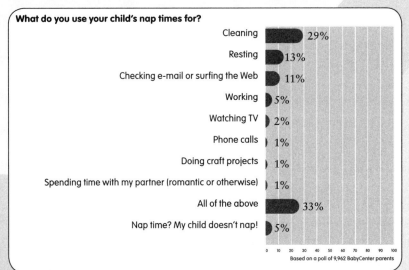

What do you use your child's nap times for?

Cleaning — 29%
Resting — 13%
Checking e-mail or surfing the Web — 11%
Working — 5%
Watching TV — 2%
Phone calls — 1%
Doing craft projects — 1%
Spending time with my partner (romantic or otherwise) — 1%
All of the above — 33%
Nap time? My child doesn't nap! — 5%

Based on a poll of 9,962 BabyCenter parents

Does your baby climb out of the crib?

Yes — 4%
No — 75%
She tries, but hasn't gotten out yet — 20%

Based on a poll of 3,244 BabyCenter parents

Have you tried sleep training?

Yes — 38%
No — 61%

Based on a poll of 3,232 BabyCenter parents

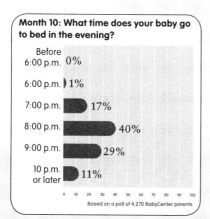

Month 10: What time does your baby go to bed in the evening?

- Before 6:00 p.m. — 0%
- 6:00 p.m. — 1%
- 7:00 p.m. — 17%
- 8:00 p.m. — 40%
- 9:00 p.m. — 29%
- 10 p.m. or later — 11%

Based on a poll of 4,270 BabyCenter parents

What comfort object does your child sleep with?

- A blankie — 32%
- A stuffed animal — 23%
- A pacifier — 21%
- Nothing — 12%
- Something else — 7%
- A favorite toy — 2%
- A bottle — 2%

Based on a poll of 36,893 BabyCenter parents

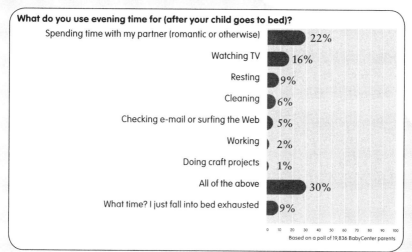

What do you use evening time for (after your child goes to bed)?

- Spending time with my partner (romantic or otherwise) — 22%
- Watching TV — 16%
- Resting — 9%
- Cleaning — 6%
- Checking e-mail or surfing the Web — 5%
- Working — 2%
- Doing craft projects — 1%
- All of the above — 30%
- What time? I just fall into bed exhausted — 9%

Based on a poll of 19,836 BabyCenter parents

the bottom line

By 12 months of age, your baby will probably be sleeping some 14 to 15 hours in every 24, with 11 or 12 of those hours at night. He'll still have two daytime naps, too, one in the morning and one in the afternoon. However, these naps begin to get shorter now, and your baby has days where he drops one of them altogether. Naps will be a feature of your baby's day for some time to come, though. About a quarter of toddlers give up daytime naps by the time they're 3, half by age 4. Another quarter continue to nap until they're age 5 or older.

sleep—
10 to 12 months

When you and your baby are feeling rested, everyone's less cranky. However, if sleep problems start to get in the way of mellow days and nights, you have plenty of tactics at your disposal to get everyone back on track.

sleep problems and the almost-toddler

It seems like some sleep problems—some old and some new—just won't rest, even at this stage of a baby's development.

your baby wakes at night

Even parents aren't always successful at getting back to sleep when they wake in the middle of the night. Babies are no exception.

why it happens

Sometimes the problem is short-lived, caused by a fever or an ear infection or because your baby simply missed a nap and his normal sleep schedule was disrupted. Nightmares can also cause a one-time waking.

babycenter **buzz**
dreaming about sleep

"In my experience, the harder I've tried to get babies to bed, the more difficult it is and the less they sleep. When I go with the flow and let them work their sleep schedules out, everyone usually ends up getting more sleep. Some people (babies included) are night owls, and some are morning people."—**Amanda**

"Finally, I found out for myself that I needed to stop nursing my son to sleep because he didn't know how to get himself back to sleep when he woke. He does much better now that he can fall asleep on his own. All babies (and adults) wake up many times in the night; it's just a matter of how quickly they can get themselves back to sleep."—**Anonymous**

"My 11-month-old only recently began to sleep through the night without coming in to our bed. My advice is to stick with your routine as rigidly as you can and take baby steps to get him to sleep alone. It's exhausting but definitely achievable."—**Melanie**

Changes to your baby's normal routine (or he may never have had a routine at all) can cause consistent wake-ups in the middle of the night. The same is true for overtiredness—when your baby is worn out with too much excitement, tiredness, and tension, but still unable to relax into sleep.

what you can do about it

- Establish regular naptimes, bedtime, and a consistent bedtime routine (see page 238).
- Put your baby to bed at the first signs of sleepiness to head off a meltdown.
- Introduce an earlier bedtime (long before you go to bed), so that your baby has a chance to settle down.
- Arrange time to play or rest quietly during the day so your baby doesn't become overly tired.
- Avoid rough-and-tumble activities before bed.

- If someone else in the house will be coming home after your baby goes to bed, make sure he or she walks through the door in "bedtime mode," talking calmly and quietly.

If these don't work: Try one of the approaches to dealing with sleep problems described on page 306.

your baby won't nap

Naptime is a welcome relief for you—a time to get odds and ends taken care of. What to do when your baby won't sleep?

why it happens

Typical causes: Your baby doesn't have a regular nap schedule or he gets overly tired.

what you can do about it

- Develop set naptimes and a naptime routine similar to your baby's bedtime routine.
- If you think your baby needs only one nap a day, after lunch is usually best; then he has a shorter stretch until bedtime.

What do experts think about napping? See the napping chart at babycenter.com.

your baby stalls at bedtime

Sometimes the best of bedtime routines starts losing its effectiveness.

why it happens

There's so much going on—your baby just wants to be part of the action. He is also beginning to understand that he's his own person and wants to assert his independence.

what you can do about it

- Teach your baby to fall asleep alone. (See page 241.)

- Don't let your baby dawdle: Anticipate all his usual requests and make them part of your bedtime routine—sing a lullaby, turn on the nightlight, and so on. A good compromise is to allow one extra request, but make it clear that one is the limit.
- Be calm, but firm: Stand your ground even if your baby cries or pleads for an exception to the going-to-bed rule. Consistency and firmness are essential.
- Keep the house relatively quiet after he's asleep.

your baby is bothered by teething

Imagine trying to get to sleep with a toothache. It's not the same as teething, but both conditions can make it difficult to doze off.

why it happens

Your toddler's molars push through between about 12 and 15 months, which can be painful. If your baby has a pacifier or sucks his thumb, the sucking will cause more pain.

what you can do about it

As much as possible, stick to your regular sleep routine, both at night and for daytime naps. Massage your baby's gums gently with one finger or give him something cold to chew on, such as a cooled (not frozen) gel-filled teething ring. With your doctor's blessing, you can also give the correct dose of infant acetaminophen.

To share your sleep concerns—and hear from other parents—log on to BabyCenter's "Sleep Problems" bulletin board at babycenter.com.

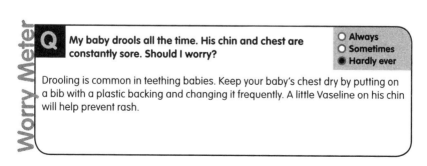

Worry Meter

Q My baby drools all the time. His chin and chest are constantly sore. Should I worry?

○ Always
○ Sometimes
● Hardly ever

Drooling is common in teething babies. Keep your baby's chest dry by putting on a bib with a plastic backing and changing it frequently. A little Vaseline on his chin will help prevent rash.

by the numbers
baby care: 10 to 12 months

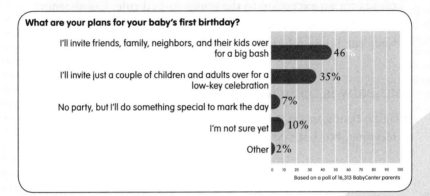

What are your plans for your baby's first birthday?

- I'll invite friends, family, neighbors, and their kids over for a big bash — 46%
- I'll invite just a couple of children and adults over for a low-key celebration — 35%
- No party, but I'll do something special to mark the day — 7%
- I'm not sure yet — 10%
- Other — 2%

Based on a poll of 16,313 BabyCenter parents

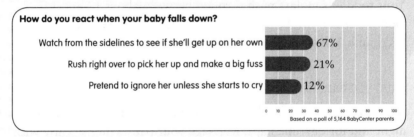

How do you react when your baby falls down?

- Watch from the sidelines to see if she'll get up on her own — 67%
- Rush right over to pick her up and make a big fuss — 21%
- Pretend to ignore her unless she starts to cry — 12%

Based on a poll of 5,164 BabyCenter parents

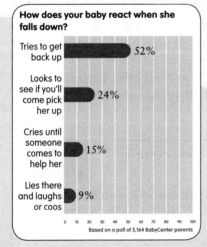

How does your baby react when she falls down?

- Tries to get back up — 52%
- Looks to see if you'll come pick her up — 24%
- Cries until someone comes to help her — 15%
- Lies there and laughs or coos — 9%

Based on a poll of 5,164 BabyCenter parents

the bottom line

Your baby's memory is developing to the point where he's used to doing certain things at certain times. If you get the stroller out, he realizes it's time for a walk. If you start to cook, he goes to his highchair. He'll get upset if something he thought was going to happen doesn't. If he cries when you go into the bathroom to clean it, it's because he thought it was bath time. Sometimes you just have to make a guess at what he's thinking, but you know him better than anyone else, so you'll get it right most of the time.

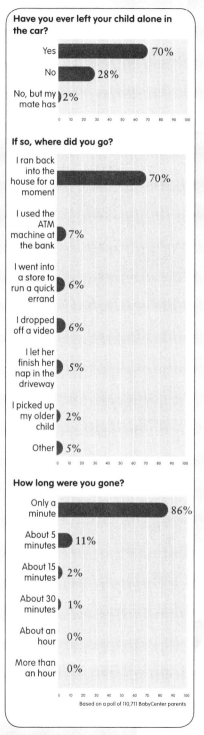

Have you ever left your child alone in the car?

- Yes — 70%
- No — 28%
- No, but my mate has — 2%

If so, where did you go?

- I ran back into the house for a moment — 70%
- I used the ATM machine at the bank — 7%
- I went into a store to run a quick errand — 6%
- I dropped off a video — 6%
- I let her finish her nap in the driveway — 5%
- I picked up my older child — 2%
- Other — 5%

How long were you gone?

- Only a minute — 86%
- About 5 minutes — 11%
- About 15 minutes — 2%
- About 30 minutes — 1%
- About an hour — 0%
- More than an hour — 0%

Based on a poll of 110,711 BabyCenter parents

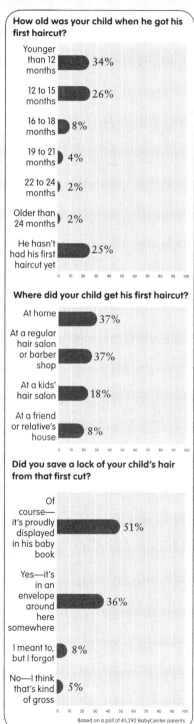

How old was your child when he got his first haircut?

- Younger than 12 months — 34%
- 12 to 15 months — 26%
- 16 to 18 months — 8%
- 19 to 21 months — 4%
- 22 to 24 months — 2%
- Older than 24 months — 2%
- He hasn't had his first haircut yet — 25%

Where did your child get his first haircut?

- At home — 37%
- At a regular hair salon or barber shop — 37%
- At a kids' hair salon — 18%
- At a friend or relative's house — 8%

Did you save a lock of your child's hair from that first cut?

- Of course—it's proudly displayed in his baby book — 51%
- Yes—it's in an envelope around here somewhere — 36%
- I meant to, but I forgot — 8%
- No—I think that's kind of gross — 5%

Based on a poll of 45,292 BabyCenter parents

baby care—
10 to 12 months

So much of what you'll be doing at this stage is in preparation for impending toddlerhood. Your baby is about to become a "tween" of sorts—no longer a baby but not quite a toddler.

managing your baby's day

Many babies drop the morning nap about this time, which can lead to a tired baby falling asleep in the very early evening and then waking up in the middle of the night. (Others don't do this until closer to 15 months.) Welcome to the awkward weeks. By juggling her schedule, you can help your baby to stay awake until a reasonable time in the evening.

At first, you may need to let your baby nap but wake her before she would usually get up herself. If, for example, she usually sleeps in the morning for an hour, start waking her after 50 minutes. A few days later, drop this time down to 40 minutes, and so on. If you find that she can manage without this nap, replace it with a quiet time when you read to her and let her play on your lap.

babycenter **buzz**
calming measures

"Whenever my baby is really cranky, I take him outside for some fresh, cool air. It seems to calm him down."—**Anonymous**

"My son loves music videos but only certain ones, so I tape them, and when it's time to get his haircut, I pop in the video and he sits still and stays quiet."—**Cee Cee**

"I found that when my son was biting me, it was because I wasn't giving him my full attention. If I was trying to type or read a book while nursing, he'd bite. If I stopped and just held him and enjoyed the moment and talked to him, he wouldn't bite."—**Jessi**

Expect dropping this nap to take a month or so of adjustment. During this bumpy phase, accept that some days your baby will fall asleep just when you wanted her to stay awake—because of a car ride at the "wrong" time, perhaps, or a fun day out with friends that exhausts her. On those days, push her bedtime back an hour or two so she'll be ready to sleep. Most babies continue with one daytime nap for at least another year and sometimes longer.

explained: baby signing

Baby signing is a way of communicating with your baby before he has the coordination to speak understandable words. Your baby's understanding of language and ability to make signs develops much faster than his ability to speak.

Both deaf and hearing babies naturally start using simple gestures, such as pointing, at around 8 to 9 months of age. At about 9 to 10 months, all babies develop a kind of gestural language. They begin to ask for things by using gestures or combinations of gestures and sounds. For example, your baby reaches out toward something he wants, opening and closing his hands, and making a whining noise at the same time. He waves bye-bye long before he can say *bye-bye*. Between 10 and 20 months, babies are so highly motivated to communicate that they often start using such symbolic gestures as a way of getting around the physical difficulties of saying words.

Building on this idea, some parents teach their babies a form of very basic sign language to help them communicate before they can talk.

what are the advantages of signing?

Giving your baby the tools to express himself may help cut down on his frustration. Some research shows that signing babies understand more words, have larger vocabularies, and engage in more sophisticated play than non-signing babies. In one study, parents of the signing babies noted decreased frustration, increased communication, and enriched parent-infant bonding.

But there's no strong proof yet that signing really offers a developmental advantage.

are there disadvantages to signing?

Some people see baby signing as another form of parents attempting to rush their children. Some speech and language therapists are also skeptical about its use, arguing that signing is a normal part of the way that parents and babies communicate anyway, and that a formal structured program simply isn't necessary. Besides, they say, parents shouldn't think that they can't start communicating with their babies until they're capable of signing.

how do I sign with my baby?

Most babies can begin to learn signs from about 6 months, but you can also start later. To begin, try using a hand signal every

by the numbers

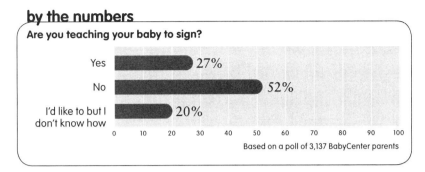

Are you teaching your baby to sign?

Yes 27%
No 52%
I'd like to but I don't know how 20%

Based on a poll of 3,137 BabyCenter parents

time you use common words. Simple signs that you could use include:

- *More:* Open and close your hand
- *Eat:* Put your fingertips to your mouth
- *Drink:* Pretend to raise a glass
- *Hug:* Put your arms around yourself

It may take a few weeks of signing to your baby before he starts making the signs back.

discipline and the almost-1-year-old

Like their parents, young children learn by doing—so when your baby tosses her peas off the highchair tray, it's because she wants to see what will happen, not because she wants to upset you or mess up the clean kitchen floor. By now, you've already told your baby more than once that bowls aren't for throwing. Before **12 months**, she begins testing your authority by refusing to follow your directions or pleas. When your baby pushes back, she's not being disobedient or willful—she's just curious. Plus, she simply can't remember things for more than a couple of seconds at a time. Even if you told her not to throw the bowl yesterday, that doesn't mean she remembers today. And if she does remember, she's doing it again because she's curious about what your response will be. Will you look annoyed and say *no* again this time—or ignore it?

Worry Meter

Q **My baby screams when I try to wash her hair. Should I worry?**

○ Always
○ Sometimes
● Hardly ever

Lots of babies hate having their hair washed. Often, hair washing frightens them. Forcing the issue won't make it any better. Your best bet is to put it off for as long as you can. Yes, your baby's hair gets dirty, but if you can wait for even a week or more, whatever was frightening him could be lost to memory. Another option: Try using a hair shield in the bath to stop the water from getting in his eyes. Or let him help you wash *your* hair in the bath a few times to give him confidence that he'll survive the process.

The best tactic is still to use a simple *no*, then distract her. Take the object away or physically move your baby away from it. Then give her an alternative. If she can't throw the peas, can she throw a ball? If she can't chew on the remote control, can she chew a teething ring? If she can't hit the cat, can she stroke it instead?

Make sure to always explain what you're doing, even if your baby is too young to really understand. You're teaching a fundamental life rule—that some behaviors aren't acceptable, and that you'll let her know when that's the case. Just don't expect your baby to change her behavior as a result of simple reasoning. The idea is to get her in the habit of hearing about rules—but developmentally she's still too young to understand and automatically change her behavior just because you "explained" what was wrong.

By around your baby's first birthday, though, there comes a turning point. Your child becomes capable of knowing when she's doing something she's not supposed to. When she looks at you with that glint in her eye and then throws the bowl anyway, it's time to take a different tack. Exploding in rage will only be very entertaining and offer the reward she was expecting when she tipped the bowl in the first place. Instead, involve her in the cleaning up. Take her out of her highchair, put her on the floor, and ask her to hand you some of the peas or the bowl, or to dab at the floor with a cloth. Let her sense that she's "helping" you deal with the problem. Just as before, talk to her about what you're doing: "There is a mess, so we have to clean it up." Then put her back in her chair and give her something else to eat, or end the meal. You're teaching your baby the concept of taking responsibility for her actions.

Another good tactic is to emphasize the positive. Pay a lot of attention to your baby when she's playing nicely or doing something you *do* like. Tell her how well she's behaving, rather than speaking up only when she's doing something wrong. That way, when she's older, you'll already be used to paying attention to her before she misbehaves, instead of trying to figure out how to punish her afterward.

It can take a bit of practice to get in the habit of rewarding good behavior rather than punishing bad, but it's far more effective in the long run.

babyproofing for a cruising or walking baby

Once your baby is upright and mobile, objects sitting at greater heights become accessible. In addition to the safety precautions you took when she started moving around (see page 318), now's a good time to get down on your hands and knees—your baby's height—and see what new safety measures you need to put in place.

- Drawers are reachable, so keep them locked if they contain pens, scissors, letter openers, staplers, and other sharp instruments, not to mention , buttons and other small choking hazards (or move everything higher up).
- In the kitchen, make sure any matches and lighters are out of reach.
- Fit a safety gate at the top of stairs and another three steps from the bottom. This prevents your baby from climbing all the way to the top only to discover that she can't reverse the process.
- Install safety gates to keep your baby out of rooms that are off-limits.

- Assume that all household cleaning products are dangerous and keep them out of your baby's reach. Even if she doesn't try to eat them, she can spray herself with them, burning her skin and eyes.

- Beware of standing water—even a mop bucket full of water is a danger as a 12-month-old can crawl or toddle over, fall in headfirst, and drown. Always drain bathtubs immediately.
- Never leave an iron or curling iron with a dangling cord where a toddler could reach it and pull the object down; even if the iron is cool, it is heavy.
- Now that your child is mobile, recheck window locks and make sure she can't access an open window.
- Secure dressers to the wall so they can't tip over if your child crawls up onto open drawers.
- Keep all pills and medicines securely locked in a cupboard out of the way. Any medicine, whether prescribed for you or for her, is dangerous. Even vitamin supplements are fatal in large doses.
- Periodically, check bare floors and carpets to make sure there are no small objects, such as coins or paper clips, which are potential choking hazards that your baby can pick up and put in her mouth.

To find out how BabyCenter parents babyproofed their homes, go to babycenter.com.

car seat turnaround?

The current recommendations are for babies to remain in a rear-facing car seat until they're 20 pounds *and* 12 months old, whichever comes later. These are the minimums. Your baby can and should stay in the rear-facing seat even after these markers, provided he still fits in the seat. If he outgrows the infant starter seat, use a larger-size car seat that's also designed to face the rear. These next-stage car seats don't have handles and are designed to remain in the vehicle all the time. Always follow the height and weight guidelines that apply to your particular car seat.

first shoes

Your baby doesn't need shoes until she's walking outside, where her sensitive feet need protection. Experts say that the longer a baby is allowed to walk without shoes, the better, as this allows her feet and lower legs to develop and strengthen without restriction. It's been estimated that a person will walk 115,000 miles in his or her lifetime, so you want to set those new feet off on the right track!

When your baby starts learning to walk indoors, have her walk barefoot, as long as the floor is clean and safe. Once she's taking a few steps confidently and starts walking outdoors on rough surfaces, protect her feet with shoes made of flexible, lightweight, and natural materials, such as soft leather, with flexible soles and nonskid bottoms.

celebrating your baby's first birthday

At 1 year old, your baby's memory is quite short, so chances are eventually she won't remember her first birthday. But don't let that stop you from making it a memorable day. It's a good time to gather together close family and friends for a special celebration; just don't feel pressured into going over the top when it comes to parties and presents. Your baby won't appreciate such extravagance,

party favors

Party favors are really superfluous at this age, and the usual goodies such as sweets and balloons are downright dangerous. One of the biggest money-wasters is overpriced plastic toys that get lost or thrown out in no time. If you really want to present a favor to your little guests, why not choose a safe soft toy or a board book to chew on?

babycenter **buzz**
how to party hearty!

"We're having a time-capsule party. Everyone is writing my daughter a letter and bringing items that represent life today to be placed inside the time capsule. We'll be sealing it at the party. She'll open it on her 16th birthday. I'm inviting everyone who's important to her."—**Charlette**

"For my baby's first birthday party, I bought a karaoke machine (inexpensive) and some tapes with popular children's songs. Of course she can't speak yet, let alone sing, but she danced and hummed while the other children— all over 3—sang to her. It was the cutest thing and we have it on videotape!"—**Angela**

"My daughter's first birthday is in 3 weeks. We're keeping it small—family mostly. We have sidewalk chalk for the kids, and we made a DVD with pictures of her first year and plan to show that. Finger foods, cake, gifts—all simple."—**Jessie**

and small is definitely beautiful at this age. All of this adds up to an intimate, low-budget family party.

Where? Remember that your 1-year-old may be fearful of strangers and new places. Home is where your baby feels most relaxed. So consider having a party in your own home or backyard, where it's easier to organize and carry out activities, and you won't have to haul food and supplies around in ice chests. If your living space is simply too small to accommodate friends and family, consider borrowing a relative's house, but make it clear that you'll do all the organizing and cleaning up. Or, if weather permits, use a local park.

When? Your baby probably has a definite daytime nap routine. You'll want to avoid the excitement of a party when your baby is tired, so an afternoon celebration, after the nap, may work well. If you're inviting other baby guests, check out their naptimes with their parents. Once one starts wailing, they all will! Keep the party brief; an hour or so is long enough at this age.

Who? Despite liking other babies, your 1-year-old won't understand how to play with them yet. Her social network will be small and intimate and that's how she likes it. She won't thank you for a house full of strangers, so it's a good idea to stick to close friends and relatives. Relatives won't want to miss this party, cameras at the ready, either, but the bigger the gathering, the more hectic it will be.

What? Keep food simple—after all, plenty of it will end up on the floor! Finger foods are excellent for both babies and adults, since eating them won't interrupt play or interaction. Parents of other babies will likely bring a bottle or cup with them containing the drink of their choice, but have water, milk, and diluted fruit juices at the ready. If you're providing food for grown-ups, keep it simple and avoid peanuts and other foods that can cause an allergic reaction or present a choking hazard to little ones.

Some babies have quite a few teeth by now and can bite into food; others are still relatively toothless, so cater the cooking for both extremes: bread sticks, tiny sandwiches with cheese spread, soft vegetables, and so on. Your mini guests will probably eat very little food, so aim for a variety of taste, texture, and color rather than quantity.

Cake with icing is delicious but messy. On the other hand, what's a birthday without a cake? If it has candles, keep your baby away from them, as she'll be more inclined to grab them than blow them out.

How? One-year-olds are too young for organized games, so save these for later years. Why not have some musical fun, such as dancing with your baby, or singing to a nursery rhyme CD? She'll appreciate a few simple games, such as peekaboo, finding toys hidden in a box or under a cloth, and, of course, helping you open

presents for a 1-year-old

Babies this age appreciate anything that makes a noise or lights up, or both, so activity centers are a good choice. It's never too early to read, and board books are great fun for your tactile baby. A push toy to encourage walking skills will be popular, and new bath toys are always welcome. Consider a big lasting present, such as a baby swing for outdoors or a rocking horse. If you already have rooms full of toys, your baby won't object if some people buy him clothes!

her presents (although the wrapping paper will be far more fun than the gift!). At this closely-attached-to-mom stage, the best way to make this a special day for your 1-year-old is to give her loads of undiluted you.

Caution: Loud bangs from party poppers and bursting balloons tend to frighten babies, and discarded poppers and balloons are a serious choking hazard at this age, so skip them.

10 tips for a successful party

1. Prepare a space somewhere clean, handy, and well-equipped for diaper changing.

2. Designate somewhere quiet for breastfeeding moms who appreciate privacy.

3. It's crawling, walking, and climbing time; safety gates are essential.

4. Stow away precious ornaments and breakables.

5. Keep pets well out of the way.

6. Keep a very watchful eye on the party area for hazards, such as forks or small objects babies can swallow, and clear them away quickly.

7. Babies will play alongside each other, but rarely together at this age, so make available a variety of toys within a large, safe floor space.

8. Don't fret about a party theme. It won't impress a 1-year-old.

9. Buy paper plates, napkins, cups, and plastic cutlery in mix-and-match colors at your local supermarket to keep dishwashing to a minimum.

10. Relax: Let your baby and her guests set the pace.

Whatever you do, don't forget to take plenty of photographs to look back on in years to come.

by the numbers
you: 10 to 12 months

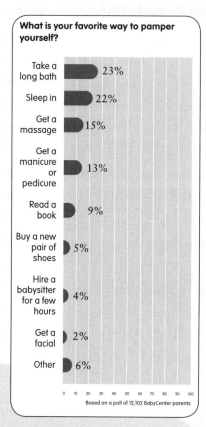

What is your favorite way to pamper yourself?

Take a long bath	23%
Sleep in	22%
Get a massage	15%
Get a manicure or pedicure	13%
Read a book	9%
Buy a new pair of shoes	5%
Hire a babysitter for a few hours	4%
Get a facial	2%
Other	6%

Based on a poll of 12,102 BabyCenter parents

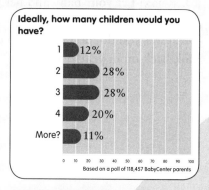

Ideally, how many children would you have?

1	12%
2	28%
3	28%
4	20%
More?	11%

Based on a poll of 118,457 BabyCenter parents

Are you and your partner ready for another baby?

No	64%
Yes	16%
I am, but my partner isn't	8%
My partner is, but I'm not	5%
I'm already pregnant	4%

Based on a poll of 3,054 BabyCenter parents

Do you get to sleep in on the weekend?

No	43%
Yes, sometimes	40%
Yes, regularly	16%

Based on a poll of 3,103 BabyCenter parents

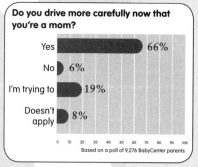

Do you drive more carefully now that you're a mom?

Yes	66%
No	6%
I'm trying to	19%
Doesn't apply	8%

Based on a poll of 9,276 BabyCenter parents

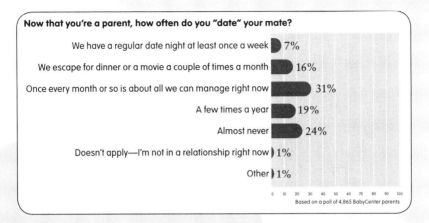

Now that you're a parent, how often do you "date" your mate?

We have a regular date night at least once a week — 7%
We escape for dinner or a movie a couple of times a month — 16%
Once every month or so is about all we can manage right now — 31%
A few times a year — 19%
Almost never — 24%
Doesn't apply—I'm not in a relationship right now — 1%
Other — 1%

0 10 20 30 40 50 60 70 80 90 100
Based on a poll of 4,865 BabyCenter parents

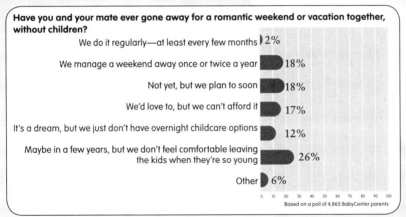

Have you and your mate ever gone away for a romantic weekend or vacation together, without children?

We do it regularly—at least every few months — 2%
We manage a weekend away once or twice a year — 18%
Not yet, but we plan to soon — 18%
We'd love to, but we can't afford it — 17%
It's a dream, but we just don't have overnight childcare options — 12%
Maybe in a few years, but we don't feel comfortable leaving the kids when they're so young — 26%
Other — 6%

0 10 20 30 40 50 60 70 80 90 100
Based on a poll of 4,865 BabyCenter parents

the bottom line

It's been an amazing year. You and your baby have changed dramatically. Whatever else you do as that first birthday approaches, give yourself a pat on the back. Your baby's first year was hard work, but you survived it. (And, of course, your 1-year-old is the most delightful baby the on the planet.)

you—
10 to 12 months

New decisions will be fast approaching—whether to wean your baby completely (if you haven't already done so)—and, incredibly, whether it's time to start thinking about growing your family, though there's certainly no reason to rush either one.

stopping breastfeeding

Your body may continue making milk for some weeks or months after your baby finishes nursing. Many women find that they have days of feeling that their breasts are heavy and full, while others hardly notice anything. Milk sometimes leaks when you take a bath or shower, or even when you hear another baby cry or see a newborn. You can wear breast pads to catch any leaks.

Gradually, your body stops making milk. Some women find this stage quite difficult, caused, perhaps, by the physiological aspects of stopping feeding and the thought that your baby is growing up. Or it may be the discomfort you feel or the hormonal changes going on inside your body. Perhaps it's a combination of all these things. Give yourself the time and mental space to come to terms

babycenter **buzz**
don't forget about yourself

"If you can find a friend to watch your child for even 30 minutes a week, you can go out for a walk, run, coffee, or take a bath at home. Just close the door, turn on music, light, candles—whatever it takes to relax and have some time to yourself."—**Anonymous**

"Well, guess what, there's finally some clear, bright light at the end of the tunnel. My twins are more independent, and I have some free time. I've even started reading books again."—**Kathleen**

with the changes. Tell your partner and family why you feel jumpy or down and remind yourself that this will pass.

Often, as milk production stops, some women find that their breasts seem to shrink. During breastfeeding, many women's breasts are significantly larger than usual, but they often feel soft and empty when you stop. Breast tissue is mostly fat, and it takes a few months for the fat stores to build up again.

If your periods ceased during breastfeeding, they'll return soon after stopping and may be a bit erratic at first.

Visit babycenter.com to see how your breasts will change after weaning your baby.

happy birthday, mom!

Sometimes being a parent seems like one long hard slog. No matter how much cooking, cleaning, or caring you do, and no matter how often your sleep is disrupted by crying bouts, no one ever says "thank you" or "good job."

(continued on page 399)

just for dads

the responsibility of fatherhood

During these months, you're probably beginning to feel like you know which end is up. Stinky diapers, juggling a baby in one arm and her dinner in the other, and even getting your baby to sleep become second nature.

And now that you're confident with the day-to-day, you'll find yourself planning new adventures, too: longer outings, different activities. Many dads discover that as their babies begin to stand, cruise, or walk, a new world of interactions opens up (and so does your vigilance as you keep an eye out for possible wipeouts).

As dessert to this delicious turn of events, you and your partner can finally grab some serious time together again—just the two of you. Now that your baby's nearly a year old, it gets even easier to leave him with a relative or a babysitter, so that you can spend an evening in your own company or in other adult company. Take advantage! If your partner is still reluctant to leave the baby, remind her that while you're crazy about your child, you're still just as crazy about her. That might help her see that stoking your relationship is just as important as baby care. And your baby won't remember at all if you go out for the evening or even out over-night, as long as you leave him in good hands.

One more surprising thing about a growing baby: There's every chance that during these months he'll say the word that's only possible because of you and the part you've played in his life so far: *Dadda*.

how to do your part

- Take turns sleeping in on the weekends so both you and your partner get some rest.

- Take part in your baby's morning and bedtime routines. You're teaching him that you can be part of his daily care. Designate at least one activity during the week that's just for you and your baby—perhaps a Sunday bath night, or a Saturday afternoon walk.

- Now that your baby enjoys books and stories, discover which ones you'll most enjoy reading together.

- Alter your play so that you encourage your baby's growing abilities and his problem-solving skills. As your baby plays with a nesting puzzle, instead of doing it for him, talk him through doing it himself. "Will the yellow cup go inside the green cup?"

- Plan your baby's first birthday. Which of *your* friends or relatives do you want to help celebrate your first year of being a dad?

test yourself) **what kind of dad are you?**

1. Childbirth is a life-changing experience. How prepared were you?

a. It took me a while to find everything to take to the hospital, but we got there with time to spare.

b. I attended every prenatal class, printed a list of the signs of labor and what to pack in the labor bag, and did a trial run to the hospital to time the trip.

c. We were already in the car when I suddenly realized I didn't have any snacks to keep me going. Oh, and we had to stop to buy batteries for the camera, but we got there just as she was ready to begin pushing, so it was okay.

d. We were out of the house and in the car in 5 minutes. I even had time to double-check we'd packed our birth plan, our hospital bag, and the cell phone to tell everyone the news.

2. You get home from work, say hello to your partner, and . . .

a. Sit down, put my feet up, and then maybe have a cuddle with my baby in my lap. We'll see where the evening takes us.

b. Take the baby off her hands, give the baby a bath, then hand her back to Mom for a last feeding before bed. Routines are the way forward.

c. Play with the baby. She really likes to play with a new toy at the moment, and I think it's good for her development.

d. Play learning games with the baby. I look through books and Web sites for new ideas.

3. What are your hopes and dreams for your child?

a. She's too young. Whatever will be, will be.

b. Once she's finished with high school, she'll go to a good college before studying law, then a partnership at a good firm. Actually, I have a friend who might be able to help.

c. As long as she's healthy and happy, I'll support her in whatever decision she makes.

d. Well, if she reaches her potential, she can do whatever she wants. Perhaps a little extra tuition would give her a little push.

4. You plan a special night out with your partner. You . . .

a. Start with a four-star film that just opened, then see where the night takes you.

b. Phone your parents to babysit, make dinner reservations, and make sure your favorite shirt is clean and pressed. You give your partner plenty of warning so she can get organized, too.

c, Buy something special to cook, surprise her with the good news, and let her take over the cooking when you can't quite get it right.

d, Research the best restaurant in your area and make sure they have her favorite wine on the list. Remember to get a babysitter at the last minute.

5. You offer to look after the baby for a day while your partner has some girl-time with her friends. What does she return to find?

a, A fabulous piece of pasta artwork. Okay, maybe glue is smeared all over the kitchen walls, paint is dripping its way down the sink, and the dog is coughing up the leftover macaroni, but we had a fun day.

b, The house still empty. We still haven't finished watching the penguins at our local zoo. I organized an action-packed day, full of happy memories.

c, We never made it out of the park. My baby can't get enough of the swings, and to be honest, neither can I!

d, Our baby is settled down for a nap. We had a busy day at music class, then at her baby gym class. All good fun—and stimulating her development. Um, was I supposed to change her diaper, too?

6. How has fatherhood changed you?

a I didn't really expect it would take up so much time and money, but it's been 100 percent worth it.

b I read all the literature and still didn't understand fatherhood until our little one actually showed up.

c I'm learning new things every day, but I love the challenge.

d I try my hardest. We have a schedule we try to stick to, but I've had to let some of my standards go. Do you think I should buy some more baby books?

(See page 398 for answers.)

ANSWERS

Mostly a's

You're a laid- back, well-intentioned dad, prepared to go with the flow when you need to, and put in enough effort to enjoy your time with your baby. The house may be a mess by the time you've finished, but everyone's had fun. Your partner may love you for your endearing enthusiasms or be driven to distraction by your lack of planning and organization. Stay sensitive to her feedback and be prepared to pull your socks up occasionally.

Mostly b's

You like life to be organized and well planned. Routines matter to you, and you consider them important for your baby, too. You'll be reliable and helpful, but sometimes this may just veer into being so infuriatingly organized that your partner loses her cool. Try to balance the organization with some time to loosen up and enjoy the here-and-now of life with a baby.

Mostly c's

You're full of good intentions. Sometimes things work out really well, but sometimes they go off track. You're learning as you go, which is a good way to approach parenthood. Your partner is likely to love you for trying most of the time. Occasionally, your ineptness may cause an argument, so be sure to watch out for the times she's really tired or frustrated and make an effort to help her more positively.

Mostly d's

You really, really want to be a good dad and—most of the time—you are. Don't let other people's standards and ideas take over; you don't have to be perfect. Your baby will love you just for being a "good enough" dad. Make sure you've mastered the basics (changing and feeding), and the safety issues, and relax about the rest.

babycenter **buzz**
planning another baby?

"Our daughter is 10 months old, and we're considering round two when she turns 1. When the new baby comes, she'll be almost 2 and I figure that's a good time. I'm 30 and I just want to be around to see our grandkids."
—**Abigail**

"I have an 11-month-old son and am expecting a daughter in 2 months. She wasn't planned, but that doesn't mean she'll be loved any less; we're very excited about her arrival. I do worry that my son will be jealous of the new baby, but everyone has told me not to—that he's too young to understand—so maybe that's a blessing."—**Anonymous**

"I'm so torn about having another baby. I love my daughter to death. I want to be able to give her all my time and attention, and I feel that a second child would take that from her. However, I also think of the other side of the spectrum: She'd have a playmate for life."—**Marci**

"We both have baby fever, but financially, it's just not feasible."—**Anonymous**

It isn't just your baby who's changed over this first year—you have, too. A year ago, you were a complete beginner. Now, you've learned not just about the practical mysteries of feeding, crying, bathing, sleeping, and childproofing but how to make your baby laugh, what makes him nervous, how to play his favorite game, and which pictures he likes to look at. It's time to celebrate your own first birthday as a mom.

Be nice to yourself. Parenting is hard work. Plan some time out, even if it's just a long bath on your own while someone else entertains your baby. If you've had a week of interrupted nights (and what parent hasn't!), plan an afternoon nap during the weekend. If your daytime conversation consists of simple speech with your baby and yet another reading of *Goodnight Moon*, treat yourself to a grown-up glass of wine in the evening with your partner, a long catch-up on the phone with a girlfriend, an extended

(continued on page 402)

test yourself **what kind of mom are you?**

Experienced mom or learning as you go? Your baby won't mind either way. Laid-back or clock-watcher? Either is fine, except perhaps if your baby is just the opposite!

1. It's breakfast time. What's your baby eating?

a. My baby is breastfeeding for the first time today, and later, at 8:17 a.m., we'll both be eating homemade baby cereal.

b. Thank goodness for breastfeeding! That's another half hour in bed. We'll have our cereal when we're ready.

c. It's *what* time? *Again*?

2. You're on your way to the baby clinic. What's in your purse?

a. My baby's health record and a list of questions to ask about upcoming vaccinations.

b. My baby's health record, three cookies (for me), and a sock.

c. My purse? I know I've seen it somewhere.

3. It's playtime. What's your baby doing?

a. Tummy time, followed by sorting, stacking, and an introduction to sifting.

b. I'll see what my baby wants to do; I try to follow his cues and provide the right toys.

c. Whatever he likes; I just make sure he's safe.

4. It's time to go out. And it's raining. What do you do?

a. But it's *raining*.

b. Hat, coat, boots—off we go.

c. Yippee! Puddles to splash in!

5. It's dinnertime. What's your baby eating?

a. Organic pureed carrots.

b. What we eat, mashed up as much as possible.

c. Whatever.

6. It's bedtime. Is your baby asleep yet?

a. Of course.

b. Not yet, but after three more songs, a drink, a pat on the back, and a walk around the room, he might be.

c. Well, I am.

ANSWERS

Mostly a's

You're a "professional" mom through and through. You like things to be in order and predictable. You probably have a to-do list, and you're checking your way through it. If your baby is equally ordered, that's great—you'll get along fine. Just remember you'll need to adapt sometimes if your baby isn't big on schedules. When he wants to stop and watch the ducks in the park and you planned to be at the supermarket 3 minutes ago, remind yourself that the store will always be there; this moment in the park won't.

Mostly b's

You're making it up as you go along, and that's fine, because your baby is, too. As long as you're meeting your baby's needs, following his cues, and having fun, your baby will have fun, too.

Mostly c's

You're laid-back, which is great if you have a laid-back baby. You enjoy the opportunities for spontaneity and freedom that these baby days offer, but you're always there to make sure your baby is safe and cared for. Some laid-back moms find, however, that they've given birth to a secret scheduler. If your baby seems to thrive when you do things by the clock, a little routine may help you get your baby ready for the more ordered world that many toddlers thrive on.

Web session while your baby naps, or an extended listen to your favorite iPod playlist while pushing the stroller. You'll get your brain back, and your baby will have a refreshed mom who's more fun to be with.

Take the long view. Remember when you thought that your baby would never sleep through the night? Right now it probably feels like he'll be clamped to your side 24 hours a day. In reality, all babies become toddlers and then preschoolers and then—with a few stages in between—teenagers. And they get easier to handle as they grow (at least until they're teens, anyway). Whenever you face a tough stage, remind yourself that this is a phase and you will get through it.

Count to 10 . . . Or 20 or 100—whatever you need to—in order to react calmly when your toddler brings you a handful of worms from the garden, spills bubble-bath on the carpet, or breaks his favorite toy. If your first thought is "No!" then stop, count, and your second thought will be a much more reasonable "Yes, they're very nice worms, but they'll be sad if you take them out of the garden." When you stay calm, your toddler learns some useful lessons about the world.

Make a safe space. Arrange your house to make it safe and fun for your baby. If your baby is learning to cruise and walk, you can either spend your time rescuing precious objects and grabbing your baby every time he goes near something dangerous, or you can do one good sweep through the house and move everything that he might break or that might harm him. You'll enjoy your baby's newfound skill in a more relaxed way, and he'll get a mellow mom who encourages him to explore.

Be ruthless about your priorities. Are your children happy, warm, and well fed? Great! Are their pajamas ironed and the flowerbed weeded? Who cares! Make your own list of priorities and stick to it. You don't have to be a domestic goddess if you don't want to. And your kids will remember a mom who played with them more fondly than one who spent time keeping house.

Keep the faith! Parenting is all about the day-to-day tasks. It's the care we give our children: the time we take to go for walks, play games, and sit and talk with them that eventually makes them into the kind of adults we want them to be.

how your toddler grows

The excitement of the first year may be over, but many rewarding changes and challenges lie ahead. If your baby isn't already walking, then during the next few months he'll take his first steps. If he's already started, soon he'll walk confidently, letting go of your hand. And then he'll run.

stepping into a whole new realm

Every step forward shows your baby is becoming his own person. But there's lots you can do to encourage his journey. In the months ahead, your baby will learn to . . .

understand the world

Through your toddler's play, he discovers so much about the world and how things work. He'll learn to bend over and pick up an object, try to lift heavy things and light things, and roll a ball back and forth. He'll fill and empty containers, pour and tip things. He'll discover that water trickles away when he turns a cup upside down, but sand stays in a pile. Water runs cold or hot. Mix water with sand and it stops being water. The world is an amazing place!

what you can do to encourage your toddler

Provide your toddler with all sorts of materials to learn about the world: sand, water, paint, play dough, blocks, and balls. Show him how things fill, pour, bend, break, tip over, mix, roll, get hot, and turn cold. A toddler is never bored. The simplest things, such as water and sand, provide many fascinating minutes on end.

Play helps your toddler's balance and walking, too. Introduce some push and pull toys. Your toddler can probably now use them as he walks, and this develops his sense of cause and effect, as well.

order the world

Sorting and ordering the world is an important part of being a toddler. Over the next few months, she'll begin sorting toys into groups, putting all the teddies and dolls together, collecting all the cars in a box, or stacking all the books together. She'll connect shapes and colors and match lids with appropriate containers, such as pots and pans.

This is a huge step in her understanding of the world—that things belong together and can be ordered. She's beginning to realize that people and things belong to groups, and she's categorizing them. The ability to order and organize is a vital first stage for later number skills, and it helps your toddler understand concepts such as today-tomorrow, more-less, and big-small.

what you can do to encourage your toddler

Let your toddler help to sort the groceries into groups when you get home: all the cans here, all the boxes there. Read her a book about mother and baby animals or provide a farmyard set so she can sort the animals into groups.

As your toddler grows, she will enjoy sorting by size, too—small things here, large things there. Once she has an idea of size, help her line things up, starting with the little ones and working up to the big ones. She needs to have a feel for physical size before she can understand the increasing size of numbers: 1, 2, 3 . . . She has to grasp the idea of "small," "bigger," and "biggest."

Building towers of blocks helps your toddler understand that it's more efficient if the biggest blocks are at the bottom and the smaller ones are on top. Building towers helps her hand control, too. Other good toys for this stage: wooden puzzles with shapes that fit in place and sorting boxes with holes of various shapes. Cups that stack in towers and that can be used in the bath or a sandbox for pouring games provide rich play opportunities, too.

find a place in the world

When your toddler copies you, he's expressing his understanding of the world. He may want to sweep the floor, weed the garden, load the car—just like Mommy or Daddy.

During the second year, the outside world becomes more impor-tant to your child, and you'll find yourself playing more in the yard or the park. Your toddler becomes much more interested in other toddlers and playing with them. He'll reach out for another toddler's toy, offer a plaything to another child (but may change his mind at the last moment and yank it back!), and watch older children playing and try to copy them. He'll stop and listen to what other children are doing or pick up a discarded toy and copy what another child did with it. Your toddler's ability to anticipate actions and reactions gets better through his play with toys and other toddlers, and his sense of what comes next grows much stronger in the toddler years, as his memory improves and he learns from what's happened before. You're still his, though, and if another child is sitting on your lap, he'll want that spot of honor.

what you can do to encourage your toddler

Taking lots of outings will broaden your toddler's world. In the yard or at the playground, he'll learn to walk, run, kick, climb, and swing. A widening world lets your toddler stretch and develop his skills. Other people become more important during this year, as well. He'll find friends to play with in the park or at daycare, visit relatives, and recognize the people he sees most days on the bus or in the grocery store. Talk to your toddler about familiar people and situations. Using language in this way helps him think about people and places, even when they're not right in front of his eyes. He may still be shy and need you to help him communicate, but he'll begin to know and recognize more people, and they'll have a place in his world.

If your child doesn't attend daycare with others, try joining a playgroup so that he can meet new friends and see how older children play. Give your toddler miniature versions of your tools when you're in the house (his own dustpan and brush, hammer, mini grocery cart, and so on). From about 18 months, your toddler will begin to take care of his stuffed animal or a doll, feeding it and wrapping it in a blanket, just as you take care of him.

Many toddlers enjoy gazing at their reflections. Stand your toddler in front of a mirror, and he'll not only realize that the toddler in the reflection is him, he can show off all the expressions he can make. Dressing up comes later, when he's beginning to invent a world, too.

invent a world

After your baby is about a year old, imaginative play really starts. It's very different from exploratory play. During your baby's first year, a block was a block. During the second year, that block will become a house, a plane, or a car. This is an important intellectual step: One thing can represent another. If your toddler cries when you move his cardboard box, it's because that cardboard box was his bus, his boat, his train, or his magic carpet. Your toddler is drawing on experiences from his memory.

Next step: Introduce toys that represent the world, and play at being in charge of that world. Your toddler will like a toy plane with miniature people to put in the seat, stacking his animals into a bus he's made out of a box, and eventually running his very own dolls' treasure hunt. He's trying out imaginary worlds where he is in charge and makes things happen.

what you can do to encourage your toddler

Provide plenty of chunky crayons to scribble with along with paint and play dough. Give your toddler lots of dolls, stuffed toys, blocks, and toys with wheels, and they'll become the focus of pretend play, and he'll play make-believe whenever he wants.

Your toddler will begin to construct pretend games about people and activities that he's familiar with. For example, he may sit on a step and pretend that he's driving a car. Or he may offer you a sip of milk from a pretend cup. He knows it's empty, really, but he'll lift it to his lips and pretend to drink from it—and hope that you will, too!

remember the world

As your toddler's memory improves, she'll remember more: where toys go, where she put her blankie, and what happens on the next page of her favorite bedtime book. Routines become important to your toddler as well as to you. In your daily walk, she'll always wave good-bye to the ducks or stop to watch the construction crew, and she'll get upset if she can't.

what you can do to encourage your toddler

Nursery rhymes and action songs come into their own at this stage. Sing them regularly, and your toddler will know what's coming next. Her ability to imagine herself as the central character in "I'm a Little Teapot" and "The Itsy Bitsy Spider" will delight her. And she'll remember the pay-off line, which is great fun for both of you. Continue offering a variety of board books and regular books that you can read to her.

For in-depth suggestions on how to start your baby on the path to becoming a bookworm, visit babycenter.com.

your baby's growing up

When it comes to milestones, your baby's first steps are a particularly magical one. One day he's sliding along the sofa, the next day he's off walking by himself. He's leaving babyhood behind. Your child's first baby steps are, after all, his first major move toward independence.

As your toddler's sense of independence develops, so does his will. He'll make a fuss when he can't do what he wants or have what he wants when *he* wants it.

Welcome to the wonderful world of toddlers!

part six

first-year
health guide

keeping your baby healthy

A healthy baby—that's what all parents want. In this chapter, you'll find out about the critical well-baby visits and immunizations that will help your baby stay well.

well-baby checkups

Regular checkups (well-child visits) are an important part of keeping your baby's health and development on track. Your child's doctor will tell you his preferred schedule. The American Academy of Pediatrics recommends seven checkups during the first year: At 2 to 4 days after birth (usually in the hospital), by 1 month (usually at 2 weeks), and at 2, 4, 6, 9, and 12 months. In the second year, they recommend checkups at 15, 18, and 24 months. After that, it's once a year from ages 3 to 21.

Some doctor's offices have separate waiting rooms for sick children and well children. If yours doesn't, be sure to mention to the receptionist that you're there for a well visit so that, hopefully, you can be moved quickly to an exam room. This is especially important with preemies, who are more vulnerable to picking up infections.

At each visit, your baby will be weighed and measured to monitor growth, and the doctor will thoroughly check her fontanelles (soft spots present on the skull at birth), eyes, ears, mouth and teeth, heart, lungs, abdomen, genitalia, hips, and legs. He'll assess your baby's developmental progress and give you guidelines regarding feeding and safety. Any scheduled vaccines will be administered at this time as well.

It's great if both parents can attend these visits. You each have different perspectives on your child and can both learn new information. Equally important, it's easier to focus on what the doctor's saying if both of you aren't also having to manage your baby. Bring a friend to help you if you have to go alone. Use this opportunity to ask any questions, large or small, about your baby's development, feeding, sleep, or behavior—or anything else that you'd like some advice on. Your pediatrician is an expert on children, so don't limit yourself to health questions. Most children's doctors are also familiar with local parenting resources. Don't neglect to check the bulletin board in the office for potentially useful notices about topics such as playgroups, upcoming speakers, and consultants (for example, lactation advisors or babyproofing companies).

Many parents find it useful to jot questions down in a notebook or on a piece of paper on the refrigerator whenever they pop up during the time between doctor visits. Be prepared to talk about the ways you notice your baby progressing (or regressing) and his eating and sleeping habits.

Be sure that you know how to reach the doctor after hours and review with the staff what you should do in the event of an emergency.

immunization guide

Immunizations are one of the most crucial steps you can take to ensure your child's health throughout life. Be sure to get your baby started with vaccinations early and keep her on schedule.

how immunization (vaccination) works

Why are shots so important? Our bodies develop immunity to many bacteria and diseases through the production of antibodies by our immune systems. If a bacteria or virus begins to invade your body, and the immune system recognizes it from a previous infection, your antibodies and immune cells can quickly attack and stop the germ from taking hold. For a few weeks after birth, newborns have "passive" immunity to some diseases because antibodies pass to the baby from the mother through the placenta.

Vaccines work by introducing a small dose of an inactive (killed) form of the germ or germ component. The inactive form doesn't cause an infection, but your body still responds as if being attacked by a bacteria or virus by producing antibodies. This primes the antibodies and immune cells to respond in the future if an active version of the germ enters your body. The immune system can quickly respond by telling the cells that made antibodies in response to the vaccine to make more to fight the infection.

Once your baby receives a full series of a vaccine (via injection or orally), he's largely protected against the disease. (Some immunizations provide close to 100 percent protection, while for others— such as chickenpox—a small percent of children will still get the disease, but in a milder form.) Some immunities last for a lifetime, while for others your child will need a "booster" shot when he's older.

herd immunity: why everybody's needed

Once enough people have been immunized against a disease, it's more difficult for that disease to get passed on to those who haven't been immunized. This is known as herd immunity. The result is that vulnerable people in the community who can't be immunized due to health problems are protected, too. The percentage of the population immunized needed for herd immunity to work varies from disease to disease, but it must be as high as 95 percent for some diseases.

Former killers that were once almost eradicated are making a comeback as some parents choose not to have their children vaccinated, usually because of fears about a vaccine's safety. Epidemics of mumps, whooping cough (pertussis), and measles have broken out in parts of the United States and in developed countries abroad, for example.

While some parents believe that not having their child inoculated will protect her from possible side effects of vaccines, they inadvertently wind up leaving the child vulnerable to the very real possibility of disease, a far greater risk, especially when large numbers of other parents do the same thing. Also, as a child grows older, she may encounter the diseases she wasn't immunized for while traveling or coming into contact with people from other lands where immunization isn't widespread for a given disease.

Although rumors still abound regarding vaccine safety and possible links to one side effect or another, all the major health organizations in the United States—including the Centers for Disease Control and Prevention, the National Institutes of Health, the American Medical Association, and the American Academy of Pediatrics—believe the currently used vaccine schedule is safe for babies and that the possible risks of side effects, usually mild, are far outweighed by the benefits immunization provides.

Vaccines have been linked in the popular wisdom to SIDS, autism, diabetes, ADHD, asthma, and multiple sclerosis. Yet despite extensive research and review in most of these cases, there's no medical evidence of any link. The idea that there are "hot lots" or bad batches of particular vaccines that can somehow be avoided is also a myth.

If you have serious reservations about vaccines, you owe it to your baby (and the society he's growing up in) to not simply duck the issue but explore it fully and also discuss it with health professionals. Immunization can be a scary prospect—nobody wants to see their baby hurt—but opting out is not a decision to make lightly.

immunization schedule: birth to 18 months

Vaccinations begin sometime between your baby's first and second month and continue throughout the first 18 months, and beyond. Here's what to expect:

Vaccination	Purpose	Doses Given
HepB	Protects against hepatitis B virus, which attacks the liver.	Three doses: At birth, between 1 and 4 months, and between 6 and 18 months
Rota	Protects against Rotavirus, a common cause of severe diarrhea.	Three doses: At 2, 4, and 6 months
DTaP	Protects against diphtheria, tetanus, and pertussis (whooping cough).	Five doses: At 2, 4, and 6 months, between 15 and 18 months, and between 4 and 6 years
Hib (Haemophilus influenza type b)	Guards against meningitis, pneumonia, and epiglottis.	Four doses: At 2, 4, and 6 months, and between 12 and 15 months
IPV (inactivated polio virus)	Protects against polio, which can cause paralysis and death.	Four doses: At 2 and 4 months, between 6 and 18 months, and between 4 and 6 years
PCV	Defends against a pneumococcal pneumonia (a common lung disease), meningitis, and ear infections.	Four doses: At 2, 4, and 6 months, and between 12 and 15 months
MMR	Protects against measles, mumps, and rubella.	Two doses: Between 12 and 15 months and between 4 and 6 years
Varicella	Guards against chickenpox.	Two doses: Between 12 and 18 months and between 4 and 5 years
HepA	Protects against hepatitis A virus, a liver disease.	Two doses: Any time between 12 and 23 months, but at least 6 months apart.

You can set up a personalized immunization scheduler for your baby at babycenter.com.

what's really at stake?

Vaccination has been widely used for many years now, and it's easy to forget what illnesses these shots and oral vaccines protect against.

Chickenpox is a viral infection that causes a characteristic rash of spots and blisters. It can cause more serious and painful symptoms in adults who never developed immunity as children through the disease or the vaccination, leading to an increased risk of getting shingles (a potentially painful skin and nerve condition) later in life, or congenital problems in the children of exposed pregnant women.

Diphtheria is a serious infection of the throat and lungs caused by bacteria that produce toxins. These toxins get into the bloodstream and affect the heart, nervous system, kidneys, and adrenal tissue. Diphtheria can cause paralysis and heart failure.

Haemophilus influenza b is a bacterial infection that can cause meningitis (a very serious inflammation of the membranes covering the brain and spinal cord) and epiglottis (a serious throat infection that can cause the airway to become completely blocked), and bacteremia (the presence of bacteria in the bloodstream, also known as blood poisoning). It can also cause septic arthritis, infection in the bones and the heart, and pneumonia. Meningitis in particular can cause long-term problems including deafness, convulsions, and neurological problems.

Measles is a highly infectious illness caused by the measles virus. Measles is usually a minor illness and rash, but it can also cause some serious complications such as pneumonia and encephalitis (inflammation of the brain), sometimes resulting in brain damage or even death.

Mumps is a viral illness that typically causes inflammation and swelling of the parotid glands (the glands under the ears that make saliva), either on one or both sides. Mumps is usually a mild illness, but it can cause complications, such as meningitis or inflammation of the pancreas, ovaries, testes, or brain. Many people associate mumps with male sterility, but this is rare even if both testes are affected.

Pertussis (whooping cough) is a highly infectious disease that causes a distressing and prolonged coughing illness, which often lasts for 2 to 3 months. Whooping cough has a number of dangerous complications that can cause brain damage and even death, particularly in babies younger than 6 months of age.

Pneumococcal infection by the pneumococcus bacterium, aka *Streptococcus pneumoniae,* can result in serious illnesses such as meningitis, bacterial infection of the blood, and pneumonia.

Polio (poliomyelitis) is a serious illness caused by one of three types of polio virus. Polio can cause severe breathing difficulties and permanent nerve damage, sometimes causing muscle wastage and paralysis of the arms or legs.

Rotavirus is a potentially serious intestinal virus that causes prolonged vomiting and diarrhea. Severe dehydration is the primary risk, and it can be fatal.

Rubella (German measles) is a mild viral infection most common in young children. In a pregnant woman, rubella infection can cause serious abnormalities in the developing baby, particularly in the first trimester.

Tetanus is an infection caused by toxins released following infection with the bacterium *Clostridium tetani.* It's a serious illness that attacks the nervous system and can produce rigidity and muscle spasms, often leading to death. Tetanus isn't transmitted from person to person but picked up from soil or manure in which tetanus spores live. There must be a puncture in the skin—such as a cut, burn, or wound—to allow the bacterium into the body. Even tiny cuts you're unaware of, such as a thorn scratch, are enough to allow lethal levels of the bacterium into the body.

Most babies are immunized according to the standard immunization schedule on page 416, which is recommended by the Centers
for Disease Control and Prevention and the American Academy of
Pediatrics.

common vaccine questions

The idea of giving shots to a baby can make parents uncomfortable, while raising certain safety concerns.

what if my baby is sick?

There's no reason to postpone a dose of vaccine if your baby has a
minor infection such as a cough, cold, or sniffles, without a fever.
Vaccination while a baby has a minor illness—such as an ear
infection or upper respiratory tract infection—doesn't make an
adverse reaction or reduced antibody response more likely.

what if my baby was premature?

Premature babies should still have their immunizations according
to the schedule from 2 months of age, irrespective of the extent of
prematurity. Antibody response and the rate of adverse reaction
aren't affected by prematurity.

what are the side effects of vaccines?

Most children have no reaction after initial crying from the shot.
Your doctor will let you know what to watch out for, since different vaccines in rare cases cause specific reactions, such as a rash
7 to 10 days after the MMR shot. In general, the most common
effects are soreness at the injection site and, less often, a fever.
Alert your doctor if you note worrisome symptoms.

Allergic reactions such as difficulty breathing, hives, paleness,
fainting, or rapid heartbeat are extremely rare but would show up
within hours of a shot; call 911 if you notice this.

will getting so many shots close together overtax my baby's immune system?

According to a 2002 Institute of Medicine report, commissioned by the Centers for Disease Control and Prevention and the National Institutes of Health, there's no proof of a connection between multiple vaccines and an increased incidence of auto-immune disease or infection. Nor do vaccinated children appear to have a higher incidence of allergy and asthma. Basically, your child's immune system is strong to begin with, and vaccination against some of the most potent and deadly diseases serves to strengthen the immune system.

can I just wait until my baby is older to have him immunized?

Your baby may seem tiny and defenseless, but there's no medical reason—and no medical advantage—to delaying immunizations until toddlerhood or later. In fact, there are good reasons not to do this. For one, children under age 2 are especially vulnerable to some of the diseases for which vaccinations are given, such as pertussis (whooping cough). Children's ages and the relative threats of various diseases have been factored into the decisions about which shots are recommended when.

should my baby get a flu shot?

Annual flu shots are recommended for infants older than 6 months. This is especially important if your child has older sib-lings. (The whole family should get vaccinated, along with caregiv-ers.) A flu shot is especially critical for high-risk kids, including those with compromised immune systems, sickle-cell disease, diabetes, or chronic illnesses. October and November—just before flu season strikes—is the ideal time to get one. The first year a child gets the vaccine he needs two shots (1 month apart); annually is sufficient after that. If you have reservations or questions about vaccines, be sure to ask your doctor, who'll also furnish additional information about each immunization.

when your baby is sick

Babies get sick quickly, but they can also get better very fast. Unlike older children, babies can't tell you that something's wrong. Sometimes you can't be sure whether your baby *is* sick and needs a doctor, or whether she'll get better with just some tender loving care.

recognizing the signs of illness

To help you decide if your baby is sick, run through this checklist:

- Is your baby drowsy and sleepy? If she's hard to rouse, or irritable when you touch her, she's likely to be ill and need medical attention.
- Will your baby look at you, respond when you talk to her, and smile back at you? If she ignores you or is hard to engage, it may be a sign that she's sick.
- Is your baby having plenty of wet diapers? Too few of these may indicate dehydration.
- Is your baby feeding? Not nursing well is common when a baby is sick, but something quite minor, such as teething or a cold, may also cause this.

- Is your baby's skin color normal? If she is pale or very flushed, it may be a sign that she's in pain or has an infection.
- Has your baby developed a rash? She may be sick for a day or more before a rash appears.
- Is your baby vomiting? Throwing up (unlike ordinary spitting up) usually signals illness.
- What are your baby's diapers like? Diarrhea, mucousy stools, or blood in the stools all indicate something's wrong.

Parental instincts are usually right. If you're worried, call your doctor. If you're told to bring your baby in for a checkup and it turns out it's "nothing serious," at least you can rest easy. You've simply made an unnecessary trip. Any doctor would rather you took that trip than not see a sick baby.

taking your baby's temperature

Most parents can tell if their baby has a fever just by the child's behavior and by touching the skin. Feverish skin feels hot when you place your fingers or wrist against it. A baby with a fever may also be sweaty, flushed, cranky, or listless. In one study, parents were right 80 percent of the time when asked to assess whether their babies had fevers.

Usually you don't need to know exactly how high your baby's temperature is in order to know that she's sick. But it's a good idea to take her temperature in order to track whether it's coming down. Your doctor may ask this information as well. There are several ways to take your baby's temperature. Don't use thermometers in the mouth of a baby or toddler (oral thermometers) in case she bites the end.

Ear thermometers are very accurate if used correctly and have the advantage of being quick. They're not especially accurate in young infants, though, nor recommended before 3 months. To use one, you place the end in your baby's ear and then read the temperature gauge. Placing the thermometer into your baby's ear at the correct angle is very important for an accurate reading, so follow instructions carefully.

Rectal thermometers give the most accurate reading. This is why they're used in hospitals. But they need careful use at home. Take care to coat the bulb end in petroleum jelly. Put your baby on his stomach, resting across your lap. Insert the thermometer ½ to 1 inch into your baby's rectum. Don't let go of the thermometer because if your baby moves, the thermometer can move also, and possibly injure her. Leave the thermometer in place for the recommended amount of time (usually around 2 minutes), remove it, and read it. A rectal temperature is generally 1°F higher than an oral reading.

Note: All thermometers used in homes or medical clinics should be digital. Don't use old-fashioned mercury thermometers.

Axillary thermometers are used in your baby's armpit, but it can be hard to persuade a baby to stay still long enough to get a reading. Place the end of the thermometer under the armpit and leave for the recommended length of time (usually several minutes longer than an ear thermometer). You need to add 1°F to the reading to get a more accurate idea of core body temperature.

Thermometer strips measure the skin rather than body temperature. This means they're not very accurate, though they're quick and easy. Using both hands, hold the strip on your baby's forehead. Keep your fingers away from the heat-measuring panels and hold it there for 2 to 3 minutes.

An adult's normal oral body temperature is about 98.6°F. In a baby, though, any rectal temperature of 100.4°F or above is considered high and is usually classed as a fever. For a baby younger than 2 months, always call your doctor to report a fever above 100.4°F, or if your older baby has a fever for 3 days, just to be safe.

Each individual child has a normal temperature range that may be different from another child, and there's argument among experts as to what counts as a high temperature. Mild increases in a child's temperature to 100.4°F can be caused by wearing too many clothes, taking a hot bath, or being outside in hot weather. Newborns are particularly susceptible to raised temperatures if they're overdressed because they can't regulate their own body temperature well.

Judge your child's general condition as well as his actual temperature. He may have a raised temperature but be happily playing and feeding as usual. Or he may have a slight fever and be very unhappy, clingy, and crying, with decreased appetite. Contact your doctor whenever you're concerned.

fever basics

Because it's measurable proof of illness, fever can be alarming. But it's important to realize that a fever is a symptom of illness and not a disease in itself. Fever helps the body fight infections by stimulating natural defense mechanisms.

The most common causes of fever are viral infections such as coughs or colds, flu, or stomach bugs. Ear infections are also often associated with fever. Your baby may run a slight fever after a routine vaccination.

treatment

If your baby is older than 8 weeks, give him liquid acetaminophen. For babies younger than 8 weeks, talk to your doctor first. Don't give your baby (or any child) any form of aspirin due to its association with Reye's syndrome, a rare but serious disease. And don't give ibuprofen before 6 months.

Other ways to bring down a fever are to take off your baby's clothes and blankets to allow him to cool down, sponge him with lukewarm wet cloths, or give a lukewarm bath.

When your baby has a fever, it's important to keep him well hydrated. Offer the breast or bottle or cool drinks. A breastfed baby may need to keep going to the breast for frequent small feedings of the watery foremilk.

Often a high temperature will come down and your baby may appear to be almost back to normal within an hour or so. If your baby has a serious infection, however, the symptoms will usually become worse. Your baby will become increasingly ill, even though you're trying to bring her temperature down. If other alarming symptoms also develop, such as an unusual rash, breathing problems, unusual sleepiness, refusing fluids, convulsions, or neck stiffness, contact your doctor or hospital.

when to call the doctor

Make an appointment to see your doctor if your baby has any of these symptoms for 24 hours or more:

- Is unusually irritable and unhappy for no apparent reason
- Pink, watery, or sticky eyes (This could be a sign of an eye infection, such as conjunctivitis. This can be infectious and needs prompt treatment if it's bacterial, though most causes are viral and need no treatment.)
- Discharge from the ears, eyes, navel, or penis (Vaginal discharge is common in the first 10 days after birth.)
- Loss of appetite and more than two missed feedings or meals
- Diarrhea that lasts several days

Seek same-day medical help if your baby has:

- A foreign body is lodged in the nose, ear, or vagina (Never try to remove objects yourself.)
- A burn larger than an inch across, particularly if the skin is blistering
- A fever for more than 2 days, or if he has other worrisome symptoms along with a fever, such as persistent crying or a rash
- Vomiting for 12 hours or more, or if he has other symptoms with it, such as fever or a rash
- Blood-streaked or green vomit or bowel movements

- An unexplained rash, particularly if it's accompanied by a fever
- A cough and makes a barking noise when he breathes in
- Sunken fontanelles (the soft spots on his head) along with other symptoms of dehydration, including dry lips, crying without tears, fewer than six wet diapers a day, and dark yellow urine
- Been crying persistently (As a parent, you know your baby's pattern of crying better than anyone; if he's crying more than usual, or if his cry sounds abnormal, see your doctor.)

Call your doctor urgently if your baby:

- Shows one or more possible signs of meningitis (brain inflammation. These include swollen fontanelles; abnormal drowsiness or unresponsiveness; floppiness; a purple-red rash that doesn't disappear when you press a finger against it (which isn't an actual sign of meningitis but of a bacterial infection that can cause meningitis and other serious infections); dislike of bright lights; or a stiff neck.
- Has a serious fall, and you suspect she may have a broken bone or sprain
- Gets a serious bump to the head, particularly if he loses consciousness or seems confused afterward
- Swallows or eats anything potentially poisonous or harmful, even if he seems well (Call the poison control center for any accidental ingestion; don't wait to see if your baby becomes sick.)

Call an ambulance if your baby:

- Is unconscious or semiconscious
- Is having trouble breathing or is breathing abnormally quickly, particularly if her skin and lips start to develop a bluish tinge (This means that she's not getting enough oxygen.)
- Becomes sick after swallowing something poisonous or harmful, such as medications meant for adults (Remember to take the packet or bottle to the hospital with you.)

If your baby has a condition or injury that's not life-threatening, but needs immediate treatment, it's best to take her straight to a hospital yourself.

what to do in an emergency

If your baby needs urgent medical attention, call 911. If you're calling from a wireless phone, be sure to give your location right away, since emergency responders can't trace this information over phone lines. Also give your cell number right away in case you get cut off; again, the responder may not be able to trace your number and call you back.

Go to a hospital if your baby:

- Has a cut that's bleeding profusely or one that's particularly deep and may need stitching (To try to stop the bleeding, apply pressure to the cut with a clean cloth and try to keep the affected part raised.)
- Has a seizure for the first time (Her eyes will roll back in her head, she'll be unresponsive, and her limbs will twitch.)

caring for a sick baby

Babies who don't feel well need plenty of cuddling and attention. You may find your baby is very sleepy and content to lie in her bed, or she cries and needs constant holding and carrying. Most sick babies need your attention most of the time, so try to plan your day so that other things can wait. You may be able to put a small baby in a sling and get things done while he snoozes close to you. Older babies may prefer a "nest" in a play yard near you. Put a sheet and blankets in the play yard and let your baby snuggle down with a few of her favorite things. Check her regularly to make sure she's not too hot and offer her plenty to drink.

Your baby may like you to rock her and sing to her, wash her face to cool her down, or just sit and talk to her so she can hear your voice.

If your baby is ill for more than a day or two, you may need help in your role as nurse. It can be very tiring reassuring a sick baby all day and throughout the night. Ask your partner, a relative, or a friend to take over while you get some sleep.

Most children regress a bit when they're ill, needing to be held more or wanting to breastfeed more often. Or your baby may refuse a cup and want drinks in a bottle. A baby who usually happily crawls everywhere may sit and cry and refuse to move around. She may cry when you put her down or try to leave her, even if it's only for a minute to two. As your baby feels better, she'll begin to get back to her usual self. Most babies start feeling better almost as quickly as they got sick.

is my baby well enough for daycare?

Your provider will undoubtedly have specific guidelines. In general, a baby shouldn't go to daycare if he has:

- Fever, irritability, lethargy, persistent crying, or difficulty breathing (These can all be signs of illness and need medical attention.)
- A respiratory illness, such as bronchiolitis (a lower respiratory infection) or influenza (If your baby has a fever, too, he should definitely stay at home, but a child with the common cold doesn't usually need to be kept home.)
- Diarrhea or vomiting (Your baby should stay at home until his condition improves.)
- A rash (Until you know what's causing it, your baby may be infectious.)
- A pink eye or yellow discharge from the eye
- Mouth ulcers that cause excessive drooling (Wait until your baby's doctor says he's not infectious.)

baby medicines

Very few over-the-counter medicines are suitable for babies under 1 year. Most parents find a pediatric syrup containing acetaminophen or (for a baby over 6 months) ibuprofen a useful standby, as it helps reduce fever and is a good pain reliever. Check with your doctor before using either with a baby younger than 2 months. For babies older than 2 months, use the medicine according to the directions and only when really necessary. It's essential to know your baby's weight as, with most medicines, the correct dosage depends on it. And never give more than the dosage recommended on the label.

Aspirin, and anything containing it, is unsuitable for any child under 16 years. Its use is linked with Reye's syndrome, a rare but dangerous condition that can affect children recovering from viral illnesses.

Always check with your doctor or pharmacist if you're buying over-the-counter medicines for infant use, even creams and ointments, which can be absorbed through the skin.

If you're interested in treatments from the universe of complementary and alternative medicine, such as homeopathic or botanical (herbal) preparations, Chinese medicine, or chiropractic medicine, be sure to do so only with an experienced practitioner who works with young children and who, ideally, is willing to work in a team approach with your regular doctor. Many conventionally trained physicians are open to complementary and alternative practices; it's useful to keep your doctor in the loop about alternative care you're trying. Herbal teas and drinks sold for babies are usually safe, but other herbal remedies may not be. Be aware that most of these products have not been FDA-approved or extensively tested on infants and children.

how to use and give medicines

Make sure you use medicines as directed. Check the timing, frequency, and dosage that's recommended or prescribed. Some medicines should be given with foods; others alone. Finish the course of any medicine prescribed by your doctor. This is particularly important with antibiotics to make sure that the infection is completely cleared. Otherwise, the infection may return, plus the bacteria may develop resistance to that type of antibiotic.

Measure the dose carefully. An oral syringe makes it easier to get a baby to take medication. Push the plunger all the way down. Then put the syringe into the medicine bottle. Slowly pull back on the plunger until the syringe fills to the right level. Put the syringe into your baby's mouth and squirt the medicine between his tongue and the side of his mouth. Avoid aiming at the back of his throat as he may choke.

When giving medicine, wrap a small baby in a large towel to keep his arms out of the way. Sit down, tuck him under your arm, and put the medicine in his mouth. If he clamps his lips tight, hold his nose and, when he opens his mouth to breathe, put the medicine in and sit him up so he can swallow. If you do it quickly, it will be over before he realizes it. You can use the same towel-wrapping technique when giving eye or ear drops.

storing medicine

Follow these guidelines when storing your baby's medications:

- Store all medicines in a cool place out of your child's reach. Some antibiotics need to be kept in the refrigerator. Check the label to be sure.
- Check the shelf life of medicines before using them. Some eye ointments, for example, have to be used within a few days of opening.
- Don't reuse medicines prescribed for an earlier condition.
- Don't give your child medicines prescribed for anyone else.
- Don't give adult medications, even in smaller doses.

you can count on it: the six most common first-year ailments

No parent rests easy when their baby is sick, or likes to even think about the possibility. Certain illnesses, however, are so common during the first year that they're almost routine. Your baby is very likely to experience one or more of the following six conditions during his first year of life. Fortunately, there's plenty you can do to comfort him when these ailments strike. *Note:* They're in alphabetical order, not ranked by how common they are.

1. constipation

A baby who cries or seems uncomfortable when moving her bowels, and who passes small, pebble-like stools, is likely to be constipated. There's no norm for how often your baby should pass stools; some babies poop after every meal while others can go 3 or more days; much depends on what they eat and drink and what's normal for them.

Because parents tend to scrutinize diaper contents as if they were secret-bearing treasure maps and monitor the frequency of changes closely, constipation is often quickly detected. It's very common, affecting about 30 percent of children at some stage. Let behavior also be your guide: If your baby is uncomfortable and not having bowel movements or is passing very hard stools, then it may be constipation.

Exclusively breastfed babies usually have very soft and runny stools and are rarely constipated. Formula-fed babies occasionally have hard stools. Check that you're making up the formula in the correct proportions (see page 104). If you're using too much formula powder in ratio to water, your baby may become dehydrated, and this can lead to constipation. Other causes of constipation include the transition to solid foods, dehydration for reasons other than formula concentrations, or sickness.

treatment

In a very young baby, it's best to consult your doctor any time you're uncertain about constipation; she may recommend offering your baby up to 2 ounces of water a day. More treatment advice: Give your baby lots to drink to soften the stools; water and diluted fruit juices (in babies over 4 months) are best, particularly fruit juices that contain fructose and sorbitol (such as prune, pear, or apple juice). If your baby eats solid foods as well as breast milk or formula, offer foods with more fiber, such as fruit, vegetables, whole grain cereals, and whole grain bread. Keep offering the milk or formula. Mix puréed prunes or other fruits in with cereal.

If you see blood in your baby's diaper, take her to the doctor; there may be a tear in the skin around the anus.

Some doctors will prescribe oral laxatives, over-the-counter stool softeners, or glycerin suppositories, although most recommend using them for a short time only. It's a good idea to check with your doctor first, even before using an over-the-counter remedy.

A study of chronic constipation in adults found abdominal massage to be helpful, and it seems logical for it to help babies as well. So you could try gently massaging your baby's tummy, starting at the navel.

2. coughs and colds

It's almost certain that your baby will catch a cold during his first year. There are literally hundreds of viruses that cause colds, and your baby can't fight them off as easily as you can because his immune system is still developing. What's more, babies explore everything with their hands and mouths, giving cold-causing viruses ample opportunity to hitch a ride into your baby's system. Colds are especially common in fall and winter, when babies spend more time indoors. And if your baby attends daycare with other children, he's also more likely to exchange cold viruses with his playmates.

The average grown-up gets two to four colds a year; the average child gets six to ten—and up to a dozen for those in daycare! (The silver lining: Little ones who attend daycare wind up with fewer colds during the school years, presumably because they've built up immunities from all those babyhood sniffles.)

Figuring out whether your baby is battling the common cold, an allergy, or a more serious illness can be tricky. The hallmarks of a cold include a runny nose (with clear or yellowish to greenish mucus), sneezing, and possibly a cough or low fever. More clues:

- Behavior. A child with just a cold is apt to continue playing and eating fairly normally. If it's a more serious illness, he's apt to be less energetic and more cranky.

- Gradual onset. A cold creeps up, worsens, and blows over in about 10 days. Illnesses such as flu tend to have a rapid onset. Allergies tend to go on and on, and they don't cause a fever.

treatment

Because colds are caused by viruses, they won't respond to antibiotics. Although you'll have a strong impulse to want to "do" something, don't give your baby any over-the-counter cold remedies. They're usually not recommended for children under 6 months of age because it's unclear whether they help, and given the high risk of side effects, they should be used only sparingly in an older child. Always consult your doctor first. You can give infant acetaminophen (never aspirin) for a fever. (See **fever basics** on page 424.) There's no evidence that zinc, vitamin C, or echinacea cure a child's colds, and because these supplements haven't been tested in infants, it's wise to discuss their use with your doctor first.

There isn't usually any need to see your doctor about an ordinary cold, unless your baby is less than 3 months old. For a baby of any age, you can offer plenty of comfort at home. If your baby's stuffy nose is making sleep difficult, try raising the head of his mattress by a few inches by placing a folded blanket under the mattress. (Don't use pillows on top of the mattress to raise your baby's head.) Use a nasal bulb syringe in the nose to help clear breathing passages. (A few drops of saltwater in the nostrils before suctioning can make breast- or bottle-feeding easier.) Running a cool-air humidifier in your baby's room helps moisten the air; a warm bath or sitting in the bathroom with the shower running helps as well. Some parents find that a few drops of eucalyptus, menthol, or pine oil—sold at health food stores—make breathing easier when added to the bath or humidifier.

Coughing is a common side effect of colds because the respiratory passages are infected. Although it can be hard to tell one kind of cough from another, here are some general guidelines:

- A wheezy cough can indicate **RSV** (respiratory syncytial virus), a very common affliction that seems a lot like a cold but is especially dangerous to premature infants.
- A deep, barking cough is the hallmark of **croup**, a common disease that causes the windpipe to narrow (and sounds much scarier than it actually is).
- A birdlike whooping inhalation before or between coughs is a sign of **whooping cough (pertussis)**, though in babies especially, the cough of pertussis is classically a long sequence of short coughs that sound as if he can't catch his breath. The onset may be sudden or more gradual like a cold, and often starts with upper respiratory symptoms. Your baby is protected if he receives the DTaP vaccine, though the level of protection depends on how many shots in the series have been received so far.
- A long-lasting cough is often a sign of **allergy.** A cough associated with a cold will start to ease up (though not go away entirely) around the 1-week to 10-day mark. Another possibility in a cough that lingers for more than 10 days is sinusitis (a sinus infection), a secondary infection of a cold. Whooping cough is also a possibility because it can occur without the characteristic whoop sound.
- A cough that gets progressively worse can be a sign of **pneumonia,** especially when accompanied by fevers, chills, and difficulty breathing. An examination and possibly x-ray will diagnose it, and usually antibiotics are prescribed.

If your baby tugs at his ear or cries when feeding, he may also have an **ear infection**, a common secondary infection to a cold, so check this out with your doctor. (See **ear infections** on page 439.)

Call your doctor about your baby's cold or cough any time you're worried or if he:

- Is younger than 3 months old, especially if the symptoms include a fever over 100.4°F or a persistent cough
- Is breathing more rapidly than normal or seems to have difficulty getting air
- Is wheezing

- Coughs up mucus that's tinged with blood
- Is excessively drowsy
- Has cold symptoms that persist for more than a week, which is the point at which they should start to improve

3. diaper rash

Diaper rash is a fact of infant life. Nearly all babies in diapers get diaper rash at some stage. Interestingly, in countries where diapers aren't used, diaper rash is almost unknown. However, here in the developed and bottom-covered world, about one in four babies develops diaper rash in the first 4 weeks alone. A diaper rash isn't a sign that you're a negligent parent, though it can certainly feel that way when you see your baby's smooth, soft skin all rough, red, and sore. If your baby cries because of the rash, it can seem like an accusation.

Contact with feces—the skin's greatest irritant—is the main cause of diaper rash. The ammonia in urine and wetness in general also contribute to diaper rash. If your baby's diaper area is wet for long periods, the skin can become macerated—it appears white or lighter than the surrounding skin—and be more susceptible to damage. Add in the raised temperature in the diaper area and some friction between the diaper and your baby's skin, and you have a recipe for diaper rash.

treatment

The main way to prevent diaper rash is to minimize contact between skin in the diaper area and the contents of the diaper. Changing diapers frequently helps, but as a newborn may urinate more than 20 times a day, it's not the complete answer. By the time babies are 1 year old, they urinate about seven times a day, which is one reason why diaper rash tends to be less of a problem as babies get older.

Some babies seem to be particularly sensitive, no matter how frequently they're changed. Steps to take to help prevent and treat diaper rash include:

- Leave your baby's diaper off as much as possible. Put your baby on a soft absorbent sheet on a waterproof mattress cover and change the sheet as soon as it's wet.
- Change your baby's diaper and clean your baby's skin more frequently.
- Dry your baby's skin by patting, not by rubbing, with a towel.
- Don't use powders such as talcum powder or cornstarch.
- Use liberal amounts of diaper cream or ointment, which typically contains zinc oxide and other soothing ingredients, after every diaper change at the first sign of redness.
- Avoid using tight-fitting plastic pants over diapers in order to allow some wetness to evaporate.
- Use one-way liners with cloth diapers to help keep the wetness away from your baby's skin.
- Fasten your baby's diaper loosely so that some moisture can evaporate.
- Use highly breathable disposable diapers, which can reduce diaper rash compared to standard disposable diapers. With cloth diapers, the plastic wrap or pants used can be important; some are more breathable than others.
- Likewise, because today's disposable wipes don't contain alcohol, they don't contribute to the development of diaper rash, but if your baby's skin is already irritated or is prone to skin problems (such as eczema), look for hypoallergenic wipes or just wipe your baby's diaper area with warm water and mild soap.

There's no difference in the effectiveness of one brand or type of barrier ointment or cream over another, so find one that you like. You may find one type easier to use than another. Creams are emulsions of oil and water; they tend to be well absorbed into the skin and easier to wash off your hands. Ointments are greasier and insoluble in water. They create a waterproof layer on the skin that's hard to wash off your hands, but that also means they protect your baby's skin well.

If there's no improvement in the rash, seek advice from your doctor. She may prescribe an anti-yeast cream or ointment to treat *Can-*

dida albicans, perhaps with a mild corticosteroid to reduce the inflammation. The diaper rash should improve rapidly. If it doesn't, then tell your doctor, who may prescribe a different treatment.

If the diaper rash still fails to improve, then your baby may have developed a secondary infection, such as staphylococcal or strepto-coccal bacteria. These bacteria usually live harmlessly on the skin, but prolonged diaper rash leaves your baby open to infection as a result of damage to the skin's protective barrier. Seek advice from your doctor.

4. diarrhea

One thing about diarrhea: You'll know it when you see it. Unlike the random loose stool, diarrhea tends to be more frequent, looser, and more watery (to very watery). It sometimes has a foul smell, too. (The normal breastfed baby produces stool that's soft but with a recognizable poop-like form; it also smells sweetish, like buttermilk, or has no real odor.) A bout of diarrhea can last for several days. Crampy pains are common and may ease between bouts of diarrhea.

Acute diarrhea is common in children; up to one in six children each year see their doctors because of an episode of acute diarrhea. Most cases in babies are caused by an infection. Bacteria, viruses, and other germs can infect the gut. Less commonly it results from food poisoning, such as *E. coli* or salmonella. Even an ear infec-tion can cause this problem. Severe diarrhea in children is most commonly caused by gastroenteritis, which is typically caused by viruses. Acute gastroenteritis is characterized by the sudden onset of diarrhea with or without vomiting, nausea, fever, and abdomi-nal pain. Sometimes food allergies or a reaction to an antibiotic medication causes diarrhea. Excessive juice is a common cause as well; the American Academy of Pediatrics recommends no fruit juice before 6 months, and no more than 4 to 6 ounces per day after that. It's best to dilute your baby's juice very well to prevent diarrhea.

Despite the frequency of diarrhea, most cases aren't serious. It's unusual for complications to develop as a result of diarrhea, but see your doctor if any of the following are present:

- Dehydration
- Blood in the stools
- Vomiting for more than 1 day, or diarrhea that doesn't start to settle after 3 to 4 days
- Pains that are getting worse
- Drowsiness or confusion

treatment

The immune system usually clears the infection within a week or so, often sooner. Your main job, aside from keeping your baby comfortable, is making sure he doesn't get dehydrated. Give your baby plenty of fluids (formula and water) or breastfeed often. If you're dealing with more than an isolated episode, ask your doctor about rehydration drinks such as Pedialyte. Contrary to what you may have heard, *don't* offer your baby Gatorade, flat soda, Jell-o, or undiluted fruit juice, all of which can worsen the condition. Yogurt with live cultures (lactobacillus) can be effective in quelling diarrhea; probiotic drinks (such as Culturelle) may reduce the duration of the attack. But offer such drinks only to babies older than 8 months with no history of dairy allergy.

Diaper rash is a risk of diarrhea, so take care to keep your baby's bottom clean and dry. Even if you don't normally use a barrier cream as a preventative, now's a good time to try it.

Good hygiene helps to prevent infectious diarrhea. Always wash your hands, and wash your baby's hands, too. Do so before and after changing diapers, before cooking, between touching raw and cooked meats, and after gardening or touching pets. If someone in the household has diarrhea, clean the toilets regularly and wipe the flush handle and toilet seat with disinfectant each time it's used.

5. ear infections

Children get more ear infections (otitis media, or OM) than any other diagnosed illness except the common cold. Eighty to 90 percent of all children get one before age 3, and some unlucky children get them again and again. Why?

First, your baby is physically predisposed to ear infections. The small space behind the eardrum is connected to the back of the throat by a tiny channel called the Eustachian tube. Anything that interferes with the function of the Eustachian tube or blocks normal drainage from the middle ear, which is normally filled with air, can increase the risk of infection. Babies tend to get ear infections more than toddlers and preschoolers because the Eustachian tube is quite flat in a baby. As a baby's head grows, the tube tilts, and this steeper angle makes it easier to ventilate the middle ear.

Second, lots of things can cause ear infections, including the common cold. Both viruses and bacteria can lead to ear infections. They're also more likely when your child is exposed to smoking, if he attends daycare, or you bottle-feed him while he's lying down. The prolonged use of a pacifier also seems to increase the risk of OM. There may be a genetic link as well; if a parent got a lot of ear infections, her child may also suffer more frequently. Sometimes an ear infection occurs out of the blue, for no apparent reason.

The most common symptoms of ear infections include:

- A sudden change in behavior—crying and irritability
- Older babies may pull or rub their ears
- Earache caused by a tense ear drum, causing persistent crying
- Fever
- Feeling sick or vomiting, generally feeling ill, and sometimes diarrhea

Runny discharge from the ear is a possible sign that the eardrum has perforated, or burst, letting out infected mucus. This doesn't typically happen with every ear infection. A burst eardrum often

relieves the pain of earache and usually heals quickly after the
infection clears. But a doctor should check to make sure it's healed
properly and your child isn't at risk for hearing problems as a result.

treatment

In most cases, the immune system will clear an ear infection
within 3 days. But most doctors like to see infants with the symptoms of ear infection in order to verify the diagnosis, rule out more
serious illnesses with similar symptoms, and, possibly, treat with
antibiotics. Although over-prescription of antibiotics for children
has become a big concern in the medical community, most special-
ists say they'd rather err on the side of caution in a very young
child. Find out what your doctor thinks.

After looking inside your baby's ear for symptoms such as pus and
a bulging or burst eardrum, your doctor may advise a wait-and-see
approach for 2 or 3 days to see if the infection clears on its own.
It's likely he'll prescribe antibiotics for severe infection or an
infection that's worsening after a few days.

More reasons for prompt medical attention: A serious infection of
the ear and surrounding bone can develop from a common ear
infection, although this is unusual. In very rare cases, meningitis
can develop.

If antibiotics are prescribed, note whether they need to be refrigerated or not. Be sure to give your baby the complete course, even
after she seems well again. If your baby doesn't seem to respond to
the antibiotic after a few days, tell your doctor; you may need a
different medicine. Meanwhile you can ease the pain and lower a
temperature by giving your baby infant acetaminophen or ibuprofen (if your baby is older than 6 months), as directed.

Some fluid may remain behind the eardrum after the infection
clears, causing dulled hearing for a week or so. See a doctor if you
think your baby's hearing is affected. If the fluid doesn't clear
properly, it can cause otitis media with effusion (OME), a condi-

tion that can cause hearing problems or loss, usually temporary, and perhaps a short-term delay in speaking.

Babies with persistent ear infections may be candidates for tympanostomy—also known as having tubes put in—the most common surgery performed on children under age 4 in North America, after circumcision. In this controversial procedure, a tiny incision is made in the child's eardrum for the placement of a millimeters-long tube that acts like a vent, allowing air in and preventing fluid from collecting in the ear. Not all physicians are convinced the tubes work, but given the potential benefit— avoiding hearing loss and learning problems—it's worth asking your doctor about it. Permanent hearing loss associated with ear infections is rare.

6. vomiting

Almost all babies throw up at some time or other. Vomiting is unpleasant for your baby—not to mention you—but it's seldom dangerous, and it has many different possible causes. It can be a sign of illness (such as viral gastroenteritis, a urinary tract infection, an ear infection, or something more serious) or of problems with feeding or just feeding too much. Other possible causes include allergy, ingesting a poisonous substance, or even just coughing or crying too much. A very upset baby can literally "make himself sick."

It's not always easy to pinpoint the cause of vomiting, so it's best to look for other symptoms as well. A viral infection causing vomiting typically brings on other problems, such as diarrhea or fever, for example. Food-related vomiting happens soon after meals.

Call your doctor if:

- Your baby's vomiting is very forceful
- Vomiting goes on for longer than 8 hours
- The vomit looks green (bilious) or contains blood
- There are other symptoms such as pain or blood in the stools

You should be aware of four other kinds of vomiting-related concerns:

Reflux is a digestive condition that causes spitting up after eating.

Rotavirus is a very common intestinal virus that once affected nearly all kids before age 3 and sometimes causes severe vomiting and diarrhea that continues for days. Though it's usually not too serious, it's known to make some children miserable, and about one in 50 children with rotavirus needs hospitalization for dehydration. A relatively new vaccine given in the first year now protects against this very unpleasant disease. (It replaces an earlier vaccine that was discontinued because of a rare complication; the new one has been found safe in large clinical trials.)

Very occasionally, persistent projectile vomiting (sudden forceful vomiting that seems out of the blue) in young babies (2 weeks to 2 months) may be caused by **pyloric stenosis,** an obstruction or narrowing at the outlet of the stomach (pylorus) preventing food from emptying from the stomach. This can lead to serious illness if left untreated. Your doctor may feel your baby's stomach as he feeds to check for a bulge next to the stomach. If you suspect pyloric stenosis because of persistent projectile vomiting, quickly take your baby to a doctor, who may recommend a consultation with a surgeon.

Vomiting in children under age 4 can also be caused by **intussus-ception,** where one part of the bowel is telescoped into another. If your baby has this condition, he may pull up his legs, go pale, and pass blood in the stools, in which case take him to see a doctor immediately.

treatment

Try to make your baby comfortable after vomiting. Rinse your baby's mouth out with water or offer water to drink to help get rid of the sour taste. The physical exertion of vomiting can leave your baby feeling cold, sweaty, and tired, so let him rest. Be alert for another bout of vomiting, as one tends to follow soon after another in some illnesses.

Keep your baby's fluid levels up to prevent dehydration. Offer breastfeeding or formula or other fluids for bottle-fed or older babies. Oral rehydration solutions (oral electrolyte solutions) contain a balanced mix of salt, sugar, potassium, and other elements to help replace lost body fluids. Doctors often suggest using these solutions to help prevent or treat dehydration.

If your baby is diagnosed with pyloric stenosis, he'll need an operation to widen the outlet of the stomach to normal size. In the meantime, your baby will be given intravenous fluids to prevent dehydration. General anesthetic is necessary for the operation, which has a high success rate. Most babies can nurse normally shortly after the operation and have no further problems. Surgery is also sometimes necessary if the underlying cause of vomiting is intussusception.

index

Boldface page references indicate photographs.
Underscored references indicate boxed text.